A *volume in the*

DOUGLASS SERIES IN EDUCATION,
edited by HARL R. DOUGLASS, Ph.D.,
DIRECTOR OF THE COLLEGE OF EDUCATION,
UNIVERSITY OF COLORADO

VOLUMES IN

DOUGLASS SERIES IN EDUCATION

STUDENT TEACHING IN THE ELEMENTARY SCHOOL—Lindsey and Gruhn

SCHOOL FINANCE—ITS THEORY AND PRACTICE—Rosenstengel and Eastmond

TEACHING IN HIGH SCHOOL—Mills and Douglass

THE HIGH SCHOOL CURRICULUM—Douglass and others

THE MODERN JUNIOR HIGH SCHOOL—Gruhn and Douglass

TEACHING IN ELEMENTARY SCHOOL—Mehl, Mills, and Douglass

EDUCATIONAL PSYCHOLOGY—Guthrie and Powers

EDUCATION FOR LIFE ADJUSTMENT—Douglass and others

PRINCIPLES AND PRACTICES OF SECONDARY EDUCATION—Anderson, Grim, and Gruhn

WORK EXPERIENCE IN HIGH SCHOOL—Ivins and Runge

SECONDARY EDUCATION—Douglass

STUDENT ACTIVITIES IN SECONDARY SCHOOLS—Johnson and Faunce

MANAGING THE CLASSROOM—Brown

PUBLIC SCHOOL ADMINISTRATION—Grieder and Rosenstengel

STUDENT TEACHING IN THE SECONDARY SCHOOL—Gruhn

BUILDING THE HIGH SCHOOL CURRICULUM—Romine

AMERICAN PUBLIC EDUCATION—Grieder and Romine

THE SCHOOL AND THE COMMUNITY—Grinnell, Young, and others

PRINCIPLES AND PROCEDURES OF CURRICULUM IMPROVEMENT—Anderson

TEACHING LANGUAGE ARTS IN ELEMENTARY SCHOOLS—Hatchett and Hughes

ADMINISTRATIVE LEADERSHIP IN THE ELEMENTARY SCHOOL—Hicks

TECHNIQUES OF SECONDARY SCHOOL TEACHING—Watkins

THE
MODERN
JUNIOR HIGH SCHOOL

By

WILLIAM T. GRUHN

PROFESSOR OF EDUCATION
UNIVERSITY OF CONNECTICUT

and

HARL R. DOUGLASS

DIRECTOR OF THE COLLEGE OF EDUCATION
UNIVERSITY OF COLORADO

SECOND EDITION

THE RONALD PRESS COMPANY ⸴ NEW YORK

6

PREFACE

This volume is a complete and up-to-date presentation of junior high school education—its historical development, its basic philosophy, and its practices. In this Second Edition of THE MODERN JUNIOR HIGH SCHOOL, the authors have tried to produce a thoroughgoing revision guided by the latest research in the field. This includes ideas and data obtained from numerous recent surveys and from a checklist study of current junior high school practices in 370 schools in all parts of the United States.

The book is intended to serve a number of purposes. It should be useful as a textbook or reference for professional courses on the junior high school; it should be helpful to teacher and citizen study groups concerned with problems in the area; and it should serve as a source book on junior high school education for administrators, supervisors, and teachers.

The authors have had in view chiefly the program under such revised plans as the 6-3-3, 6-2-4, 6-4-4, and 6-6, giving special and repeated attention to problems of the junior high school grades in six-year high schools. However, the philosophy and program discussed here is quite suitable, with adaptations, to schools under the 8-4 plan. In short, the book should be of value to administrators, supervisors, teachers, and parents who are concerned with the program in grades seven, eight, and nine, regardless of the type of grade organization.

The book aims at a comprehensive and genuinely helpful treatment of its subject. Such matters as curriculum guidance, extraclass activities, and administrative problems, as well as historical development and basic philosophy, are amply covered. Although the book gives a great deal of information about current practices, it does much more than that. It also summarizes various attitudes toward these practices, including the points of view of the authors. It is not expected that the book will supply ready-made answers, but rather that it will provide much information and many suggestions to help teachers, administrators, and citizens find answers appropriate to their own situations.

WILLIAM T. GRUHN
HARL R. DOUGLASS

January, 1956

ACKNOWLEDGMENTS

The authors are greatly indebted to many persons, professional organizations, school systems, and publishers who have contributed in one way or another to the preparation of this manuscript. Several hundred principals provided much information by replying to the checklist survey of junior high school practices, sending materials for their schools, and responding to other requests. For this information concerning current practices the authors are deeply grateful.

They appreciate the valuable contributions to the chapters on the curriculum which were made by the following: Professor Howard H. Nelson, University of Minnesota; Professor Delbert Oberteuffer, The Ohio State University; Professor Lucien B. Kinney, Stanford University; Professor Elise Ruffini, Teachers College, Columbia University; Professor Ella J. Rose, University of Minnesota; Professor G. Robert Carlsen, University of Texas; Professor Walter V. Kaulfers, University of Illinois; Professor Edwin R. Carr, University of Colorado; Professor James L. Mursell, Teachers College, Columbia University; Professor Stanley A. Brown, University of Colorado; Professor V. Ronald Nelson, Augustana College; Professor Erich Hopka, St. John's College, Winfield, Kansas; and Professor Herbert T. Tonne, New York University.

The authors appreciate the privilege of quoting from the published materials of various school systems, especially the following: Wauwatosa, Wisconsin; New Britain, Connecticut; Allentown, Pennsylvania; Newton, Massachusetts; Wellesley, Massachusetts; Shaker Heights, Ohio; Denver, Colorado; Eugene, Oregon; District of Columbia; Long Beach, California; New York, New York; Muscatine, Iowa; Battle Creek, Michigan; Springfield, Massachusetts; Philadelphia, Pennsylvania; and Baltimore, Maryland.

They appreciate permission to quote from the publications of a number of professional organizations, publishers, and authors, including the following: National Education Association, National Association of Secondary-School Principals, American Vocational Association, New York State Education Department, Minnesota State Department of Education, New Mexico Department of Public Instruction, Washington State Board of Vocational Education, United States Office of Education, North Central Association of Colleges and Secondary Schools, *The Mathematics Teacher*, American Book Company, Harper & Brothers, The Macmillan Company, and the American Crayon Company.

Several doctoral dissertations were made available to the authors with permission to use materials and data. They are particularly grateful to Dr. Richard S. Byers, Rockville Centre, New York; Professor Edward G. Fennell, University of Massachusetts; and Professor W. C. Wood, Fort Hays Kansas State College.

The authors also appreciate the suggestions of a number of their colleagues who read various parts of the manuscript.

W.T.G.
H.R.D.

CONTENTS

PART I

History and Philosophy

CHAPTER   PAGE
1 GROWTH OF THE JUNIOR HIGH SCHOOL   3
2 PHILOSOPHY OF THE JUNIOR HIGH SCHOOL 22
3 ADVANTAGES AND LIMITATIONS OF THE JUNIOR HIGH SCHOOL . . 45

PART II

The Instructional Program

4 CURRICULUM TRENDS AND ORGANIZATION 61
5 THE CORE CURRICULUM 82
6 THE CURRICULUM FIELDS: INDUSTRIAL ARTS, HEALTH AND PHYS-
     ICAL EDUCATION, MATHEMATICS, ART 100
7 THE CURRICULUM FIELDS: HOME ECONOMICS, THE LANGUAGE
     ARTS, FOREIGN LANGUAGES, AND THE SOCIAL STUDIES . . . 128
8 THE CURRICULUM FIELDS: MUSIC, BUSINESS EDUCATION, AND
     SCIENCE 161
9 DIRECTING LEARNING ACTIVITIES 178
10 MEETING INDIVIDUAL DIFFERENCES 202

PART III

Guidance and Extraclass Activities

11 THE GUIDANCE PROGRAM 237
12 THE HOMEROOM 263
13 EXTRACLASS ACTIVITIES 284

PART IV

Organization and Administration

CHAPTER   PAGE

14   EVALUATING, REPORTING, AND RECORDING PUPIL PROGRESS . . 313

15   PROBLEMS OF ORGANIZATION AND ARTICULATION 340

16   STAFF PROBLEMS 359

PART V

Looking Ahead

17   PROBLEMS FACING THE JUNIOR HIGH SCHOOL 379

    SELECTED READINGS 391

    NAME INDEX 411

    SUBJECT INDEX 415

Part I

HISTORY AND PHILOSOPHY

Chapter 1

GROWTH OF THE JUNIOR HIGH SCHOOL

1. The Junior High School—A Growing Institution

Present Growth of the Junior High School. For the second time in its short history, the junior high school today is experiencing rapid development. The first such period came immediately after World War I, when the junior high school was a new addition to the American school system. Not until the 1920's did the junior high school, however, become firmly established as an administrative unit in the American schools.

As in the 1920's, a tremendous increase is now taking place in elementary and secondary school enrollments. Community after community is engaged in an extensive school building program to meet this increase. Because of its position between the elementary school and the high school, the junior high school frequently provides a ready solution to the pressure of increased enrollments. A time when new buildings are being constructed is, therefore, an appropriate time in some communities to introduce the junior high school plan of organization.

In most communities today, however, the junior high school is much more than a housing convenience. In those communities which are still on the 8-4 plan, many parents who have themselves had the benefits of a junior high school education are demanding a similar educational program for their children. In some communities a separate junior high school is most appropriate to meet the community needs, while in others a combined junior-senior or six-year high school is more suitable. *What is important, however, is that the advantages of the broad program offered in a junior high school type of organization are so widely recognized that most communities faced with building a secondary school today are giving serious consideration to the establishment of a junior high school type of program.*

Definition of the Junior High School. At this point it might be appropriate to define the term "junior high school," because it is used in different ways by different people. Some think of a junior high

3

school as the building which houses grades seven, eight, and nine. Others think of any school which includes grades seven, eight, and nine as a junior high school, but would not so term other combinations, such as grades seven and eight or grades seven to ten. Some educators and parents characterize the junior high school as one that has certain administrative features, such as departmentalization, promotion by subject, and homogeneous grouping.

In a sense, all these statements are appropriate in explaining what is meant by a junior high school. Although a junior high school is most commonly thought of as including grades seven, eight, and nine, there are many schools that include grades seven and eight, and others grades seven through ten, which are called junior high schools. Likewise, it is important to have a building for a junior high school, and also to have appropriate administrative features and characteristics. But a building, a particular grade arrangement, or certain administrative practices alone do not constitute a junior high school.

If we examine the early history and background of the junior high school, we find that particular attention was given to the needs of boys and girls during early adolescent years. It was suggested again and again in the early reports out of which the junior high school developed that the schools under the 8-4 arrangement were not adequately meeting the needs of boys and girls in grades seven and eight and also to some extent those in grade nine. In other words, these reports suggested many times that the grade arrangement of the school system should be reorganized so that a more satisfactory educational program could be provided for early adolescents. This thinking has been predominant in the minds of junior high school educators to the present time. It seems appropriate, therefore, to define the junior high school as follows: *The junior high school is an educational program which is designed particularly to meet the needs, the interests, and the abilities of boys and girls during early adolescence.* A school building, grade organization, and certain administrative features are important in the junior high school only to the extent that they have a bearing on that educational program.

The Junior-Senior High School. From the beginning of the reorganization movement, the emphasis was on the development of a six-year secondary school program, rather than on separate junior and senior high schools. The reports on reorganization suggested that a division between elementary and secondary education on a 6-6 basis would be desirable. The early reports on reorganization did not propose a division of the secondary school into a junior and a senior high school.

This does not mean that there was opposition to a separately organized junior high school. Rather, it means that the early reports on reorganization emphasized the development of a well-articulated six-year secondary school program. It was believed that the secondary school program should begin in grade seven and end in grade twelve without any break along the way, irrespective of whether the grades were all housed in one building or in different buildings. Furthermore, recommendations for a six-year program of secondary education grew out of the conviction that the needs of pupils in grades seven, eight, and nine could and should be more adequately met.

In other words, there is nothing contradictory between the junior high school and the six-year high school. In meeting the educational needs of early adolescents, they serve the same purposes. The decision as to whether there should be separate junior high schools or a combined six-year school is based, in most communities, on the number of pupils enrolled. Consequently, in the large cities one is more likely to find separately organized junior high schools, while in medium-sized and small communities the six-year school is more common.

It is important to recognize the common purposes of the junior high school and the six-year high school. It is true that the six-year high school has certain peculiar problems, particularly in the development of the program for pupils in the lower grades. At the same time, the basic philosophy, the curriculum, the guidance and extraclass activities, and the organizations which are suggested for a junior high school are equally appropriate for grades seven, eight, and nine in a six-year high school. The discussions in the chapters that follow are therefore designed to help principals and teachers whether they are developing a program for a separate junior high school or for the junior high school grades in a six-year secondary school.

2. Movement for Reorganization of the 8-4 Plan

Origin of the 8-4 Plan. Little is known of the reasons for having an eight-grade elementary school and a four-year high school. Some historians contend that the idea of eight elementary grades was introduced from Prussia, but others insist its origin is definitely American. We do know that the eight-grade idea became the practice in America about 1810 to 1830, at a time when many American educators were studying Prussian education. In any case, there is no evidence that there was any extensive discussion of the number of grades that are best for the elementary school, nor were any experimental schools developed to try different types of grade arrangement. About all we know concerning the origin of the eight-grade elementary school is that it came into being during the years from 1810 to 1830, and by the end of that time it was generally accepted in most states, except in the South, which had seven-year elementary schools, and in New England, where the nine-year school prevailed.

The origin of the four-year high school is just as uncertain as that of the elementary school. The first English high school was introduced in Boston in 1821, but it was not until after the Civil War that the idea spread rapidly. In some states there were, at the beginning, three-year high schools; in others they consisted of four years; and a few had five-year schools. By 1900, however, the four-year idea generally prevailed in the United States. As with the elementary school, there is no evidence that the four-year high school came about after serious study and experimentation.

A thorough study of the literature on the origins of the eight-year elementary school and the four-year high school leads to certain conclusions that have a bearing on the movement to reorganize the 8-4 plan, and on the later development of the junior high school. *First, there is no evidence that the eight-year elementary school and the four-year high school were influenced in their origin and early development by any recognition of the nature of the physical, social, and psychological growth of children. Second, the elementary and the secondary schools began as two entirely separate institutions; furthermore, throughout much of their early history there was little or no attempt to bring about satisfactory articulation between them.* These two conditions were significant in initiating the reorganization movement in upper elementary and secondary education that culminated eventually in the development of the junior high school.

Dissatisfaction with the 8-4 Plan. By 1900, the 8-4 plan was the predominant form of grade organization in all parts of the United States, except in the South and in some New England communities. But the 8-4 plan had hardly become generally accepted in practice before criticisms were directed at certain inherent weaknesses. Strangely enough, the first criticisms came not from leaders in elementary or secondary education, but from representatives of colleges and universities.

Educators at the elementary and secondary levels became immediately aware of this dissatisfaction and soon were participating actively in the investigations designed to improve the educational program below the collegiate level. From 1890 to 1910, there was a series of events which included discussions at educational conferences, addresses by educational leaders, and reports by committees representing various professional bodies, all directed toward the improvement of certain features of the 8-4 plan. These events are known in the history of American education as the reorganization movement in upper elementary and secondary education. We shall briefly summarize the events in that movement and then trace in more detail the influences which gave birth to and nourished the growth of the junior high school.

First Notable Attack on the 8-4 Plan. The first criticism of the 8-4 organization stressed that, from the standpoint of the college and the university, the program of elementary and secondary education was undesirably long. President Charles W. Eliot of Harvard called attention to this problem as early as 1872-73, when he pointed out that the entering age of freshmen at that institution had gradually risen until it was then a little over eighteen years.[1] The Harvard faculty believed, he said, that the entering age should not go higher.

Apparently little was done to correct this situation, because in 1885-86 Eliot again referred to it, stating that then two-fifths of the freshmen at entrance were over nineteen years of age. The Harvard faculty took some specific steps to bring about earlier admission to college and faster completion of the college program. It made admissions requirements more flexible, urged parents to send boys to college earlier, and studied ways of having superior students complete college in less than the usual time. From the standpoint of the reorganization of secondary education, however, the most important action was President Eliot's proposal that the total period of elementary and secondary education be shortened so that young men could enter college earlier. President Eliot first made his proposal to shorten the period of elementary and secondary education to the National Education Association in 1888.[2] But a later address before the same body, in 1892, has more significance because it led to the beginning of a series of committee investigations that form an important part of the reorganization movement in secondary education.

Appointment of Committee of Ten Through Eliot's Influence. Although President Eliot undoubtedly was more interested in reducing the college-entrance age than in the improvement of elementary and secondary education, his public pronouncements led, in 1892, to the appointment of the Committee of Ten on Secondary-School Studies. This committee was authorized to arrange "a conference

[1] Frank F. Bunker, *The Junior High School Movement: Its Beginnings* (Washington, D.C.: F. W. Roberts Co., 1935), *passim*, is the source for this summary of reform measures emanating from Harvard.

[2] Charles W. Eliot, *Educational Reform: Essays and Addresses* (New York: The Century Co., 1898), pp. 151-76.

of school and college teachers of each principal subject which enters into the programs of secondary schools in the United States . . . each conference to consider the proper limits of its subject, the best methods of instruction, the most desirable allotment of time for the subject, and the best methods of testing the pupils' attainments therein . . ." [3] President Eliot very appropriately was appointed to serve as chairman of the Committee of Ten, as this group came to be called.

Apparently it was not intended that the Committee of Ten should make recommendations for the reorganization of the entire school system. Nevertheless, it was inevitable that an investigation of the time to be allotted to the various secondary school studies should lead to some consideration of the appropriate place in the program for these studies to begin. When the committee organized for its work, it included the following question among those formulated to serve as a guide for each of the subject conferences: "In the school course of study extending approximately from the age of six years to eighteen years—a course including the period of both elementary and secondary education—at what age should the study which is the subject of the conference be first introduced?" [4]

Earlier Introduction of Secondary School Studies Recommended by Committee of Ten. In most of the conference reports of the Committee of Ten, some reference was made to instruction below the high school level, several suggesting that some material from such subjects as English, arithmetic, natural history, and geography be introduced as early as the primary grades. It was also urged that well-organized instruction in Latin be introduced at least a year earlier than was then the custom; that German or French be offered as electives at the age of ten; and that at about the age of ten systematic instruction in concrete or experimental geometry should begin.

In the final report of the Committee of Ten, issued in 1893, the recommendations for introducing pupils to secondary school studies at an earlier age were summarized in these words:

> In preparing these programs, the committee were perfectly aware that it is impossible to make a satisfactory secondary-school program limited to a period of four years and founded on the present elementary-school subjects and methods. In the opinion of the committee, several subjects now reserved for high schools—such as algebra, geometry, natural science, and foreign languages—should be begun earlier than now, and therefore within the schools classified as elementary; or, as an alternative, the secondary-school period should be made to begin two years earlier than at present, leaving six years instead of eight for the ele-

[3] National Education Association, *Report of the Committee of Ten on Secondary-School Studies* (New York: American Book Co., 1894), p. 3.
[4] *Ibid.,* p. 6.

mentary-school period. Under the present organization, elementary subjects and elementary methods are, in the judgment of the committee, kept in use too long.[5]

The report of the Committee of Ten, which is generally recognized as one of the great documents in the history of American education, exerted a tremendous influence on subsequent developments in the reorganization of upper elementary and secondary education. Almost every significant pronouncement on educational reform by investigating committees during the next two decades showed the influence of this report. But the specific proposals of the committee with respect to the introduction of secondary school studies at an earlier age were not widely introduced into the schools at that time. It was these proposals which, after 1910, were reflected in the early programs of junior high school education.

Better Articulation Recommended by Committee of Fifteen. Several months before the Committee of Ten presented its report in 1893, the Department of Superintendence of the National Education Association appointed a Committee of Fifteen to investigate the organization of school systems, the coordination of studies in primary and grammar schools, and the training of teachers. Compared with the Committee of Ten, the Committee of Fifteen was more directly charged with problems that concerned the reorganization of elementary and secondary education.[6]

In organizing its activities, the committee divided its work into three parts, appointing a subcommittee to direct the work for each. One of these concerned itself with the division of time between elementary and secondary education. As a basis for its report, the subcommittee submitted seventeen questions to qualified persons in education throughout the country. Of these questions, two that had a direct bearing on the reorganization of upper elementary and secondary education were stated as follows:

1. Should the elementary course be eight years and the secondary course four years, as at present? Or, should the elementary course be six years and the secondary course six years?
2. Should . . . Latin or a modern language be taught in the elementary-school course? If so, why? [7]

Those who replied to the subcommittee's questionnaire in general expressed concern regarding the suggestion that the elementary school

[5] *Ibid.,* p. 45.
[6] National Education Association, *Journal of Proceedings and Addresses* (Denver, 1895), p. 232.
[7] *Ibid.,* pp. 233 f.

course be shortened to six years, while on the question of introducing Latin or a modern language earlier in the school program there was a division of opinion. The replies to these two questions in the subcommittee's investigation may be summarized as follows:

1. The objection to shortening the elementary course to six years, held commonly by those replying to the first question, was the fear that such a step would cause many children to leave school.

2. In respect to beginning Latin or a modern language in grades seven and eight, the responses were about equally divided between those who considered language study profitable and those who held that the mind is not mature enough to profit from it until the high school age.

In its report, the subcommittee consequently opposed revision of the 8-4 type of grade organization. Even so, this committee made some contribution toward the reorganization of upper elementary and secondary education through its recommendation for closer articulation between the elementary and the secondary school, as well as its suggestion that certain secondary school studies begin earlier. More specifically, it suggested that algebra begin in grades seven and eight, and Latin in grade eight. It suggested further that the earlier introduction of these subjects should be used to make the transition easier from the elementary to the secondary school. Both the recommendation that certain high school subjects should begin earlier and that there be better articulation between the elementary and the secondary schools point toward the thinking which is basic to the junior high school philosophy which developed a few years later.

Six-Year High School Urged by Committee on College Entrance Requirements. At the meeting of the National Education Association in 1895, a committee was appointed to consider the question of bringing about "a better understanding between the secondary schools and the colleges and universities in regard to requirements for admission. . . ." [8] This was a joint committee representing the Department of Secondary Education and the Department of Higher Education. Although this committee was authorized primarily to investigate the problem of college-entrance requirements, as with the Committee of Ten, it seemed that a discussion of reforms in upper elementary and secondary education was inevitable. In its report, in 1899, the committee expressed itself unequivocally in favor of a unified six-year high school course of study beginning with the seventh grade. In

[8] National Education Association, *Journal of Proceedings and Addresses* (Los Angeles, 1899), p. 633.

support of this recommendation, the committee expressed itself as follows:

The seventh grade, rather than the ninth, is the natural turning-point in the pupil's life, as the age of adolescence demands new methods and wiser direction. Six elementary and six high school, or secondary, grades form symmetrical units. The transition from the elementary to the secondary period may be made natural and easy by changing gradually from the one-teacher regimen to the system of special teachers, thus avoiding the violent shock now commonly felt on entering the high school.... Statistics show that the number of students leaving school at the end of the sixth grade is comparatively small, while the number is very large at the end of the eighth grade. By the proposed change, the students in the seventh and eighth grades would gradually gain the inspiration of the high school life, and the desire to go farther in the languages and sciences which they have already begun under favorable conditions. The result would doubtless be a more closely articulated system, with a larger percentage of high school graduates.[9]

The work of the Committee on College Entrance Requirements is particularly significant in the reorganization movement because, with its proposal for a six-year high school, it became the first professional group to formulate a specific plan for reorganizing the 8-4 plan. Although previous committees had suggested that secondary education should begin earlier, none had presented a definite plan for effecting this change.

Then, too, the Committee on College Entrance Requirements outlined a number of specific advantages for the earlier introduction of secondary education which had not been mentioned in the reports of previous committees. The chief argument for reorganization before this time had been the need for shortening the period of elementary and secondary education. The Committee on College Entrance Requirements urged as further reasons for a 6-6 plan that (1) the seventh grade as compared with the ninth grade coincides more closely with changes in the growth of the child, (2) the transition from elementary to secondary education could be made more gradually, and (3) there would be greater retention of pupils in the upper-elementary grades and in the high school. More than a decade later these arguments for reorganization were to figure prominently in the junior high school movement.

3. Growing Sentiment for a 6-6 Organization

Support for the 6-6 Plan by the Department of Secondary Education. It has already been suggested that the Department of Secondary Education, of the National Education Association, supported the idea

[9] *Ibid.*, p. 659.

of a 6-6 organization as early as 1899 through the report of its Committee on College Entrance Requirements. The Department of Secondary Education gave further indication of an interest in a 6-6 plan by appointing, in 1905, a standing committee on the equal division of time between elementary and secondary education. In its first report, in 1907, this committee came out strongly for a 6-6 plan, presenting the following advantages for it: [10]

1. Pupils could be taught by teachers specially trained in the various subject fields.
2. Departmentalized instruction would give seventh and eighth grade pupils contact with several teacher personalities.
3. The 6-6 plan would make laboratories available so that elementary science could be introduced earlier.
4. Manual training shops would be more readily accessible to upper-grade pupils.
5. The work in the modern languages could be begun earlier and continued longer than at present.
6. The transition from the elementary to the secondary school would be less abrupt.
7. More pupils would be likely to enter the ninth grade than under the traditional plan.
8. An equal division of the twelve years would make the system more nearly self-consistent, as is shown by the European secondary schools.
9. The six-year secondary course would give pupils more time to prepare for college.
10. The lengthening of the high school course to six years would help extend the curriculum to include some of the newer subjects.

It should be noted that several arguments for a six-year secondary school which were not emphasized by earlier committees on reorganization received considerable attention in this report. Among them were the belief that under the 6-6 plan better-trained teachers could be obtained, conditions for better teaching could be developed, and departmentalized instruction could be introduced. Some of these advantages were to be stressed greatly later on by proponents of the junior high school.

As a basis for a later report, in 1909, the committee carried on extensive correspondence through both individual and circular letters with city superintendents concerning their attitude toward a 6-6 organization. On the basis of this correspondence the committee con-

[10] Gilbert B. Morrison (chairman), "Report of the Committee on an Equal Division of the Twelve Years in the Public School Between the District and the High Schools," *Journal of Proceedings and Addresses of the National Education Association* (Los Angeles, 1907), pp. 705-10.

cluded that sentiment for a 6-6 plan was definitely growing. It stated further:

> There is a general impression revealed by this and other correspondence that the whole course of instruction, both elementary and secondary, should be simplified; that the differentiation of pupils' work should begin at the end of the sixth grade; that time is wasted on nonessentials and on impractical topics; that there should be greater flexibility in the promotion of pupils; that the whole system should be reorganized....[11]

Contributions of the Committees on Six-Year Courses. The reports of the Committees on Six-Year Courses did more than to urge again the desirability of a 6-6 organization. In these reports are expressed more clearly than in any previous statement the reforms that were so urgently needed in the administrative organization and the educational program of the 8-4 plan. Some of these reforms had been suggested before, but others were here urged for the first time. In the decade following the reports of these committees, most of their recommendations were to be incorporated into the junior high school and were to become the characteristic features of that institution. The work of the Committees on Six-Year Courses is of interest for another reason; namely, *these were the first committees of national standing to be appointed expressly for the purpose of studying the reorganization of the 8-4 plan.* The reports of these committees were exceedingly influential in gaining support for the reorganization of the 8-4 plan, and, later, for the introduction of the junior high school.

Emphasis on Economy of Time in Education. One of the most interesting developments in the reorganization movement was the emphasis on economy of time in education. It was particularly the college and university people who were concerned with this aspect of reorganization. No doubt this interest developed in part from the early emphasis on economy of time by President Eliot of Harvard. Some of the leaders in the economy of time movement suggested that the total period of elementary and secondary education be shortened, while others favored introducing some college subjects into the upper high school grades.

In 1903, the concern for economy of time in education led to the appointment of a standing committee by the National Education Association. Known as the Committee on Economy of Time in Education, it made periodic reports over a period of years, emphasizing particularly that the total period of elementary and secondary education could be shortened by two years without necessarily reducing the value of that education. In a comprehensive report in 1913, this com-

[11] *Ibid.,* pp. 502 f.

mittee made the following suggestions which tended to support some of the early thinking underlying junior high school education:

1. Saving of time can be effected by selecting the most important topics and subjects for study; by differentiation of methods for various types of courses; by vitalizing subjects and relating them to life; by adapting instruction to the interests, capacities, and mental development of pupils; by simplifying courses of instruction; and by ceasing the multiplication of subjects.
2. The last two years of the elementary school should be included in secondary education, and the study of foreign language, elementary algebra, constructive geometry, elementary science, and history should begin two years earlier than at present.
3. The following divisions of general and special education are proposed:

Elementary education .... 6 to 12
Secondary education
(2 divisions—4 years and 2 years) .... 12 to 18
College .... 16 to 20
University
(graduate school and professional schools) ...... 20 to 24 [12]

The reports of the Committee on Economy of Time in Education, coming from 1903 to 1919, are important in this discussion because they appeared at a time when the junior high school movement was just getting under way. The basic philosophy of this committee supported that of other committees on reorganization, and its numerous specific suggestions on changes in the educational program had much influence on the developing program of the junior high school after 1910.

Influence of the Various Committees on the Junior High School. It is an interesting fact that the idea of an intermediate school, such as the junior high school, was not seriously considered by any of the committees on reorganization until after the junior high school was established. The Committee on Economy of Time, in a report in 1913, recommended such an intermediate school. But by that time several junior high schools had already been established in the United States. We must conclude, therefore, that the plan of grade organization which included the junior high school was not a direct outcome of the recommendations of the various committees on reorganization.

The fact that the precise plan of grade reorganization which included the junior high school did not originate with any of the com-

[12] James H. Baker (chairman), *Report of the Committee of the National Council of Education on Economy of Time in Education,* United States Bureau of Education Bulletin No. 38 (Washington, D.C.: Government Printing Office, 1913), pp. 10-19.

mittees on educational reform does not mean that these committees had little or no influence on the development of the junior high school. *Actually, the basic philosophy and virtually all the important administrative and instructional features of the early junior high schools were largely the outgrowth of the recommendations of the various committees that served for two decades beginning with the Committee of Ten in 1892.* For instance, basic concepts underlying the junior high school idea which were stressed by the various committees on reform included: (1) better provision for the needs of young adolescents, (2) better provision for exploration by the pupils of their interests and abilities, (3) better individualization in the instructional program, and (4) better articulation between elementary and secondary education.

4. Other Influences Toward Reorganization

Experience With the 7-4 Plan. In addition to the various professional committees, a number of other factors played a part in the reorganization movement. One of these was the experience of Kansas City, Missouri, with the 7-4 organization, dating back to 1867. In an address before the Department of Superintendence in 1903, Superintendent James M. Greenwood of Kansas City said that his experience with the plan led him to believe that "all that is really valuable to the child in a ward-school course can be learned in seven years. Furthermore, I do not hesitate to affirm that, in view of all facts, an eight-year course is one year more than pupils of average ability need to do the work." [13] In support of his recommendation of the seven-year elementary course, Greenwood showed that a larger proportion of youth in Kansas City continued into high school than in any other city of the same or larger size in the United States. Greenwood's report on the apparent success of the shorter school course in Kansas City gave further encouragement to the proponents of economy of time in education.

Influence of Pupil Elimination Studies on Reorganization Movement. Recognition of the need for educational reforms undoubtedly was stimulated during the first decade or so after 1900 by the studies of pupil withdrawals which were made by Thorndike (1907), Ayres (1909), and Strayer (1911). Frank F. Bunker, who, as superintendent of schools in Berkeley, California, reorganized the school system there beginning in 1910, summarized the main conclusions from these three

---

[13] James M. Greenwood, "Seven-Year Course for Ward-School Pupils," *Journal of Proceedings and Addresses of the National Education Association* (Boston, 1903), p. 258.

studies, as they relate to pupil withdrawals in the upper elementary and early high school grades, as follows:

> Of every one hundred children annually entering the first grade of our schools, practically all reach the end of the fifth grade. Between this point and the first year of high school, from 60 to 67 per cent of those reaching the fifth grade will be lost, leaving but from seventeen to twenty-five of the original one hundred pupils who will reach the second year of high school. Out of this number, only from eight to ten will finally complete the high-school course.[14]

Coming at a time when interest in the reorganization of the 8-4 plan was already high, the studies of pupil withdrawals served as further objective evidence of the need for reforms in the educational program of the upper elementary and high school grades. These studies emphasized particularly the fact that many pupils failed to make the transition from the eighth grade in the elementary school to the ninth grade in the high school. The evidence was sufficiently convincing to encourage many communities where there already was dissatisfaction with the 8-4 plan to hasten the reorganization of that plan.

5. Growth of the Junior High School

Departure from 8-4 Plan Before 1910. There were some departures from the traditional plans of grade organization before 1910. Unfortunately we know little about either the number or the form of these early reorganized systems. The information available must be credited largely to Superintendent Frank F. Bunker of Berkeley, California, who made a survey in 1911 to ascertain the type of grade organization prevalent in cities with a population of eight thousand or more.[15]

Bunker found that, of 669 cities investigated, only 24 had introduced a type of grade organization which was a departure from the traditional plans. In view of the fact that by 1911 the problem of reorganization had been under serious study for two decades, that number of reorganized city systems was certainly not large. It does indicate, however, that some beginnings were being made to introduce reforms in the traditional program of elementary and secondary education.

[14] Frank F. Bunker, *Reorganization of the Public School System*, United States Bureau of Education Bulletin No. 8 (Washington, D.C.: Government Printing Office, 1916), p. 101.

[15] Frank F. Bunker, *The Junior High School Movement: Its Beginnings* (Washington, D.C.: F. W. Roberts Co., 1935), p. 75.

The first city to introduce a modified grade organization was Richmond, Indiana, which in 1896 placed the seventh and eighth grades in
a separate building. This was not merely a housing reorganization,
for it included some significant program changes as well. Curriculum
changes for the seventh and eighth grades made before 1900 in Richmond included modifications in English, mathematics, social studies,
music, and art, and the introduction in these grades of practical arts
and a foreign language. New features in organization and administration included departmentalized teaching, elective courses, promotion by subjects, and homerooms with faculty advisers.[16] Richmond
undoubtedly has a strong claim to the honor of establishing the first
intermediate school with a functional reorganization that is similar
to the junior high school as it developed after 1910.

A number of other cities soon followed Richmond in the introduction of an intermediate school for grades seven and eight, although
it is not clear that these systems effected any substantial reforms in
their educational programs. Lawrence, Kansas, in 1901, and New
York City, in 1905, were among the early cities to introduce an intermediate school. A number of cities in Bunker's survey reported a
6-6 organization, among them Ithaca, New York; Rahway, New
Jersey; and Saginaw, Michigan.

Several practices were fairly common in many of these early reorganized systems; they included the tendency to consider grades
seven and eight as part of the secondary school, the introduction of
departmentalized teaching, promotion by subjects, and elective courses
and curriculums below the ninth grade. Experience with these practices in the early reorganized schools was undoubtedly of value to
leaders in the junior high school movement after 1910.

Introduction of the First Junior High Schools. The school year
1909-10 is ordinarily considered to mark the beginning of the junior
high school movement. In that year two city systems—Columbus,
Ohio, and Berkeley, California—introduced the 6-3-3 organization.
During the years immediately following 1910, these cities attracted
nationwide attention to this new type of intermediate school. Other
cities studied the experiments in Columbus and Berkeley, and many
were so favorably impressed that the 6-3-3 plan was rapidly introduced elsewhere. From the time that the junior high school was first
introduced in these two cities it seemed to be the answer to the prob-

---

[16] The information about the program in the Richmond, Indiana, schools is based
on a report left by N. C. Heironimus, who was principal of the intermediate school
there in 1896 and for many years thereafter. This report was made available to the
authors by the Richmond school authorities.

lem of reorganization which had been so earnestly discussed for two decades.

The story of the junior high school in Berkeley is typical of that of other early junior high schools.[17] The immediate reason for reorganization was apparently an overcrowded high school building. But the two "introductory high schools" established in Berkeley constituted from the start more than a rearrangement of the grades merely for housing purposes. A modified instructional program was immediately introduced in these schools, including the offering of elective courses, the introduction of foreign languages, enrichment in the content and methods of instruction, and departmentalized teaching.

It is debatable as to which city was the first to introduce an intermediate school corresponding to a junior high school organization. Richmond, Indiana, with the introduction in 1896 of an intermediate school for grades seven and eight, apparently was the first city to establish such a school for these two grades. After 1896, the program in Richmond was modified considerably, and by 1910 it embodied many of the practices which later became part and parcel of the junior high school. Columbus, Ohio, claims to have had the earliest three-year intermediate school, established in September, 1909, and it also was the first to call the new organization a "junior high school." The two "introductory high schools" in Berkeley, established in January, 1910, were the first three-year intermediate schools, according to Bunker, to introduce a modified program especially designed to meet the needs of early adolescents. What is more important, however, is that these communities pointed the way for others in the establishment of the junior high school.

Growth Since 1910. The success of the junior high school idea in Richmond, Columbus, Berkeley, and other cities attracted nation-wide attention, with the result that junior high schools were soon introduced in many communities in the United States. In small communities the 6-6 plan spread rapidly, while in large communities the 6-3-3 plan was more popular. Frequently, building and administrative considerations influenced communities to introduce the 6-2-4 plan, or some other type of reorganized school. By 1920 there was a sufficient number of reorganized schools to justify the conclusion that the 6-6 division between elementary and secondary education was quite generally recognized as being desirable.

The first period of rapid growth of junior and junior-senior high schools came during the 1920's when both elementary and secondary school enrollments were increasing rapidly. Although there were only 55 junior high schools in 1920, by 1930 this number had grown to 1,842 (Table 1). The number of combined junior-senior high schools and separate senior high schools likewise increased tremendously during the same period.

TABLE 1

NUMBER AND VARIOUS TYPES OF SECONDARY SCHOOLS, 1920-1952

Type of School	1920	1930	1938	1946	1952
Junior high schools	55	1,842	2,372	2,653	3,227
Junior-senior high schools	828	3,287	6,203	6,360	8,591
Senior high schools	22	648	959	1,312	1,760
Regular high schools	13,421	16,460	15,523	13,797	10,168
Total	14,326	22,237	25,057	24,122	23,746

Source: Walter H. Gaumnitz and J. Dan Hull, "Junior High Schools Versus the Traditional (8-4) High School Organization," *Bulletin of the National Association of Secondary-School Principals,* XXXVIII (March, 1954), 112-21.

Since World War II there has again been a tremendous growth in the number of reorganized secondary schools. The largest growth is in the junior-senior or six-year high schools, the number increasing by one third from 1946 to 1952. Because the six-year high school is so appropriate for rural and small urban communities, this growth will no doubt continue. There has also been a considerable growth, however, in the number of junior high schools, their number increasing more than one fourth from 1946 to 1952.

In a number of respects the year 1952 may be considered a significant one in the development of the reorganized secondary schools. An examination of statistics published by the United States Office of Education reveals that, for the first time in our history, by 1952 the reorganized schools were clearly the predominant type of school organization in America.[18] This was true not only so far as the number of schools was concerned, but also in the number of pupils enrolled in the various types of schools. More specifically, the situation in 1952, with respect to the various types of reorganized secondary schools was as follows:

1. The number of reorganized secondary schools in the United States exceeded the number of regular high schools, 57 per cent being of the reorganized type.
2. The number of pupils in reorganized secondary schools far exceeded those in regular high schools, with 75 per cent enrolled in reorganized schools.

[18] Walter H. Gaumnitz and J. Dan Hull, "Junior High Schools Versus Traditional (8-4) High School Organization," *Bulletin of the National Association of Secondary-School Principals,* XXXVIII (March, 1954), 112-21.

3. The number of pupils in grades seven and eight in reorganized schools exceeded those in regular elementary schools, with 54 per cent enrolled in the reorganized schools.
4. The separate junior high school was developing quite definitely as an urban school, with 81 per cent in communities of 10,000 or more population.
5. The junior-senior or six-year high school was developing primarily as a rural and small urban school, with 77 per cent in communities of less than 10,000 population.

6. Conclusion

When President Eliot first pointed the way toward educational reforms before the turn of the century, it was impossible to foresee the far-reaching influence which his recommendations were to have. Certainly, it is evident from our study of the history of American education since 1890 that our schools were ready for some reforms. The intervening years have seen a thoroughgoing discussion of the type of grade organization best suited to the needs of young adolescents; the introduction of the 6-6 and 6-3-3 plans of grade organization; and the growth of the reorganized plans until they predominate throughout much of the United States.

If one is to judge from present trends, it appears that this growth of reorganized secondary schools will continue. The majority of the schools which are being built today to meet rapidly increasing enrollments are either separate junior and senior high schools or combined six-year high schools. In the years ahead the reorganized secondary schools should increase in numbers with a corresponding decline of the four-year high school. The junior high school and the six-year high school have indeed come to stay as a prominent part of the American school system.

Questions and Exercises

1. From a study of various sources in American educational history, describe the elementary schools before 1800, the Latin grammar school, the academy, the first high schools.

2. Locate all the information you can about the development of the high school in your state, tracing the development of the four-year high school and of the reorganized secondary schools.

3. From a study of available sources, trace the development of the secondary school in your own community. Old files of a local newspaper, records of the board of education, superintendents' reports, and older citizens are sources of such information.

4. What was the most significant contribution of each of the committees on reorganization?

5. Assume that you were a superintendent of schools in 1910 in a community which was contemplating the introduction of the 6-3-3 plan. Prepare a summary of arguments for such a reorganization, basing it on the committee reports included in this chapter.

6. It is frequently stated that the junior high school makes most growth in a period of increasing school enrollments. Explain fully why this has been true.

7. Why do you suppose the movement for economy of time in education did not make more headway? That is, why did not more school systems shorten their programs of elementary and secondary education in harmony with the recommendations of the leaders and committees in this movement?

8. Study the most recent statistics in the Biennial Survey of Education in the United States, published by the United States Office of Education, and prepare a summary of trends in the growth of the different types of secondary schools in the United States.

9. Consult the statistical reports of the department of education in your state and prepare a summary of trends in the growth of the different types of secondary schools.

10. Obtain all the copies you can of brochures and booklets used in communities in your state where there has recently been an effort to change from an 8-4 to a 6-6 or a 6-3-3 plan. Summarize the reasons given for the change.

Chapter 2

PHILOSOPHY OF THE JUNIOR
HIGH SCHOOL

Three subjects should receive attention in studying the philosophy of the junior high school: (1) the objectives of junior high school education; (2) basic points of view on junior high school education; and (3) the particular functions that the junior high school should serve. The purpose of this chapter is to present a discussion of these aspects of the philosophy underlying the junior high school.

1. OBJECTIVES OF JUNIOR HIGH SCHOOL EDUCATION

Objectives of Secondary Education. The objectives of all secondary education are generally accepted as the objectives of the junior high school as well. The objectives of secondary education have been variously formulated from time to time. The statement known as the "Seven Cardinal Principles of Secondary Education," formulated in 1918 by the Commission on the Reorganization of Secondary Education of the National Education Association, has been most widely used. When this statement was formulated, the junior high school movement was well under way, and the junior high school was already recognized as a part of our system of secondary education. Except for its emphasis on vocational preparation, this statement is as appropriate for the junior high school today as it was in 1918. It can be useful in giving direction to any program of junior high school education.[1]

More recently, the Educational Policies Commission of the National Education Association developed a statement of purposes for both elementary and secondary education in America, including, of course, the junior high school grades. Although this statement is long, it is so helpful in giving an overview of the objectives to be achieved through a program of junior high school education that it is quoted here in its entirety. For interpretation and implications of these ob-

[1] See *Cardinal Principles of Secondary Education,* United States Bureau of Education Bulletin No. 35 (Washington, D.C.: Government Printing Office, 1918), pp. 10-11.

jectives, the entire volume in which the statement appeared should be thoroughly studied.[2]

In presenting its statement of the purposes of education, the Commission first stated the over-all purpose of American education:

> The general end of education in America at the present time is the fullest possible development of the individual within the framework of our present industrialized society. The attainment of this end is to be observed in individual behavior or conduct.[3]

The Commission then developed this over-all purpose in more detail under four groups of objectives, as follows: [4]

THE OBJECTIVES OF SELF-REALIZATION

The Inquiring Mind. The educated person has an appetite for learning.
Speech. The educated person can speak the mother tongue clearly.
Reading. The educated person reads the mother tongue efficiently.
Writing. The educated person writes the mother tongue effectively.
Number. The educated person solves his problems of counting and calculating.
Sight and Hearing. The educated person is skilled in listening and observing.
Health Knowledge. The educated person understands the basic facts concerning health and disease.
Health Habits. The educated person protects his own health and that of his dependents.
Public Health. The educated person works to improve the health of the community.
Recreation. The educated person is participant and spectator in many sports and other pastimes.
Intellectual Interests. The educated person has mental resources for the use of leisure.
Aesthetic Interests. The educated person appreciates beauty.
Character. The educated person gives responsible direction to his own life.

THE OBJECTIVES OF HUMAN RELATIONSHIP

Respect for Humanity. The educated person puts human relationships first.
Friendships. The educated person enjoys a rich, sincere, and varied social life.
Cooperation. The educated person can work and play with others.
Courtesy. The educated person observes the amenities of social behavior.
Appreciation of the Home. The educated person appreciates the family as a social institution.
Conservation of the Home. The educated person conserves family ideals.
Homemaking. The educated person is skilled in homemaking.
Democracy in the Home. The educated person maintains democratic family relationships.

---

[2] Educational Policies Commission, *The Purposes of Education in American Democracy* (Washington, D.C.: National Education Association, 1938).
[3] *Ibid.*, p. 41.
[4] *Ibid.*, pp. 50, 72, 90, 108.

The Objectives of Economic Efficiency

Work. The educated producer knows the satisfaction of good workmanship.

Occupational Information. The educated producer understands the requirements and opportunities for various jobs.

Occupational Choice. The educated producer has selected his occupation.

Occupational Efficiency. The educated producer succeeds in his chosen vocation.

Occupational Adjustment. The educated producer maintains and improves his efficiency.

Occupational Appreciation. The educated producer appreciates the social value of his work.

Personal Economics. The educated consumer plans the economics of his own life.

Consumer Judgment. The educated consumer develops standards for guiding his expenditures.

Efficiency in Buying. The educated consumer is an informed and skillful buyer.

Consumer Protection. The educated consumer takes appropriate measures to safeguard his interests.

The Objectives of Civic Responsibility

Social Justice. The educated citizen is sensitive to the disparities of human circumstance.

Social Activity. The educated citizen acts to correct unsatisfactory conditions.

Social Understanding. The educated citizen seeks to understand social structures and social processes.

Critical Judgment. The educated citizen has defenses against propaganda.

Tolerance. The educated citizen respects honest differences of opinion.

Conservation. The educated citizen has a regard for the nation's resources.

Social Applications of Science. The educated citizen measures scientific advance by its contribution to the general welfare.

World Citizenship. The educated citizen is a cooperating member of the world community.

Law Observance. The educated citizen respects the law.

Economic Literacy. The educated citizen is economically literate.

Political Citizenship. The educated citizen accepts his civic duties.

Devotion to Democracy. The educated citizen acts upon an unswerving loyalty to democratic ideals.

Needs of Junior High School Youth. Some years ago, a committee for the National Association of Secondary-School Principals prepared an excellent statement of the needs of youth which has received widespread acceptance by leaders in secondary education.[5] This statement has been exceedingly helpful in giving direction to the program of education in many secondary schools.

[5] William L. Ransom, "How Well Does Your High School Rate on the Imperative Needs of Youth," *The Bulletin of the National Association of Secondary-School Principals,* XXXIII (October, 1949), pp. 8-46.

Recently, a group of junior high school administrators in California participated in a workshop to reconsider the purposes of the junior high school. They felt that a statement of pupil needs such as the one developed for the National Association of Secondary-School Principals could be exceedingly useful as a basis for developing programs of junior high school education. Although the earlier statement of pupil needs was in their opinion excellent for secondary school youth, they did not feel that it was as appropriate for junior as for senior high school pupils. Consequently, after much study, they re-formulated the statement so that it was pointed more directly toward the junior high school group. The following are the "Ten Imperative Needs of Junior High School Youth" developed by the California committee.[6]

1. All junior high school youth need to explore their own aptitudes and to have experiences basic to occupational proficiency.
2. All junior high school youth need to develop and maintain abundant physical and mental health.
3. All junior high school youth need to be participating citizens of their school and community, with increasing orientation to adult citizenship.
4. All junior high school youth need experiences and understandings, appropriate to their age and development, which are the foundation of successful home and family life.
5. All junior high school youth need to develop a sense of the value of material things and the rights of ownership.
6. All junior high school youth need to learn about the natural and physical environment and its effects on life, and to have opportunities for using the scientific approach in the solution of problems.
7. All junior high school youth need the enriched living which comes from appreciation of and expression in the arts and from experiencing the beauty and wonder of the world around them.
8. All junior high school youth need to have a variety of socially acceptable and personally satisfying leisure-time experiences which contribute either to their personal growth or to their development in wholesome group relationships, or to both.
9. All junior high school youth need experiences in group living which contribute to personality and character development; they need to develop respect for other persons and their rights and to grow in ethical insights.
10. All junior high school youth need to grow in their ability to observe, listen, read, think, speak, and write with purpose and appreciation.

[6] M. E. Herriott (chairman), "Organizing the Junior High School," *The Bulletin of the National Association of Secondary-School Principals*, XXXV (December, 1951), 14-19.

A statement of needs such as this can indeed be of much value to a faculty as it develops a program of education for junior high school youth. Its use is similar to that of any statement of objectives or purposes; namely, it indicates the goals that need to be achieved when a curriculum is developed, learning activities are planned, or classroom instruction is carried on.

2. Basic Philosophy of the Junior High School

A School for Early Adolescents. From the very beginning, it was emphasized that the junior high school should provide an effective program of education for early adolescents. This was, in fact, the chief purpose underlying its origin and early development. Educators of half a century ago believed that they were doing reasonably well in meeting the needs of elementary school children and of the older adolescents in the upper high school grades. Many of them questioned seriously, however, the effectiveness of the program for early adolescents, particularly the work offered in grades seven, eight, and nine. In fact, by the turn of the century, as previously noted, many teachers were convinced that the educational program of these grades was so unsatisfactory that there was urgent need for change in its organization, content, and methods.

There was much evidence to support this point of view. Teachers and parents were fully aware of the chronic indifference toward school displayed by early adolescents. Children who enjoyed school during their early and middle elementary grades seemed to find it uninteresting, if not actually distasteful, when they reached grades seven and eight. Some teachers were inclined to blame the children for this indifference to academic learning. The more discerning educators and parents realized, however, that if so many children found the educational program distasteful, the school itself might be at fault.

Concern about the attitudes of early adolescents toward school was accentuated by studies of elimination from school made soon after 1900 (described in Chapter 1). For children to be uninterested in school was serious enough, but to have them drop out in large numbers beginning in grade seven caused even more concern to both teachers and parents. What is more, these studies revealed that lack of interest in school was a major cause of early pupil withdrawal from school. *It is not surprising, therefore, that the junior high school movement from the very beginning was dominated by a desire to develop a program of education which would effectively meet the needs, interests, and abilities of early adolescents.* This point of view is the basis on

which the philosophy of junior high school education has been developed. It has continued to the present time as the dominating purpose of the junior high school.

Emphasis on All Aspects of Child Growth. If the junior high
school is to provide a program for young adolescents, it follows quite
naturally that all aspects of child growth and development need to be
emphasized. Such emphasis was lacking in the program of the 8-4
schools half a century ago. Then the chief concern in grades seven,
eight, and nine was to continue an education in the academic subjects
begun in the earlier elementary grades with almost exclusive emphasis
upon intellectual growth narrowly conceived—the "three R's," historical facts, and the like. The child's growth as a person was badly
neglected.

During the early adolescent years, more than at any other age level,
educators need to be concerned with the social, emotional, and personal development of the child. During these years the child develops
new social relationships with those of the other sex; he undergoes
physiological changes which have a considerable bearing on his emotional development; and qualities begin to emerge which will be a
definite part of his personality and character as he grows toward adult-
hood. During the early adolescent years he develops interests in
music, creative hobbies, participating sports, and certain types of community participation. It is essential that the program of junior high
school education should recognize these various aspects of child growth
and development.

This statement does not imply that subject matter skills, information, and understandings are unimportant. In fact, just the opposite
is true. If the young adolescent is to mature into a competent and
self-assured adult, he needs to be well informed, to be able to speak
effectively and fluently, and to write well. Thorough preparation in
subject matter, therefore, is an integral part of the child's social, emotional, personality, and character development. The education of the
child in all these respects is basic to an effective program of junior high
school education.

Recognizing Each Child as an Individual. In the junior high
school we find boys and girls at all stages of physiological, physical,
and social maturity. In fact, at no other level in the entire school
system do we find greater differences among boys and girls. These
differences are of particular concern to the teacher of physical education and athletics, to the director of the glee clubs and the chorus, and
to those who are planning social activities for the school. Some of the
boys are sufficiently well developed to participate in the more rugged

sports of the secondary school, while others are much more like the youngsters in grades five and six. The girls may be interested in dating, while many of the boys in their classes shun the opposite sex. The voices of the boys in the chorus and the glee club are changing so rapidly that the director finds it difficult indeed to plan more than a few weeks ahead.

Even in the academic subjects these extreme differences among pupils create difficult instructional problems. The maturity of the pupils has a bearing on their reading interests in the English class; their physical development may cause reluctance to participate in oral activities before a group; and their desire for physical activity may make it difficult for them to sit still for a long part of the day in the academic classes. Then, too, the range of differences increases tremendously in the achievement level of pupils in certain fundamental skills. For instance, it is not at all unusual to find pupils in the eighth grade whose reading skills are at the fourth-grade level, while others are reading as well as the typical twelfth-grade pupil. Similar differences exist among pupils in arithmetic, spelling, oral and written expression, and penmanship. These wide differences among early adolescents tax the ingenuity and resourcefulness of the teachers of the academic subjects as they attempt to work effectively with all pupils.

The earliest literature on the junior high school emphasized the need for developing a program which would recognize each pupil as an individual. This is particularly important because the junior high school is, as a rule, a larger school than the elementary school from which the child has come. It is so easy for the junior high school to take on the aspects of a large secondary school which has an impersonal attitude toward the individual child. That situation should not exist in an educational program for young adolescents. In an effective junior high school program, there is an awareness of every pupil as an individual personality; there is a curriculum which recognizes all levels of pupil ability and interests; and there is a broad offering of extraclass activities which gives every child an opportunity to have satisfying and worth-while educational experiences. Recognizing each child as an individual is indeed basic to the philosophy of junior high school education.

General Rather Than Specialized Education. The program of the junior high school should emphasize general, rather than specialized, education. General education provides learning experiences that are of interest and that may be useful to all pupils in everyday living. General education does not deny pupils some elective opportunities to meet individual needs and interests. It does emphasize that pupils should delay decisions concerning educational and vocational goals until the senior high school or later. Pupils should not be expected to decide during the junior high school years whether they want to go to college, teachers college, nursing school, or some other specialized school.

In most junior high schools the work in grades seven and eight is largely general education. Grade nine is apt to be somewhat different. In many junior high schools, pupils must make a choice at the beginning of the ninth grade concerning curricula or courses which lead to some specialized educational or vocational goal, particularly if they want to go to college. If pupils are to complete admissions requirements of certain colleges, it may be necessary to begin foreign languages in the ninth grade. Even so, these languages should be taught in such a way that they are largely exploratory in nature; they may be of some interest and value to pupils who do not have college as a goal. Furthermore, the curriculum in the senior high school should be so planned that pupils may begin their college-preparatory subjects in the tenth grade. In so far as possible, the program of the ninth grade, as well as that of the seventh and eighth, should emphasize general education.

Preparation in Basic Skills and Knowledge. Because the junior high school is considered a secondary school, its responsibility for instruction in the fundamentals is sometimes misunderstood. It is a mistake to believe that instruction in the fundamentals can and should be completed in the elementary school. Such instruction should be continued as long as pupils may profit from it. It is clearly the responsibility of the junior high school to continue instruction in the basic skills and knowledge.

We must be careful, however, not to place a narrow interpretation on the meaning of the fundamentals. They include, of course, reading skills, penmanship, the ability to express oneself clearly and forcefully, and arithmetic skills. But the interpretation today of what is included in the fundamentals goes far beyond the traditional "three R's."

Skill in speaking, for instance, is as important as ability in written expression. Yet oral expression all too often is not given much emphasis in the traditional program of instruction in the fundamentals. Then, too, we have come to recognize study skills as being important for further learning in the junior high school, the senior high school, and college. Basic information in the social sciences, the natural sciences, and other areas of knowledge is also important. Effective skills in human relationships are being emphasized. In other words, although we still consider the traditional three R's as being exceedingly important, we recognize that there are other skills and knowledge which are equally fundamental to further learning and effective living. The junior high school has a peculiar responsibility in the teaching of the fundamentals. Not only should instruction in the basic skills be continued as it has been in the elementary school, but an effort should be made for these skills to become more functional. It is the particular responsibility of the junior high school to provide opportunities for the various basic skills to become more useful in the everyday activities of the child. This responsibility should be accepted in the entire program of the school. Not only in the classroom but also in the various extraclass activities of the junior high school, opportunities can be provided to help make the fundamental skills become more functional for every child. This end cannot be achieved by accident. It can result only from careful planning on the part of every teacher.

The School as a Community. From the very beginning, it was emphasized that the junior high school should be more than a place where pupils go from room to room and from class to class. Rather, the junior high school should be considered a community where young adolescents spend three important years of their lives. It is a community where the major activities and interests of the pupils are centered, a community toward which they develop a strong feeling of loyalty and in whose life they play a significant part.

A good classroom program is, of course, an essential part of such a school community. Alone, however, it is not sufficient. In addition to the instructional program in the classroom, there need to be many activities outside the classroom which bring pupils together from all classes and from all grade levels. These activities should include pupil participation in the administration of school affairs, in assemblies, clubs, school publications, and sports activities. Through such activities the pupils should develop a feeling of belongingness and loyalty to their school community. Such loyalties are usually developed by having pupils make some contribution to the community life of the school. The development of a functioning school community is essential to an effective program of any junior high school.

3. FUNCTIONS OF THE JUNIOR HIGH SCHOOL

Meaning of Functions. The fundamental ways in which the junior high school operates to achieve its objectives are usually stated in terms of functions. The term "function," as used in this sense, refers to *the responsibility for providing those conditions or elements in the program of the junior high school which will lead most directly to the* *satisfactory realization of the ultimate aims of education.* For example, we know that pupils are more likely to reach the ultimate aims of education if there is satisfactory articulation between the elementary and secondary schools. Similarly, pupils are more likely to succeed in school, and consequently to achieve the goals of education, if there is a satisfactory program of guidance. Therefore, in terms of the definition, *articulation* and *guidance* are recognized as functions that should be assumed by the junior high school.

Functions are sometimes confused with aims or objectives. There is, however, a difference between these terms. *An aim or an objective is usually defined as a goal of the educational process, while a function of a school unit, such as the junior high school, is a modus operandi which will facilitate the realization of that goal.* Dr. Leonard V. Koos, one of the early writers on junior high school education, made this distinction when he used the term "function" in the sense of a *proximate* aim as compared with an *ultimate* aim. With reference to the functions of the secondary school, he said: "They are for the most part in the nature of conditions under which secondary education must go forward the better to achieve the 'ultimate' goals." [7]

Statement of Functions. During the early history of the junior high school, a number of different statements and studies of the functions of the junior high school were prepared. Several of these studies summarized the thinking and opinions of various leaders in the junior high school movement. Others were statements of the point of view of one person. The student of the history of the junior high school movement would do well to study the early statements of functions.

These statements served in part as a basis for that which is presented here by the present authors. It is believed that the best current thinking concerning the functions to be served by the junior high school have been incorporated in the following statement. *similar statement by GruhN, NASSP Feb '62 p 3-13.*

FUNCTION I: INTEGRATION

To provide learning experiences in which pupils may use the skills, attitudes, interests, ideals, and understandings previously acquired in such a way that they will become coordinated and integrated into effective and wholesome pupil behavior.

To provide for all pupils a broad, general, and common education in the basic knowledges and skills which will lead to wholesome, well-integrated behavior, attitudes, interests, ideals, and understandings.

FUNCTION II: EXPLORATION

To lead pupils to discover and explore their specialized interests, aptitudes, and abilities as a basis for decisions regarding educational opportunities.

---

[7] Leonard V. Koos, *The American Secondary School* (Boston: Ginn & Co., 1927), pp. 156 f.

To lead pupils to discover and explore their specialized interests, aptitudes, and abilities as a basis for present and future vocational decisions.

To stimulate pupils and provide opportunities for them to develop a continually widening range of cultural, social, civic, avocational, and recreational interests.

FUNCTION III: GUIDANCE

To assist pupils to make intelligent decisions regarding present educational activities and opportunities and to prepare them to make future educational decisions.

To assist pupils to make intelligent decisions regarding present vocational opportunities and to prepare them to make future vocational decisions.

To assist pupils to make satisfactory mental, emotional, and social adjustments in their growth toward wholesome, well-adjusted personalities.

To stimulate and prepare pupils to participate as effectively as possible in learning activities, so that they may reach the maximum development of their personal powers and qualities.

FUNCTION IV: DIFFERENTIATION

To provide differentiated educational facilities and opportunities suited to the varying backgrounds, interests, aptitudes, abilities, personalities, and needs of pupils, in order that each pupil may realize most economically and completely the ultimate aims of education.

FUNCTION V: SOCIALIZATION

To provide increasingly for learning experiences designed to prepare pupils for effective and satisfying participation in the present complex social order.

To provide increasingly for learning experiences designed to prepare pupils to adjust themselves and contribute to future developments and changes in that social order.

FUNCTION VI: ARTICULATION

To provide a gradual transition from preadolescent education to an educational program suited to the needs and interests of adolescent boys and girls.

4. CHANGING EMPHASES ON FUNCTIONS

The functions accepted for the junior high school were quite well recognized by 1920. Although various statements of functions have been formulated since that time, they continue to express much the same basic point of view as the earlier ones. There have indeed been some changes in the thinking on the functions of the junior high school, but they have been largely changes in interpretation, emphasis, and methods of implementation. These changes are briefly presented in the succeeding pages.

Trend Toward Integration. Although integration was generally accepted as a function of the junior high school by the 1920's, it is only recently that significant progress has been made toward implementing it. Twenty-five or more years ago there was much emphasis *about 1930*

on correlation between subjects. It was believed that this would be one step toward integration in a highly departmentalized school program. With this point of view there was little disagreement. Actually, there was little correlation on the part of teachers of the various subjects. What correlation took place was largely incidental, rather than a basic part of the planning by teachers in related subject areas.

In recent years, however, some educators believe that integration can be achieved in the junior high school program only by a serious modification of the highly departmentalized system. They feel that certain subjects can be combined and taught by one teacher and that as a result there will be better integration of learning outcomes. This is believed to be particularly true of English and social studies, and of mathematics and science. The trend toward the reorganization of subject areas is the most significant development in integration in the curriculum of the junior high school in recent years.

For many years the unit approach to planning and teaching learning activities has predominated in some subjects of the junior high school curriculum. At first these were largely subject matter units. Even so, some encouragement was given by the unit approach to the better correlation of learning outcomes between subject areas. Later, especially in the 1930's, the activity unit received more attention. The latest development in unit teaching is the experience-centered unit. In the experience-centered unit there is a tendency to reach beyond narrow subject matter lines and to draw upon the previous learning experiences of pupils in many areas both within and without the program of the school. It is obvious that the experience-centered unit, effectively used, may also lead to better integration of learning outcomes.

Broader Emphasis on Exploration. In the early literature on the junior high school, exploration was considered to be closely related to guidance. Attention was given particularly to the exploration of vocational interests and talents. Because of the high percentage of pupil drop-outs, this emphasis was natural in the early junior high schools.

The concept of exploration was broadened considerably in recent decades. With increased retention of pupils in school, vocational exploration at the junior high school level has lost some of its urgency. At the same time it has become important that pupils have an opportunity to try out their interests and abilities in educational activities, especially in those activities that have a bearing on later elective programs in the senior high school and in college. Furthermore, it is believed today that the schools should also give pupils an opportunity to find themselves in cultural, social, recreational, and avocational pursuits. In other words, exploration today is concerned not only with vocational activities but also with every other area of human interest and endeavor.

In early junior high school programs, exploration was carried on largely through certain courses developed especially for that purpose, such as survey courses in industrial arts, homemaking, general language, and general business. Although such exploratory courses are still being offered, today exploration is not confined to these areas. Rather, every subject in the curriculum and every extraclass activity is thought to have some contribution to exploration. The language arts provide an excellent example of this new point of view. It is believed the language arts provide opportunities for pupils to explore interests in literature, public speaking, journalism, and many other areas through the oral and written activities of the language arts class. Many opportunities for exploration may also be found in the social studies, physical education, music, art, and other subjects. In other words, every subject in the curriculum should be examined to see what opportunities it may provide for the exploration of pupil interests and talents.

Exploration is not achieved merely through course offerings. It is as much a matter of teaching methods as course content. In methods that encourage exploration of pupil interests and abilities, pupils are given much freedom to participate in planning learning activities and to choose activities of interest to them. The teacher may suggest activities which pupils may pursue, but the pupils may select those which give the greatest opportunity to explore their interests. A regimented assignment which is uniform for all pupils does not give the freedom of choice which is essential as a basis for exploratory activities. Flexibility in the methods of teaching is therefore considered essential if exploration is to be most effective. This emphasis on flexibility in the methods of teaching the various subjects is one of the most significant developments in the implementation of the exploratory function of the junior high school.

Guidance in Personal Development. Guidance, like exploration, is as old as the junior high school itself. In fact, guidance was one of the functions most often emphasized in the early literature urging the development of junior high school programs. However, like exploration, the concept of guidance has been considerably broadened since the first junior high schools were introduced. In the beginning, vocational and educational guidance were particularly emphasized, because of the large number of drop-outs during the junior high school years.

This situation has changed greatly. Instead of being a terminal institution for a large number of pupils, the junior high school is merely another step toward the completion of a high school education. With increased retention in school, guidance with respect to definite choice of a vocation is being left more and more to the senior high school level.

In place of emphasis on vocational guidance, there has been much more attention in the junior high school to helping pupils with personal, social, and emotional problems. It is only natural that this development should have taken place. In the past twenty-five years we have learned much about the psychological, physiological, and emotional development of young adolescents. In recent years, numerous books have been written on mental health and its relation to the educational program. The implications of these writings have been particularly significant for the junior high school grades. As a result, guidance in the junior high school today is directed toward helping boys and girls with all the problems and adjustments that they face. These include problems dealing with their educational progress, social development, emotional growth, and adjustments to new situations.

Attention to Individuals Within Classes. In the 1920's, much of the discussion concerning the individualization of the junior high school program centered around homogeneous grouping. Somehow, homogeneous grouping seemed to be the panacea for all the difficulties of meeting individual differences among pupils. It was believed that, if boys and girls could be placed in groups of approximately equal ability, the teachers could, with little difficulty, meet their different needs, interests, and abilities by adapting both the content and the methods of instruction. This thinking led to the development of differentiated marking systems, multiple-track curriculums, and other formal plans for differentiated teaching which would be appropriate in classes arranged according to ability.

It soon became evident, however, that no one plan of school organization would easily resolve difficulties of meeting individual pupil needs, interests, and abilities. It was especially evident that administrative devices, in and of themselves, would have little effect in meeting individual differences. It was true that such devices might help, but the important thing was the ingenuity and resourcefulness which the individual teacher displayed as he worked with boys and girls in every situation in school. *How teachers worked with pupils, rather than peculiar administrative devices, became the main focus of thinking on individualization of instruction.* Consequently, today there is much attention to developing methods of teaching which make it possible to meet more effectively the needs, interests, and abilities of individual pupils.

The changes which have taken place in the unit method of teaching are characteristic of this new emphasis. The unit approach, with its emphasis upon supervised learning activities instead of recitations, has long been recognized as one method of better meeting individual pupil needs. This approach is still basic to the planning of instructional activities for most junior high school classrooms. It has been considerably modified, however, during the many years in which it has been used. Today, the large-unit plan provides for much pupil participation in planning learning activities, numerous small-group activities, a variety of instructional activities, and self-evaluation by the pupils of their own progress. Through such flexible methods of teaching as the unit approach, rather than through administrative devices, we attempt today to meet the needs, interests, and abilities of individual pupils. Furthermore, we are emphasizing individualized teaching in all aspects of the school program, including guidance and extraclass activities as well as the classroom program.

Socialization Is Living Together. There has not been as much change in the interpretation of the socialization concept as in some of the other functions. Extraclass activities have always played an important part in achieving socialization. In fact, until recently little attention was given this function except in such activities. It was believed that participation in activities like the student council, assemblies, clubs, and various types of service organizations would contribute a great deal to the effectiveness with which young adolescents would be able to live with each other.

The contribution of extraclass activities to the socialization function is still generally accepted. In recent years, however, a change has taken place in some classroom methods, with the result that the classroom program today provides excellent opportunities for socialization. There have been many modifications in teaching methods which make better socializing activities possible. For example, in order that boys and girls may learn to work together effectively in planning and carrying on learning activities, there has been an increasing emphasis on small-group activities, particularly in language arts and social studies, but sometimes in other subjects as well. The emphasis on small-group activities is in part a result of the attention which has been given in both school and adult life to group dynamics. Other classroom methods related to socialization are also being used more often, such as pupil participation in planning, large-group discussions, skits and dramatizations, field trips and excursions, and other activities that give a prominent place to pupil planning and direction. With methods of teaching such as these, it is believed that junior high school classrooms, as well as extraclass activities, give pupils experiences which lead to more effective living together.

More Emphasis on Articulation. The articulation function was emphasized in the early literature on the junior high school more than any of the others. There was little suggestion, however, as to exactly what articulation meant or how it was to be implemented. It was assumed that somehow the introduction of the junior high school in and of itself would take care of articulation between the elementary and the secondary programs. As a result, with the introduction of the junior high school, little was done to improve articulation through specific practices and devices.

Although the point of view concerning articulation has not changed greatly, it is recognized today that this function can be implemented only if attention is given to specific articulation practices. Consequently, some school systems today are giving serious study to practices that seem to have a bearing on articulation. The more common articulation activities include workshops, faculty meetings, and curriculum study activities which bring teachers together from all grade levels. It is this increased emphasis on bringing teachers from all grade levels together to improve articulation, rather than any particular change in thinking concerning it, that constitutes the chief development in this function.

5. Developing a School Philosophy

Importance of a School Philosophy. The importance of having a well-formulated statement of philosophy for every junior high school cannot be overemphasized. A statement of basic philosophy can be exceedingly helpful in giving direction to any program of junior high school education. Such a statement should be clearly formulated and should be understood and accepted by the faculty of the entire school system. This is essential if there is to be satisfactory articulation between the program of the junior high school and that of the elementary and the senior high schools, and also satisfactory integration between the various learning activities within the junior high school itself. Agreement by the faculty on a basic philosophy is the first step toward the development of an effective program of junior high school education.

In many school systems today there is a well-formulated statement of philosophy for the entire school system. In a study at the University of Connecticut, Richard S. Byers found that of 130 school systems in the United States replying to a checklist, 59 per cent have written statements of philosophy. In most instances, staff members from all grade levels participated in formulating the statement.[8] This simplifies the task of the junior high school faculty in developing its own statement of philosophy. The philosophy of the junior high school should, of course, conform to the basic thinking of the statement for the school system as a whole. Even so, it might be desirable to have an additional statement for the junior high school itself, which would express in more detail those aspects of the philosophy of the entire system which are particularly appropriate to a program of education for young adolescents.

The statement of philosophy for a junior high school should contain a number of elements, among them the following:

1. *The ultimate goals of education for the entire program of education in the junior high school.* This statement, of course, should be much like that for the school system as a whole.
2. *A statement of basic point of view underlying a program of junior high school education which will readily achieve the ultimate goals.* This should include the point of view of the faculty concerning children and how they learn, the organization of the curriculum, methods of teaching boys and girls, the administration of the school, and relations with parents and other members of the community.
3. *A statement of suggestions for implementing this basic point of view.* This statement need not be prepared in great detail, but it should be sufficiently explicit so that it is clear to members of the faculty how the philosophy of the school can best be achieved.

The form which the statement of philosophy should take will depend, of course, upon the preferences of the faculty concerned. In any case, however, the statement of philosophy should be sufficiently brief and well outlined so that it can be readily examined, studied, and understood by all members of the staff.

Procedures for Formulation. There is no one pattern for the formulation of a statement of philosophy which will fit every junior high school. The statement will need to be developed in terms of the size of the individual school, the size of the entire school system, and the preferences of the faculty. In any case, however, the first step will be to create a feeling on the part of the faculty that such a statement of basic point of view is highly desirable, if not essential. Until that is

[8] Richard S. Byers, "Articulation in the Junior High School" (Unpublished doctoral thesis, University of Connecticut, Storrs, Conn., 1955), pp. 63-66.

done, members of the faculty are not likely to cooperate enthusiastically in preparing such a statement. How to develop this feeling on the part of the faculty is not easy to suggest. Sometimes a faculty, in working on a problem dealing with the curriculum, extraclass activities, or the administration of the school, finds that agreement on a statement of philosophy is essential before work on the other problem can satisfactorily proceed. Occasionally, however, a faculty can agree with a little encouragement that a statement of basic philosophy is so essential as a basis for an effective program of education that it is willing to formulate one.

Other suggestions concerning procedures for formulating a philosophy for a junior high school include the following:

1. All persons concerned in any way with the philosophy of the school should have a part in formulating it. This means that all members of the faculty, parents, and representatives of the elementary and the senior high school staffs should participate.
2. It is preferable that agreement be reached by consensus rather than majority vote. It is more likely that members of the staff will try to implement a philosophy with which they are in essential agreement.
3. The discussion of the philosophy should not be hurried, but should continue for a sufficiently long time and in enough detail so that all members of the participating group have an opportunity to contribute and to think through various points of view. Thorough study and discussion of the points of view that ultimately are included in the formulated philosophy not only lead to a better statement, but also result in more complete understanding and acceptance of that philosophy by the faculty.

Some attention should also be given to ways of implementing the formulated philosophy in the program of the school. It is so easy to spend much time in preparing a splendid statement of point of view and committing it to print, and then to lay it aside while the faculty continues with the program of the school much as before. Some of the following practices may be helpful in implementing the philosophy of the school:

1. The statement of philosophy should serve as an introduction to, and as a basis for, the development of any curriculum materials, curriculum guides, or statements of practices and policies for the school.
2. The faculty as a whole should refer occasionally to the statement of philosophy and discuss ways of implementing it in the program of the school.

3. There should be some provision for helping teachers who are new to the school to become acquainted with the philosophy and to study its implementation in practice.

4. The statement of philosophy needs to be reviewed occasionally in order that consideration might be given to needed changes. This is particularly true in a school where frequent changes are taking place in the faculty. Every new faculty member should have the feeling that he has participated in developing a statement of the point of view underlying the program of the school.

Philosophy Developed in Newton, Massachusetts. The procedure employed recently in formulating a philosophy of education for the Jonathan Weeks Junior High School, Newton, Massachusetts, provides an excellent example of how this may be done. The faculty of the Weeks Junior High School became concerned about the marking and reporting systems employed in the school. A survey by a faculty committee indicated that there was sufficient disagreement concerning the marking and reporting systems to justify studying ways of improving them. The immediate problem, therefore, was not to develop a philosophy for the school, but rather to develop a more effective marking and reporting system. The faculty had not proceeded far with this project, however, before it became evident that some agreement needed to be reached with respect to the basic points of view of the school's program before they could seriously approach the problem of modifying the marking and reporting system.

Much of a year was devoted by the Newton faculty to a discussion of points of view underlying junior high school education. An outcome of these discussions was the formulation of a well-developed statement of philosophy with some suggestions for its implementation. This statement was set up in such an attractive and well-organized form that it was readily understood by both teachers and parents.

The following aspects of the procedure employed at the Weeks Junior High School are of particular interest:

1. Although participation by the faculty was not compulsory, 80 per cent of the professional staff participated in a workshop which met weekly after school to study this problem. Furthermore, there was a faculty steering committee for the workshop elected by the staff, with the principal and assistant principal as ex-officio members. The workshop was, therefore, largely initiated and directed by the faculty itself.

2. Parent representatives were appointed from each elementary district served by the Weeks Junior High School. The first year, there were twelve parents and the second year eighteen, who

attended the meetings regularly and participated actively in all of the discussions.

3. Agreement by consensus rather than majority vote was considered desirable in developing various points of view that were included in the formulated statement of philosophy.

4. An editing committee was appointed to integrate the thinking of the faculty and to develop the points of view into a well-organized statement.

5. The final statement developed by the editing committee was thoroughly discussed by the faculty and, with some modification, was finally adopted.

6. The entire statement was developed into an attractive booklet and made available to teachers, administrators, supervisors, and interested parents.

6. EXAMPLES OF FORMULATED STATEMENTS OF PHILOSOPHY

WEEKS JUNIOR HIGH SCHOOL
NEWTON, MASSACHUSETTS

The philosophy at the Weeks Junior High School is an extensive statement which includes a philosophy for the school as a whole and for each of the subject areas. Because the statement is so long, only the basic outline can be included here.

Education at Weeks

The over-all purpose of education at Weeks Junior High School is to help boys and girls develop their potentialities and assume individual and group responsibilities for effective participation in our American democratic society.

This Is Our Basic Point of View

Weeks Junior High School exists as an integral part of the community to provide the best means it can for the individual and group development of its boys and girls—intellectually, physically, emotionally, morally and socially.

Toward Successful Living

That boys and girls at Weeks may live most successfully we are endeavoring to base our program upon:

What teachers know about the pupils they are teaching and the way these pupils learn.

What teachers believe should be important provisions of the school program if it is to be consistent with this knowledge.

What teachers expect of themselves if they are to work in harmony with what they know and believe.

JUNIOR HIGH SCHOOL
WELLESLEY, MASSACHUSETTS

Philosophy of Junior High School Education

We believe that a junior high school should offer opportunities to all pupils:
—to develop to the extent of their ability in fundamental subject matter fields,
—to pursue their special fields of interest,
—to develop good habits of character and citizenship.

In the accomplishment of the above aims the following procedures seem desirable:

I. Orientation and adjustment to bring about a gradual transition from elementary to secondary education.

II. A pupil guidance program which will follow the individual child through his junior high school years and will steer him into that course in the senior high school which will be for him desirable and suitable.

III. An enriched and varied program of studies which will provide a wide selection of subject matter to meet individual differences in abilities, interests and aptitudes.

IV. Teaching techniques which recognize that all children cannot proceed at the same pace; but that all children should be taught good study habits and good work habits.

V. A wise use of classroom time so that there will be more than "hearing of lessons"; there will be supervision and direction of *study* to the end that pupils may develop good study habits and good work habits right in the classroom.

VI. Evidence that the school is putting the *child* first, not the school or the subject.

VII. Provision for work of the activity or laboratory type so that the pupil may learn by doing and may have opportunity for self-evaluation and for measuring progress in terms of his own development.

VIII. As the use of the English language is so essential to all of life, we should strive for excellence in oral and written expression to the extent of potentialities in all children. This is not only the responsibility of the English teacher but of *all* teachers in *all* classes and *all* the time.

IX. A program of pupil activities which will meet the needs of adolescent youth for self-expression. Children at this age are active, energetic, and enthusiastic. We should aim to harness this energy and direct it into proper channels. Well-organized activities such as clubs, assemblies, class organizations and an intramural sports program serve as healthful outlets for the enthusiasms of youth. They have their basis in adolescent psychology.

X. A wholesome school morale which is the outgrowth of a well-planned organization, good teaching, purposeful activities, and genuine teacher interest in the welfare of boys and girls.

JUNIOR HIGH SCHOOL
SHAKER HEIGHTS, OHIO

Our Philosophy

Foreword: A Working Philosophy

We believe that the philosophy of our school should be a working instrument, one which we should all use to reach common ends. As individuals and as a group we express our philosophy whenever we define our problems to carry them out in school activities; we reveal our philosophy by the way we live with each other and with the boys and girls.

In writing this statement of our philosophy we have tried to put down those fundamental beliefs and purposes on which we now have majority agreement. We intend to refer to this statement as a guide and standard as we continually re-examine our school program, keeping what we conclude is good or making changes that seem wise.

Our Philosophy: A Way of Living

In our school we are trying to make understandable and real the democratic way of living.

Our Practice of the Democratic Way

In order to help youth understand that individual happiness and group welfare are interdependent, our school provides experiences in which:

The pupil, through an increasing sense of the worth of every individual, gains in self-confidence and in concern for others.

The group recognizes that every individual has something of value to contribute.

The pupil more and more assumes responsibility for his own acts and for the welfare of the group.

The individual and the group come to judge their acts in terms of the common welfare.

The pupil increasingly uses the scientific method of thinking and recognizes it as the best method of solving individual and group problems.

Our Conception of the Learning Process

We recognize that the physical, emotional, intellectual and social factors that make up a child's personality cannot be treated separately; therefore subject matter in various fields will be used as means for the development of the whole child, not as separate ends in the various fields.

The individual learns most readily when he feels a real need, when he has a share in planning an experience, when a purpose important to him will be advanced, or when he can test his new learning by making immediate use of it.

QUESTIONS AND EXERCISES

1. Be able to define each of the following terms: function, aim, and objective.

2. How may a faculty use each of the following in developing an effective curriculum for a junior high school: Seven Cardinal Principles of Secondary Education; The Purposes of Education in American Democracy; and the Needs of Junior High School Youth?

3. Would you modify in any way the statement of Needs of Junior High School Youth? Study the statement carefully with this in mind.

4. Would you modify in any way the statement of functions of the junior high school? Study the statement carefully with this in mind.

5. What changes have taken place in the interpretation of each of the functions of the junior high school since about 1920?

6. How has the tendency of youth to continue in school brought about changes in emphasis in some of the functions of the junior high school?

7. Outline in some detail the steps a faculty should follow in developing a statement of philosophy for its school.

8. What steps can a faculty take to be sure that its accepted statement of philosophy will be implemented in the instructional program of the school?

9. Develop a statement of philosophy for a junior high school.

Chapter 3

ADVANTAGES AND LIMITATIONS OF THE JUNIOR HIGH SCHOOL

From the beginning of the junior high school movement, many claims have been made concerning the advantages of the junior high school, and at the same time some disadvantages have been claimed. As the junior high school developed, thinking changed concerning the new institution. Some aspects which were claimed as advantages forty years ago are not so considered today; e.g., the early introduction of college-preparatory subjects and the complete departmentalization of the school program. Other factors formerly called advantages have lost their purpose because of changing conditions in school and society. The early introduction of vocational preparation, for example, has less point in a discussion of the advantages of the junior high school today than after World War I because a larger percentage of our youth now continue into the senior high school, where vocational education is more appropriate. Moreover, some early claims for the junior high school have not been substantiated, either through objective studies or experience.

The early objections to the junior high school likewise need to be studied in terms of almost half a century of experience. A number of the early criticisms have proved to be false, or at best seem to have little merit. Others have been directed at certain practices which are not necessarily basic to an effective junior high school program, such as the objections to complete departmentalization, highly regimented plans for homogeneous grouping, and promotion by subjects. Some objections which have merit are really cautions against dangers that can be avoided in a well-developed junior high school program.

On the following pages there will be presented a discussion of the advantages, limitations, and possible dangers of the junior high school type of organization and program. These will be grouped under the following headings: (1) the curriculum, the teaching staff, and other aspects of instruction; (2) achievement of pupils; (3) provisions for guidance, meeting pupil needs, and retention of pupils; and (4) housing, equipment, and cost.

1. Considerations Relative to Instruction

The Curriculum Is Broader. From the beginning of the junior high school movement, the claim has been made that an adequate program of instruction in home economics, industrial arts, music, art, and physical education can be provided at a reasonable cost more easily in a junior high school than in an elementary school. The same claim is made of a number of extraclass activities, such as sports, clubs, assemblies, and the music organizations. In grades seven and eight, these subjects and activities demand special facilities and teachers with special skills that cannot be readily provided in the elementary school.

The reasons, of course, are obvious. The laboratories and shops needed for industrial arts, homemaking, and art are expensive, and their use is quite specialized. The facilities and staff needed for a school band, an orchestra, and glee clubs also are not ordinarily available in the elementary school. The relatively small number of pupils in grades seven and eight in the typical elementary school does not justify the staff or facilities for these subjects and activities. Furthermore, even if the cost were not a factor, the limited number of pupils in the upper grades of elementary schools hinders the development of the type of programs in intramural sports, music, clubs, and assemblies that are possible in the junior high school, which draws its students from several elementary schools.

Curriculum Changes Are More Easily Made. It also seems to be true that curriculum changes for pupils in grades seven, eight, and nine are made more readily in junior high schools than in schools under the 8-4 plan. A number of factors appear to account for this greater flexibility. First, with grades seven to nine in a separate school, it is easier to study the needs of pupils in this age group and to develop a program to meet those needs. Second, with building facilities and the staff available in many subject areas and activities, a faculty is provided which has a wider variety of backgrounds and experience than in the upper grades of the elementary school. Third, the fact that the junior high school is a new institution, reasonably free from the limitations of tradition, encourages curriculum change. Fourth, the junior high school frequently is established in a new building with new leadership, a situation which is conducive to curriculum changes. Perhaps, as the junior high school becomes more mature and established as a part of the American school system, these conditions will not continue. For the present, however, they seem to have a decided influence in encouraging study and experimentation in curriculum developments in the junior high school.

Pupil Activities Are Readily Developed. One of the most important advantages of the junior high school is that it can provide a broad
program of extraclass activities suitable for young adolescents. Educators have long recognized the importance of such activities in the
educational growth of the child, particularly as he enters early adolescent years. Such activities as clubs, assemblies, student council, publications, and sports offer desirable educational experiences which
cannot be duplicated in the usual classroom program. These activities
help the young adolescent develop poise and self-confidence; they help
develop the social graces; they encourage attitudes of civic and social
responsibility; they provide an opportunity to work cooperatively
with other youth; and they help establish firm friendships through
common interests. These things are exceedingly important in the life
of the young adolescent and contribute to his educational growth and
development.

Under the 8-4 plan, it is difficult to provide an adequate program of
extraclass activities for young adolescents. In the elementary school,
the physical facilities—gymnasium, auditorium, laboratories, and shops
—are often lacking. Then, too, the number of pupils in grades seven
and eight is usually too small to justify or sustain a broad program of
activities. Finally, the small number of teachers in grades seven and
eight of the elementary school limits the variety of faculty talent that
is essential for such activities. In the ninth grade of the four-year high
school the facilities and staff may be available, but upper-grade pupils
tend to dominate these activities and to crowd out the younger pupils.
In other words, it is much easier to provide an adequate program of
extraclass activities for young adolescents in a junior high school than
in schools under the 8-4 plan.

Better-Qualified Teachers. A strong argument for the junior high
school has been that it attracts better-qualified teachers than grades
seven and eight in the elementary school as the result of higher salaries,
greater prestige, departmentalized teaching, and better opportunities
for promotion to administrative and supervisory positions, among
other things. In the junior high school, the number of years of college
work which teachers have had tends to be higher than in the elementary school. Then, too, the junior high school has attracted more men
than the elementary school, thus giving pupils more contact with men
teachers. The departmentalized program in the junior high school
makes it possible for teachers to concentrate on one or two subjects,
giving them an opportunity to be more thoroughly prepared in the
subjects they teach. These factors all tend to improve the effectiveness of the teaching staff in the junior high school.

It is true that similar changes have been taking place in the elementary school. Many school systems, for instance, have established salary schedules that are uniform for all grade levels. The amount of college preparation of elementary teachers has increased considerably, with many having advanced degrees. In recent years, the elementary school has also attracted more men teachers. Even so, sufficient improvement has been sustained in these respects in the junior high school so that in most communities it continues to have a better-prepared teaching staff than the elementary school.

Criticisms of the Instructional Program. In spite of these apparent advantages, the instructional program of the junior high school has been subjected to some criticisms. One has been directed at a practice that was quite common in the early junior high schools; namely, *that it is undemocratic and educationally unsound to introduce pupils so early to specialized education through vocational courses and differentiated curriculums.* Although this criticism may have been justified some years ago, it is not equally valid today. In recent years, vocational courses have been largely postponed until the senior high school. Furthermore, differentiated curriculums have almost disappeared from grades seven and eight. Although in some schools differentiated curriculums are still offered in the ninth grade, even there a single curriculum is rapidly becoming the prevailing practice.

A second criticism of the instructional program has been concerned with the high degree of departmentalization in the junior high school. Elementary school educators, who tend to favor keeping pupils with one teacher, were particularly strong in their opposition to departmentalized teaching for pupils in grades seven and eight. There is little doubt that this criticism is justified. Departmentalization was an imitation of a practice in the four-year high school. Many educators today believe it never was appropriate in the same way in the junior high school. Consequently, some reaction to the highly departmentalized program has developed in recent years. Usually this has expressed itself through the core curriculum, block-scheduling, common learnings, or some other practice for combining subjects and having pupils remain with the same teacher for several periods. The criticism of departmentalization in the junior high school is therefore rapidly becoming less valid.

A third criticism of the instructional program has been that there are not enough teachers available who are well prepared in the philosophy, program, and organization of the junior high school. For many years this was truly a decided disadvantage of the junior high school. Administrators and teachers for a new junior high school were usually drawn from the four-year high school and grades seven and eight in the elementary school. These people often continued the practices to which they were accustomed, instead of developing new ones that were appropriate for the junior high school.

Although finding a well-qualified professional staff for the junior high school continues to be a problem, the situation has improved tremendously. Teacher-education institutions are offering more programs designed especially for junior high school administrators and teachers. Furthermore, salaries in the junior high school are rapidly approaching the level of the senior high school, with the result that well-qualified people are more willing to make the junior high school their career. Consequently, the supply of well-qualified professional staff for the junior high school has improved greatly in the last decade.

2. Considerations Relative to Pupil Achievement

Achievement in the Junior High School. Many educators and parents have been concerned lest the achievement of pupils, especially in the fundamentals, might suffer in the junior high school. They have feared that such new studies as home economics and industrial arts, as well as the program of extraclass activities, would interfere with the older subjects. Obviously, for evidence on this point we must rely on studies of pupil achievement in the junior high schools as compared with schools on the 8-4 plan. The studies which are available were made some years ago. However, the conclusions from these studies seem to be equally valid today.

In studies made by Carpenter [1] in two Indiana schools, by Childs [2] in two Indiana counties, and by Porter [3] in the Minneapolis schools, there were no significant differences in achievement in standard tests between the pupils in grades seven and eight in the 8-4 schools and those in the junior high schools.

When schools were paired on the basis of the type of community in several Massachusetts school systems, both Mills [4] and Beatley [5]

[1] L. H. Carpenter, "A Study of the Effects of the Junior High Organization of Wabash, Indiana" (Unpublished master's thesis, University of Chicago, 1918).

[2] Hubert G. Childs, *An Investigation of Certain Phases of the Reorganization Movement in the Grammar Grades of Indiana Public Schools* (Fort Wayne, Ind.: Fort Wayne Printing Co., 1918).

[3] W. A. Porter, "A Comparative Study of the Scholastic Achievements Made by Junior and Non-Junior High School Pupils in Minneapolis, Minnesota" (Unpublished master's thesis, University of Minnesota, Minneapolis, 1927).

[4] H. C. Mills, "The Comparative Efficiency of the 8-4 and 6-3-3 Systems of Schools" (Unpublished doctoral thesis, Graduate School of Education, Harvard University, Cambridge, Mass., 1931).

[5] Bancroft Beatley, *Achievement in the Junior High School*, Harvard Studies in Education, No. 18 (Cambridge, Mass.: Harvard University Press, 1932).

found that, in spite of smaller time allotments for the fundamentals because of the addition of such subjects as home economics and industrial arts, pupils in the junior high schools did just as well on standard tests as those in the 8-4 systems. Similar results were found by Smith [6] in a study of pupil achievement in the junior high schools of Syracuse, New York. From these studies, one concludes that pupils in the junior high school are not at a disadvantage in the fundamentals as compared with pupils in the 8-4 schools, even though pupils in junior high schools have broader opportunities through such subjects as home economics and industrial arts and a time-consuming program of extra-class activities.

Achievement in the Senior High Schools. Another approach to the study of pupil achievement in the junior high schools is to see how their records compare with pupils from 8-4 schools when they get into the senior high school. Porter [7] found that junior high school graduates did as well as, but no better than, graduates of the eight-year elementary schools when they entered the senior high schools. In Porter's study the pupils were paired on the basis of I.Q., sex, nationality, and economic status. Lillian Glass [8] reported similar results for fifty pairs of seniors in the Frankford High School, Philadelphia. A study by Clem and Roberts [9] showed similar findings for two groups in Central High School, Syracuse, New York, while Landsittel [10] reported similar results with respect to marks made in the senior high school and in the freshman year in college. In other words, pupils from junior high schools are certainly not at a disadvantage when they compete with pupils from other schools in the senior high school and college.

Factors Influencing Studies of Achievement. Some considerations make it difficult to interpret the results of the studies regarding the influence of the junior high school on pupil achievement. One important factor in all of these studies was the newness of the junior high school in communities where the studies were made. In most cases

[6] Harry P. Smith, "The Relative Efficiency of the Junior High School vs. the Conventional 8-grade Type of School," *Journal of Educational Research*, XXIX (December, 1935), pp. 276-80.

[7] Porter, *op. cit.*

[8] Lillian Glass, "The Relative Achievement in Senior High School of Graduates and Non-graduates of Junior High Schools" (Unpublished master's thesis, University of Pennsylvania, Philadelphia, 1930).

[9] O. M. Clem and H. M. Roberts, "The Tenth Year Progress of Junior High School and Elementary School Pupils," *Journal of Educational Research*, XXI (April, 1930), pp. 288-96.

[10] F. C. Landsittel, "Scholastic Accomplishment in the Junior High School," *Journal of Educational Research*, XVIII (March, 1929), pp. 127-35.

the reorganized plan had been in effect so short a time that an adequately modified program had not yet been developed.

Furthermore, when many of these studies were made the teachers were largely unprepared in the philosophy, curriculum, and methods of the junior high school, most of them having recently transferred from schools on the 8-4 plan. In many of the schools even the principal was new to the junior high school program. With an inexperienced staff and a new educational program, one could hardly expect pupil achievement to improve in the junior high school during the first few years.

Besides the inexperience of the staff and the newness of the school program, several other factors have a bearing on the validity of the early studies of achievement in the junior high school. For instance, in interpreting the findings from the studies in which achievement tests were employed, the following factors must be considered:

1. The standard achievement tests employed in the early studies were developed largely to fit the factual content and the memory-type methods prevalent in the traditional 8-4 schools. Consequently, they may not have been so well adapted to the modified content and the socialized methods of the junior high school. Pupils in the 8-4 schools should therefore have excelled on these tests.

2. In the junior high schools, there has been ordinarily a smaller time allotment for the fundamental subjects usually covered by the achievement tests. This is true because a considerable portion of the school day in the junior high school has been devoted to such new subjects as home economics, industrial arts, foreign languages, and vocational studies, as well as to guidance and other extraclass activities. If other things are equal, pupils in the 8-4 schools should therefore show up better on the achievement tests.

3. Achievement tests as a rule measure only one type of educational outcome, namely, the mastery of subject matter. But in the junior high schools many learning outcomes other than mastery of subject matter are emphasized through socialized classroom methods, new subjects in the curriculum, and extraclass and guidance activities. Since these outcomes were not included in the studies of achievement, the results of those studies do not give a complete picture of the achievement of junior high school pupils.

Efficiency of the Junior High School as Judged by Authorities.
There are no recent studies in which achievement in the junior high school has been compared with that in other types of schools. However, an excellent recent study by W. C. Wood at the University of Colorado ascertained the thinking of leaders in secondary education on this point. Wood's study shows that almost all of 66 recognized

authorities on secondary education favored either the 6-3-3 or the 6-4-4 organization as compared with other types of organization. While 25 of the 66 authorities gave first rank to the 6-3-3 plan and 32 to the 6-4-4 organization, not one gave first rank to the 8-4 type of organization and only three gave it second rank.

TABLE 2

NUMBER AND PERCENTAGE OF TYPES OF ORGANIZATION RANKED BY AUTHORITIES
IN ORDER OF PREFERENCE FIRST, SECOND, AND THIRD

Types of Schools	First		Second		Third		Weighted Total
	No.	Per Cent	No.	Per Cent	No.	Per Cent	
6-3-3	25	38	24	39	5	9	128
6-4-4	32	48	11	18	6	10	124
6-6-(2)	3	4	13	21	22	38	57
5-7-(2)	—	—	—	—	2	3	2
8-4-(2)	—	—	3	5	7	12	13
4-4-4-(2)	—	—	4	6	4	7	12
9-3-(2)	2	3	1	2	3	5	11
7-5-(2)	—	—	2	3	7	12	11
Miscellaneous.	4	7	3	6	2	4	20

Source: W. C. Wood, "An Analysis of the Structural Organization of the Public Schools" (Doctoral dissertation, University of Colorado, Boulder, Colo., 1951).

Weightings for the different types of organization were obtained by first rank with 3 points, second rank with 2 points, and third rank with 1 point.

3. CONSIDERATIONS RELATIVE TO GUIDANCE, MEETING PUPIL NEEDS, AND RETENTION OF PUPILS

Better Guidance Facilities Are Possible. In the early literature on the junior high school, it was contended that better guidance facilities could be provided for early adolescents in a school which had a sufficient number of pupils to justify the employment of qualified guidance personnel. It was urged that this was particularly important in grades seven, eight, and nine because of the many educational problems that are found among early adolescents. In grades seven and eight of the elementary school, the number of pupils in any one school is too small to justify the staff and facilities needed for an adequate guidance program.

The claim that better guidance activities can be provided in the junior high school has been fully justified in practice. It is almost universal in the junior high school today to have some type of homeroom organization, with a homeroom teacher who has some guidance responsibilities for his group. Furthermore, most medium-sized and large schools have guidance specialists who devote much or all of their time to planning and administering the guidance program and to conferences with teachers and pupils on guidance problems. There is no doubt that the guidance activities of the junior high school are far superior to those of the upper grades in the elementary school.

Better Provision for Individual Differences. From the days of the earliest junior high schools, it has been contended that, in this type of school, it is much easier to make adequate provision for the different needs, interests, and abilities of boys and girls. Since a wide range of individual differences is particularly characteristic of early adolescents, providing for individual differences is indeed an important consideration in an educational program for grades seven, eight, and nine.

Meeting individual differences always has been, and still is, difficult in a school with limited enrollments, as is true in grades seven and eight of the typical elementary school. Almost all the practices for meeting individual differences which have been employed in the junior high school would be difficult or impossible with the small number of pupils in grades seven and eight of a single elementary school. The practices for meeting individual differences emphasized most in the early junior high schools were elective courses and curriculums, ability grouping, and promotion by subjects. To employ these practices effectively requires the large enrollments made possible by the junior high school.

In recent years these practices have been giving way to others that today seem to be more appropriate for early adolescents, such as a broad program of extraclass activities, remedial classes for pupils with learning deficiencies, and more effective methods of working with small groups or individual pupils within classes. Some of these practices likewise demand the larger enrollments and the type of administrative organization made possible by the junior high school. *The claim that individual differences among early adolescents can be met more adequately in the junior high school continues to be justified by the various practices which are being employed so effectively for this purpose.*

Better Exploratory Opportunities. As in the case of meeting individual differences, provision for adequate exploratory opportunities has been one of the strong claims for the junior high school. From the beginning of the junior high school movement, there is reason to believe that this claim has been realized. In the early junior high schools this was accomplished largely through elective courses and so-called "try-out" or exploratory courses. In fact, exploratory courses in industrial arts, home economics, business, and general language were among the distinguishing features of the early junior high school curriculum.

Recently exploration has not been limited to a few courses but has extended into every subject in the curriculum. Furthermore, it is being provided through a broad program of extraclass activities. Flexible methods of teaching in the classroom are also being employed more effectively for this purpose. *There is every reason to believe that the junior high school continues to justify the claim that, in this type of school, better opportunities for exploration can be provided.*

Pupils Are Retained Longer. The junior high school movement was given much impetus by the early studies of pupil elimination which revealed that pupil withdrawals were particularly high in grades seven, eight, and nine. It is common knowledge that pupil retention has improved tremendously in the past thirty to forty years, not only in the junior high school, but in the senior high school as well. It is difficult to ascertain how much of this increased retention is due to the introduction of the junior high school, as compared with other factors that obviously must also have had an influence on it. *There is much reason to believe, however, that the junior high school has had some influence in retaining pupils in school by offering an educational program that is more attractive to young adolescents.*

In recent years there have been no objective studies to evaluate the influence of the junior high school in retaining pupils in school. In the 1920's and 1930's, however, there were a number of such studies, all leading to the same conclusion, namely, that the junior high school has some influence in retaining pupils in school.[11] In the study by Fritz, which included junior high schools, eight-year elementary schools, and four-year high schools, there was a definite indication that more pupils in the junior high school tended to complete the ninth grade, but that there was little difference in retention beyond the ninth grade. Even so, this conclusion means that, in the junior high school, pupils tend to remain in school for one year more than in other types of schools.

Less Retardation in Ninth Grade. Without question, fewer pupils are retarded in the American schools today than a generation or two ago. There is little evidence, however, to indicate what influence, if any, the junior high school has had on the extent of retardation. We do know that fewer pupils are failed, and therefore not so many are retarded, in the ninth grade of the junior high school as compared

---

[11] These studies include: Childs, *op. cit.*; Carpenter, *op. cit.*; J. O. Powers, "Is the Junior High School Realizing Its Objectives?" *School Life*, XIV (December, 1928), 77-78; Ernest C. Witham, "Holding Powers of Junior and Non-Junior High School Cities," *School Executives Magazine*, XLVIII (January, 1929), 451-53; Ralph A. Fritz, *An Evaluation of Two Special Purposes of the Junior High School, Economy of Time and Bridging the Gap*, University of Iowa Studies in Education, No. 143 (Iowa City, Iowa: University of Iowa, 1927).

with that grade in the four-year high schools. Ninth-grade teachers in four-year high schools tend to have a more severe attitude concerning the promotion and failure of pupils than do teachers in the junior high schools. In the ninth grade, therefore, the junior high school has tended to reduce failures and retardation.

Economy of Time Not Achieved. Early in the reorganization movement one of the strong arguments for the junior high school was that it would make possible a reduction in the total number of years required for elementary and secondary education. College educators were especially interested in this claim. Junior high school educators, however, never took seriously the proposal to shorten the period of elementary and secondary education. The introduction of junior high schools has not reduced the years of elementary and secondary education. Furthermore, it is many years since there was a serious desire on the part of many educators that it should do so.

Articulation Has Improved. One of the earliest claims for the junior high school was that it would bridge the gap between the elementary and the secondary school. There is reason to believe that this claim has been substantiated. It is true that, in some communities, the junior high school introduced two breaks where only one existed before. At the same time, these breaks were not so severe as that between the eighth and the ninth grades under the 8-4 plan. Much still needs to be done to improve articulation between the elementary and the junior high school, and between the junior and the senior high school, particularly along the lines of gradual introduction of departmentalization. Nevertheless, the transition from the elementary to the secondary school is much smoother in most communities which have a junior high school than under the 8-4 plan.

Discipline Is Better. It was believed by some proponents of the junior high school that the disciplinary situation would be better if grades seven and eight were removed from the elementary school. Although there is no objective evidence to support this claim, it is the opinion of many educators that this is true. They contend that the disciplinary situation for the younger children in the elementary school is better without the influence of seventh- and eighth-grade pupils. Furthermore, the older pupils find the junior high school program, with its new subjects and many pupil activities, much more interesting. They are, therefore, happier and better adjusted in the junior high school, with the result that the disciplinary situation is more satisfactory.

4. Considerations Relative to Housing and Costs

Better Facilities for Grades Seven and Eight. It has long been argued that better buildings, equipment, and other facilities can be provided for pupils in grades seven and eight, if they are placed in a junior high school. There is little doubt that this claim has been realized. As compared with the eight-grade elementary schools, the junior high schools usually have better libraries, gymnasiums, auditoriums, science rooms, guidance rooms, shops, home economics laboratories, music rooms, and arts and crafts rooms. Such facilities are necessary if an educational program appropriate for young adolescents is to be provided.

The location of the junior high school is, ordinarily, more appropriate for young adolescents than the elementary school or the high school. The elementary school is typically a neighborhood school with travel distances appropriate for young children, while the high school is usually a central school located at some distance from the homes of the pupils. The junior high school provides an excellent transition in travel distance for pupils, because its location is usually somewhere between the elementary school and the senior high school.

Costs Are Reasonable. It is difficult to compare the costs of the junior high school with those of the 8-4 plan because the junior high school usually offers a superior program for grades seven, eight, and nine. *Educators generally agree that a program that is suitable for young adolescents can be provided at less cost in a junior high school than in schools under the 8-4 plan.* This becomes obvious if one recognizes that it is exceedingly expensive to provide adequate shops, auditoriums, music rooms, libraries, laboratories, and athletic fields for seventh- and eighth-grade pupils in all the elementary schools because the number of upper-grade pupils in the elementary schools is usually so small that such facilities would be used only part of the day. Furthermore, ninth-grade pupils do not need as expensive facilities for special services and activities as are ordinarily provided in the high school. In the junior high school, special facilities and equipment can be provided for grades seven, eight, and nine at a lower cost per pupil than in either the elementary school or the high school.

The cost of providing appropriate staff for the special services and activities of the junior high school also is usually less than in schools under the 8-4 plan. It is expensive to provide for seventh- and eighth-grade pupils in the elementary school the services of teachers for band, orchestra, and glee club; for industrial arts, home economics, and arts and crafts; a school librarian; and guidance specialists. In the elementary schools such staff members would have to serve several schools, at best an unsatisfactory plan. Competent staff for special activities and services for grades seven, eight, and nine can be most economically provided in the junior high school.

5. Summary of Conclusions Concerning Advantages and Disadvantages

The following conclusions may be drawn from this discussion of the advantages and disadvantages of the junior high school as compared with schools under the 8-4 plan:

I. *Conclusions relative to instruction*

1. The curriculum of the junior high school is broader and provides for more enriched learning experiences than does the 8-4 system, especially for pupils in grades seven and eight.
2. It is easier to introduce changes in the curriculum, especially when the junior high school is first introduced.
3. A broader program of extraclass activities can be provided. This is possible for ninth-grade pupils as well as those in grades seven and eight.
4. Teachers with better preparation, particularly in the special subject fields, can be attracted.
5. It is easier to attract men teachers than in grades seven and eight of the elementary school.
6. The supply of well-qualified administrators, supervisors, and teachers for the junior high school has been increasing in recent years.

II. *Conclusions relative to pupil achievement*

7. Pupils in junior high schools do as well in the fundamentals as pupils in schools under the 8-4 plan, even though they spend less time on these subjects because they take a number of new subjects and participate in extraclass activities.
8. Pupils from junior high schools do as well as those from other schools when they enter the senior high school.

III. *Conclusions relative to guidance, meeting pupil needs, and retention of pupils*

9. Better guidance personnel, facilities, and activities are provided.
10. It is easier to make provision for individual differences in the junior high school because the number of pupils in grades seven and eight is larger than in an elementary school.
11. There are usually more opportunities in both the curricular and the extraclass programs for pupils to explore their interests, abilities, and talents.

12. Pupils tend to remain in school longer, usually through the ninth grade.
13. There are fewer failures and less retardation in the junior high school, especially in the ninth grade.
14. Articulation between the elementary and the secondary school has improved in most communities where the junior high school has been introduced. However, much still needs to be done to achieve satisfactory articulation.
15. Although evidence is lacking on this point, many educators believe that the disciplinary situation, both in the elementary school and in grades seven and eight of the junior high school, is better when the older pupils are separated from the younger ones.
16. Ninth-grade pupils are less likely to develop early sophistication because they do not have contact with older high school pupils. Furthermore, they can usually participate more fully in pupil activities in the junior high school than in the four-year high school.

IV. *Conclusions relative to housing and costs*

17. Better building facilities, equipment, and athletic fields can be provided, especially for seventh- and eighth-grade pupils.
18. The cost of providing an adequate educational program for young adolescents is less in the junior high school. If comparable facilities were provided for grades seven and eight in the elementary school they would need to be duplicated in every school.

Questions and Exercises

1. Evaluate the relative strength and weakness of each of the claims and of the objections made for the junior high school with respect to (a) improving the curriculum; (b) improving the teaching staff; (c) better adjustment to the individual; (d) retention, rates of pupil progress, articulation, and economy of time; (e) improving the opportunities for pupil socialization; (f) housing, equipment, and finance; (g) effects upon the elementary and the senior high school; and (h) any other claims you can think of.

2. Locate recent studies on the effectiveness of the junior high school and prepare a report on one such study.

Part II

THE INSTRUCTIONAL PROGRAM

Chapter 4

CURRICULUM TRENDS AND ORGANIZATION

1. Basic Concepts Concerning the Curriculum

Changing Concept of the Curriculum. For many years the curriculum was regarded more or less as a fixed body of subject matter, a different portion of which was to be mastered each year by the pupils as they passed from grade to grade through the educational program of the elementary and the secondary school. During the years when this point of view was generally accepted, educational psychologists were concerned primarily with finding means for measuring and increasing the degree of efficiency and thoroughness with which mastery of subject matter might be attained.

In recent years the point of view with respect to the curriculum has undergone much modification. It is not believed today that the curriculum is even relatively fixed and static or that it is confined to what we have thought of in the past as "subject matter." Rather, today *the curriculum is coming to be thought of as consisting of the total controlled environment created under the direction of the school, for the purpose of stimulating, influencing, and contributing to the wholesome growth and development of boys and girls.*

Philosophy Underlying the Curriculum. This new concept of the curriculum recognizes that, during the years of growth, the child is in a continuous process of change—physically, mentally, emotionally, and morally. The nature of that growth is determined by two factors—heredity and environment. The development of the child is shaped by the characteristics transmitted to him by his ancestors and by the impact upon him of the surroundings in which he lives. These hereditary characteristics and extraschool environmental factors tend to set the limits within which the curriculum provided by the school can influence the development of the child. How the child acts and thinks in the future will depend, therefore, not only on his school experiences, but also on his congenital nature and on his environmental experiences outside the school.

61

In primitive societies the child learned chiefly from real-life experiences. Little effort was expended in creating situations especially for the purpose of shaping his growth and development, particularly his intellectual growth. Even in American society today, the child learns much from extraschool situations, perhaps even more than from the experiences provided for him by the school and other formal educational agencies. But today, as compared with primitive society, much more attention is given to the development of a relatively controlled environment, the primary purpose of which is the education of the child. Boys and girls are taken from their homes and, for a great portion of the day, are placed in schools where they engage in activities and participate in learning situations that will accelerate their growth toward desirable and accepted educational goals. This environment, created under the direction of the school, constitutes the curriculum of the elementary and secondary schools as we are inclined to think of it today.

If we accept the point of view that the development of the child is influenced significantly by his environment, then it becomes highly important that the environment be the one that will be most favorable to his growth and development. That environment may be one which the child finds in any ordinary real-life situation, or it may be one that is created especially to meet his peculiar educational needs. Certainly, if the natural environment of the child furnished him with completely satisfactory learning situations, that in itself would suffice so far as his educational growth is concerned. But, from an educational standpoint, it is obvious that the child's natural environment is far from adequate. Consequently, society has found it necessary for educational purposes to provide a supplementary environment, one that has been developed and is controlled to meet the educational needs of the child. To provide this controlled environment for the more effective education of the child, the school and certain other educational agencies were created.

This brief discussion of the philosophy underlying the curriculum leads to the formulation of the following basic principle: *the selection for the curriculum of any learning activities, subject content, or instructional techniques should be determined primarily by their contribution to the growth and development of the child toward accepted educational goals.* It is not an easy matter, however, to evaluate curriculum materials in terms of this principle. Such an evaluation should recognize the demands of life in the world, both of today and of tomorrow, the nature of the child to be educated, and a number of other factors. But, difficult though it may be, the values of the entire curriculum must ultimately be assessed in the light of this basic principle.

Relation of the Curriculum to Objectives. It is evident from the preceding discussion that the curriculum of the school is merely a means to an end, a means contributing to the achievement of accepted goals of education. Therefore, in developing a curriculum for the school, we are concerned not only with the nature of the child, but also with the goals that have been set up for his educational program.

As a basis for selecting and organizing the content of the curriculum, it is highly important that the faculty of a school formulate a statement of the goals of education. In the junior high schools, the formulation of such goals is far too uncommon. The goals for effective formal action should be stated in terms of specific types of pupil growth. They should include important information and principles to be understood and learned; habits and skills to be acquired—social, physical, and intellectual; and specific ideals, appreciations, attitudes, and interests to be developed. Such a formulation of goals should be thought through in terms of the over-all goals of all elementary and secondary education, of which the goals to be achieved at the junior high school level are a part. Typical statements of philosophy and goals found in junior high schools are rather high-sounding and impressive, but they suffer from three grievous faults: (1) they are not specific; (2) they are not sufficiently comprehensive and inclusive; and (3) they are "lip service" statements to be made rather than to be used as a guide for teaching.

In a majority of the junior high schools today consideration is being given by teachers to the relationship between the educational program of the junior high school and the goals of education. The most common way to insure understanding and implementation of this philosophy and these goals is to have frequent discussions and reference to them in various types of teachers' meetings. They should also be discussed in supervisory conferences. Provision should be made for orienting, informing, and indoctrinating new teachers coming into the school system with respect to these goals. Listing them in the teachers' handbooks and courses of study is useful, but in itself it is far from sufficient. There should be ample opportunity for discussion by teachers to insure understanding of the goals in terms of jobs to be done and to make certain that they will not be forgotten when the work from day to day is being planned and carried out. Only through specific activities such as these are educational objectives likely to give the direction to the curriculum which is desirable in carrying on a forward-looking and effective educational program.

Curriculum Terminology. Educational terminology has never been standardized, and it is particularly confusing in the area of the curriculum. As a matter of fact, with respect to curriculum terminology, the confusion has become greater in recent years by reason of the fact that so many new terms have been coined and different people use curriculum terms to mean different things. Following are some of the more commonly used definitions which are acceptable to a large group of workers in secondary education.

Curriculum: (a) The sum total of the various courses of study and of the learning experiences conducted by or under the auspices of the school. (b) The systematic arrangement of a number of courses into a unit group for differentiated groups of pupils is a type of curriculum, for example, the college-preparatory curriculum.

Field: A broad, relatively homogeneous area of learning, for example, mathematics, history, biological science.

Broad fields: The combination of two or more subjects or closely related fields, for example, English, journalism, and speech; general science; general social studies; arts and crafts.

Subject: A specific area of learning, usually within a field, for example, algebra in the field of mathematics.

Program: The total educational offerings of the school including the curriculum, the co-curriculum, and the guidance facilities.

Program of studies: The list by years of all high school courses of instruction (for example, physics and algebra) offered for study in a given school without reference to grouping into curriculums.

Course of study: A guide for teachers and learners of a subject or curriculum. It should, and usually does, include: (a) statements of objectives; (b) suggested learning materials and activities for a given period of time, for example, course of study for algebra or course of study for the core curriculum; (c) suggestions for their use in the school; and (d) suggestions for evaluation.

Resource unit: An outline of learning activities involving usually two to four weeks, and a reservoir of optional course of study materials and learning activities as suggestions for the teacher and learners.

Core curriculum: A large block of the curriculum contributing to the objectives of general education, involving materials from two or more subjects and organized around life problems or foci of life interests; usually involves or overlaps one or more other concepts, such as fusion or integrated curriculum, social living and experience curriculum.

Fusion: The combining of all, or nearly all, of the materials of two or more subjects, not necessarily in the same broad field, on one or more grade levels, for example, English and the social studies, and mathematics and physics.

Correlation plan: Two or more subjects taught with simultaneous intercorrelation, for example, colonial history and English literature of the colonial period.

Experience curriculum: A curriculum organized with a view to employing as far as possible the current normal life experiences of the learners as the fundamental criterion for the selection and organization of learning materials and activities.

Constant: A subject which is required of all pupils for graduation, no matter what curriculum is elected.

Curriculum prescription: A subject not required of all pupils in the school, but required of all pupils in a given curriculum, for example, algebra in a college-preparatory curriculum.

Limited elective: One of two or more subjects, not all of which are required of all pupils of the school or of a given curriculum, but from which one must be elected by the pupils.

Free elective: A subject not required of a pupil in the curriculum which he is following, but which he may choose.

2. CURRENT TRENDS IN THE CURRICULUM

Summary of Current Trends in the Curriculum. Among the more significant trends in the content and organization of the junior high school curriculum are the following:

1. The trend toward closer interrelation between the various subjects. It has taken several forms, including organization into broad fields, fusion of subjects, correlated courses, integrated or core courses, and the experience curriculum.
2. The trend toward greater participation by pupils in planning learning activities.
3. The trend toward the organization of course-of-study material and learning activities into large units.
4. The trend toward the use of resource units in place of, or as a supplement to, the typical conventional course of study.
5. The trend toward less dependence upon the textbook and greater flexibility in its use.
6. The trend toward correlation of the curriculum with real-life activities outside the school.
7. The trend toward preparation for intelligent consumership and effective home life.
8. The trend toward more adequate preparation for intelligent citizenship.
9. The trend toward postponement of college-preparatory and vocational studies.
10. The trend away from large numbers of differentiated curriculums and courses and toward differentiation within curriculums and courses.
11. The trend toward general education as compared with special education; in other words, the trend toward emphasis upon teaching for the common needs of all youngsters rather than upon elective subjects in fields of special interests.

Trend Toward Correlation Between Subjects. Among the various definitions of correlation, two seem to be more commonly accepted. According to one definition, correlation has meant teaching two subjects in such a way that interrelationships are developed between them. This involves careful planning and timing. For example, in correlating history and literature, there would be reading and discussion of the literature in relation to the period in history to which it pertains. In correlation between history or the other social studies and the language arts, the language arts would be correlated day to day with the work in history or other social studies. This artificial plan never was widely employed and has lost considerable ground in recent years.

A second definition of correlation between subjects is the practice of teaching a relationship between one subject and another as that relationship seems to occur and wherever it seems to make the work more meaningful, practical, or interesting. For example, in mathematics there are many occasions when it is desirable to relate the material being studied to science, scout work, home living, business, and recreation.

The teaching of subjects in isolation one from another in a highly developed system of departmentalization has not proved effective and is rather vigorously condemned by most educators today. Even so, a considerable minority, if not a majority, of teachers have not yet greatly changed their practice with respect to correlation. An effective practice to improve correlation is to have teachers keep in touch with each other as they plan units of work. For example, English teachers may profit by consultation with teachers of social studies, as well as teachers of other subjects, to keep informed about the learning activities being carried on in those subjects and how the work in English may be correlated with them. In some schools planning periods for teachers to work together are arranged before school, after school, or on school time.

Trend Toward Fusion of Related Subjects. In the traditional eight-year elementary school, the program of studies was divided into eight, ten, or more different subjects for each of the upper grades. Spelling, penmanship, grammar, composition, reading or literature, history, civics, hygiene, arithmetic, nature study, art, and other subjects were included in the typical school program. This extreme form of compartmentalization in the program of studies, so prevalent in the traditional elementary school, has been modified considerably in the junior high school by combining subjects in closely related areas and teaching them as single courses. Following are the broad fields in which fusion has most commonly been achieved:

1. Most common of all: spelling, grammar, literature, etc. into English
2. In a large majority of schools: history, geography, civics, and community problems into the social studies
3. In about two-thirds of the schools: hygiene, nature study, and elementary materials from physics, chemistry, geology, botany, zoology, biology, bacteriology, astronomy, and meteorology into general science
4. In a large majority of schools: cooking, sewing, child care, household care, and home management into home living
5. In about two-thirds of the schools: woodwork, metalwork, electricity, and other arts and crafts into general shop courses
6. In the ninth grade as an elective, in a great majority of schools: arithmetic, algebra, and geometry into general mathematics

Among the factors which have encouraged this fusion of related subjects in the curriculum of the junior high school are (1) the example of fused courses in the senior high school, (2) the advantages of having fewer classes in schedule-making, and (3) the tendency toward longer class periods and supervised study in the junior high school. But more significant than any of these influences has been the growing belief in recent years that the compartmentalized curriculum is in conflict with certain modern concepts of education, particularly the concept of integration. Educators who hold this view point out that the satisfactory attainment of learning outcomes cannot be achieved if the learning experiences of the child are broken up into too many separate and specific subject areas. The fusion of related subjects into a few broad fields is believed by many educators to be in harmony with the present emphasis on integration. In the junior high school this trend toward the fusion of related subjects already has gone a long way.

Trend Toward Integration—The Core and Unified Studies. Many educators believe that the fusion of related subjects into broader courses of instruction is a step in the right direction, but that it fails to go far enough. They contend that the satisfactory integration of learning outcomes demands far more fusion and unification in the instructional program of the school than is made possible by such fused or combined courses as English, social studies, and general science. As an outgrowth of this demand for further unification and fusion in the curriculum, integrated "core" courses have been introduced in some schools which combine two or more subject fields, such as

English and social studies. The core has spread so widely among the junior high schools in the United States and is seemingly so sound a plan of curriculum organization that a special chapter in this volume is devoted to it. The core type of integrated curriculum most commonly includes English and the social studies and sometimes parts of one or more of the following fields: art, science, mathematics, and music.

Trend Toward Pupil Participation in Curriculum-Planning. The first carefully planned courses of study and curriculums in the United States were prepared largely by administrators and supervisors and were placed in the hands of teachers who were expected to follow them closely. Later, courses of study prepared by the teachers themselves were introduced into the schools. In marked contrast to these two methods of curriculum development is the recent suggestion by some educators for pupil participation in planning courses of study and the curriculum as a whole.

Whether this proposal is a gesture toward democracy in the American schools or constitutes a well-conceived effort toward improving the learning situation, we do not know. It may be both. One should be inclined, however, to be somewhat cautious in embracing too quickly and too heartily this method of curriculum development. It is quite probable that there should be gradual introduction of pupil participation in planning and that it should be extended as both the teachers and the pupils come to understand it better and as they develop appropriate skills in managing it.

Pupil participation in the planning of the curriculum has certain rather obvious advantages. The more important ones include (1) increased pupil interest in the curriculum, (2) the development of creative abilities, (3) greater pupil responsibility for a desirable learning situation in school, and (4) the development by pupils of such character qualities as initiative and resourcefulness. But there are also some rather serious objections to this practice, such as (1) the time consumed by this method, (2) a lack of sufficient pupil background, and (3) difficulty in getting representative pupil ideas.

Trend Toward Lay Participation in Curriculum-Planning. In recent years there has been greatly increased participation by parents and other lay people in the community in the planning of the curriculum and other aspects of the program of the school. Much can be said in favor of lay participation in curriculum development. Laymen bring a point of view to curriculum-planning which may be quite different from that of teachers. Furthermore, since the public supports the schools, its point of view deserves serious consideration.

Laymen are not expected to participate in the technical aspects of curriculum-building, but they may contribute much in shaping the philosophy of the curriculum, the objectives, and the over-all content.

At Cornell University, Edward G. Fennell made a study of lay participation in the development of the program in a group of outstanding junior high schools in the United States.[1] The number of schools, among 224 studied, having various lay groups participating in program development is as follows, with the extent of use indicated:

Lay Group	Much	Some	Little	Total
School board	50	97	39	186
Parent-Teacher Association	32	83	59	174
Homeroom mothers	11	41	47	99
Lay advisory group	12	44	54	110
Pupils	39	100	51	190
Meetings of parents	11	64	34	109

Trend Toward Unit Organization. Most teachers are familiar with the present practice of preparing teaching plans in terms of long units covering several weeks, as compared with the daily lesson plan of a few decades ago. There has been a similar trend toward the unit approach in the courses of study which have been developed at the junior high school level in recent years. The trend toward the unit plan, both in classroom teaching and curriculum development, is an outgrowth of the current emphasis on integration in the school program.

In course-of-study construction and curriculum development the unit is thought of as a plan of organization for the objectives, activities, materials, and methods of instruction of a given block of work that is to extend over a period of several weeks. The unit plan of organization is the one most prevalent in the junior high school today. It is most commonly employed in social studies, science, and English.

Particularly in recent years, there has been a trend toward the increased employment of a resource type of unit. A resource unit differs from others in that it is a reservoir of suggestions on instructional materials and learning activities which may be employed. From this reservoir the teacher selects and organizes those materials and activities which seem to him to be most effective for a particular learning situation. He is not restricted to the materials and activities mentioned in the resource unit and may supplement them in any way that he sees fit.

In a study of junior high school practices the authors found that courses of study are organized on the unit plan in many schools. In

[1] Edward Glenn Fennell, "An Analysis of Programs of Outstanding Junior High Schools in the United States" (Unpublished doctoral dissertation, Cornell University, 1953), p. 220.

fact, in one-third of the schools it is employed in practically all subjects. The percentage of 370 junior high schools in which courses of
study are organized on the unit plan is as follows:

Practically all subjects	34%	Mathematics	6%
Social studies	20%	No subjects	5%
Science	17%	Others	6%
English	12%		

Trend Toward Correlation with Real-Life Activities. In older
textbooks and courses of study there was little relationship between
the things learned in school and real-life situations outside the school.
In the hours from nine to four the pupil devoted his efforts to the
acquisition of a large fund of facts and information. In his language
classes, for instance, he memorized definitions and an immense store
of terminology which was of little direct value either in speech or
written work. Dates, wars, treaties, and the names of presidents and
kings constituted much of the history that was taught.

Although mathematics courses did contain some problems meaningful to the child and useful later in adult life, there were also many
that dealt with situations rarely experienced by the average person—
problems involving the speed of trains, the movement of boats on a
river, and even the jumping of frogs in a well. Such materials suggest
that there is either poverty in the school subjects with respect to real-
life applications, or a lack of practical experiences and resourcefulness
on the part of the authors of textbooks. The character of the early
courses and textbooks was largely justified, however, on the theory
that there would be transfer of training from the impractical learning
situations in school to the more practical problems of adult life outside
the school.

There has been an increased recognition in the interpretation of
the principle of transfer of training that, if materials are to be well
understood, retained, and used effectively in life activities, the materials should be taught in connection with their application to, and use
in, life situations. The Education for Life Adjustment movement,
which has influenced the curriculum in many secondary schools in
the United States, is based in part upon this principle. Indeed, it is
one of the fundamental principles of the core curriculum, the experience curriculum, the integrated curriculum, and all other curriculum
movements which involve the close relationship of instructional materials and activities with real-life uses.

Throughout the country teachers of all subjects, particularly of
science, social studies, mathematics, art, industrial arts, and health
education, are relating their instruction more and more to life situa-

tions. Developing skill in correlating work in school with life activities is a slow process for most teachers, since their own experiences
have been so highly academic. It is necessary for them to read, study,
and participate in community life with a definite view to increasing
their own orientation to activities outside of school. This is a first
step toward the improvement of correlation between learning situations in school and life activities outside the school.

Some schools have gone much further than others in reorganizing
the curriculum in terms of real-life activities. The most extreme form
of such reorganization is that which is known as the *experience curriculum*. In the experience curriculum, the learning situations for the
various subjects are not outlined in courses of study in the usual way.
Instead, they are developed cooperatively during the school term by
teachers and pupils from the interests and experiences of the pupils
themselves. The experience curriculum is still very much in the experimental stage and for the present is used only in a very limited way
in a few junior high schools. In those schools in which the experience
curriculum seems to be succeeding best, it has been introduced gradually, and the result is a compromise between the experience approach
and more traditional ones. It is rare that a teacher is able to succeed
in developing a course of study effectively around the experiences of
the youngsters for an entire year. Indeed, there are so many important future needs with which the youngsters at their stage of maturity are not cognizant that the experience approach must be limited
to certain parts of the work in any subject. *Even so, the experience
approach is so sound in theory that teachers should develop skill in
using it and should apply the thinking basic to this approach in as
many learning situations as possible.* Progress in developing a more
effective instructional program will not be made if we avoid employing new approaches to teaching just because they are difficult.

**Trend Toward Preparation for Intelligent Consumership and Ef-
fective Home Life.** For two important reasons, an increasing amount
of attention has been given in recent years to the preparation of youth
for more intelligent consumership. In the first place, this trend is
part of the movement to make school work more functional and to
teach materials in their relationship to problems of everyday living.
Perhaps of equal importance is the fact that, in the last few decades,
the extent and effectiveness of advertising and other sales pressures
have increased so greatly that the need for the education of young
people in the problems of buying and repair of materials has become
much greater. The best art, music, theatrical, and dramatic talent is
employed on television and the radio, in the newspapers, and in period-

icals to influence people to spend their money in ways that are of profit to the advertisers. Because young people have more spending money than in previous generations, there are more opportunities for teaching wise consumership in correlation with out-of-school activities.

Furthermore, since a far greater share of the goods consumed in the home is produced elsewhere, the home is not as self-sufficient as it has been in the past. Another complicating factor is the greatly increased commercialization of amusement and recreation. Increased use of installment-buying and other forms of borrowing has contributed heavily to the need for consumer education.

In the junior high school the recent emphasis on consumer education has led to the introduction of materials on consumership into practically all subjects of the curriculum and many extraclass activities as well. Consumer education is an important part of most junior high school courses in home economics, arithmetic, and general mathematics. In a few schools there are special courses in consumer education, although such courses have not become popular at the junior high school level. In the study by the authors, consumer education is included in various subjects in the percentage of schools indicated:

Mathematics	35%
Home economics	31%
Business	15%
Social studies	15%
Special courses in consumership	1%
Others	3%

Consumership is only one of the more important activities in home and family living which are being taught in the junior high school today. In fact, there is hardly a phase of the junior high school curriculum which does not include some materials related to the attitudes, skills, and ideals that are essential for effective home and family living. For girls, these materials are being taught especially in home economics classes. But for both boys and girls, materials on home and family living are also included in the homeroom activities, social studies courses, school assemblies, industrial arts courses, school clubs, and English classes.

Trend Toward Preparation for Citizenship. At no time in the history of America has there been a greater need for an intelligent citizenry. The past several decades have seen one national or international crisis after another. The dislocation of economic life in the early 1920's, the boom period late in the same decade, the world-wide depression of the 1930's, the recent attacks on democracy—both political and military—on practically every continent have presented very serious problems for the present generation of American citizens. Furthermore, the problem has become greatly complicated by the activities of political opportunists hoping to improve their political status by rash and unproven charges against organizations and individuals. While in the last few years curbs have been placed upon the worst of these enemies of real democracy and the people have become wiser in the ways of political opportunists, the threat is still sufficiently grave to challenge the efforts of school people to prepare future citizens to distinguish sound and patriotic leadership from the dangerous types.

For some years, educators, parents, and the public in general have recognized the demands which these problems make on the intelligence of citizens in a democracy like ours. As early as 1920, in the aftermath of World War I, the secondary school program was carefully analyzed to ascertain the educational needs of our people for effective citizenship. That scrutiny revealed that certain areas of citizenship training were badly neglected. For instance, before 1920, there was scant attention to the study of social, economic, political, and international problems. Then, too, there had been some question as to the appropriateness of our classroom methods as preparation for democratic citizenship. As a result of this critical study, initiated more than two decades ago, increasing attention has been paid in recent years to citizenship education in the American schools. At the junior high school level new courses in citizenship have been introduced, the organization and content of the social studies have been modified, and teaching methods that emphasize problem-solving skills rather than the mastery of subject matter have been increasingly employed.

Education for citizenship must be carried on through both instructional activities and daily living. In classroom studies and in various extraclass activities there are opportunities for young people to develop the ideals, skills, habits, and general orientation that are needed for democratic living and democratic relations at their best. The homeroom, clubs, the student council, and school service organizations are especially effective channels for giving pupils experience in democratic citizenship.

Trend Toward Postponement of College-Preparatory and Vocational Studies. In the early years of the reorganization movement, it was urged that secondary school studies should begin earlier than the ninth grade. These early proposals were stressed especially by representatives of the colleges and universities who were concerned primarily with shortening the total period of elementary and secondary education so that higher education could begin earlier. The secondary school studies to which they referred were chiefly foreign languages and mathematics. It was quite natural, therefore, that in the first junior high schools such studies as Latin, French, algebra, and geometry were frequently introduced in the seventh and eighth grades.

Vocational studies were also urged for the early years of the junior high school. Proponents of the vocational studies pointed out that, since pupil withdrawals were particularly heavy from grades seven to nine, many pupils would receive no vocational education unless it were given in the junior high school grades. Vocational subjects consequently were introduced into the curriculum of the early junior high schools to meet the needs of those youth who were not likely to remain in school beyond the eighth or ninth grades.

In recent years these practices in the junior high school with respect to college-preparatory and vocational subjects have been largely outmoded and reversed. Beginning in the 1920's, foreign languages and advanced mathematics were postponed increasingly to the senior high school. In fact, in many schools today algebra and geometry, traditionally taught in grades nine and ten respectively, are each being offered a year later, while foreign languages are not being offered at all in many junior high schools. However, in the past few years there has been some tendency to introduce at least one foreign language in the elementary school or the seventh grade of the junior high school. It is too early to know whether these are just isolated instances, or whether they are part of an emerging trend to introduce foreign languages earlier. In any case, the foreign languages recently introduced into the elementary grades have been thought of as general education, not as preparation for college.

Vocational subjects, likewise, have been postponed increasingly to the senior high school years. Courses in home economics and industrial arts, it is true, still have a place in the junior high school curriculum, but today they are taught largely for general education rather than vocational purposes.

One significant advantage of the postponement of college-preparatory and vocational studies is the opportunity it has offered to enrich the junior high school curriculum. In place of those studies many new materials have been introduced in various subjects, pupil activities and projects are being used more widely, and instructional aids and materials have been expanded to include more audio-visual materials, field trips and excursions, and a variety of books, pamphlets, magazines, and other reading materials. Parallel to this enrichment in the classroom, there has been considerable expansion in such extraclass activities as clubs, assemblies, social functions, sports, pupil publications, and speech activities. This enrichment would hardly have been possible had the college-preparatory and vocational studies been retained in the junior high school program.

Trend Toward Differentiation Within Curriculums and Courses. Before the establishment of the junior high school, the four-year high school had made some progress toward individualizing the school program in terms of the needs, abilities, and interests of the various pupils. The most prevalent practice for individualizing the curriculum in the four-year high school of several decades ago was the offering of elective curriculums and courses. One of the early arguments for the junior high school, it may be recalled, was the recognized need for individualizing the program of the seventh, eighth, and ninth grades. It was therefore quite natural that, in the first junior high schools, the plan of offering elective curriculums and courses as a means of individualizing the program should have been copied from the four-year high school.

In the last decade or two, however, there has been a change in our point of view concerning the desirability of elective curriculums and courses at the junior high school level. More and more educators today feel that differentiation within the various courses is a more satisfactory method for meeting the needs, interests, and abilities of the individual pupil, than the offering of a variety of elective curriculums and courses. This approach to the problem of differentiation has come about in part because of the many new teaching aids and materials which are now available in the various subjects, as well as from a better understanding by teachers of methods and techniques for individualizing instruction. Especially in the seventh and eighth grades, the differentiation of instruction within courses is rapidly replacing the practice of meeting individual pupil needs through the offering of a large variety of elective curriculums and courses.

3. Curriculum Organization and Development

Types of General Organization. In the secondary schools of the United States as a whole, the plan of organization for the curriculum may be classified into two general types: (1) the single curriculum, and (2) the multiple curriculum. The single curriculum with electives provides for one program of studies which is taken by all pupils, with certain courses required and others offered as electives. For instance, under this plan all pupils in the ninth grade, regardless of their future educational or vocational goals, may be required to take such courses as English, social studies, algebra, and physical education, while they may have a choice of one other course from a group which includes such subjects as French, junior business training, industrial arts, and home economics. The multiple curriculum provides for the grouping of all courses in the program of studies into several curriculums, usually in terms of the educational or vocational goals of the pupil. The most common curriculums under this plan are college preparatory, business, general, industrial arts, and home and family living curriculums. Usually in each of these curriculums the pupil is required to take certain subjects, but is also permitted one or two elective courses from a limited group.

Until recently, a single curriculum with a few electives was commonly employed in grades seven and eight, followed by a multiple curriculum in the ninth. In recent years, there has been a noticeable trend toward employing the single curriculum with electives through the ninth grade. There is also a trend toward having the pupils in the ninth grade carry as many subjects as pupils in grades seven and eight. Ninth-grade pupils are being scheduled increasingly with few if any separate study periods. The trend toward the single curriculum with electives for all junior high school grades is in harmony with the recent point of view that the pupil should postpone specialization in his studies until he reaches the senior high school, a view that has been encouraged by the fact that an increasing proportion of youth is continuing its education into the senior high school.

Principles of Curriculum Organization. Certain principles of curriculum organization are generally accepted by curriculum specialists at secondary school levels. Some of these principles having particular appropriateness in a study of the junior high school curriculum are as follows:

1. For every pupil the curriculum should include some instruction for each of the aims of secondary education, such as health, citizenship, vocation, avocation, home life, fundamental skills and knowledge, and character.
2. The curriculum should provide opportunities for exploration of the potential interests and capacities of each pupil, preferably through activities and materials which will also have other values.
3. The curriculum should make a definite contribution to the integrative, differentiative, and adaptive functions of secondary education.
4. The curriculum should be so organized that the portion completed by any student withdrawing from school will not be greatly dependent for realization of its values upon the study of that portion of the curriculum which he has not taken.

5. The curriculum should provide opportunities for pupils of inferior and of superior abilities.

6. The grade placement of courses in the curriculum should be guided by the social and economic as well as the intellectual maturity of the pupils.

7. Those subjects for which a certain and important need may be predicted for all pupils should be required of all pupils, with provision being made for adaptation to the individual ability to learn.

8. The curriculum of the junior high school should be closely articulated with those of the elementary and the senior high school.

Characteristics of a Good Curriculum. Among the more important characteristics of good junior high school curriculums are those listed in "A Design for Early Secondary Education in New York State—An Abstract."

1. Every subject area is closely integrated with every other subject area as well as with the extraclass portion of the program.

2. The total offering is closely articulated with that of the elementary and of the senior high school grades.

3. For the most part, the emphasis at the early secondary level is on general education, specialization being delayed until the senior high school grades.

4. Throughout the various subject areas, attention is given to pupil growth and development in health, personality, and character, as well as in academic skills and knowledge.

5. There is considerable flexibility in the program to provide for the varied and changing needs, interests, and abilities of pupils at this level.

6. Learning activities take place in a class situation which arouses and capitalizes the pupils' interests and stimulates pupils to put forth their best efforts.

7. Learning activities are selected in part on the basis of suitability for the individual pupil.

8. Learning activities are organized around fairly large units.

9. Pupils share in planning a unit of study and in developing activities which contribute to their understanding of the unit.

10. When a unit is being studied by a class, subtopics may be developed by individuals or by small groups of pupils.

11. Basic skills are made functional.

12. Pupils are helped to gain insights into the personal and social significance of the topics they study.

13. When a certain goal can be attained best through systematic learnings, the teacher plans a sequence of logically related developmental lessons.

14. In developing learning activities, judicious use is made of various community resources.

15. Frequent and comprehensive evaluations are made to discover evidence of pupil growth as a result of learning activities and to determine unmet pupil needs.[2]

Summary of Trends in Curriculum Organization and Development. There are rather distinct trends in the way in which course of study and curriculum materials are developed and organized in the junior high school. These may be summarized as follows:

From	*To*
1. Separate departmentalized subjects.	Broader subject fields.
2. Courses of study which are little more than broad outlines.	Suggestions of instructional materials and learning activities.
3. Organization of materials and learning activities around subject matter as topical divisions.	Organization of subject matter and learning activities around problems in everyday life of children or adults.
4. No orientation or basic philosophy related and developed to be in harmony with the fundamental philosophy of education.	A knowledge, cognizance, and observation of a sound broad basic philosophy of education.
5. The evaluation of the growth of the pupil through paper-and-pencil tests.	Evaluation from a wide variety of sources and techniques, including daily observation of growth in all areas.
6. No definite setting of aims and objectives except in terms of separate subject-matter coverage or mastery.	Definitely formulated aims and objectives in terms of specific types of growth of learners.
7. Determination by higher authorities of what curriculum materials and learning activities should be employed.	Selection of learning materials and activities by the teachers and the learners.
8. Confining learning materials to those contained in the textbooks.	The use of textbooks along with a variety of materials and activities of other types and from other sources.
9. Rather exclusive emphasis upon intellectual activities and intellectual growth, such as the acquisition of factual information.	Emphasis upon growth in all areas—social, physical, intellectual, and emotional.
10. Following closely courses of study prepared by a committee of teachers, a supervisor, or an administrator.	The planning of learning materials and activities by each teacher for the particular subject, grade, and group of pupils concerned.
11. A concept of uniform minimum essentials as the goal for everyone.	A recognition in practice as well as in theory that children vary greatly in their ability to learn and in their individual needs.

[2] *A Design for Early Secondary Education—An Abstract*, State Department of Education, The University of the State of New York (Albany, N. Y., 1954), pp. 9-10.

4. Typical Programs of Studies

LONGFELLOW JUNIOR HIGH SCHOOL
WAUWATOSA, WISCONSIN

Seventh Grade
Required

1. English
2. Social Science
3. Mathematics
4. Homemaking, Industrial Arts
5. Art and Music
6. Physical Education (Gym, Pool, Health, Safety, First Aid, Water Safety)

Eighth Grade
Required

1. English
2. Social Science
3. Mathematics
4. Homemaking, Industrial Arts
5. Physical Education (Gym, Pool, Health, Safety, First Aid, Water Safety)

Electives
(Choose One)

Instrumental Music (Band and Orchestra)

Vocal Music

General Science

General Business

Arts and Crafts

Typing (For personal use)

Ninth Grade
Required

1. English
2. Social Science
3. Physical Education (Gym, Pool, Health, Safety, First Aid, Water Safety)

Electives
(Choose Three)

General Science (Required in either grade 8 or 9)

Algebra

General Mathematics

General Business

Industrial Arts

Homemaking

Latin

Art

Instrumental Music (Band and Orchestra)

Typing (For personal use)

ROOSEVELT JUNIOR HIGH SCHOOL
NEW BRITAIN, CONNECTICUT

Seventh Grade Required	Periods	*Eighth Grade* Required	Periods
English	5	English	5
Social Studies	5	Social Studies	5
Arithmetic	5	Arithmetic	5
Science and Hygiene	3	Science and Hygiene	3
Physical Education	2	Physical Education	2
Industrial Arts ⎫ Homemaking ⎭	2	Industrial Arts ⎫ Homemaking ⎭	2
Music	1 or 2	Music	1
Art	2	Art	1
Club	1	Typewriting	2
Assembly	1	Guidance and Safety Education	1
Manners and Morals or Religious Education	1	Assembly	1
Guidance and Safety Education	1	Manners and Morals or Religious Education	1
		Club	1

Ninth Grade

Required	Periods
English	5
Algebra or General Mathematics	4 or 5
American Democracy	4 or 5
Physical Education	2
Assembly	1
Guidance and Safety Education	1
Religious Education or Manners and Morals	1

Electives
(Elect 10 or 12 periods to make a total of 30)

World History	4 or 5
General Science and Hygiene	4
Latin	1 or 2
Art	1 or 2
Typewriting	1 or 2
Music	1 or 2
Home Economics } Industrial Arts }	2 or 4
Study	1
Club	1

To meet the varying needs of individual pupils, the hours per week in each subject may, where circumstances warrant it, be altered to meet those needs.

ALLENTOWN, PENNSYLVANIA, JUNIOR HIGH SCHOOL
PROGRAM OF STUDIES

Seventh Grade	Periods
Language Arts (Grammar, Composition, Spelling, Library, Penmanship, Reading and Study Skills, and Reading Appreciation)	7
Social Studies	9
Mathematics	5
Health	3
Fine Arts (Arts and Crafts, Music)	2
Practical Arts (Industrial Arts, Homemaking)	2
Physical Education	2
School Life Activities (Homeroom, Assembly, Student Government, Music, Dramatics, School and Community Welfare, School Paper)	5
	35

Eighth Grade	Periods
Language Arts (Grammar, Composition, Spelling, Library, Penmanship, Reading and Study Skills, and Reading Appreciation)	7
Social Studies (Integrated Units in Geography)	9
Mathematics	5
Science	3
Fine Arts (Arts and Crafts, Music)	2
Practical Arts (Industrial Arts, Homemaking)	2
Physical Education	2
School Life Activities (Homeroom, Assembly, Student Government, Music, Dramatics, School and Community Welfare, School Paper)	5
	35

Ninth Grade

	Periods
English I (Library)	5
Social Studies (Pennsylvania History and Government)	4
Algebra I or General Mathematics	5
General Science	4
Major Electives (Latin I, Spanish I, Music, Arts and Crafts, Business Education, Homemaking, Industrial Arts)	4
Health and Physical Education	3
Fine Arts (Arts and Crafts, Music)	2
Practical Arts (Homemaking, Industrial Arts)	2
Guidance	1
School Life Activities (Homeroom, Assembly, Student Government, Music, Dramatics, School and Community Welfare, School Paper)	5
	35

QUESTIONS AND EXERCISES

1. State fully and evaluate the various points of view developed in this chapter about the nature of the curriculum.

2. What part does the individual teacher play in determining the curriculum of the junior high school?

3. Rewrite in your own words definitions of the various terms employed in the discussions of the curriculum.

4. Select any two of the current trends in junior high school curriculum theory and practice and be able to discuss them in class.

5. Summarize briefly in your own words all the current trends in the junior high school curriculum.

6. Be able to explain and evaluate each of the principles given in the section on curriculum organization.

7. What do you regard as the three most important current trends in the junior high school curriculum? Explain.

8. Which of the following plans of curriculum organization do you consider the most appropriate for the junior high school: (a) single curriculum, (b) single curriculum with variables, or (c) multiple curriculum? Be able to substantiate your answer.

9. Prepare a program of studies for a junior high school with which you are familiar. Indicate the size and type of the community and the enrollment of the school.

10. Under what conditions should controversial matters be discussed in junior high school classes?

Chapter 5

THE CORE CURRICULUM

1. BASIC POINT OF VIEW

Development of the Core Curriculum. The most significant development in the junior high school curriculum in recent years is the core curriculum. Although the term "core" was used as early as the 1920's, it was then applied only to the required subjects in the curriculum—those studies which were the "core" of the program for every pupil. Since the 1930's the "core" has referred to a new type of curriculum organization and a new approach to teaching. It is in this sense that the term is being used today. Other terms are frequently used in the same sense as "core" curriculum, such as "common learnings," "unified studies," "integrated courses," and "block scheduling." Whatever the term used, the purposes, content, and organization are much the same.

In some schools there has been a studied attempt to avoid calling the core curriculum by any particular name. Sometimes this is due to prejudices on the part of teachers against new terminology, to a fear that some new name may disturb parents or citizens, or to the fact that core curriculum, common learnings, and other terms are not particularly appropriate for the sort of thing that a faculty wants to do. _For the purpose of the present discussion, we shall include under "core curriculum" any attempts that are being made to break down artificial barriers between subjects and for which a block of time longer than one class period is arranged_.

Because the term "core curriculum" is used in so many different ways, it is difficult to learn how many junior high schools have a program of this type. From the studies available on the subject, two things are evident. First, the core curriculum is much more common in grades seven and eight than in grade nine. Second, English and social studies are most often combined in the core classes. In a recent study by Byers, schools were asked whether they had pupils in grades seven, eight, and nine remain with the same teacher for more than one period in certain basic subjects. The percentage of 130 schools employing this practice in each grade is as follows: grade seven,

40 per cent; grade eight, 35 per cent; and grade nine, 18 per cent.[1]

The present authors used another approach to find out how many schools use the core curriculum. In a checklist study of 370 junior high schools, they asked what subjects are combined into one course and taught in a core class. The percentage of schools combining various subjects is as follows:

English—social studies	40%
English—social studies—science	7%
Social studies—science	1%
Other combinations	12%
No integrated courses	40%

Departmentalization Overemphasized. The core curriculum is in part a reaction against the extremes to which departmentalization was carried in the early junior high schools. It was only natural that over-departmentalization should have occurred at the beginning. The early junior high schools imitated many features of the four-year high school, of which departmentalization was most frequently copied. As a result, one of the basic characteristics of the junior high school thirty or more years ago was that it was a departmentalized school.

It is doubtful, however, that much thought was given to the manner and extent to which departmentalization was appropriate for young adolescents. For instance, it hardly seems desirable from the standpoint of articulation to have pupils remain with one teacher all day long in the sixth grade, and then to meet a different teacher for every period in the seventh grade. In fact, an examination of the departmentalized practices in contemporary junior and senior high schools reveals that in many medium-sized and large schools, seventh-grade pupils have more different-teacher contacts during a school week than those in grades eleven and twelve. There is little doubt but that the abrupt change from one teacher in the elementary school to many different teachers in the junior high school has no support in any sound philosophy of the junior high school.

The proponents of the core curriculum do not suggest that departmentalization be discontinued in the junior high school and that there be a return to one teacher for a group of pupils for the entire day. Such a complete change would obviously sacrifice too much in those subjects where a specialist is necessary, particularly in industrial arts, music, art, physical education, homemaking, and similar fields. In these subjects junior high school pupils are ready for experiences

[1] Richard S. Byers, "Articulation in the Junior High School" (Unpublished doctoral thesis, University of Connecticut, Storrs, Conn., 1955), p. 103.

that require far more preparation, talent, and skill on the part of the teacher than would be possible if they remained with one teacher for the entire day. Rather, it is suggested by proponents of the core curriculum that the extreme departmentalization which has been common in the junior high school needs to be modified sufficiently so that pupils may have the security of knowing a few teachers well, that teachers may become intimately acquainted with their pupils, and that better integration may be achieved. The core curriculum, it is believed, will achieve these results.

Integration Is Important. One of the most serious shortcomings of a highly departmentalized program is the difficulty that it creates in bringing about satisfactory integration between the learning activities in the various subjects and in the guidance and extraclass activities of the school. With the emphasis on subject-matter mastery in the early junior high schools, the lack of integration did not seem to be a serious problem. In the past twenty-five years, however, our entire approach to learning has changed. Instead of being concerned primarily with the mastery of unrelated bodies of subject matter, we are now emphasizing the need for having pupils study subject matter in a setting that will lead to its effective use in a real-life situation. This includes skill in reading, oral and written expression, and mathematics, as well as basic information and knowledge. Obviously, the real-life activities of both the child and the adult are not departmentalized, at least not on the same pattern that has been traditionally followed in school.

The core curriculum is the first major step toward providing the basis for better integration in the program of the junior high school. The core makes it possible for a teacher to remain with a group of pupils for more than one period, and to be responsible for their learning activities in more than one subject. Consequently, in this type of program the junior high school teacher has much the same opportunity as the elementary school teacher to achieve integration in learning outcomes. Language skills are not confined merely to the language arts period, but may be emphasized equally well in social studies, science, and other subject areas. As a result, the core curriculum should lead to more effective instruction in the language skills and other basic learnings because of the attention they receive in many different learning situations.

Although improved instruction in the basic learning skills is one of the outcomes of better integration, it is not the only one. The same may be said of all learning outcomes, including pupil ideals and attitudes, the ability to work together, personality growth and development, problem-solving skills, and many others. In this discussion, however, the advantages of the core curriculum for improving basic language and other skills are emphasized because they are so often overlooked. They are among the really significant outcomes of an effective core curriculum.

Knowing Individual Pupils. Meeting the needs, abilities, and interests of individual pupils was emphasized very early as one of the significant purposes for which the junior high school was established. A highly departmentalized program has, however, imposed serious difficulties in achieving this purpose. A teacher who meets five different classes daily may well have as many as 150 different pupils, if not more. The situation is even more serious in subjects that are taught in some schools on alternating days, such as music, physical education, art, and science. In these subjects, teachers may have 300 or more different pupils. In that situation, individualization of instruction indeed becomes an impossibility. It may well be that the teacher will not even know the names of his pupils much before the end of the term.

For some years junior high school educators have been groping for a way to reduce the pupil load of teachers so that teachers may become better acquainted with the backgrounds, learning difficulties, abilities, and interests of individual pupils. The core curriculum provides this opportunity. It lengthens the amount of time that a teacher spends with every group and at the same time reduces the number of pupil contacts that he has. For instance, if two subjects are combined under one teacher, he will have half or two-thirds as many pupils and meet them for twice as long. This should indeed improve the opportunity for knowing individual pupils and meeting their different needs, interests, and abilities.

Guidance Is Improved. In the past there has been much the same difficulty in providing adequate guidance for pupils in the junior high school as in individualizing instruction. For effective guidance to take place, some person in the school must know each child intimately and must have the opportunity to spend much time with him. The homeroom was intended to provide this opportunity. In this respect, it has been only a partial success. In most schools, the time that a teacher has to spend with his homeroom group is far too little for him to get to know all the pupils well and to give them individual help with their problems, interests, and adjustments.

By having pupils remain with one teacher for more than one class period daily, there is a better opportunity to provide adequate guidance. In some schools, the homeroom is combined with certain classes that form part of the core curriculum. Where that is done, the homeroom ceases to stand apart from the program of the school, and instead may become well integrated with it. When the homeroom is combined with core classes, guidance may be carried on through activities that are ordinarily considered to be English or social studies. In other words, the usual subject areas provide splendid opportunities for guidance. In this way, the core curriculum may greatly improve the guidance activities of the school.

Conditions for Better Teaching. In some discussions of the core curriculum, the administrative features seem to be greatly emphasized. It is true, of course, that they are important. However, the really significant thing about the core curriculum is the opportunity that it gives to employ more effectively some of the newer approaches to teaching. It is in the field of methods rather than curriculum organization that the core curriculum can make its greatest contribution to the program of the school.

The forty-minute class period in the departmentalized school was established at a time when the assign-study-recite approach to teaching generally prevailed. As new methods of teaching were developed, the forty-minute period appeared to limit the extent to which they could be used. One of the first steps was to lengthen the period to fifty or sixty minutes. Even with the longer period, it was difficult to use effectively some of the new methods of teaching. The core curriculum usually provides for a double class period, and sometimes more. This longer block of time makes it much easier to use effectively some of the new methods of classroom teaching.

Some of the methods which are encouraged in the core curriculum are working more effectively with individual pupils, group activities, cooperative pupil-teacher planning, more effective use of audio-visual materials, better opportunity for field trips, and provision for evaluation of pupil progress by the pupils themselves. For classroom methods such as these, teachers need to know their pupils well, and they need to be free from the strict limitations of a short class period. The opportunity which the core curriculum gives for using more effectively some of these methods of teaching is perhaps its greatest contribution to the program of the junior high school.

Summary of Purposes of the Core Curriculum. This, then, is some of the basic thinking underlying the core curriculum in the junior high school today. The essential purposes of the core curriculum as it is found in most schools may therefore be summarized briefly as follows:

know important

1. It draws upon various subject areas to improve the learning situation, rather than giving undue emphasis to arbitrary subject-matter lines.

2. It encourages the correlation and integration of learning outcomes in the various subject areas through having teachers responsible for more than one subject and through cooperative teacher-pupil planning.

3. It permits better individualization of teaching, smaller total pupil loads, and longer blocks of time with a given group.

4. It encourages the use of a variety of approaches to teaching through longer blocks of class time, thereby permitting more field trips, better use of audio-visual materials, large- and small-group activities, and similar learning activities which may demand more than one class period.

5. It encourages pupil participation in planning and carrying on learning activities.

6. It permits the more effective teaching of certain fundamentals, especially the language skills, by correlating all subjects more effectively with the language arts.

7. It encourages attention to some commonly neglected fundamentals, such as oral expression, problem-solving skills, and the ability to work together.

8. It permits a more relaxed social situation in the classroom, with pupils assuming some responsibility for maintaining an atmosphere where effective learning can take place.

9. It encourages self-evaluation by pupils of their progress in school, both of the group as a whole and of individuals within the group.

2. Types of Core Programs

Life-Problems Approach. One approach to developing the core curriculum is to build the learning activities in certain subject areas around real-life problems of the pupils. These problems are not confined to any one subject area, but ordinarily draw upon materials and skills from several related subject areas. The activities are planned cooperatively by the teacher and pupils, but clearly grow out of the interests and experiences of the pupils. These problems ordinarily are centered in the language arts–social studies areas. However, they may also draw upon the pupils' backgrounds in science, mathematics, art, industrial arts, music, and all other subject areas.

The traditional basic skills, as well as basic information, are taught in this approach to the core curriculum, but ordinarily they do not stand out prominently as distinct learning outcomes. Rather, such skills as written and oral expression, spelling, penmanship, reading, and arithmetic are taught as pupils study the problems which they have selected and are developing. In this approach it is expected that pupils will do far more reading, creative work, and study than in a more traditional approach to teaching. It is also intended that sufficient attention will be given to the various basic skills so that pupil progress in those skills will be as good as, if not better than, in a more formal approach to teaching.

It is not often that the life-problems approach to developing the core curriculum is used in isolation from other approaches. Usually this approach is combined with some of the others that will be discussed subsequently. Where the life-problems approach is used most effectively, there is cooperative planning on many learning activities by teachers from all subject areas. In fact, such cooperative planning on the part of teachers is essential if the life-problems approach is to be used effectively.

Basic-Subjects Approach. In the basic-subjects approach to the core curriculum pupils remain with the same teacher for all the basic subjects, such as language arts, social studies, science, and mathematics. In some schools, as in the Darien, Connecticut, Junior High School, this plan is confined to the seventh grade. In the Valley Regional High School, Deep River, Connecticut, a six-year secondary school, pupils in grades seven and eight remain with the same teacher for the basic subjects. This approach is particularly appropriate in the seventh grade because it avoids an abrupt change from the single teacher of the sixth grade to the more highly departmentalized program of the junior high school.

Where this plan is followed pupils frequently remain with one teacher for half a day, and then devote the other half day to subjects that demand the help of specialists. The teacher is free to use the time in this long period in any way that he thinks best. At times the various basic subjects will be taught as separate subjects, while at other times the work will be developed around a problem that may cut across several or all basic subjects. The teacher is free to give pupils "breaks" during the half day that he has with the group, so that they may go to the drinking fountains, washrooms, and into the corridors.

There are a number of advantages in having the pupils remain with the same teacher for the four basic subjects. Perhaps the most obvious is the improvement in articulation from the sixth grade to the seventh, which this plan provides. It means that, in the seventh and possibly the eighth grade, pupils will spend much of the day with one teacher, as they did in the elementary school. Other advantages of the basic-subjects approach are that (1) it improves integration between the basic subjects, (2) pupils have the security that comes from knowing one teacher well, (3) teachers are much better acquainted with individual pupils and their problems, (4) guidance is likely to be more effective, and (5) teachers have a better opportunity to get acquainted with parents.

There are also, however, some disadvantages to the basic-subjects approach. Perhaps the most prominent is the difficulty in finding teachers who are well prepared in all of the subjects concerned. The subject that is most likely to suffer under this plan is science. It usually is so important to have a teacher who is well prepared in the language arts that this subject and the social studies receive first consideration in the selection of a teacher for this type of program. It is difficult, indeed, to find a teacher who is well prepared in the broad field of general science, as well as in the language arts, social studies, and mathematics.

In some schools teachers are responsible only for language arts, social studies, and mathematics. Since mathematics in grades seven and eight consists primarily of arithmetic, it is not difficult to find teachers with adequate subject-matter preparation for it. Hence a specialist can be employed for general science. This plan tends to relieve somewhat the objection that it is difficult to find well-qualified teachers in all four subject areas.

The effectiveness of the basic-subjects approach to the core curriculum depends upon the background, experience, and preparation of the teacher concerned. If the teacher is well qualified in all the subject areas, is conversant with methods of teaching in these areas, and has resourcefulness and imagination in developing well-integrated learning activities, the basic-subjects approach can indeed provide an effective learning situation. The teacher should also have an unusually sympathetic understanding of children and their problems, he should be skilled in the use of the various instruments for studying children, and he should have some competence in guidance. This is asking for a great deal in one teacher. But if these qualities are lacking, the teacher may continue to teach the basic subjects with little more effectiveness than in a highly departmentalized school. Even so, in the basic-subjects approach to the core curriculum, the teacher is better able to become acquainted with the pupils, there is a longer block of time to carry on learning activities, and there is a smoother transition from the elementary to the junior high school.

Related-Subjects Approach. The most common approach to the development of the core curriculum is to combine certain related subjects under one teacher. This may be called the related-subjects approach. Usually English and social studies are combined in this way, frequently with the homeroom included. In fact, these two subject areas are so frequently combined that many educators think of the core curriculum primarily in terms of an English–social studies combination.

Under the related-subjects approach, a group of pupils remains with the same teacher for more than one class period daily. This teacher is responsible for the usual material covered in language arts and social studies. If the schedule permits, these classes are consecutive, but in some schools where that is not possible they may come at different times of the day. In the related-subjects approach, as with the other approaches to the core curriculum, the longer block of time is not the primary characteristic. Better correlation between the subjects concerned, more effective teaching methods, better individualized instruction, and improved guidance are also major outcomes of the related-subjects approach.

The West Junior High School, Kansas City, Missouri, provides an excellent example of the related-subjects approach to the core curriculum. In this school it is called the common-learnings program, but in every respect it fulfills the essentials of the core curriculum as outlined earlier in this chapter. At West Junior High School a group of pupils remains with a teacher for two and a half class periods daily. The periods are sixty minutes in length. The schedule was planned this way in order that approximately the equivalent of one period daily may be devoted to language arts, a second period to the social studies, and a half period to homeroom activities. In practice, such a division of time is not discernible. Rather, learning activities are developed in terms of the needs and interests of the pupils, and then are carried on during the two-and-a-half-period block of time in whatever way seems most appropriate. The common-learnings teacher has two such groups every day. He serves as the homeroom teacher for these groups as well as teaching the work in language arts and social studies. At West Junior High School the periods are taught consecutively.

A similar plan is in effect at the Jonathan Weeks Junior High School, Newton, Massachusetts, where pupils remain with the same teacher for twelve forty-minute periods a week. During that time, the usual activities included in language arts, social studies, and homeroom are covered. As at the West Junior High School, teachers at the Weeks Junior High School have two such class groups.

At the Weeks Junior High School, the class periods are arranged consecutively in so far as possible. However, this cannot be arranged in all cases. In the beginning, it was planned that approximately five periods of this time should be devoted to language arts, five periods to social studies, and two periods to the homeroom. However, teachers are encouraged to integrate the work in the various subjects as much as possible and to use the total time in such a way as to produce the most effective results.

In some schools science and mathematics are taught as a combination by one teacher, with English and social studies being taught by another. This plan is followed at the Central Junior High School, Granite School District, Salt Lake City, Utah. In grades seven, eight, and nine, English and social studies are taught to a group of pupils by the same teacher, while in grades seven and eight mathematics and science are also taught by one teacher. Although mathematics and science do not lend themselves as readily to integration as language arts and social studies, there are certain times in the program when integrated activities in these subject areas may be carried on. That is especially true when there are summarizing activities, especially late in the school year.

There is particular need for combining science with another subject in the core curriculum because science so often is not taught every day. Especially in grades seven and eight it is taught on days that alternate with some other subject. That is, in grade seven science may be taught on Tuesday and Thursday, while in grade eight it may come on Monday, Wednesday and Friday. Where this is done, it is difficult for the teacher to become well acquainted with pupils and to teach them as individuals. That is obvious because the teacher may have ten or more different groups of pupils during the course of a week. However, by combining science with mathematics, a teacher may meet these pupils for seven or eight periods weekly, and become sufficiently well acquainted with them to meet their individual interests, needs, and abilities. At the Strickland Junior High School, Alice, Texas, a rather unique plan is used for this purpose. There the basic period in the day is thirty minutes long. The social living class meets for four thirty-minute periods, or a total of two clock-hours. The mathematics-science class meets for three thirty-minute periods, or a total of one and a half clock-hours. In this way it is possible to meet the needs of pupils in both of these areas and yet give a greater amount of time to those subjects that, in the thinking of the faculty, need the most time.

Cooperative-Planning Approach. In some schools the purposes of a core curriculum are achieved largely through cooperative planning by the teachers of the various subjects. Often this approach is combined with one of the others, as is true in the Jonathan Weeks Junior High School, Newton, Massachusetts. This school exemplifies particularly well the cooperative planning approach to the core curriculum, although it is combined with the related-subjects approach. There is a daily planning period for teachers from 8:00 to 8:45 A.M. Various groups of teachers meet according to a prearranged weekly schedule. For instance, it may be that on Monday morning the seventh grade teachers will meet, Tuesday morning the eighth-grade teachers, Wednesday the ninth-grade teachers, and so on. The schedule of meetings is arranged by the chairman of the groups, and depends upon current needs.

The purpose of the planning sessions in Newton is for teachers to discuss the activities that each one is carrying on with his classes and to make plans for future learning activities. In this way the teacher of the English–social studies class is always in touch with what is taking place in mathematics, science, art, music, and the other subjects. The work in those subjects may be correlated, therefore, with the learning activities that are carried on in basic language skills. Furthermore, classes in art, music, industrial arts, and similar subjects may make a considerable contribution to the learning activities that are being carried on in English, social studies, science, and mathematics. In other words, with the cooperative planning approach to the core curriculum, the teachers are able to function as a team in planning and carrying on the learning activities in all subjects for any group of pupils. There is an opportunity also to plan the classroom activities so that they are well correlated with extraclass activities. Through such cooperative planning week by week, teachers are able to achieve more fully the purposes of the core curriculum.

The most difficult part of the cooperative-planning approach, of course, is to find time during the day when all teachers can be free for such meetings. In the Killingly Memorial School, Danielson, Connecticut, teachers of the upper grades meet during the noon hour occasionally for such planning sessions. Where there is a long noon hour, it is possible for such meetings to be arranged. In most schools, however, the cooperative-planning period for teachers may have to come either before or after school. This period need not be a long one. Even thirty minutes a week is sufficient for teachers to get together and keep informed concerning learning activities in the various subject areas.

3. Introducing Core Programs

Avoid Spectacular Introduction. The core curriculum has not always had a smooth history in the schools where it was introduced. In some communities where, according to the faculty, it appeared to be exceedingly successful, it was discontinued because of opposition from parents and other citizens. In several cities, in fact, it became the focal point of criticism by militant parents and citizens who were dissatisfied with the schools. This has happened in enough communities so that the best method of introduction deserves some consideration in any discussion of the core curriculum.

In some of these communities a spectacular approach was employed in introducing the core curriculum. It was publicized as something unusual, modern, progressive, and new. Furthermore, in some communities the terms that were used to identify the core program raised suspicions. Parents and citizens seemed to believe that the schools were going to discontinue teaching English and social studies, and introduce in their place a new course called core, common learnings, unified studies, or block program. Obviously, these new terms meant little if anything to many parents, other citizens, and even teachers.

In introducing the core curriculum, a school should try to avoid giving the impression that this is something new and unusual. Actually, many features of the core curriculum are very old indeed. For instance, the idea of having a teacher remain with a group of pupils for more than one period in grades seven and eight is certainly not new. In fact, in the traditional eight-grade elementary school this was and is still the usual practice. Many other features of the core curriculum have been discussed and used by some teachers for years. Examples of such features are individualizing the work of the class, cooperative teacher-pupil planning, correlating the work in English with that of other subjects, and the use of a variety of instructional materials and aids. These and some of the other practices common to the core curriculum have been used by effective junior high school teachers for more than a quarter of a century.

In introducing the core curriculum to teachers, parents, and other citizens, it seems best, therefore, to point out that the core curriculum is not something spectacular or entirely new. Rather, it is an arrangement of the program of the school so that teachers can use more effectively some of the better methods of instruction. Furthermore, it should be suggested that this is a modification of the highly departmentalized program which was copied from the four-year high school in the early days of the junior high school. It might also be added that the core curriculum merely encourages teachers to use some of the effective methods of instruction which some of the better teachers have been using for many years.

Furthermore, it might be wise to caution a faculty against the use of new terms. *After all, it is not so important what we call the program, but it is exceedingly important what approach we use in work-*

ing with youngsters in the program. In one community, the principal stated that it was the intention to avoid using any new term for the core curriculum. In discussing the program with parents, the faculty in this community suggested that English, social studies, and the homeroom were being combined under one teacher so that these subjects might be taught more effectively. It was pointed out that the language skills particularly would receive more adequate attention in the new program. Furthermore, in this community the subjects in the new program were still designated separately as English and social studies, instead of substituting a new term for the combined subjects. In other words, "English" and "social studies" continued as before on pupil-progress reports and on office records. Consequently, in this community there was little opportunity for critics of the schools to use the new program as a target. This approach to the introduction of the core curriculum did not call attention to spectacular changes in the program of the school. Rather, it suggested that many of the old things were being taught but that this instruction was being given in a little different setting.

Cooperative Faculty Study. If the core curriculum is to be effective, it is indeed important to have the understanding and support of all the teachers concerned. It seems appropriate, therefore, to introduce the core curriculum by a period of intensive faculty study of the purposes that this curriculum is to achieve and the ways in which teachers may work most effectively with it. This study might well be concerned with the shortcomings of the departmentalized program, with the methods of teaching which are not now being used as effectively as may be desired, with ways of correlating and integrating work between the subject areas, and with other emphases that are appropriate in the core curriculum. It is always helpful to have the assistance of parents, elementary teachers, and senior high school teachers in such a study. Each group brings a different point of view to bear on the discussions.

It is not essential for every teacher in school, or for that matter all those who are directly concerned with it, to be enthusiastic at the beginning about the core curriculum. In fact, it is unlikely that unanimous enthusiasm can ever be obtained for any new program. But it is important to have one or two teachers who are willing to try such a program, at least experimentally. As they gain skill and confidence in their work, they may be observed by other teachers and they help in other ways to extend the program throughout the school. In many schools such a gradual introduction of the core curriculum has been brought about.

Furthermore, it is not necessary that a teacher try to achieve all the purposes of the core curriculum during the first year or two. In fact, in one junior high school of about 1200 pupils, all teachers of English and social studies were asked if they would be willing to keep the same groups for these two subjects. It was suggested that they might go as far with correlation and integration as they wished, but that they would not be expected to introduce any method or activities of which they did not approve. As a result, some teachers for the first year or two continued to teach English and social studies as separate subjects, except that they had the same group of pupils in these subjects for two periods. Some other teachers went a long way toward introducing immediately a well-integrated approach to teaching, employing many of the methods which are suggested by the core enthusiasts. The principal, however, stated that even the teachers who continued to teach the subjects separately were doing a better job of teaching English because the basic language skills could be so readily taught during the social studies period. At the end of one year, all the teachers in the program agreed that having pupils take their work in English and social studies with the same teacher was preferable to a more highly departmentalized program.

In another school of about 900 pupils, two teachers volunteered to take experimental classes in which English, social studies, and the homeroom were combined. They became so enthusiastic about their work with these groups that other teachers asked to participate in a similar program the second year. By the beginning of the fifth year, all of the English and social studies teachers in the school had asked for groups that were organized on this basis. Although some of the teachers were more effective than others in developing good core activities, even the less effective teachers felt that they were doing better teaching under the new arrangement than under the old.

It is important that faculty study of the core curriculum be continued even after this program is introduced. In other words, the study of a core program should be a continuing thing. Furthermore, teachers may learn a great deal from each other as they try out new things and as they gain experience with the program. It is particularly helpful to have parents continue with such a study group. They can give the reaction of youngsters as they hear them at home, as well as their own thinking concerning the experiences of teachers with the program.

Facilities That Are Needed. Although it is not essential to have certain types of facilities and equipment for the core curriculum, it is much easier to carry on such a program if suitable facilities are available. For instance, there should be movable furniture so that pupils may work in committees, that the seats may be arranged for informal class discussions, and the furniture may be arranged for other types of activities. There should be a variety of furniture, such as a table or two, a work bench or counter, ample display space, and adequate cupboard and storage space. It is desirable to have the classroom sufficiently large so that furniture may be rearranged for committee and small-group activities, for large-group discussions, for laboratory and other similar activities, and for dramatizations and other oral presentations. It is also desirable to have ample reference materials in the classroom, adequate library materials, audio-visual equipment, and other supplies and materials that make it possible to carry on a variety of learning activities.

It should be pointed out, however, that the imagination, resourcefulness, interest, and skill of teachers are of far more importance than any physical facilities and equipment that may be provided. In one school observed by the writer, classrooms were quite small, there was very little display space, and the furniture in most of the core classrooms was fixed. Yet in that school there was an excellent core curriculum as compared with some others that have more ample facilities. A junior high school faculty should not permit inadequate facilities to prevent the introduction of a core curriculum.

Developing the Core Program. It is absolutely essential that the core curriculum for a given school be developed by its faculty, the administration, and the parents of the community. It cannot be a sheer imitation of the program in another school, no matter how successful that program might be in its present situation. Although there is some advantage in studying the programs of other schools, this should be done only to obtain background for developing a school's own program.

The traditional type of course of study is not appropriate for a core curriculum. Rather, it is helpful to have curriculum guides which offer many suggestions concerning the content of the program, the methods of teaching, and the materials that may be used. It may be helpful, also, to indicate that certain basic skills and content should be covered in a given grade. In any case, there must be every opportunity for the individual teacher to develop the learning activities which are most appropriate for the group of pupils concerned. Furthermore, the teacher should have freedom to adapt the curriculum to the many different interests, abilities, and needs that he finds among his pupils. A broad framework for the year's work certainly should be provided, but within that framework the individual teacher needs to have much freedom to plan and carry on appropriate learning activities.

Attention to Basic Skills. Because the work in basic skills is not definitely outlined, there is danger that they may be neglected in the core curriculum. Every effort should be made to avoid this possibility. It should be understood that each semester the basic skills should receive attention. In a core curriculum there needs to be some formal instruction in reading, oral expression, written expression, and the other basic skills. Furthermore, that instruction needs to be carried on in a well-planned manner. There is, however, some difference between the instruction in basic skills in the core curriculum and that of a more traditional program. In the core curriculum the instruction in basic skills is given as part of a functional learning situation in which pupils have an opportunity to make extensive use of the various skills.

In planning a core curriculum, it is essential that provision be made for an extensive program of evaluation and testing. There should be periodic diagnostic and achievement tests in all the basic skills to ascertain the difficulties and the progress of individual pupils as well as of the class as a whole. Fortunately, many schools in which a core curriculum has been introduced are now making provision for such a testing program. The information which that program gives is exceedingly helpful to teachers in studying the progress of their pupils in the fundamental skills.

Evaluation of the Core Curriculum. Once a core curriculum has been introduced in a school, there should be provision for evaluating its effectiveness. Such evaluation should begin immediately and should be carried on continuously. That is the only way information for improving the core curriculum may be accumulated. If achievement tests are regularly given, this information may be useful for evaluating the core curriculum, especially if it can be compared with the results under the previous curriculum. It is especially important, through such a testing program, to evaluate the progress of pupils in the fundamental skills.

Adequate evaluation of the core curriculum, however, should go far beyond a testing program in the fundamental skills. It is important to know how the faculty, parents, and pupils react to the new program. For instance, one needs to know whether teachers find the preparation unduly heavy; whether there are adequate materials, supplies, and equipment; whether the disciplinary situation in the classroom is affected; and whether teachers find it easier to work with pupils on personal problems. Similarly, it would be helpful to know the reaction of pupils to the core curriculum. For instance, one should know whether pupils are happy in this type of situation; whether they feel that their individual interests are being satisfied; whether they have sufficient opportunity to assume leadership responsibilities; and whether they are satisfied with the progress that they are making in the basic skills. If such information from teachers, parents, and pupils is systematically accumulated from time to time, much information may be gathered which will be useful in improving the effectiveness of the core curriculum.

Discipline Should Not Be a Problem. The informal nature of the learning activities frequently carried on in a core curriculum demands informal pupil-pupil and teacher-pupil relationships. This is essential in order that the most effective learning situation may obtain. In the hands of an inexperienced teacher, however, pupils may take undue advantage of such informality.

Nothing can destroy the effectiveness of the core curriculum more quickly than an unsatisfactory disciplinary situation. Teacher and pupils alike need to understand that the informality and freedom obtains for one reason only; namely, that pupils may work more effectively together on common learning problems. It is essential that the human relations in the classroom be such that pupils and teachers may work together most effectively in planning and carrying on learning activities.

4. Conclusion

The core curriculum is indeed an interesting development in junior high school education today. It has much to contribute to the implementation of the basic philosophy of the junior high school. In a way, it is still in the experimental stage. Yet it has been so successful in many of the schools where it has been introduced that it seems to be on the way to becoming accepted junior high school practice.

Questions and Exercises

1. Summarize in your own words the basic philosophy of the core curriculum.
2. What methods of teaching are particularly appropriate for the core curriculum?
3. Explain in some detail how you would proceed to introduce a curriculum in a junior high school.
4. What are the advantages of having pupils in grades seven and eight remain with the same teacher for all the basic subjects? What are the disadvantages?

5. If the homeroom is a part of the core curriculum, how would you integrate the homeroom activities with the work in the language arts?

6. If you were to include only two subjects in a combination for core classes, which would you combine? Give your reasons.

7. What are the more serious difficulties that you see in the core curriculum?

8. What aspects of the philosophy of the junior high school are achieved particularly through the core curriculum?

Chapter 6

THE CURRICULUM FIELDS:
INDUSTRIAL ARTS, HEALTH
AND PHYSICAL EDUCATION,
MATHEMATICS, ART

1. INDUSTRIAL ARTS [1]

Objectives of Industrial Arts Education. The general objectives of industrial arts should be related to the all-school aims of education. All objectives should be considered by the teacher as being made up of three distinct phases. First, he should translate them into descriptions of behavioral changes in pupils which should result from a particular experience. Second, the teacher should decide which learning activities are most likely to bring about the desired changes. And, third, he should determine what kinds of evidence can be gathered to ascertain the level of pupil attainment. The industrial arts objectives of the junior high school should not prove hazy, remote, or difficult of attainment when treated to the critical examination suggested in these three steps.

The nine most commonly accepted industrial arts objectives are listed below. They should be considered as suggestive of the broad goals worthy of attainment in this subject area. Although these nine objectives are widely accepted, each teacher should formulate his own statement of objectives in the light of his philosophy, the needs of youth in his school, and the potentialities or limitations of his own teaching situation.

1. *Interest in industry. To develop in each pupil an active interest in industrial life and in the methods and problems of production and exchange.* Young people are alert and curious as to what goes on about them. Many homes and communities do not afford opportunities for observing and understanding industrial life with its problems and opportunities. The schools, and particularly the industrial arts teachers, should aid in providing that understanding. Information

[1] This section was prepared by Howard H. Nelson, Associate Professor of Industrial Education, University of Minnesota.

should be given and insight developed to improve the pupil's social-mindedness and to broaden his view of vocational possibilities and requirements.

2. *Appreciation and use. To develop in each pupil the appreciation of good design, materials, and workmanship, and the ability to select, care for, and use industrial products wisely.* One of the most important functions of industrial arts is the development of "consumer literacy" and a sense of esthetic values. Pupils should be led to distinguish between the bizarre effects that prevail for a time and the quieter designs and constructions that are more clearly based upon simplicity, adaptability, proportion, and harmony.

3. *Self-realization and initiative. To develop in each pupil the habits of self-reliance and resourcefulness in meeting practical situations.* This is a responsibility of all teachers, but one for which industrial arts teachers possess peculiar readiness. They have unusual opportunity to build self-confidence, judgment, self-discipline, idealism, reliability, respect for authority or valid custom, and self-expression.

4. *Cooperative attitudes. To develop in each pupil a readiness to assist others and to join in socially accepted group undertakings.* We are concerned here with helping to develop individuals who are unselfish, able to get along with their fellows at work or play, and inclined toward the support of what makes for progress and the common good. We want pupils to desire to make others comfortable, not because of a rule or requirement, but because there is pleasure in "doing a good turn," in cooperative activity, and in common courtesy. School is the place to impress the fact that harmony is a requisite of happy home and community life and that good attitudes are highly conducive to advancement in most earning situations.

5. *Health and safety. To develop in each pupil desirable attitudes and practices with respect to health and safety.* We recognize that industrial arts subjects afford exceptional facilities and situations for advancing the interests of pupils in this area. Teachers certainly need to be conscious of their responsibilities for it. Information provided and habits established should have observable effect in the school shop and should carry over to adult home and vocational life.

6. *Interest in achievement. To develop in each pupil a feeling of pride in his ability to do useful things and to develop certain worthy free-time interests, particularly in the crafts.* We assume that abilities in these respects may be a strong incentive to good citizenship. Every pupil should be encouraged and instructed until he can do at least a few things well. This approach to the development and maintenance of self-respect should not be neglected.

7. *Habit of orderly performance. To develop in each pupil the habit of an orderly and efficient performance of any task.* It is a worthy use of school time to emphasize the importance of planned, orderly, and efficient work. In the shop and elsewhere, there is much value to be gained from efficient work habits. Pupils should develop habits of thoughtful, careful, and efficient work.

8. *Drawings and design. To develop in each pupil an understanding of all kinds of common graphic representations and the ability to express ideas by means of drawings and sketches.* Drawing is a universal language, and everyone should have a certain proficiency in interpreting or performing it. Industrial arts affords effective means for the development of reading knowledge and the ability and desire of self-expression, both freehand and with the use of instruments.

9. *Shop skills and knowledge. To develop in each pupil skill in the use of common tools and machines and an understanding of the problems involved in common types of construction and repair.* It is important to have pupils become proficient in the occasional minor mechanical and electrical tasks encountered by the average adult. They should have some knowledge of the principles of tool use and simple machine operation.[2]

Offerings in Industrial Arts. In a majority of the 370 schools included in the survey by the authors, industrial arts is required in grades seven and eight, usually for two semesters in each grade. In the ninth grade, industrial arts is usually an elective subject. The percentage of schools which offer industrial arts either as a required (R) or an elective (E) subject is as follows:

	Two Semesters		One Semester	
	Percentage of Schools	Average Periods Weekly	Percentage of Schools	Average Periods Weekly
Seventh grade:				
General industrial arts (R)	57	3.4	18	3.7
General industrial arts (E)	4	5.0	2	4.5
Eighth grade:				
General industrial arts (R)	57	3.6	21	4.6
General industrial arts (E)	18	4.6	2	4.6
Ninth grade:				
General industrial arts (R)	21	3.5	1	2.0
General industrial arts (E)	68	4.7	4	4.9
Home mechanics (E)	1	5.0		
Woodworking (E)	1	3.5		
Printing (E)	1	3.5	1	

[2] American Vocational Association, *A Guide to Improving Instruction in Industrial Arts* (Washington, D.C.: The Association, 1953), pp. 19-28.

Planning Learning Activities. The content and activities of instructional shopwork are drawn from all phases of industrial life. This practice precludes limiting the work to manipulative-constructive exercises in woodwork alone. The multifaceted structure of industry today presents numerous logical avenues from which to select classroom activities. Few, if any, of these activities should be employed as ends in themselves; rather, they should serve as the vehicles by which to attain certain desired skills or understandings. These various avenues indicate the broadness of the offering and also suggest its limitations, for:

These several points of departure—that is, the materials, tools and processes of industry; science and invention applied to industry; the social and economic contributions of industry—define the scope of the industrial arts program.[3]

Historically, industrial arts evolved from the village crafts; that is, the industry of individuals. Industrial arts has been, and should continue to be, characterized by work in the shop—sound manipulative-constructive activities—permitting an interest in things industrial to develop out of depth, rather than breadth, of experience. This basic concept has been well expressed as follows:

Those who participate in industrial arts programs receive orientation in the areas of production, consumption, and recreation through actual experiences in planning, producing, servicing, and repairing various types of consumer goods in common usage. Through these experiences, young people learn about material goods. They learn how to use and maintain them intelligently. They develop general skill and resourcefulness in working with things, technical and mechanical. They learn facts, principles, and procedures about tools, materials, processes, mechanics, and design. They learn about woods, metals, plastics, ceramics, textiles, paper, and other industrial materials. They learn about electricity, motors, engines, structures, and other items of importance, interest, and concern to all people at home, on the farm, at work, and in recreation. They learn to do critical thinking in solving problems related to these matters.[4]

Examples of Class Activities. An ingenious industrial arts teacher finds many approaches for the selection of industrial arts activities which he may use for the purpose of providing learning experiences within certain areas of industry under investigation. Once an activity is selected, ways of facilitating its use as a vehicle of instruction are determined. For example, a junior high school teacher and his class may have decided to produce as a class project a simple program for the all-school Christmas play. They may also have planned to enhance the attractiveness of the program covers by using an appropriate

[3] *Ibid.*, p. 10.
[4] American Vocational Association, Industrial Arts Planning and Policy Committee, *Industrial Arts in Education* (Washington, D.C.: The Association, 1953), p. 3.

linoleum block cut. The industrial arts teacher then introduces a unit from the graphic arts area which involves the planning, preparation, and production of linoleum block cuts for the project.

During the course of the unit, the teacher may provide enrichment for the class by bringing in some of the more interesting aspects of the history of printing. For instance, the class may learn about the earliest attempts at duplicating words or messages, the stories crudely scratched into rocks by primitive men, the later advancements exemplified in the picture-writing of the Egyptian hieroglyphics, and the clay tablets employed by ancient Babylonians for recording their messages.

The instructor may arrange activities that will enable pupils to learn of the laborious tasks of the monks in copying manuscripts by hand. They may learn about the first pieces of movable type cut from wood, and how later pieces of type came to be cast from metals. They should study the development of printing presses. The names of Gutenberg, Coster, Caslon, and Benjamin Franklin should take on new meaning through a study of the graphic arts.

The class should also study printing today. They can become acquainted with the kinds of presses. The term "automation" should take on new meaning in relation to modern printing processes. Classes should learn about the qualifications of printers, the working conditions, wages paid, avenues of advancement, security of the job, and other interesting facts about the graphic arts.

The teacher can make use of field trips, movies, charts, specimens, models, reproductions, and samples to raise the level of appreciation and understanding. Through these experiences pupils may learn about relief and offset printing, and also learn how to judge the quality of printed materials. They can become wiser consumers of these goods. The pupils may also begin to understand the terminology of the graphic arts trade and thus be able to speak more intelligently about it.

It should not be assumed that every class should cover the entire group of activities suggested. These should be selected in terms of the interests and needs of the group and the time, materials, and facilities available.

Experience Areas in Industrial Arts Program. The experience areas in the industrial arts program of the junior high school, while conforming to no set pattern, reflect what people do or should know to get their job done in industry. Experience areas must be limited, certainly, by practical considerations faced when adapting selected portions of industrial work to school shop experience.

If there is one area which can be designated of greatest importance in the total program, it is the general drawing and planning area. This part of the shop work incorporates the facilities and furnishings necessary for the thinking and planning required by every other area or activity in the program. The remaining areas are often selected from a series consisting of general wood, general metals, general graphic arts, general crafts, and general power, including electricity. None of these separate areas need to be thought of as unitary subjects in themselves, but rather, they should be considered as parts of the total program. The separate areas support and strengthen each other to form a well-rounded total series, and together they constitute the minimum number of activities through which to explore present-day industry.

One of the most comprehensive studies of industrial arts experiences for junior high school pupils was made by administrators, supervisors, classroom teachers, and teacher trainers working at the invitation of Dean M. Schweickhard, Commissioner of Education for the State of Minnesota. The committee was asked to revise the industrial arts curriculum for the state. Proposals by this group were prepared during 1947 and 1948 and were submitted for criticism and revision to teachers of the state. In this manner, all interested persons were permitted to react to the proposals of the committee. The outcome of this work by the committee and teachers of the state was a printed guide which presents a suggested program in industrial arts education. A summary of these suggestions is presented below.

Suggested Industrial Arts Program for the Junior High School [5]

Seventh-Grade Industrial Arts. An effective program at any grade level must start with a consideration of the students being served. The typical seventh-grade student can be characterized as:

1. Being highly active
2. Lacking in fine coordination in skills
3. Having short interest retention
4. Liking to work with others—is a social being
5. Being easily motivated
6. Acting before he thinks
7. Being interested primarily in immediate and personal values
8. Having a wide range of aptitudes and unknown abilities
9. Being inquisitive

[5] *A Guide for Instruction in Industrial Arts,* Curriculum Bulletin No. 13, Part I (St. Paul: State Department of Education, 1950), pp. 30-34.

In view of these characteristics, the following guiding principles will prove helpful in organizing industrial arts experiences at the seventh-grade level:

1. Short jobs, lessons or projects (two to four hours in length)
2. Simple manipulative work (may include package type of projects or pre-cut materials)
3. Projects or jobs similar for all in the class

Eighth-Grade Industrial Arts. The offering on the eighth-grade level must take into consideration both mental and physical maturation. The eighth-grade student being a year older—conditioned to a greater extent by innate and environmental factors—can best be described by a direct comparison with the seventh-grade student. The typical eighth-grade student then can be characterized as:

1. Having more purposeful activities—becoming aware of his limitations
2. Having better muscular coordination dealing with hand skills
3. Having improved and lengthened interest span
4. Being more selfish in so far as he begins to like to do things by himself and for himself, and probably is more self-critical of what he is doing
5. Being harder to motivate, but possessing a higher competitive spirit
6. Possessing more ability to think before acting and being more conscious of shop safety
7. Being interested in deferred and projected values
8. Being more able to evaluate his products and those of his fellow students
9. Being more restrained

In view of these characteristics the following guiding principles will prove helpful in organizing industrial arts experiences at the eighth-grade level:

1. Jobs, lessons, and projects requiring more time—less in number— up to ten hours
2. Manipulative work requiring the use of a greater number of hand tools
3. A wider range of related study
4. Projects to reflect some individual tastes

Ninth-Grade Industrial Arts. The industrial arts program in the seventh and eighth grades consists of experiences with a wide variety of materials, simple elementary skills, and a minimum of related information. It is chiefly manipulative in nature.

The following points have been considered in suggesting a program for the ninth-grade student, who may be characterized as:

1. Having advanced to a marked degree beyond the eighth-grade student in stature and muscular coordination
2. Having made noticeable improvement in acquiring skills and applying shop knowledge
3. Being ready to assume a good deal more responsibility in working on projects
4. Being ready to assimilate much more related information
5. Being physically much larger and able to handle heavier objects and equipment
6. Having enough coordination of hand and eye to be able to use selected power equipment
7. Having become more safety conscious through observing many demonstrations and study of safe working practices

The time has come to have the student do more individual planning and to record this planning through the accepted practices of correct mechanical drawing procedure. The subject areas should be fewer in number allowing more time for planning, construction, and related information.

SUBJECT AREAS AND GRADE PLACEMENT

Grade Level	Required		Elective	
Seventh:	1. Metal [6]		Sketching	Rubber
	2. Wood		Ceramics	Paper and Fiber
	3. Plastics		Textiles	Glass
	4. Graphic Arts		Keene Cement	Models
	5. Leather		Rope and Cord	Fly-tying
	6. Disassembly and Assembly			

Minimum time in one area—12 clock hours
Maximum time in one area—30 clock hours

Eighth:	1. Drawing	Metal
	2. Electricity	Wood
	3. (elective)	Graphic Arts
	4. (elective)	(additional electives chosen from seventh-grade list)

Minimum time in one area—18 clock hours
Maximum time in one area—45 clock hours

Ninth:	Plan A	Plan B	Metal
	1. Drawing	1. Drawing	Graphic Arts
	2. Woodwork	2. Woodwork	Electricity
		3. (elective)	

Plan A—90 clock hours in each area
Plan B—60 clock hours in each area

[6] "General" implied, i.e., general metal, general wood, etc.

2. Health and Physical Education [7]

Physical education in junior high school should make a significant contribution to the development of the total personality of the child. Objectives in physical education grow out of a recognition of some of the basic facts of man's biological nature and social beliefs, as well as the educational philosophy of the times. Through participation in the sports, games, and dances of the people, not only are organic growth and psychological development enhanced, but contributions are also made to an understanding of the prevailing social and political culture. The modern teacher in physical education views his opportunity as one far broader than mere entertainment, wider than merely "conditioning," and deeper by far than any device invented to relax children from the more serious business of education.

The teacher of physical education views the gymnasium, playing fields, and swimming pool as laboratories for human development, and he plans and conducts the physical education program accordingly. He sees the potentialities of physical education as transcending the bounds of "the physical" and bearing in an important way upon the total cultural development of the child. He renounces the cult of the physical alone as readily as he does that of the intellect alone, because he realizes that each has an important bearing on the other.

Principles Underlying the Program. To construct a program of physical education which reflects the foregoing point of view requires thoughtful effort on the part of curriculum-makers. The program should become neither a patchwork of games chosen to amuse children nor a series of formalized body-building activities. It should seek to educate through the motor experiences, consider games as educative media, and recognize the need of children for developmental activities.

From the study of man, his nature, and his society have come principles which may be used as guides in curriculum-building and in the administration of physical education. The following principles are basic to the development of an effective program of physical education in the junior high school.

1. *The program should be developed in terms of the interests and abilities of all the pupils.* In physical education, the pupils who are poor in ability, the "dubs," and the handicapped have as much right to participation, to good instruction, and to space, time, and equipment as the superior student and the athlete. Every child should be served.

2. *The program should seek to develop self-direction, self-deter-*

[7] This section was prepared by Professor Delbert Oberteuffer, College of Education, Ohio State University.

mination, and self-control in pupils by allowing them opportunity for decision-making, planning, and active participation in those phases of the program which involve the making of choices. No modern program should consist merely of exercises directed by the adult and of unthinking muscular exercise as the sole outcome to the students.

3. *The program should cultivate leadership by allowing ample opportunity for pupils to choose, elect, lead, and follow in the limitless opportunities which play situations provide.* The physical education teacher should seek to give children rotating and full opportunities for all to share in leadership.

4. *The program should seek the development of personal resources —creative ability, ability in self-appraisal, resources in self-entertainment and self-sufficiency.* In a sense, physical education should whet the appetite of students for continuous lifelong participation in the games, sports, and dances chosen in accordance with differences in age, sex, and physical condition.

5. *The program should make a constructive contribution to the development of emotional control.* The physical education experience should be fun, and it should produce relaxation, friendship, and understanding.

6. *The program should provide for the pupils an important group experience.* The physical education teacher is, in a sense, a "group worker." The team, squad, club, or class becomes the social unit which, by using some physical education activity as a medium, may lead to those desirable outcomes in personal development which are peculiarly derivative of group experience. Group standards of behavior, ethical value, and morality can be taught through the multitude of interpersonal relationships which arise in physical education situations.

7. *The program should help pupils understand that competition may be used as a means of furthering the goals of a democratic culture.* Competition, when ruthless, may be antithetical to things we hold dear, but in the hands of wise teachers it may be controlled to be a healthy force in social growth.

8. *The program should help pupils believe in the essential worth of each human being.* This thought often has been cited as the very essence of the democratic culture. There are many opportunities in physical education to have children come to know, understand, appreciate, and enjoy one another. Furthermore, this thought suggests that, where there are wide differences in ability, the better performers should help and encourage those who are less skilled. There is danger of developing a hierarchy of superior performers, leaving the poor performer relegated to a hopelessly inferior position. This criterion

suggests that we consider the pupil with little ability as good as the star, not in performance, of course, but surely in deserving an equal opportunity to learn and an equal regard while he is learning.

9. *The program should allow for progression in learning, with a minimum of repetition in activities, and it should give students consecutive time to learn instead of jumping from one activity to another to maintain interest.* It should allow for cooperative student-teacher planning, utilize activities which are inherently interesting, and make provision for the teaching of those "learnings" normally associated with motor activities, such as appreciations, ethical and social controls, health factors, and the elements of consumer education related to sports and recreation.

10. *The program should seek to preserve and develop the health of its participants.* It should never condone the sacrifice of the best health interests of the child for the sake of some irrelevant value. The program should be dependent upon medical cooperation for original classification and thereafter should be fully attentive to the need for medical supervision, accident prevention, emergency care, disease control, and health-counseling.

Offerings in Physical Education. In the junior high school it is almost the universal practice to require physical education in all three grades, usually for two semesters. This is in harmony with the thinking of leaders in junior high school education. Most authorities on this subject also believe that pupils should have physical education daily. However, it is the usual practice to have physical education on alternate days. In the survey of 370 schools by the authors, the percentage of schools which offer physical education either as a required (R) or an elective (E) subject is as follows:

		Two Semesters		One Semester	
		Percentage of Schools	Average Periods Weekly	Percentage of Schools	Average Periods Weekly
Seventh grade:					
Physical education	(R)	93	3.1	6	3.9
Physical education	(E)	2	4.3		
Eighth grade:					
Physical education	(R)	93	3.1	5	4.2
Physical education	(E)	3	3.8		
Ninth grade:					
Physical education	(R)	88	3.2	6	4.0
Physical education	(E)	5	4.7	2	4.0

Special Problems in Junior High School. There are two problems associated with physical education in the junior high school which require particularly careful study. *The first of these, and the most controversial one, is the problem of interscholastic athletics.* Unless the organized competitive program of athletics is considered only as extracurricular amusement, it should be expected to contribute to the educational and developmental needs of junior high school boys and girls. With respect to the popular games of football and basketball—both of them played intensively and under pressure conditions—there is some serious question as to their advisability in the junior high school. Often they are organized to give boys experience prior to their effort to make the senior high school varsity team. They may well command the interest of such boys before they are psychologically and physically ready for them. At the junior high school level there should be a broad, varied program of activities for all pupils, with the highly organized interschool competitive contests postponed until the years of greater maturity.

A second problem receiving attention today in the physical education curriculum of the junior high school is that of integration. The field of physical education can be an important resource for core projects in those curriculums using some kind of integrated plan. Since it is usually thought of as a special subject virtually unrelated to any other area, physical education thus far has made little contribution to the enrichment of core programs. However, in developing an understanding of the culture of our people, physical education has much to offer in the planning of core programs and activities.

Similarly, within the physical education program itself the concept of integration may be applied. Instead of consisting only of a series of different sports activities, the work in physical education may center on a study of "Recreation in Our Town," or some other unified study, which may include not only the usual skills but also understandings of the place of such skills in everyday living. Integration within physical education itself is a hopeful area of investigation and experimentation.

A Typical Physical Education Program. There is, of course, wide variety among physical education programs in junior high schools. There is virtually no standard practice. From the many programs available, the following has been selected as representative of the best:

Boys' Physical Education [8]

Seventh Grade. Introduction of simple coordination exercises is made here with emphasis on response, rhythm, and balance, with attention given to group games of low organization, relays, and modified team-game skills. Good sports-

[8] By permission from the Cleveland, Ohio, Public Schools, *What We Teach*, 1950, pp. 102-3.

manship and desirable personality reactions are urged in all activities. Health education emphases are brought into actual practice by regular shower programs, care of the feet, prevention of infections, proper clothing, safety practices, and proper sleeping and eating habits.

Eighth Grade. The program in the eighth grade includes seasonal sports such as basketball, softball, volleyball, track, and noncontact football, with an opportunity to play the game in learning situations where the emphasis is on fundamental skills and rules of play. Elementary tumbling and apparatus are included as are conditioning exercises and command-response activities.

Ninth Grade. More advanced skills in games and sports are included here. Tumbling, stunts, and apparatus activities are progressively more challenging to the boys' ability. Motor-ability testing and self-testing activities are given, as well as a proportionate increase in the amount of body-building exercises. Social dancing and co-recreational games are favorably received. Progressive upgrading of all activities is maintained from the seventh through the ninth grade.

GIRLS' PHYSICAL EDUCATION

Seventh Grade.   Activities are geared to the needs, abilities, and age level of the groups. In general the program includes familiar group games such as dodgeball, club snatch, and bombardment; relays of various types; simple stunts, tumbling and pyramid building, athletic and recreational game skills; seasonal team games with modified rules, such as basketball, volleyball, soccer, and softball; rhythmic activities and simple dances; posture, body-building and conditioning exercises; and self-testing activities. Incidental health activities are provided through general class procedure, discussions, shower periods, and class projects. The entire program is supplemented by the use of visual aids in each specific teaching area, for example, sports, dance, or posture. After-school intramural games are offered.

Eighth Grade. The instruction is a continuation of the preceding grade, but all activities are on a progressively higher skill basis. More difficult team games are played, and much more difficult dances are introduced in the program. New recreational games, such as paddle-tennis, shuffleboard, and badminton, are introduced.

Ninth Grade. In the final year of junior high school, the girl begins to develop real competence in a wide variety of sports, recreational skills, and rhythmic activities. Team games including volleyball, softball, basketball, and speedball begin to show a greater degree of teamwork than in the two previous years. Official rules are introduced in several sports. New and more difficult types of dance are taught. Folk and square dances are executed with real skill. Classes in social dance with boys fill a need for the girl. At this age level co-recreational games are enjoyed.

Program of Health Education. A program of health education should have its origin in the lives of people. It should seek to discover and meet the needs of children in school and of the general population. It should be dedicated to the transmission of the knowledge and wisdom of science as it affects human life and to the prevention of the disasters of disease, accident, and handicaps as they may affect school children.

In junior high schools, the health program is developing with the following features:

THE HEALTH NEEDS OF THE SCHOOL AND COMMUNITY [9]
MAY BE MET BY:

A Program of Instruction and which is founded upon *An Appraisal of Information Needs* which are organized into a *Course of Study and Curriculum* requiring *Skilled Teachers* who constantly attempt an *Evaluation of Results* to determine whether *The Needs Are Met*	*A Program of Service* which is also founded upon *An Appraisal of Needs* leading to an appropriate program of *Medical, Dental, Psychiatric, and Educational Activity* requiring *Skilled Personnel* who constantly attempt an *Evaluation of Results* to determine whether *The Needs Are Met*

With such a program of instruction and service, the purposes of the health program should become clear. They are (1) to inform children concerning matters pertaining to health, (2) to assist in the total effort to aid children to remain or become fit to receive an education, (3) to give children experience with the best of scientific health services, and (4) to secure for them a school environment favorable in every respect to their healthy growth and development.

Principles Underlying the Health Program. In developing the health program for the junior high school, certain basic principles should be kept in mind. The most important of these include:

1. *The health education program requires the coordinated efforts and talents of parents, teachers, administrators, physicians, nurses, dentists, psychiatrists, nutritionists, sanitarians, and many others.* No one group can safely feel that the program is its monopoly. Administrative responsibility for the program should remain, of course, in the hands of school authorities, but the services and resources of many different people and groups should be employed.

2. *The health program should recognize the needs of children.* These needs are discovered from analyses of morbidity and mortality tables, home and environmental analyses, investigation of health interests through expressed curiosities, and observation of the reading and listening activities of pupils. Such interests and needs as may be discovered should serve as the bases for programs of health instruction and health services. Adult judgment of pupil needs is not wholly re-

[9] By permission from Delbert Oberteuffer, *School Health Education*, p. 31. Copyright, 1951, Harper & Bros., New York.

liable. The facts of child life should be studied, and programs should then be developed to meet the needs of the children concerned.

3. *The program of health education should be developed from a study of human problems.* The teaching of anatomy and physiology without reference to a living problem is not particularly effective.

4. *The program of health education should have personal action as its principal and ultimate objective.* One never affects the public health by any device whatsoever except as one touches the personal life of an individual. Health education should seek to affect favorably the way people live. Changes in behavior are more significant than the acquisition of knowledge or the development of attitudes. The latter may be important as they lead to personal action, but in any analysis it is the way the junior high school pupil lives that counts. All instruction, all services in the program, are effective only in the degree to which they bear upon the way in which people live.

5. *The program of health education should provide for the development through cooperative effort by teachers, parents, and the health staff of certain health activities and services.* These include appraisal or screening activities, such as physical examinations or tuberculin tests; controls for the prevention of disease; nutrition and growth activities, such as school lunch programs; dental programs; sight-saving and hearing activities; and psychological or psychiatric services. Cooperative development of these activities is important because the teacher has many functions in the health program of the junior high school. Screening for children who need the services of the specialist is one of the principal functions, while utilizing the findings or following through on a recommended health program is another. Without full teacher participation the program of health services is seriously handicapped. In organizing such programs of health education, the school is not engaged in the practice of medicine. What it does, it does for educational purposes, either to discover and remove those conditions which obstruct the education of the child or to educate the child into better and more effective living. It should be clear that a nonmedically trained person should never perform a diagnosis of any kind, nor should information about the health of a given child be passed on except to those who have need for that information and who will use it professionally in the child's welfare.

6. *The program of health education should provide for close cooperation with family physicians, both in the use of information about pupils and in developing health activities for them.* The final authority on all matters affecting the child's relation to the school program must, however, be centered in the school medical or administrative personnel. When differences of opinion occur, the school personnel

must accept and discharge its responsibilities in terms of what is best for the school as a whole, as well as for the individual child.

7. *In the program of health education the school should not finance extensive medical or dental activities.* Physicians and dentists should not be asked to donate their time, but should be paid for their services in the screening activities. Extensive dental, medical, or surgical treatment suggested as a result of the school's services should be provided by the family or the public assistance agencies, not from the school budget.

3. MATHEMATICS [10]

Functions of the Program. The mathematics program has the same major purposes in the junior high school as at any other level. These have been well defined by the Commission on Post-War Plans as follows:

1. To insure mathematical competence for the ordinary affairs of life, to the extent that this can be done for all citizens as a part of general education.
2. To provide sound mathematical training for future leaders in science, mathematics, and other learned fields.[11]

From elementary school through high school these constitute the guiding purposes for mathematics teaching on the basis of which results must be evaluated.

It is true, however, that in designing the mathematics program for any age level the characteristics of the pupils must be taken into account. These characteristics determine how the purposes of mathematics are to be achieved and may even indicate some concomitant purposes for the program. At no other level are the pupil characteristics more significant for the educational program than in the junior high school.

In the junior high school three functions are basic to the mathematics program. These are based on the characteristics of junior high school pupils.

1. *Attention to individual differences.* Although they increase as pupils proceed through the elementary grades, individual differences are at their peak in the junior high school. Two pupils, for example, with I.Q.'s of 92 and of 108, who differ in mental age by only one year at age six, differ in mental age by two years at age twelve when they

[10] This section was prepared by Lucien B. Kinney, Professor of Education, Stanford University.

[11] "The Second Report of the Commission on Post-War Plans," *The Mathematics Teacher*, XXXVIII (May, 1945), 195-221.

enter the junior high school. In the senior high school, the differentiated curriculums tend to reduce the range of differences in any one class. In the junior high school, the emphasis is on general education, rather than specialized preparation, and the classes are less homogeneous. Hence, wide differences in such characteristics as these occur in any class in the junior high school: abilities, interests and plans, home backgrounds, study habits, experiences, and sex.

In the mathematics class these differences mean that each child must be studied by the teacher and taught as an individual. In providing for these differences it is necessary to:

1. Make the work real, interesting, and important to pupils of a variety of backgrounds and different educational goals
2. Provide for slow-learning pupils by:
   a) Careful regulation of rate of progress
   b) Continued help with fundamentals and problem-solving
   c) Keeping problem situations concrete by leading from the familiar to the new
   d) Careful attention to vocabulary
   e) Providing variety in the fields of mathematics used—arithmetic, algebra, geometry
   f) Helping to develop efficient study habits
3. Provide for rapid-learning pupils by:
   a) Problem situations requiring greater insight, ingenuity, and ability to organize
   b) Progressing farther into mathematical abstractions

2. Orientation and guidance. Perhaps the function most typical of junior high school mathematics is that of orientation and guidance. It is also one of the most important, since, on leaving the junior high school, the pupil will need to choose one of the various curriculums of the senior high school. In most school systems a choice between algebra and general mathematics is expected on entering the ninth grade. If this is to be an intelligent choice, more needs to be known about the ability and plans of the individual pupil than is now the case in many schools.

Not only the pupil, but society as well, has an important stake in the intelligence of this choice. This is becoming clear as the shortage of trained leaders in our society becomes more acute each year. The shortage in two of these leadership groups—teachers and scientific leaders—has forced itself on the attention of everyone, but similar shortages exist in all leadership groups. These shortages emphasize the responsibility of the junior high school teacher to discover and develop the talents and aptitudes needed for leadership in our society.

In this country, of course, we are committed to the idea that each individual is free to choose his own career. He should be encouraged to do so in the light of adequate information about the nature, requirements, and rewards of the vocation, and of his own aptitudes, abilities, and interests. For the mathematics teacher in the junior high school, this means that he should help pupils explore the fields of mathematics and their vocational applications. Recent texts and syllabi show how this can be done so that the pupil can sample the fields of algebra, geometry, and trigonometry. As a result, the teacher and pupil both have some evidence to serve as the basis for the choice of mathematics that must be made at the beginning of either grade nine or ten.

3. *The transitional function.* Pupils in the junior high school are confronted with the task of developing the self-direction and competence for independent study that are required for success in high school and college. Through the elementary grades, pupils have had the continuous and day-long attention of one teacher who, in most instances, was responsible for not more than 30 to 40 other pupils. In the high school, pupils need to adjust to several teachers, each of whom may have contact weekly with 100 to 200 different pupils, or even more. In college, the relationship is still more impersonal, with the result that responsibility for success or failure rests largely with the student himself.

This is, of course, only part of the adolescent task of acquiring independent adult status. But it is an important part of the task, and one that particularly concerns the junior high school. It emphasizes the share each junior high school teacher has in helping pupils to develop academic self-direction through effective study habits, to develop the ability to budget time, and to define personal standards of workmanship. This responsibility of the junior high school has been termed the *transitional* or *articulation* function.

In mathematics the pupil needs to become self-reliant, to adopt a systematic approach in attacking problems, and to develop the ability to identify and diagnose his difficulties. With appropriate learning experiences under careful teacher guidance, these abilities can be developed. The mathematics teacher in the junior high school should help pupils engage in learning activities that emphasize these abilities.

Offerings in Mathematics. In the junior high school, either general mathematics or arithmetic is a required subject in grades seven and eight in practically all junior high schools. In the ninth grade, it is the most common practice to require a course in mathematics. In many schools the pupil may choose between algebra and general mathematics. In the survey of 370 schools by the author, the percentage of schools which offer mathematics either as a required (R) or an elective (E) subject is as follows:

		Two Semesters		One Semester	
		Percentage of Schools	Average Periods Weekly	Percentage of Schools	Average Periods Weekly
Seventh grade:					
Arithmetic or gen. math.	(R)	97	5.0	2	4.6
Arithmetic of gen. math.	(E)	1	5.0		
Remedial mathematics	(R)	1	5.0		
Eighth grade:					
Arithmetic or gen. math.	(R)	97	4.9	3	4.7
Arithmetic or gen. math.	(E)	1	5.0		
Remedial	(R)	1	5.0		
Ninth grade:					
Algebra	(R)	8	5.0	1	4.5
Algebra	(E)	49	5.0	1	4.9
Algebra or gen. math.	(R)	36	5.0	1	4.6
Gen. math.	(E)	48	5.0	3	5.0

General Curriculum Trends. An examination of textbooks and courses of study in seventh- and eighth-grade mathematics and ninth-grade general mathematics reveals the following trends:

1. *There is an increasing tendency to develop problem situations which are related to the present life experiences of the pupil.* This tendency has been encouraged (a) by the desire to capitalize on and redirect the present interests of the pupils, and (b) by emphasis on mathematics in real-life situations outside the school. The tendency to relate classwork to life experiences is readily seen in the topics in the newer textbooks. Thus, business ownership is introduced in some junior high school textbooks with a description of how a pupil may become the proprietor of a fruit and vegetable stand. The teacher and the textbook writer have the problem of finding life situations which are sufficiently real to boys and girls who live in all types of communities in various sections of the country. The teacher can do much to make the problem situation real and alive by seizing every opportunity that may arise in an incidental way, either in the classroom or in life outside the school, to bring to the attention of the pupils the social significance and utility of number and its application in life.

2. *Mathematics is being utilized as a means of developing an understanding of social institutions and processes.* There is a definite tendency to use the methods of quantitative thinking to increase the pupil's understanding of home, business, and community problems. Practically every course of study in junior high school mathematics today includes such business topics as banking and insurance, and

many include a study of government as an outgrowth of the topic of taxation or vice versa. Recent textbooks also include units on communication, transportation, travel, and the production of goods.

3. *There is a trend toward the utilization of mathematics as a means of educating for intelligent consumership.* The consumer topics most often included in mathematics courses are economy in purchasing, budgeting and accounts, and thrift and savings. In recent textbooks and courses of study it is the practice to combine narrow or specific topics on consumership into broad units or problems. Thus savings, investments, and life insurance are all seen as parts of a larger unit on providing for one's future. This functional grouping of materials and topics on consumership is a recognition of the proper role of mathematics in the life of the literate consumer.

4. *There is a tendency to utilize whatever fields and principles of mathematics are available for studying a particular topic and developing an adequate understanding of it.* In the literature on the teaching of mathematics it has been recognized for some time that the content of the course must be both socially significant and mathematically meaningful. Thus there is a tendency away from segregation of the fields of arithmetic, algebra, geometry, and numerical trigonometry, and a trend toward the organization of these materials in such a way that they will contribute to a satisfactory development of meanings in each subject field throughout the junior high school mathematics program. The usual criteria for selecting mathematical processes for this purpose are: (a) the readiness of the pupil to use them effectively, (b) the value of these processes for analyzing and contributing to the understanding of the social problems that are being studied, and (c) the necessity for developing a logical sequence in mathematical operation.

Curriculum Trends in the Ninth Grade. Whether the ninth grade is, in actual practice, a part of the junior high school or the beginning of the senior high school is an open question. If the former, then general mathematics rather than algebra should be taught in the ninth grade. Otherwise, mathematics for general education is terminated at the end of the eighth grade. These two alternatives are described in a recent joint report of committees for the Mathematics Association of America and the National Council of Teachers of Mathematics.

A recent survey reveals that, in approximately one-fifth of the schools reporting, the introduction of formal algebra is postponed to the tenth grade.[12] In schools where the introduction of algebra is

[12] Kenneth E. Brown, *Mathematics in Public High Schools,* United States Office of Education Bulletin No. 2 (Washington, D.C.: Government Printing Office, 1953), p. 10.

postponed, a practical mathematics course is frequently taught in the ninth grade which emphasizes direct applications to problems of the home, farm, shop, business, leisure time, safety, and health. In such a course there is usually an effort to develop interests, attitudes, and appreciations that arise from an understanding of the importance of mathematics in real life today.

If algebra is offered in the ninth grade for the college-preparatory group, the noncollege group is provided for according to one of three plans:

1. *The offering of no courses in mathematics for the noncollege group beyond the eighth grade.* Under this plan, it is assumed that the mathematics needs of noncollege pupils have been fully satisfied by the end of the eighth grade, a most doubtful assumption.

2. *The requiring of ninth-grade algebra for all pupils, a practice which is being continued in only a few schools.* Under this plan, the teacher may employ for all pupils (a) achievement standards ordinarily expected of the college-preparatory group, or (b) those achievement standards which are suited to the abilities and interests of the pupils as a whole, including both college and noncollege groups. Under the first plan, there would probably be a high failure rate among the noncollege pupils; while, under the second, the best interests of the college-preparatory group may be sacrificed. A third possibility is to vary the achievement standards for different groups of pupils. For this purpose, pupils would have to be grouped according to their intentions concerning college.

3. *The offering of algebra for the college-preparatory pupils and general mathematics for the noncollege group.* This plan is based on two assumptions: (a) that ninth-grade pupils are ready to make decisions concerning their education beyond high school, and (b) that those taking algebra need no further mathematics for general education. These assumptions are questionable. Furthermore, when the distinction between algebra and general mathematics is made in terms of college preparation, there is an undesirable tendency to consider general mathematics as a course for "dumbbells." This attitude on the part of teachers and pupils tends to limit the effectiveness of general mathematics. Frequently this attitude results in confining the course largely to a continuation of drill on fundamentals.

Problems in the Ninth-Grade Program. Efforts so far to solve the ninth-grade dilemma have created more problems than they have solved. Among the major problems are:

1. *The necessity for making a decision in the ninth grade between general mathematics and the college-preparatory sequence.* The col-

lege-preparatory sequence must be protected against an influx of students who, from lack of either interest or ability, may tend to lower standards to the point where success in the courses is no longer indicative of college ability. On the other hand, general mathematics should not be stigmatized as being less respectable or challenging than algebra.

2. *The problem of guidance.* In actual practice the pupil's selection of algebra or general mathematics is usually based on pupil and parental preference, along with intelligence and achievement, rather than on the need for college preparation. Such a basis for selection is indeed unsatisfactory. Guidance programs need to give more help to pupils in their choice of ninth-grade mathematics courses.

3. *Course construction.* The courses for leaders should be a challenge to pupils with demonstrated interests and abilities. Alternative courses should be provided for the general student, equal in prestige and quality to the more difficult mathematics courses. So long as teachers, pupils, and parents feel that general mathematics is inferior in status to the college-preparatory courses, the administration will be subject to pressures to dilute the quality of pupils in the college-preparatory program and be unable to hold the line on standards. At the same time, it will be difficult to attract able teachers to the general mathematics program.

4. *Curriculum design.* Flexibility is required in the two- or three-track pattern to enable pupils to move easily from one program to another. Even with the best data and counseling, mistakes occur. These should be easily remedied.

Trends in Instructional Procedures. Important trends in the instructional procedures employed in the teaching of mathematics are:

1. Increased use of diagnostic and remedial procedures for individual pupils who have specific difficulties in computation and problem-solving
2. More recognition of the importance of vocabulary difficulties and the need for special attention to vocabulary development
3. Increased use of out-of-class activities, such as field work with instruments, surveys related to purchasing, and the like
4. Increased use of reference materials, displays, geometric models, graphs, and bulletin boards
5. More recognition of individual differences in the capacity of pupils to appreciate and utilize abstract mathematical principles, as well as differences in the interests, attitudes, and personality qualities of pupils that may have a bearing on achievement in mathematics. Every teacher of mathematics recognizes the need for providing for those variations within each class which make every pupil virtually a special case.

4. ART [13]

Basic Principles. Art can and should provide an abundance of opportunity for establishing sound and accepted educational values. If art as a school subject sometimes fails to function as it should, this may be due to lack of understanding of the subject and of its vast potentialities for the general education of our youth. Art has many facets of expression other than drawing and painting, many of which are frequently overlooked. *When art becomes the full, rich area of instruction that it should be, when its educational scope is realized, it assumes a highly significant place in the total program of the junior high school.*

Educators seem agreed that, although our world is rapidly changing and the curriculum should be kept flexible to meet new conditions, there are basic concepts that are constant and should be retained. In brief, there are moral and cultural values, tested and proved, that are fundamental to our society. *Art is infinitely flexible. It is adaptable to changing conditions. At the same time, it embraces and accentuates the accepted and unchanging moral and cultural values.*

Every school system rests upon the premise that adults should guide and direct the experiences of youth so that those youth may become something better than they are or better than they would be if left to themselves. Schools exist to provide the knowledge, skills, attitudes, appreciations, and loyalties that will develop innate capacities for enriched living and for responsible citizenship. An understanding of art is a broad, inviting avenue to a fuller life for the individual. At the same time, art is so interwoven in the pattern of living that it deepens the concept of community responsibility.

The relationships, interests, and activities that are experienced in school affect each child individually and uniquely. The very essence of education in a democracy is to nurture the individual while concurrently developing respect for the rights of others and acceptance of the principles of community living. To insure personal growth, problem-solving and creative expression are essential to the curriculum. Art answers these educational needs because it is intensely personal and it is also inevitably social.

On the one hand, art is personal and practical; on the other, it is intellectual and cultural. *All art activities should stem from the child's natural interest in himself, his home, school, and community.* This approach vitalizes art. It is the spark that ignites creative urge and expression, while stimulating curiosity and expanding intellectual

[13] This section was prepared by Professor Elise Ruffini, Teachers College, Columbia University.

growth. It also insures some development of the ego so that each child remains "something special"—as he should.

At the junior high school level, interest in art is especially pronounced.

Girls and boys at this level are interested in facts. They place a new evaluation on art, because they have a new point of view. They want to be practical and are interested in art that has meaning in their lives. They are receptive to ideas that tie in with home furnishings and decoration, with dress and with social activities. Industrial arts, such as woodworking and metal work, fit their scheme. They willingly take part in group projects, if the projects are those of which they approve and in which they are interested. They will pursue art with avidity if they consider it an answer to their needs and interests. At this age, children like activity. They like *doing*. But they like to get things done, and activities must not be of too long duration.[14]

Offerings in Art. In a majority of the junior high schools, some work in arts and crafts is required in grades seven and eight. In the ninth grade it is usually offered as an elective. Few schools offer art more than two or three periods a week. This is unfortunate indeed. Much more can be accomplished in a creative subject like art and crafts if pupils devote some time to it each day. Furthermore, it is difficult for the teacher of art to work effectively with individual pupils if he sees them only two or three times a week. Some authorities believe it is better to have art and crafts offered four or five times a week for only one semester, instead of less frequently for two semesters. In the survey of 370 schools by the authors, the percentage of schools which offer art and crafts either as a required (R) or an elective (E) subject is as follows:

		Two Semesters		*One Semester*	
		Percentage of Schools	Average Periods Weekly	Percentage of Schools	Average Periods Weekly
Seventh grade:					
Art and crafts	(R)	50	2.2	24	4.4
Art and crafts	(E)	14	3.5	1	5.0
Eighth grade:					
Art and crafts	(R)	43	1.9	18	4.1
Art and crafts	(E)	28	3.6	2	4.8
Ninth grade:					
Art and crafts	(R)	16	1.7	3	1.5
Art and crafts	(E)	69	3.8	2	4.3

[14] Elise E. Ruffini and Harriet E. Knapp, *General Discussion in Teaching Reference and Course of Study for Book Seven of the New Art Education Series of Art Textbooks* (Sandusky, Ohio: The American Crayon Co., 1947).

Areas in the Art Curriculum. All areas in the art curriculum overlap in interest, content, and objectives. All have a common basis in stimulating self-expression and in the use of color and design. A consciousness of art elements and their arrangement is basic in resolving every art problem. It is in fact fundamental in all art education. The outline of areas which follows should be considered a flexible one. It is only suggestive, but it may serve as a point of departure that permits emphasis based on local conditions.

1. *Personal art area.* Dress and personal appearance, one of the personal art topics, provides a subject of interest and meaning in the art program. Problems in this area should always be treated objectively and tactfully. Discussion and analysis of basic art principles, together with their use in the actual solution of problems, should lead to an understanding and to improved use of line, color, texture, and related factors in problems of personal attire. Stress should always be on design rather than on cost, not only because embarrassing comparisons are to be avoided, but also because design is the basic factor.

Painting and drawing are other aspects of personal art which offer a challenge to most pupils of junior high school age. They should permit individual choices of subject, medium, and treatment. They should include some instruction and research, not only in techniques but also on historical and contemporary developments. In drawing, cartooning is sometimes a means of stimulating interest.

Crafts offer a boundless variety of expression and, in one form or another, are of unfailing interest to junior high school pupils. They are potentially rich in experience and expression and must not be allowed to deteriorate into the production of mere knickknacks. Design and arrangement of art elements must be the foundation of all crafts expression.

2. *Home art area.* Interior design is of immense interest to girls and boys alike, especially if they can gain some help with their own home problems. The teacher must use tact in order to avoid embarrassing economic comparisons. Interior design is an ideal vehicle for the use of line, form, color, texture, and other art elements. For enrichment, practical problems should be accompanied by research and discussion. Flower arrangement, table setting, picture framing and hanging, and the choice of furnishings and their arrangement are a few of the many possible activities. Pupils may paint pictures for their own rooms at home, or they may have other practical problems to work out.

Exterior design may lead to a consideration of the effects of different types of planting and of ways to enhance the outside appearance of the home. It may lead also to a study of home architecture. Supplementary reading and research should be encouraged to provide a background for this study. Academic problems may be worked out in the classroom, but actual problems are often solved at home. Exterior design may become a community problem and foster pride in the appearance of the neighborhood.

3. *School art area.* Most art education problems are solved, at least in part, in school. But here we are considering the use of design and various techniques for improving the visual aspects of the school itself. Art should be a factor in the life of the school. Many of the school art problems serve to make art come alive both for the individual and for the group.

School art may find expression for each student in many personal ways. It should apply, for instance, in such matters as keeping an orderly desk, making attractive notebooks, and being meticulous about the appearance of papers to be handed in. These are and should be emphasized as art practices.

As to group activities, there are many possibilities. These might include designing and painting group murals for halls, for the cafeteria, for classrooms, and for offices; designing sets and costumes for school plays; making posters for school functions; planting classroom window boxes; keeping a classroom beauty spot; working together to produce an art assembly program; arranging bulletin boards; and so on.

4. *Community art area.* Junior high school pupils should be aware of art and design as manifested in the visual aspects of their community. They should know how, when, and where art may function. They should realize the importance of civic planning, of street layout, of the location and arrangement of parks, playgrounds, and recreational centers, and of what is necessary to make the community more useful and beautiful. They should do research in books and magazines to gain a background of knowledge. Such knowledge is an integral part of civic and social consciousness.

There are a number of simple and obvious contributions that students might make to enhance the appearance of the community. They might, for instance, institute "clean up" week, clear out unsightly rubbish from vacant lots, and often do something about their own yards. They might cooperate with local merchants by lending a hand in window display. Merchants welcome this kind of interest under the guidance and direction of a competent teacher. Some schools put on an annual fashion show in which girls and boys model clothes from neighborhood shops. In some communities, the art department of the school is invited to place exhibits of school art in the public library. The library sometimes permits students to make special displays featuring certain books. There are many other possibilities for community art expression.

QUESTIONS AND EXERCISES

1. Industrial Arts

1. What are the desirable behavior changes that are likely to result from a well-chosen industrial arts experience?

2. What relationship exists between behavior changes and industrial arts course objectives?

3. What kinds of evidence show that a pupil has made a change in behavior?

4. How would you describe these behavior changes so that they might become a functional part of evaluation?

5. How are industrial marks affected when an evaluation of behavior changes is incorporated into marking?

6. Why are the broad objectives of industrial arts and those of the junior high school difficult to attain when industrial arts experiences are limited to woodwork and drawing, as so often happens?

7. What minor revisions or adjustments to an existing industrial arts department will enable an instructor to offer richer experiences with new materials and processes?

8. Why is industrial arts a part of the general education of junior high school boys and girls?

2. Physical and Health Education

1. Secure a copy of the course of study in health and physical education from your State Department of Public Instruction. Analyze it for a reflection of modern principles based upon the need of individuals.

2. In the foregoing material on physical education, principles were cited which are useful in curriculum-building. Which ones refer particularly to the society or culture in which we live? Which ones to the biological nature of man?

3. Of what importance is it that physical education programs spring from the life of the people?

4. How would you estimate the role of a good physical education program in junior high school with reference to its potentialities for the development of leadership?

5. What is the problem presented to children by the proposal to organize interscholastic football and basketball at the junior high school level?

6. What are the essentials of a health education program for junior high school?

7. Select any school in a community familiar to you. Study the personnel actually concerned with the health of school children and study their interrelationship.

8. In the same school, evaluate the health education program in terms of the principles mentioned in the text.

3. *Mathematics*

1. *a*) Select a topic in one of the fields of junior high school mathematics: algebra, geometry, or arithmetic. Show how you could design it so as to explore some important vocation.

b) Select another topic in the same field and plan a series of lessons designed to test the aptitudes and interests of pupils for further study in the field.

c) In each of the topics, show how you would provide for the differences you expect to find among your pupils.

2. Examine at least two modern series of mathematics textbooks for the junior high school, and compare them as to: (a) extent to which they provide for each of the major functions of the junior high school; (b) interests you think they would have for the pupils; (c) effectiveness of the program in the basic skills in arithmetic, algebra, and geometry; and (d) effectiveness in exploring the advanced fields of mathematics.

3. There is considerable interest at present in devising two-track or three-track plans to take care of groups of pupils with different needs in mathematics in the ninth grade. Try to locate such plans in practice and analyze their effectiveness.

4. Visit a high school and find out how the guidance of pupils into secondary mathematics courses is administered:

a) Who advises the pupils?

b) What information do the pupils and advisers have on pupil aptitudes, interests, and needs?

c) What determines which pupils take general mathematics?

d) Are pupils in the algebra classes selected with sufficient care so that adequate college-preparatory standards may be maintained?

e) What practical suggestions can you make for improving the procedures?

4. *Art*

1. What art courses should be required of all pupils? Which ones should be elective? At what grade levels?

2. Which is the better practice: (a) to teach art daily for one semester, or (b) to teach art every other day for two semesters?

3. What areas should be included in an arts and crafts program in the junior high school? What facilities and equipment are needed?

4. How can the art program be integrated with other subjects in the curriculum? Be specific in your suggestions.

5. How can the art program be correlated with various extraclass activities? Be specific in your suggestions.

Chapter 7

THE CURRICULUM FIELDS: HOME ECONOMICS, THE LANGUAGE ARTS, FOREIGN LANGUAGES, AND THE SOCIAL STUDIES

5. HOME ECONOMICS [1]

The recent development of home economics education in the secondary school has resulted from several important factors: (1) changes in economic and social conditions related to family life, (2) scientific discoveries and their practical application to home and family life, (3) federal legislation related to home economics education, and (4) developments in educational philosophy and psychology. Each of these factors has exerted an influence on the goals, the content, and the organization of the home economics curriculum.

Influences on the Content of the Home Economics Curriculum. One of the strongest influences on the content of the home economics curriculum in the junior high school is the great change that has taken place in our home and family life. The early American family was quite self-sufficient, not only in the production of household goods and services, but also in the education of children for home living. But this self-sufficiency has been greatly modified in the last fifty years. Industry has taken from the home much of the production of food and other necessities of life. It has made available many new kinds of food products, fabrics, and household equipment. As a result, a more complex pattern of living makes the problems of selection and consumption increasingly important.

In many instances, the family has been transplanted from a rural setting into an urban environment. The relationships among family members have also been modified. Young people today are associated much less with their parents than in former days. Increasing numbers of women are combining wage-earning and homemaking, thus placing

[1] This section was prepared by Ella J. Rose, Professor of Home Economics Education, University of Minnesota.

more responsibility for home activities on other members of the family. The problems of management and human relations are of great importance. These changes in the family situation have caused the school to provide more instruction in personal and family living.

Changes in economic and social conditions resulting from wars and depression have been reflected in the home economics curriculum. Attempts to help families to adjust to these changes have resulted in less emphasis on cooking and sewing skills and increasing emphasis on nutrition, conservation of food and household materials, clothing economics, housing, consumer efficiency, and time and money management.

The growth of science is another factor which has been influential in redirecting the organization and content of the home economics curriculum. Early in the present century, Ellen H. Richards, a sanitary chemist and a homemaker, saw the need and the possibilities for utilizing the resources of the rapidly developing sciences in solving problems of food, clothing, and shelter. She advocated that the school should teach children certain things about family living which they were no longer learning at home, e.g., habits of practical hygiene, cleanliness, and sanitation. She believed that the root of all social progress was education for the improvement of living conditions, costs, and efficiency.[2] Through the leadership of Mrs. Richards, early emphasis in home economics education was placed on the study of food composition in relation to physiological processes, food sanitation, and the cost of food, clothing, and shelter. For some time the application of science to home living was one of the major aims of home economics education.

New concepts of educational and social philosophy and psychology, stressing the importance of child growth, personality development, and human relationships in democratic living, have contributed toward the recent emphasis in the curriculum on child development and family relationships.

Trends in Goals and Content. In the early 1920's, the emphasis in home economics, as in other educational fields, was on preparation for adult activities. Later, there was a growing interest in the natural activities of boys and girls as a basis for instruction in home economics. Teachers were encouraged to survey the activities of their pupils as a basis for the curriculum content. However, foods and clothing still assumed a major role in the home economics curriculum.

[2] Ellen H. Richards, "Home Economics in Elementary and Secondary Education," *Journal of Proceedings and Addresses of the National Education Association* (Cleveland, 1908), pp. 486-91.

In the depression years after 1930, some new units were introduced to help pupils and their families meet the problems in homemaking caused by reduced incomes, unemployment, increased leisure time, and crowded housing conditions. These covered such topics as consumer buying, housing, and family and social relationships. Courses were extended to include units in clothing, foods, and nutrition; in personal, social, and family relationships; in care of the house, child development, health and home nursing, consumer buying, and home management.

Some of the early goals for the home economics curriculum were the development of skills, worthy home membership, preparation for adult homemaking, and education for present homemaking activities. More recently the emphasis is being placed on helping the individual grow into the kind of person and family member who can meet personal, family, and community problems with satisfaction to himself and to others. This emphasis requires a different curriculum organization.

Trends in Curriculum Organization. Besides reflecting the social and economic changes in the home and the community, trends in the organization and teaching procedures of the home economics curriculum reflect a new educational and social philosophy. That new philosophy includes: (1) a belief in the importance of the individual in relation to a democratic social living in the home, school, and community; (2) new understanding of the psychology of learning; (3) the concept of the dynamic individual—his physical, intellectual, and emotional interaction to his environment; and (4) recognition of the learning that takes place through real experiences in living. These points of view have had considerable effect on the organization, as well as the content and methods, of the home economics curriculum.

General trends in the organization of the home economics curriculum are especially prominent at the junior high school level. The more important of these include:

1. A trend from specialized courses covering limited subject areas, such as cooking and sewing, toward broader and more general areas with a series of units on various related topics dealing with personal and family living.
2. A trend from logically organized subject materials, toward materials developed around problems in everyday living at the child's level of maturity, such as Improving Ourselves, Adventures with Foods, or Enjoying Young Children.
3. A trend from separate courses covering single subject areas, toward core curriculums which include materials from several fields

and are based on the developing needs, interests, and abilities of youth in their personal, home, and community living.

4. A trend toward the integration of school experiences with those of the home and the community.

Trends in Curriculum Content and Teaching Methods. The trends just mentioned are those which concern the general organization of the home economics curriculum. Other trends are evident in methods of developing the curriculum, planning of instructional materials, and teaching procedures employed in home economics.

1. *There is a trend toward including in the home economics curriculum materials which contribute to the personal and social adjustment of boys and girls in the home and the community.* An example is the core program in home living which was developed for the seventh grade at Aberdeen, South Dakota, by teachers of science, art, music, health, industrial arts, and home economics. The major objective of the Aberdeen program is to help boys and girls solve the basic problems which they meet in everyday living. As a basis for the program, parents were consulted concerning the needs of their children in home living. Some of the units deal with interesting things about home life in Aberdeen, personal and social health, social relationships, better home and family membership, leisure-time activities, a safer home in which to live, and the home as a desirable part of Aberdeen.[3]

2. *There is a trend toward the increased use of home and community resources by the home economics teacher.* If the teacher of homemaking is acquainted with the home of each individual pupil, she can more readily help the pupil meet her needs as a member of her family group. Home and community experiences are especially important in the program of the ninth grade. Pupils are being encouraged increasingly to have the family help them select home activities which will contribute to their own learning and which may also prove of interest and satisfaction to the entire family. This practice provides opportunities for many interesting creative activities.

3. *There is a trend toward cooperative planning of the home economics curriculum with pupils, parents, and teachers of other school subjects.* Many home economics teachers in the junior high school are planning activities with pupils which will help them to be better groomed, to get along with their peers and their families, to share the family tasks, to maintain health through good nutrition, and better to manage their time and money. Some teachers are including parents

[3] *A Core Course in the Making: Cooperative Plans and Procedures* (Board of Education, Aberdeen, S. D., 1950).

and administrators in the curriculum planning. The program at Aberdeen, South Dakota, where parents were consulted regarding the needs of their children in home living, has already been mentioned. Cooperative planning in the core curriculum places emphasis on integration between the various subject areas in the school program. Teachers from several subject areas constitute a planning committee.

4. *There is a trend toward meeting pupil needs in solving complex problems of personal development and family living.* The report of the Joint Committee on Curriculum Aspects of Education for Home and Family Living [4] shows that opportunities are being provided increasingly for problem-solving activities, for pupil participation in planning and evaluating those activities, and for cooperation between the school, the home, and the community in studying problems related to home life. The committee believes, however, that there are still not enough such opportunities to provide a really adequate program for family living. The trend in the next few years appears likely to move toward increased cooperation among the agencies concerned in solving problems of family living.

5. *There is a trend toward evaluation of the home economics program in terms of individual and social behavior.* This evaluation is based on such factors as: (1) the ability of the pupil to solve his individual problems with respect to food, clothing, housing, and health; (2) the pupil's understanding and appreciation of his own behavior and that of his family; (3) his ability to employ that understanding in making satisfactory adjustments to home and family situations; (4) his interest in the activities of home life; (5) his growth in independence and ability to direct his own behavior in relation to the social group; (6) his ability to weigh values with respect to problems in home and family living; and (7) his ability to live cooperatively with others in the school, the home, and the community.

6. *There is an emerging trend toward the increasing use of home economics materials in a program of general education.* Home economics can contribute to the core curriculum for all boys and girls in two ways. In the University High School, Tallahassee, Florida, the home economics teacher taught the unit on Family Living and the core teacher served as a resource person. In Prince George's County, Maryland, the home economics teacher served as a resource person in a ninth-grade core on Achieving and Maintaining Good Family Relationships. If this trend continues, there should be increased integra-

---

[4] National Education Association, Home Economics Department, and the Society for Curriculum Study, Committee on Curriculum Aspects of Education for Home and Family Living, *Family Living and Our Schools* (Washington, D.C.: National Education Association, 1950).

tion of home economics materials with other subject areas; these materials should be organized around the home problems of the individual pupil; and there should be closer cooperation between the home and the school.

It is obvious from this brief summary of trends in the home economics curriculum that the organization, content, and teaching methods employed in that curriculum are passing through a period of considerable study and modification. In some instances the changes have already made great progress. In others, they have barely got under way. If this interest in the reorganization of the home economics program continues, the next few years should see much development toward a curriculum designed to meet the needs of boys and girls of junior high school age.

Offerings in Home Economics. In most schools home economics is a required subject for girls in grades seven and eight, and an elective subject in grade nine. General home economics courses are far more common today than separate courses in foods and clothing. Among the 370 schools included in the survey by the authors, the percentage which have required (R) and elective (E) courses in home economics is as follows:

		Two Semesters		*One Semester*	
		Percentage of Schools	Average Periods Weekly	Percentage of Schools	Average Periods Weekly
Seventh grade:					
General home economics	(R)	29	3.5	11	3.5
General home economics	(E)	3	4.5	1	2.0
Foods	(R)	15	3.5	11	3.9
Foods	(E)	1	5.0	1	4.5
Clothing	(R)	19	3.4	10	3.9
Clothing	(E)	1	5.0	1	4.5
Eighth grade:					
General home economics	(R)	34	3.8	13	4.7
General home economics	(E)	11	4.4	2	4.8
Foods	(R)	13	3.6	9	4.0
Foods	(E)	4	3.7	2	5.0
Clothing	(R)	12	3.1	9	3.8
Clothing	(E)	3	4.4	2	5.0
Ninth grade:					
General home economics	(R)	16	4.1	1	5.0
General home economics	(E)	41	4.8	4	4.3
Foods	(R)	4	3.7	4	3.7
Foods	(E)	16	4.4	8	4.5
Clothing	(R)	6	3.6	4	3.7
Clothing	(E)	17	4.4	9	4.6

TABLE 3

Suggested Units for Junior High School Homemaking

State	Grade Level	Personal, Social, and Family Relationships	Foods and Nutrition	Health and Accidents	Housing and Home Furnishing	Clothing and Textiles	Child Guidance	Vocations	Consumer Problems and Home Management
Minnesota	Early adolescence	Improving ourselves	Adventures with foods	Preventing accidents in the home	Making my room attractive	Tips on clothing	Enjoying young children	Working for others	
	Middle adolescence	Understanding ourselves	Three meals a day	Home care of the sick	Improving my home and its surroundings; worthwhile crafts	Perking up my wardrobe		Planning for a career	Managing my income
Washington	8	Being a likable person in your home (3-5 wks.)	Preparation of lunch (12-14 wks.)			Learning to sew (12-14 wks.)	Children are fun (3-4 wks.)		Relate consumer education to other areas of family living
	9	Feeling successful in high school years (2-3 wks.)	Helping with food preservation (12-14 wks.)		Girl's own room (3-4 wks.)	Grooming; textiles; care & repair of clothing; construction of garment (12 wks.)	Emphasis to some phase not included in the 8th grade		Relate consumer education to other areas of family living

TABLE 3—Continued

State	Grade	Family relationships	Foods	Home care / housing	Clothing / personal appearance	Child care	Money management
New Mexico	7	You and your friends (3-4 wks.); fun for family and guests (4 wks.)	Learning to cook (8-10 wks.)	Helping with the care of the house (2-3 wks.)	Learning to sew (8-10 wks.)	Helping to care for younger children (3 wks.)	
	8	You and your family (2-3 wks.)		When there is sickness in the home (3-4 wks.); Improving our homes (4 wks.)			Our families' money (3 wks.)
	9	Growing up happily (2-3 wks.)	Simple family meals (9-10 wks.)	The attractive bedroom (3 wks.)	A pleasing appearance (4 wks.); clothing for myself (8-10 wks.)	The child at play (4-5 wks.)	Managing personal resources (2-3 wks.)
New York	7-8	Living happily with family and friends	Selecting and preparing foods for health	As part of foods and clothing	Making myself more attractive through personal care & posture; helping with my clothes	Playing with and caring for small children	As part of housing; planning the spending of my money
	9	Getting along with family and others; understanding ourselves and others	Food for my family	Meeting home emergencies		Understanding needs of children and why they act as they do	As part of foods—developing standards and ability in meal management; buying and storing foods; as part of personal and family relationships—sharing in family money management

135

Sources: Minnesota—A Guide for Instruction in Home Economics, Curriculum Bulletin No. 12 (St. Paul, Minn.: State Department of Education, 1951); Washington—Homemaking Education, Guide for Planning (Olympia, Wash.: State Board for Vocational Education, 1953); New Mexico—Homemaking, Suggestive Guide for Planning Learning Experiences (Santa Fe, N. M.: Department of Public Instruction, 1951); New York—Planning Guide, Homemaking Education (Albany, N. Y.: The University of the State of New York, The State Education Department, Bureau of Home Economics Education, 1950).

Home Economics Programs. Several states have developed home economics curriculum guides which provide suggestions for planning, organizing, and evaluating the junior high school curriculum. In these guides materials are frequently suggested from the following areas: personal and family relationships, child guidance, housing, health, management and consumer buying, food and nutrition, clothing and textiles, and vocations. Resource units suggest goals or outcomes, activities (school, home, community), source materials, and evaluation devices which help teachers and pupils plan suitable learning activities. The units are concerned both with the individual's own activities and with his activities as a member of a family or social group. The titles of units from several of the recent state curriculum guides are summarized on pages 134-35.

6. The Language Arts [5]

The span of education now covered by the junior high school was originally so dominated by instruction in language that its very name was "grammar" school. The tradition of the "grammar" school still dominates the language arts programs of some junior high schools. In some schools there is still a group of separate subjects such as spelling, handwriting, grammar, composition, and reading taught by separate teachers in separate periods of the school day. In other schools the tradition lives in the single period devoted to English, where the instructional program consists of attacking the language skills separately in rotation.

In recent years many changes have been taking place in the formal language arts program. As a result of numerous investigations, we have been learning much about the junior high school child—his interests, habits, motivations, and goals. A number of these investigations have been concerned with the development of language, with reading interests, and with spelling and reading skills. As a result of such influences a different kind of language arts program is emerging.

Offerings in the Language Arts. Practically all junior high schools offer a required course in general English in grades seven, eight, and nine. In a few schools remedial reading and speech are required of all pupils who need it. In most schools, however, all the language arts are included in a course in general English. In the survey of 370 schools by the authors, the percentage of schools which offer various elective (E) and required (R) courses in English is as follows:

[5] This section was prepared by G. Robert Carlsen, Associate Professor of Education, University of Texas.

| | | Two Semesters | | One Semester | |
		Percentage of Schools	Average Periods Weekly	Percentage of Schools	Average Periods Weekly
Seventh grade:					
General English	(R)	94	5.1	2	4.7
Remedial reading	(R)	3	3.8	1	2.0
Speech	(R)			1	2.0
Spelling	(R)	1	5.0		
Eighth grade:					
General English	(R)	96	5.1	2	4.7
General English	(E)	1	5.0		
Reading	(R)	2	4.0	2	2.7
Speech	(R)	1	3.5		
Ninth grade:					
General English	(R)	97	5.0	1	4.5
General English	(E)	1	7.0		
Speech	(R)	2	5.0		
Speech	(E)			1	2.0
Journalism	(E)	1	5.0		
Creative works	(E)	1	5.0	1	2.0
Drama	(E)	1	3.5		
Reading	(R)	1	5.0		

Basis for a Language Arts Program in Junior High School. Increased understanding of early adolescents, a changing philosophy of education, and new points of view about the language arts suggest that certain points of view should influence the development of the language arts program for the junior high school. These points of view are summarized as follows.

1. *The early adolescent period is the one in which maximum interest in reading is reached.* By the junior high school years, the child has gained control over the reading process. Reading has become easy for him. Furthermore, he has time for reading because he has not yet been caught up in the multitude of activities of later adolescence and adult life. Thus, in early adolescence the average child spends more time in reading than at any other single period of his life.

This statement has been substantiated by the experience of junior high school teachers who have given their pupils the motivation and the opportunity to read widely. Many pupils read as much as a book a day if the right kind of material is readily available to them. For this reason, the junior high school years offer rich possibilities for giving children many kinds of human experiences through literature. Concentration on teaching the language skills to the neglect of literature, as is the practice in many schools, does not seem to be in harmony with interests of early adolescents. At this age an enjoyment of reading may be developed which will continue into adult life.

2. *The reading interests of junior high school pupils fall into relatively rigid patterns.* Generation after generation of early adolescents have recorded their strong preferences for the same kinds of reading experiences. These preferences differ according to sex, to be sure, but the patterns for the sexes also show some amazing similarities. Early adolescents like animal stories, adventure, mystery, sports, heroes, and slapstick comedy.

These interest patterns seem to indicate a basis for selection that teachers should use in their classes. The junior high school pupil must read his way through such periods if he is to arrive eventually at normal and desirable adult patterns of behavior. The job of the teacher is not just to introduce literature that boys and girls would not ordinarily read by themselves, but rather to share the child's enthusiasm for the materials he instinctively likes and to help him find better books within his interest patterns.

3. *The typical early adolescent is in the process of accepting a code of values that will stay with him for the rest of his life.* Through his random and multitudinous activities, he is finding out which sorts of things have appeal for him and which do not. Early adolescence is a period of wavering values, when stealing car horns and collecting money for a Boy Scout drive may have equal appeal. Slowly but surely, however, the adolescent begins to build a system of values in which such mutually exclusive activities seem incongruous to him.

The language arts teacher has an unusual opportunity to influence the development of values through the literature he presents. Young people in this period almost universally tend to model their activities in part after those of a hero. Thus, this is a period when much can be accomplished through the use of simple and appealing biography of individuals within the child's scope of interests. Biographies of athletic stars, of men and women of science, of social workers, of people who have struggled against seemingly insurmountable difficulties, may do much to give young readers a picture of values that they may take for their own.

4. *The early adolescent is attempting to classify his world in order that he may understand it.* He is in a period of exploration of what is around him. One day he may start an elaborate collection of match covers and try to find a basis on which to organize them. Such a collection may be abandoned in a moment as his interest veers swiftly to snakes or oriental magic. Such different interests suggest that a language arts program may serve a real purpose as a center of communication where children may constantly exchange ideas with each other.

Children should be encouraged to "talk out" their hobbies, to "write out" their enthusiasm.

In the other areas of the child's academic program the subject matter dictates rather specific limits to the topics that may be discussed. In the language arts, where teachers are constantly searching for ways of encouraging the use of language, there is an opportunity to allow children the freedom to examine diverse ideas and concepts that is not found elsewhere in the school program. The teacher therefore needs to encourage freedom of expression rather than to confine it by undue emphasis on rigid forms and adherence to stated language patterns.

5. *Language grows with and through experience.* Language is an integral and inseparable part of the total experiences of the individual. If he is to increase his language power, the individual must first broaden his range and variety of experiences. Language cannot be taught in a vacuum with the hope that what is taught will later be applied in daily life. Rather, the teacher has to set up a program in which the child sees, hears, feels, and deals with new ideas and materials at first hand. Out of a background of rich and interesting experience, language takes on added richness and depth. Many teachers of the language arts in the junior high school have filled their classrooms with an engine block, model airplanes and ships, collections of bee hives, a terrarium, and the like. Out of the richness of this material can come an excited interchange of ideas and the development of an expanded vocabulary and more ability in oral and written expression.

6. *Language patterns seem to follow rather specific developmental patterns.* Just as children learn to crawl before they learn to stand, and learn to stand before they learn to walk, so the development of abilities in language follows rather clearly defined stages that may not coincide with the internal logic of the subject matter itself. Roughly, the developmental pattern proceeds, over a period of years, from simple to more and more complex structures. Children at first have a view of the world where each item seems separate and equal in importance. As they mature, they see relations between the separate items of their environment. This change is reflected in language growth as they move from the use of simple words and statements to more complex language structure.

It is interesting that, in spite of the countless hours of effort spent in school on the more complicated aspects of the language, teachers have little effect on the language patterns that children use. Most investigators have come to feel that teachers are facing a developmental pattern that is not subject to change through education until the child has matured sufficiently to be ready himself for the next step. The junior high school pupil must use his own language patterns until his ideas have matured to the point where he needs new patterns for effective expression. Thus the teacher's responsibility is to provide the child with the opportunity for extensive practice in the various language activities and to help the child perfect the resources of the language that he is already using. The teacher must also watch for signs that indicate pupil readiness for the presentation of a more complicated language structure.

Basic Organization for Junior High School Program. The emphasis changes after the second or third grade from "learning to read" to "reading to learn." Similarly, emphasis must change from "learning to speak" to "speaking to say something." To practice writing activities, the child has to write about something. To practice speech skills, he has to speak about something. The debate in language arts curriculum-making today concerns the point at which we should make our frontal attack—*the writing, the speaking, the reading, and the listening as skills, or the topics and problems on which these skills are to be practiced.*

The weight of expert opinion seems to favor the latter. According to this point of view, the course of study should be organized in terms of the experiences that children should have and around which they should have the opportunity to practice the language skills. This point of view breaks sharply with the old grammar school concept of drill on specific parts of the language.

The first source of the content of ideas around which pupils should read, write, speak, and listen is the normal interest patterns of boys and girls at the age level concerned. As noted above, children of junior high school age are interested in their collections, in mystery, adventure, and heroes, both real and legendary. The interests of young people are not trivial fancies of the moment, but a part of their normal evolution toward maturity. To help the child explore his interests, to enjoy them, to read, write, and speak about them serves a real need.

Second, certain civic needs and problems of our society may serve as the basis for the reading, writing, speaking and listening activities of the pupils. The study of the patterns of home and family life, of various religions, and of problems of conservation have been used as central themes in language arts programs. The use of literature to make such problems a living reality to the child is immediately apparent. In such units, use is also made of outside speakers, simple community questionnaires, debates, panel discussions, oral and written reports, and creative writing. Thus they provide real situations for performing the language activities of daily life.

A third source of content for the reading, writing, speaking, and listening of children may lie within the language arts themselves. The study of the various media of mass communication may serve as a center of interest. Young people need to become aware of these media as social instruments. They should understand how radio, television, periodicals, and motion pictures may serve the ends of the small group of people who control them. They should know, too, the tremendous value of these media for keeping people in a democracy well informed and the importance of freedom of expression through them. Here, then, is a topic that pupils may study in the language arts program. Around this topic the teacher may develop a number of projects to give students practice in the various language skills.

A curriculum guide in the language arts for the junior high school should suggest a number of "content" or "experience" units around which the language skills may be practiced, units with such titles as "Our Animal Friends," "Chills and Thrills," "Periodicals," "Conservation of Resources," instead of "Nouns," "Writing a Composition," "Building Paragraphs," or "Discussion Techniques." Such a framework gives the pupils adequate opportunity to explore, through language activities, the exciting world in which they live. It gives them a chance to engage in a multitude of interesting activities, and it provides them with many significant language experiences.

Teaching the Language Skills. A given unit of instruction, such as "Animal Friends," may call for a number of language activities, such as interviewing people about their pets, writing an imaginary conversation between one's pet and oneself, reading a series of animal stories, inviting a sportsman to come to class to tell about some of the interesting things he has observed animals do, and telling about personal experiences with animals. The teacher should draw upon such activities to teach the various language skills, taking time to teach the specific skills as the unit develops. The unit itself will involve a set of words appropriate for spelling: *animal, friend, forest, prairie, leaves, silent, stealthy.* The written work should emphasize the use of not more than two or three points at a time, such as the use of proper end marks of punctuation, simple capitalization, and varied patterns of sentence construction.

Many teachers find it advisable to keep individual pupil "error cards." These are simple sheets of paper or cards on which the pupil or the teacher can tabulate language difficulties as they occur. At the end of a unit, the teacher may set aside a few days to study and drill on the common errors before introducing the next unit.

Such a program presupposes that study and drill on language usage will be determined by the needs of the class concerned. The course of study should not define the specific language content to be covered. Rather, it should permit the individual teacher to determine the content in terms of the readiness and needs of the class, which can be discovered by analyzing the language performance of the pupils.

The grammar that is studied may be determined by asking the pupils, "What is the simplest vocabulary necessary for teacher and pupil to talk intelligently about the language the pupil is trying to learn?" One good list of terms includes: sentence, subject, predicate, noun, pronoun, verb, complement, compound, phrase, clause, modifier, and connective. With such a simple list, the teacher is able to show students how to improve their language structure without the burden of elaborate grammatical terminology. Such a list of terms has to be taught directly, of course, but it can be taught quickly when compared with the time that is now spent in most schools in presenting grammatical nomenclature.

Individualizing Language Arts Instruction. The idea unit offers adequate opportunity for adjusting instruction to individual differences without the artificiality of ability grouping. Any unit contains a variety of reading materials on the topic of discussion. Materials may be selected to present a range of levels of reading difficulty. Some may be factual, some imaginative. Some may be primarily feminine in appeal, some masculine. The teacher, through discussion and stimulation, should try to help each pupil find something of interest and enjoyment in the unit. Thus materials are individualized without any particular consciousness on the part of the class of what is easy or difficult.

The language activities to help round out the "idea" are similarly varied. There is adequate opportunity for different groups of pupils to carry out different kinds of activities. Furthermore, the teacher, in keeping error cards for individual pupils, sets up a sliding scale. He calls attention to a few difficulties for each pupil, but these differ from pupil to pupil.

The language arts program should place the pupil in a number of situations which demand of him the use of the language skills of daily life. He should use the telephone, take part in discussions, ask and answer questions, make relatively informal oral presentations, read for enjoyment and information, write many kinds of letters, prepare simple reports of his activities, and occasionally write a story or sketch to express an inner feeling. He should have these experiences under the supervision of a competent teacher who can help him see and overcome his difficulties in different kinds of expression. The class period should be used essentially as a laboratory period during which work is planned through group action, ideas are germinated, and the actual work of figuring out answers goes forward.

7. FOREIGN LANGUAGES [6]

Enrollments in Foreign Languages. Most pupils in the public schools begin the study of a foreign language in the ninth grade.[7] More than half the students of foreign languages are enrolled in ninth-grade beginning classes. Approximately one-third drop out by the end of the first year and three-fourths or more by the end of the second year. In schools which have not made fundamental curriculum changes during the past quarter of a century, failures during the first year sometimes still exceed 20 per cent.[8] In 1949, the total foreign-language enrollment in the public junior high schools of the nation was 11.4 per cent of the total number of pupils enrolled in these schools.

Foreign Language Offerings. In the smaller junior high schools usually only one foreign language is offered, but in the larger schools two or three languages may be taught. The offerings commonly reported are, in order of popularity, Latin, Spanish, French, and German. In 1949, general language as a survey course enrolled over 13,000 pupils, most of them pupils of junior high school age.[9] Originally introduced as a try-out course in several languages to enable pupils to explore their interest in and aptitude for the different languages, the emphasis in general language has shifted to a survey of the languages and cultures of other lands.

In many junior high schools the study of languages in general language classes is now often limited to the amount needed to dramatize simple, practical dialogues, to sing representative songs, or to learn short, effective poems, proverbs, or quotations. Film strips, sound films, recordings, readings in English about foreign lands, visiting speakers, and excursions to places in the vicinity which are representative of the foreign culture are now common in many programs. Some

[6] This section was prepared by Walter V. Kaulfers, Professor of Education, University of Illinois.

[7] "Offerings and Enrolments in High-School Subjects, 1948-1949," *Biennial Survey of Education in the United States* (Washington, D.C.: Federal Security Agency, Office of Education, 1951), chap. v.

[8] Clarence Wachner, "Challenges to Change," *Modern Language Journal*, XXXVII (April, 1953), 167-73.

[9] Walter V. Kaulfers, "Mid-Century Enrolments in High-School Foreign Languages," *The School Review*, LVI (April, 1953), 232-36.

general language courses place major stress upon the nature and development of language, with special emphasis upon those languages which, like the Classical, Romance, and Germanic, have contributed significantly to English.[10]

The foreign languages are still primarily a ninth-grade offering. Only a few schools have foreign languages in grades seven and eight, and these are usually courses which have exploration as their chief objective. Latin continues to be offered more frequently than any other foreign language, and it is usually begun in the ninth grade. Among the 370 schools studied by the authors the percentage which offer various foreign language courses is as follows:

		Two Semesters		One Semester	
		Percentage of Schools	Average Periods Weekly	Percentage of Schools	Average Periods Weekly
Seventh grade:					
Undesignated	(R)	2	3.0		
Undesignated	(E)	1	2.0		
Spanish	(R)	1	5.0		
Spanish	(E)	2	5.0		
Eighth grade:					
Undesignated	(R)	3	4.4	3	4.4
Undesignated	(E)	12	3.7	2	5.0
Latin	(R)	1	5.0	1	4.0
Latin	(E)	1	4.0	1	4.0
Spanish	(E)	4	4.8		
French	(R)			1	4.0
French	(E)	1	5.0		
Ninth grade:					
Undesignated	(R)	4	4.3	1	5.0
Undesignated	(E)	30	4.8		
Latin	(R)	3	4.8		
Latin	(E)	34	5.0	1	5.0
Spanish	(R)	1	5.0		
Spanish	(E)	11	5.0		
French	(E)	7	5.0	1	5.0

In the checklist replies, quite a number of respondents indicated that a foreign language was offered, but they did not indicate the language. These replies are listed as "undesignated" in the table.

Aims and Objectives of Foreign Languages. The ultimate aims of foreign language programs most commonly listed in courses of study for junior high school youth include the following:

---

[10] A comprehensive discussion and outline of a general language course in terms of aims, content, and activities is given in Walter V. Kaulfers, *Modern Languages for Modern Schools* (New York: McGraw-Hill Book Co., Inc., 1942), pp. 275-335.

1. To develop ability to read, write, and speak a foreign language through content and activities that supplement or enrich the program of general education
2. To promote accuracy and facility in the use of English through such comparisons and contrasts as the study of another language conveniently affords
3. To develop an understanding of foreign peoples in terms of their influence upon our way of life and of ours upon theirs
4. To encourage the development of a lifelong interest in those contributions to literature, music, and art which foreign cultures have made or are continuing to make to Western Civilization
5. To afford young people the opportunity to increase their vocational usefulness in areas where knowledge of a foreign language is always a convenience and sometimes a necessity

Change in Status of Foreign Languages. The most significant trend in the foreign languages in the junior high school has been the marked decline in percentage of all the pupils in school who are enrolled for a foreign language. In 1933, the foreign languages enrolled 36 per cent of the pupils attending public secondary schools, but by 1949 the percentage of the total enrollment in the languages had declined to 22.[11] Because of the increase in the total number of pupils now attending secondary schools, this loss is not so obvious as it would be if the school population were static. If the same percentage of all the pupils were enrolled in the foreign languages today as in 1933, however, the number of individuals enrolled would be almost twice as great.

An analysis of the change in enrollments in the various languages might be of interest. For instance, the percentage of all high school pupils enrolled in French and Latin was, in 1949, less than half of the percentage in 1933. German had been the heaviest loser. Spanish had shown a net gain of 2 per cent. However, it had by no means absorbed the losses in French, German, and Latin. If all pupils who formerly enrolled in these languages had transferred to Spanish, the percentage gain in Spanish would have been eight times as great as it actually was.

Since 1950, a concentrated effort to reverse the trend has been initiated by the various language associations. As a result, foreign language instruction has been introduced on a voluntary basis into the elementary schools of many communities. In some elementary schools and junior high schools foreign languages are given as electives in the seventh and eighth grades.

[11] Mabel C. Rice, *National Summary of Offerings and Enrollments in High-School Subjects, 1948-1949*, United States Office of Education, Statistical Circular No. 294 (Washington, D.C.: May, 1951).

An equally significant trend in the high schools in the past two decades has been the change in status of the foreign languages from required to elective subjects. During this period, college entrance requirements have been modified so drastically that hardly a third of the institutions which formerly demanded at least two years of foreign languages for admission do so today.[12] Even medical schools, which formerly gave strong support to French, German, and Latin, have noticeably relaxed their entrance requirements in this respect. Of 79 leading medical schools in the United States, only 11 per cent now specifically require for admission either French or German, none require Latin, and 44 per cent require no foreign language at all. The recent abolition of the foreign language requirement for graduation from many colleges and universities does not give promise of a reversal of the trend away from foreign language entrance requirements.

At present the large majority of foreign language courses depend for their strength upon popular demand from below rather than, as formerly, upon coercion from above. The uncompromising conservative attitude of many influential members of past generations of foreign language teachers regarding desirable or needed changes in objectives, textbooks, contents, or methods is no longer tenable today. Although many teacher-education institutions have successfully adapted themselves to the changed status of the foreign languages in the American schools, many obstacles still remain to be overcome before a security in this new status is generally achieved.

Other Trends in the Foreign Languages. There are a number of other significant trends in the foreign languages in the secondary schools, among them the following:

1. Increased interest in the development of the ability to understand and speak a second language as a first objective. Even teachers of Latin have revived the oral approach in elementary classes as a means of giving interest and zest to the work.
2. Increased use of sound films, recordings, film strips, and tape recorders as integral, rather than as supplementary, learning aids.
3. Increased use of community resources, including representatives of the foreign culture in the community as guest speakers or as informants to answer questions concerning the culture of the people whose language is being studied.
4. Increased use of textbooks which explain the mechanics of the foreign language in more intelligible terms than the terminology of formal grammar.

[12] Thornton C. Blayne and Walter V. Kaulfers, "College Entrance Requirements and the High Schools," *Modern Language Journal*, XXXVII (April, 1953), 195-97.

5. Increased use of varied types of interest-stimulating devices for providing effective practice in a foreign language in pleasurable but educative ways. Some of these are modern classroom adaptations of old-time parlor games.

6. Increased interest in starting foreign language study in the seventh grade of the junior high school, especially for pupils for whom other work of the school presents little challenge.

7. Increased use of devices for evaluating growth in social-cultural insights and in the ability to understand and speak a language. Reliable objective tests for measuring the ability to understand a foreign language, as well as rating scales for ability to speak it, are now available. Techniques for evaluating gains in insights and attitudes and the information supporting them are also becoming more widely used by foreign language teachers.

8. THE SOCIAL STUDIES [13]

Offerings in the Social Studies. In the great majority of junior high schools some work in social studies is required in grades seven and eight. Most schools also require social studies in the ninth grade, but this requirement is not as general as in grades seven and eight. Among the 370 junior high schools included in the survey by the authors, the percentage which offer various required (R) and elective (E) courses is as follows:

		Two Semesters		*One Semester*	
		Percentage of Schools	Average Periods Weekly	Percentage of Schools	Average Periods Weekly
Seventh grade:					
Geography	(R)	69	4.9	5	4.7
U. S. history	(R)	21	4.8	3	4.8
State history	(R)	1	4.0	7	4.9
State geography	(R)			1	5.0
Gen. soc. studies	(R)	1	6.0	9	4.8
World history	(R)			4	4.8
Ancient history	(R)	1	3.0	2	5.0
Eighth grade:					
U. S. history	(R)	77	4.9	3	4.8
U. S. history	(E)	1	4.0		
Civics	(R)	6	4.7	4	5.0
State history	(R)	3	5.0	1	5.0
Geography	(R)	9	4.8	1	5.0
Gen soc. studies	(R)	7	4.7		
Vocational guidance	(R)	1	5.0		

[13] This section was prepared by Edwin R. Carr, Professor of Education and Economics, University of Colorado.

		Two Semesters		One Semester	
		Percentage of Schools	Average Periods Weekly	Percentage of Schools	Average Periods Weekly
Ninth grade:					
Gen. soc. studies	(R)	45	4.9	4	4.7
Gen. soc. studies	(E)	8	5.0	1	5.0
World history	(R)	9	5.0	1	5.0
World history	(E)	6	5.0	1	5.0
Civics	(R)	19	4.8	2	4.5
Civics	(E)	2	5.0	1	4.5
State history	(R)	3	4.5	2	4.7
Ancient history	(E)	2	4.8	1	5.0

Trends in Content. Many new topics, units, and subjects have been absorbed into the social studies curriculum, while many others are seeking admission. The more recent and significant trends in content are discussed on the following pages.

1. *Guidance.* Although guidance is often regarded as being separate from all subjects, social studies teachers have particular responsibilities in this area. For instance, units on orientation, which are taught in most junior high schools, are usually included in the social studies program; vocational and educational guidance activities are often provided; consideration is given to person-group relations; and activities are provided to help pupils understand themselves better. While the social studies program must inevitably emphasize the *social* group, it cannot ignore the *individual* who seeks to identify himself with the group.

2. *International understanding.* In an attempt to help our citizens toward increased literacy in world affairs, the study of other countries and peoples has been increased at all grade levels. In the junior high school this has included a study of the structure and functions of the United Nations and its related organizations. There has been promotion of understanding in the social studies between American children and children in other lands through correspondence with pen pals, exchange of photographs and scrapbooks, and providing foreign children with some materials from our schools. The study of geography of other nations, usually taught in the seventh grade, is becoming a course in global geography. In some schools a ninth grade course in world or global geography has been introduced. The modifications in the social studies program are being effected to produce real understanding of our relations with other nations and our responsibilities in world affairs.

3. *Human relationships.* Our growing social sensitivity has led to the introduction of activities in the social studies program which

should develop better human relationships. Pupils are being taught respect for the individual, consideration for others, consideration for other points of view, races, and nationalities, and skill in working with others.

4. *Consumer education.* The times have made consumer education more important than ever. Constant bombardment by advertisers, the vulnerability of Americans who have more money to spend than ever before, and the pressures that encourage sellers to extend installment purchases all point to the need for better understanding by consumers about how to handle their money. Consumer education cannot be postponed to the senior high school on the supposition that it is more appropriate there, since junior high school pupils today have much money to spend. Furthermore, they need to understand the financial problems faced by their families. More consumer education is being included in the social studies, sometimes as separate courses, but more often as units or topics in other courses.

5. *Critical thinking and propaganda analysis.* Definite education is necessary to help pupils learn how to enjoy, appreciate, and interpret radio programs, public speeches, television programs, and articles in newspapers and magazines. In some schools attention is directed toward this problem by adding units on critical thinking. In many others, teachers seize on the opportunity to teach critical thinking whenever it presents itself.

6. *Democracy and democratic behavior.* The events of recent years have alerted social studies teachers to the fact that Americans need a deeper understanding of our way of life, our form of government, and our democratic ideals. In junior high schools, there are units on democracy and its competitors, or simply on democracy alone, to give pupils a deeper understanding of what democracy means. Included are such topics as how democracy differs from other forms of government, the tremendous sacrifices which individuals have made through the centuries to bring democracy into being, what it has accomplished, and what remains to be done. Democracy is studied as a living, vital, growing concept, not simply as an accomplished fact. Gaining increased attention, too, is the study of civil rights and civic responsibilities. Teachers try to help pupils recognize and practice democratic behavior. Democracy is usually taught through present courses, rather than new ones.

7. *School and community.* Teachers of social studies, particularly those who teach civics and citizenship courses, are extending learning situations into the community. Local history, excursions, interviews with local residents, surveys, trips to industrial plants and governmental agencies, community improvement programs, and a host of other

sources and activities are being used to accomplish this end. Using community resources enables pupils to see social, economic, and political processes in action and helps them identify themselves with community matters.

Trends in Methods, Techniques, and Evaluation. Progress in instructional techniques and methods in the social studies has kept pace with changes in the content and organization of the curriculum. New instructional materials, new methods of planning for and directing pupil learning, and more effective techniques of evaluation have been introduced, the more important including the following:

1. *The social studies teacher is striving for ways to enrich the curriculum and to make it more meaningful.* Teachers are recognizing the difficulty of many of the concepts in the social studies and the need for a rich background of experience before the concepts become meaningful. Teachers provide this background for pupils by using a variety of direct and vicarious experiences. Direct experiences are provided through field trips, interviews, action programs, and similar activities. Vicarious experience comes through reading biography, imaginative literature, books of travel, pamphlets, and the like; through films, filmstrips, radio programs and recordings; and by engaging in socio-drama. An abundance of good materials for such activities is becoming available, much of it at low cost. Through appropriate techniques and materials, the teacher can help pupils gain real understandings rather than mere verbalizations, which have been characteristic so often of social studies in the past.

2. *The social studies curriculum tends increasingly to be taught in large units, problems, or themes.* Though the textbook teacher is by no means extinct, he is rapidly losing ground to his more imaginative and resourceful fellows. Teachers have come to see that a textbook assignment followed by a recitation does little to help pupils relate the material studied to the large movements, ideas, concepts, broad understandings, attitudes, and appreciations which constitute the major objectives of social studies instruction. This trend has been facilitated by better textbooks and resource units.

3. *There is an increasing use of pupil-teacher planning.* Pupils are more enthusiastic about carrying on activities when they have had some share in planning and directing them. Cooperative pupil-teacher planning provides better motivation, helps pupils to a better understanding of goals, aids teachers in identifying pupil interests and needs, helps to locate sources of information which the teacher has overlooked, and brings about a higher level of pupil achievement. Pupil-teacher planning works best when problems or units grow out of pupil

interests or needs. However, pupil-teacher planning can be used regardless of the type of unit or curriculum organization employed.

4. *There is an increasing use of group techniques in social studies classes.* Because one of the skills of citizenship is the ability to participate effectively in group activities, the social studies teacher frequently arranges small or large group work as the occasion dictates. In addition, he uses the small group technique to stimulate discussion in the larger group, as well as to build self-confidence in pupils. The teacher recognizes that pupils are not born with the ability to engage in group activities, but that they must be taught these skills.

5. *Social studies teachers are increasingly conscious of the need for good classroom conditions.* This means that the atmosphere of the classroom must be conducive to learning, that the room must be orderly yet not repressive, that good feeling must prevail, that pupils must feel free to express their views, and that the physical facilities in the classroom must be chosen and arranged to facilitate a variety of activities. The teacher respects the individuality of his pupils, makes them feel at ease, endeavors to make sure that the class functions democratically, and encourages pupils to participate. The pupils should help keep the room attractive, they should work at tables or desks which can be easily moved, and they should have adequate materials, supplies, and books.

6. *Social studies teachers are increasingly concerned with evaluation.* They make use of a greater number and variety of evaluative techniques. Evaluating instruments are better constructed, with more attention being given to item construction, as well as to reliability and validity. Emphasis on social studies skills is greater than before in evaluation activities, the skills including critical thinking, the ability to discuss, the ability to participate in group undertakings, the ability to locate and evaluate information, and the ability to make maps, graphs, and similar materials. Attempts to evaluate growth in attitudes, interests, and desirable behavior are more numerous and more productive. Pupils are being helped with self-evaluation of their progress through the use of checklists, inventories, and more informal devices. Finally, evaluation tends to be continuous, rather than occasional or periodic.

Content of American History Courses. Because American history is taught in the middle elementary grades, the junior high school, and the senior high school, it is important to know what should be emphasized at each level. Without such agreement there may be needless duplication or serious omissions of subject content and skills. This problem seemed so important a few years ago that a Committee on American History in Schools and Colleges was appointed to make recommendations on the teaching of American history and to propose how it should be differentiated at the various grade levels in (1) content, (2) chronology, and (3) subject skills.[14] Although the entire report should be studied to obtain a comprehensive understanding of the recommendations, the following summary gives some indication of the points of emphasis that are proposed for American history in the junior high school grades.

Proposed Major Themes:

Middle grades—How the people lived
Junior high school—The building of the Nation
Senior high school—A democratic Nation in a world setting

Proposed Chronological Emphasis:

Middle grades 1492-1789
Junior high school 1776-1876
Senior high school 1865-present

Topics for the Junior High School:

1. The American Revolution: As the outgrowth of colonial development with attention to outstanding military events, the government during the war, the Articles of Confederation, and the Constitution.

2. The Rise of Industrial Northeast, Plantation South, and Free-Farm West: With attention to the geographic and economic factors which promoted sectionalism; sectionalism *versus* national interests.

3. Territorial Development, the Struggle Over New States, and the Civil War: With attention to the use and influence of public lands, and the strengthening of national unity.

4. The Development of Waterways, Highways, Railways, and Airways, and of Domestic and International Trade: With attention to pertinent inventions, trade routes, and the social effects of cargoes carried.

5. Recreation, Sport, and Social Life: The rise of typical American games, and of resorts and vacation trips, of social clubs and organizations, of theaters, music, movies, and other commercialized amusements.

[14] Edgar B. Wesley (director), *American History in Schools and Colleges,* Report of the Committee on American History in Schools and Colleges of the American Historical Association, the Mississippi Valley Historical Association, and the National Council for the Social Studies (New York: The Macmillan Co., 1944). The statement presented here was summarized largely from chap. vi.

6. The Rise and Influence of Major Communication Industries: Postal service, press, telegraph, telephone, and radio; with attention to pertinent inventions, the industrial organization of these agencies, and their cultural power.

Representative Dates for Emphasis in the Junior High School:

Beginning of the Revolutionary War, 1775
Declaration of Independence, 1776
Surrender of Cornwallis, 1781
The Drafting of the Constitution, 1787
Inauguration of Washington, 1789
Invention of Cotton Gin, 1793
Fulton's Steamboat, 1807
War with England, 1812
Missouri Compromise, 1820
Invention of Telegraph, 1844
Civil War, 1861-1865
Transcontinental Railroad, 1869

Representative Persons for Emphasis in the Junior High School:

Samuel Adams
John Jacob Astor
Clara Barton
Alexander Graham Bell
Jefferson Davis
Thomas A. Edison
Cyrus W. Field
Henry Ford
Robert Fulton
Charles Goodyear
Ulysses S. Grant
Nathan Hale
Alexander Hamilton
Patrick Henry
James J. Hill

Elias Howe
Andrew Jackson
Thomas Jefferson
John Paul Jones
Robert E. Lee
Abraham Lincoln
Henry W. Longfellow
Cyrus McCormick
Samuel F. B. Morse
Thomas Paine
Samuel Slater
George Washington
Eli Whitney
Orville Wright
Wilbur Wright

Study Skills for Emphasis in the Junior High School:

1. Ability to interpret pictures, charts, diagrams, and cartoons.
2. Study of more maps and of more complex maps (than in the elementary school).
3. Ability to make simple outlines.
4. Locating library materials and using supplementary volumes efficiently.
5. Training in making and criticizing generalizations.
6. Ability to summarize.
7. Expansion of the vocabulary of American history.

Examples of Social Studies Programs. The following outlines of social studies programs are summarized from curriculum guides developed in a number of school systems. They are typical of some of the new social studies programs that are being developed.

DENVER, COLORADO [15]

Grade Seven—Patterns of Culture

Unit I. How Did Early Man Develop? (2-3 weeks)
Creation and development of the earth
Prehistoric man and his achievements
Modern man and his environment
Role of the scientist

Unit II. What Were Some of the Contributions of Past Civilizations? (9-10 weeks)
Growth of early civilizations
Early inventions and use of scientific principles
Contributions in government, law, science, literature, art, and other fields
Influence of religion

Unit III. What Contributions Were Made by People Who Lived in Europe During the Middle Ages? (4-5 weeks)
Effect of the Crusades
Growth of the Church
Development of organized government
Growth of towns

Unit IV. How Do People of the Eastern Hemisphere Live Today?
Africa —3-4 weeks
Europe—6-8 weeks
Asia   —6-8 weeks

Grade Eight—Our Heritage: How We Built Our Life Together

Unit I. How Did Europeans Discover and Explore a New World? (2 weeks)

Unit II. Why Did People from Different Lands Come to America? (2-3 weeks)

Unit III. How Did the Colonies Achieve Independence from Britain? (3 weeks)

[15] *The Social Studies Program of the Denver Public Schools,* Board of Education, Denver, Colorado, 1954.

*Unit IV.   How Did the New Nation Form a Union? (4 weeks)

*Unit V.   How Did Democracy and Patriotism Develop During the 1800's? (3-4 weeks)

*Unit VI.   How Did the United States Acquire and Settle the West? (3-4 weeks)

*Unit VII. How Did Internal Conflict Help to Confirm the Union?

*Unit VIII. How Did Industrial Expansion Effect Changes in Living in the United States? (4-5 weeks)

Unit IX.   What Is the Role of the United States in Today's Interdependent World? (6 weeks)

Grade Nine—Human Relations: How People Live Together

Unit I.   Denver, a Metropolitan Area (6 weeks)
Denver's Charter
Governmental agencies and their functions
Plans for the future
Denver's problems

Unit II.   Colorado, the Land and the People (8 weeks)
Geographic features and their effect on the growth of the state
Contributions made by various ethnic groups
Development of state government

Unit III. How the Nation Is Governed (9 weeks)
Constitution of the United States
Functions of executive, judicial, and legislative branches
Responsibilities, rights, and privileges of citizenship

Unit IV.   How We Work with Other Nations (4 weeks)
Beginnings of regional and world organizations
Pan American Union
United Nations

EUGENE, OREGON [16]

Grade Seven: How the People of the Pacific Northwest Contribute to the World Today

Recommended Units:
Orientation (guidance unit)
History of the Oregon Country

* Required units.

[16] *The Social Living Program,* Board of Education, Eugene, Oregon, 1953.

Lumbering
Power, mining, and manufacturing
Agriculture
Fishing
Preservation of natural beauty

Grade Eight: How the American People Have Developed Their Culture

Recommended Units:
Orientation (guidance unit)
Our heritage of freedom
Development of the West
The United States becomes a world power

Grade Nine: How Americans Strive Toward Intelligent, Productive Citizenship

Recommended Units:
Orientation (guidance unit)
Local, state, and national governments
Vocations
Minority groups in the United States

WASHINGTON, D.C. [17]

Grade 7A—World Background (for American History)
(one semester, required)

First Half—Early World Background (to 17th Century)

I. The Beginnings of Civilization

II. The Greeks

III. The Romans

IV. Leading Events of the Middle Ages

V. Life in the Middle Ages

VI. The Transition to Modern Times

Second Half—Modern World Background
(optional treatment by biography or by country)

Treatment by Biography

VII. Despots and the Struggle for Liberty on the Continent of Europe

VIII. Britain through the Victorian Age

IX. Europe's Progress toward Better Living

[17] *Curriculum Guide in Social Studies for Junior and Senior High Schools*, Board of Education, Washington, D.C., 1951.

X. Empires and Freedom Outside Europe

XI. Changing Nations and World-Wide Conflicts in the 20th Century

Treatment by Country

VII. France and Her Struggles for Democracy

VIII. Britain as a Leader in Modern Government and Trade

IX. Germany's Rise as a Great Military Power

X. Italy's Struggle for Unity and Place in the Modern World

XI. Russia from the Tsars to the Soviets

XII. The Far East and Its Western Contacts

XIII. America and the World Today

Grade 7B—American History (*chiefly to about 1850*), *Local History and Civics* (one semester, required)

I. The Transplanting of European Civilization to the New World

II. Beginnings of a Free Nation in the New World

III. Expansion and Internal Development

IV. The Nation's Capital

Grade 8A—Geography of the United States (one semester, required)

I. The United States in its World Setting

II. Agriculture

III. Hunting, Fishing, and Forestry

IV. Minerals and Power

V. Manufacturing

VI. Bringing Producers and Users Together

Grade 8B—American History and Government (one semester, required)

I. American Government

II. Division and Reunion

III. Domestic Progress and Problems

IV. The United States as a World Power

Grade 9. Optional courses in ancient and medieval history (two semesters, elective), *world geography* (one semester, elective), *and civics* (one semester, elective)

Long Beach, California [18]

Theme: Man's Adjustment to the Social and Physical Environment

The Immediate Environment Seventh Year	The National Environment Eighth Year	The World Environment Ninth Year
1. Our School: How the school environment provides for the needs of pupils.	1. Orientation: Personal problems of growing up (taught as needed throughout the year).	1. Orientation: How to understand ourselves and others.
2. Our Families: How families provide for the physical and social needs of their members.	2. How America was discovered and colonized.	2. Maps and Globes: How to understand the world in which we live.
3. Our Town: How the community (particularly Long Beach) developed to meet the needs of its citizens.	3. How the United States won freedom and became a nation (stressing origin and structure of the national government).	3. Possessions and World Power: How the United States has grown into a world power.
4. Our State: How the resources of California are used in meeting human needs.	4. How the United States expanded to the West and developed the American way of life.	4. Our American Neighbors: How countries of the western hemisphere have become interdependent.
5. Our Country: How the resources of the Southwest and other regions of the United States are used in meeting needs.	5. How sectionalism almost divided the nation.	5. Resources of the World: How global interdependence has developed.
6. Our World: How a recognition of cultural similarities among peoples leads to international understanding and cooperation.	6. How the Industrial Revolution and the Machine Age changed living conditions.	6. Peoples of the World: How the peoples of the world have become interdependent.
	7. How the United States is meeting changing conditions.	7. Vocational Orientation: How to prepare for high school.

[18] *The Social Living Program*, Board of Education, Long Beach, California, 1953.

QUESTIONS AND EXERCISES

5. Home Economics

1. In what ways may home economics contribute to a core program in a junior high school?

2. Should home economics be offered for boys in the junior high school? Explain the plan for such an offering, including grade, number of periods, content, and methods.

3. What are some home and community experiences that a ninth-grade pupil might plan and carry out while in a home economics course?

4. How much home economics would you require for girls? At what grade levels? What elective offerings would you have?

5. Plan the home economics suite for a junior high school, showing in detail the nature and location of facilities and equipment.

6. List the units or topics you would include in the home economics courses at each grade level.

6. The Language Arts

1. Pick an item of questionable usage, such as "he don't," and make a collection of its occurrences in conversation or writing during a week's period. Record the situations in which you find it, and estimate the educational and vocational background of the user. Can you map the social situation in which the item seems to be most prevalent?

2. Keep a record of the language activities for at least a class period. How much formal instruction have you been given in language arts classes in the performance of these activities?

3. Pick a characteristic interest of junior high school pupils, such as collecting, adventure, hero worship, and, using the *Standard Catalogue for High School Libraries,* find books that would satisfy this interest.

4. Read a sample of eight or ten comic books and analyze what accounts for their high level of appeal for junior high school students.

5. Examine the pattern of organization of literary selections in at least three of the standard anthologies designed for junior high school pupils.

6. Plan a reading program for pupils with reading deficiencies. Indicate class arrangement, types of reading materials, equipment, and methods.

7. Explain in some detail how you would teach spelling in the junior high school, indicating in what classes it would be taught, methods used, and other significant suggestions.

7. Foreign Languages

1. What is the present status of foreign language teaching in the lower and upper elementary grades and junior high schools as shown by reports of the Modern Language Association of America?

2. What seems to be the major concerns of foreign language teachers as reflected in articles published in recent issues of the *Classical Journal, French Review, Hispania,* and *Modern Language Journal?*

3. What organizations of foreign language teachers are active in your state? What projects or activities have they promoted in recent years?

4. From reviewing the contents of several recent issues of the professional magazines listed in the Bibliography, what benefits, would you say, accrue to a foreign language teacher who subscribes to these publications?

5. To what extent is the United States becoming aware of the increasing need and value of ability in foreign languages?

6. What basic textbooks in the foreign languages are especially suitable for pupils enrolled in grades seven to ten? What are their distinctive features?

7. Plan a program of foreign language offerings for a junior high school. Assume that you have complete freedom in preparing what you consider to be an ideal program.

8. Social Studies

1. How much social studies would you require in the junior high school? Would you offer any electives?

2. Do you favor combining social studies with some other subject to develop a core curriculum? What subjects? Justify your answer.

3. What should be the nature of the ninth grade course in social studies? Explain in some detail, listing the topics or units to be included.

4. Frequently geography is neglected in the social studies program. Explain how you would avoid this.

5. Examine several social studies curriculum guides or programs. Summarize the content and methods.

6. Explain in some detail how you would use small group activities in the social studies.

Chapter 8

THE CURRICULUM FIELDS: MUSIC, BUSINESS EDUCATION, AND SCIENCE

9. Music [1]

General Character of the Program. Music in the junior high school should be part of a continuous sequence that begins in the elementary school and runs through the senior high school. In the junior high school the music program reaches an important turning point, which is at the same time a culmination and a reorientation.

If the music program in the elementary school has been adequate, pupils will enter junior high school with appreciable musical experience, with an interest in music, and with some of the more important technical controls and insights. Even where the elementary program has been inadequate, or perhaps wholly lacking, junior high school pupils have reached a level of maturity at which music can be brought to them as something both attractive and feasible. In junior high school pupils should gain genuine musical momentum. Previous experience should now bear fruit, or the lack of such experience should be satisfied. Musical horizons should be broadened, new musical possibilities should reveal themselves, and technical controls should become more specific and independent. All this can be achieved by introducing more challenging musical activities and richer and more complex materials than would be appropriate for younger pupils. Thus there may be developed a deeper and stronger interest in music in general and at least the beginnings of specialization based on aptitude and interest.

Some Specific Suggestions. Some of the more specific suggestions appropriate for the music program at the junior high school level are the following:

1. *Few children will be able to develop any independent skill in music reading by the end of the sixth grade.* In some schools, a small percentage of fairly good music readers is produced by the sixth grade,

[1] This section was prepared by Professor James L. Mursell, Teachers College, Columbia University.

161

but this is accomplished only by an indefensible sacrifice of other factors, including musical enjoyment. Secondary school teachers are unfair to complain that the elementary schools do not turn out competent music readers. But the elementary schools can and should develop a strong interest in music and a reasonable insight into the music concepts symbolized by the notation. In the junior high school this combination of interest and insight can be transformed into a fairly practical music reading skill.

In certain junior high schools, some pupils come from elementary schools where music reading is strongly emphasized, while others come from schools where it is ignored. Yet within three months it has been found that these two groups are indistinguishable in so far as music-reading skill is concerned. However, any expectation that large numbers of junior high school pupils may become expert sight readers is sure to be disappointed. In fact, comparatively few professional musicians are expert sight readers. But there is no reason why many junior high school pupils should not develop some music-reading skill.

2. *It is quite proper to expect that considerable numbers of junior high school pupils will develop the beginnings of competence in some kind of instrumental performance.* Pupils at this level are mature enough to cope with the technical problems of the standard instruments. For many of them, the experience of instrumental performance has great educational and personal value. To achieve these values, two things are necessary: (1) expert instruction, both elementary and intermediate, to insure speedy progress and to eliminate the early frustrations that often put a stop to instrumental study; (2) opportunities for ensemble performance which provide both prestige and musical value.

3. *Junior high school pupils should be encouraged to sing throughout this period of their educational careers.* This proposition applies to boys as well as girls. The idea that it is harmful or undesirable to sing while the voice is changing seems to have been carried over from the choir schools of Europe, where a boy's voice was recognized as being at its best just before the break, after which it immediately became unusable. The point of view of American music educators is opposed to this idea. If material which is attractive to boys is provided, if the pupils are free from strain or embarrassment, and if the changing voice is carried gradually downwards, there seems to be no period in the lives of young people when they cannot or should not sing. Singing is one of the most rewarding of activities, both musically and personally.

4. *Junior high school pupils have reached a level of development at which active encouragement of musical exploration may bear good fruit.* Many of them are likely to be interested in mechanical contrivances, such as the phonograph, the radio, and the television set. It is by no means difficult to direct some of this interest toward music, pointing towards listening to, discussing, and collecting records, and musical programs on the radio and television.

Some Features of the Music Program. Many music educators maintain, and with much justice, that a course in general music should be the core of the program in the junior high school. According to this point of view, the general music course should be a substantial offering with an adequate time allotment, preferably continuing for two years as a required course. The content of the course should be varied, attractive, and geared to the interests, needs, capacities, and backgrounds of the pupils concerned. There should be projects of various kinds, involving pupil planning, research, and active musical participation by large groups, small groups, and individuals. Opportunities should be provided for listening, some organized by the pupils and others by the teacher. Pupils should make active contact with as many aspects of music as possible. Furthermore, there should be an opportunity for creatively reviewing what has been learned about music concepts and techniques in the elementary school, and for a further development of specific notational skills.

It is exceedingly desirable that informal and semiformal musical experiences and activities be disseminated as widely as possible throughout the school. Many such opportunities can be found by an energetic and enterprising music staff which remembers that the real content of the program is not made up of formal courses but of significant experiences.

Class instruction in instrumental performance is a proper and desirable part of the junior high school music program. There should be performance classes for beginners, as well as for those who have already begun the study of an instrument in the elementary school or elsewhere. Today many experienced music educators are convinced that, for many instruments, expert class instruction is more effective than individual instruction. Be this as it may, instruction of this type is appropriate and feasible at the junior high school level.

Experience has amply demonstrated that creditable instrumental ensembles are entirely possible in the junior high school. Not a few schools have impressive orchestras, and good junior high school bands are fairly common. The choice between having an orchestra and a band should be made entirely on the basis of the school situation and the needs and backgrounds of the pupils. The orchestral repertoire is, no doubt, superior to that of the band, but this is not the major consideration. The important thing is that it is difficult to find adequate string players of junior high school age. A band, as well as an orchestra, can make a significant contribution to the educational program of the school.

Offerings in Music. In a majority of the junior high schools, music is required in grades seven and eight. In the ninth grade it is usually an elective. In some schools, band, orchestra, or glee club may be substituted for the required course in general music, but in others the music organizations are carried in addition to the required course. In the 370 schools studied by the authors, the percentage which offer music as a required (R) or an elective (E) course is as follows:

		Two Semesters		One Semester	
		Percentage of Schools	Average Periods Weekly	Percentage of Schools	Average Periods Weekly
Seventh grade:					
Music	(R)	63	2.2	15	4.4
Music	(E)	21	3.5	1	5.0
Eighth grade:					
Music	(R)	57	1.9	8	4.1
Music	(E)	36	3.6	4	4.8
Ninth grade:					
Music	(R)	19	1.7	1	1.5
Music	(E)	79	3.8	2	4.3

10. BUSINESS EDUCATION [2]

Early Trends in Business Education. During the first decade or so of the junior high school movement, there was a tendency to transfer traditional secondary school studies to the newly developed junior high school. Beginning courses in typewriting, shorthand, and bookkeeping were shifted from the tenth and eleventh to the eighth and ninth grades.

But as young people remained in school longer, courses in business education for vocational training purposes could not be justified at the junior high school level. Pupils in the junior high school grades were obviously too young to grasp these subjects as they were taught in the early business courses. Furthermore, for junior high school youth,

[2] This section was prepared by Herbert A. Tonne, Professor of Business Education, New York University.

entrance upon a vocational career was still so far distant that any skills and materials that might be mastered would no doubt be largely forgotten before they were used. Formal vocational courses therefore were not considered desirable at the junior high school level, and consequently they were soon largely discontinued.

As a substitute for such purely vocational courses as shorthand and bookkeeping, a more general course in business came to be introduced in many junior high schools. In some schools this course consisted of little more than a fusion of penmanship, spelling, and arithmetic, while in others it included a study of general business and clerical training. In the general courses there was a definite effort to coordinate the content from the specific subject areas and to replace much of the formal drill on tool subjects with a study of business relationships. In schools where guidance and acquisition of general business information were stressed, the elementary phases of business were sometimes required of all seventh- and eighth-grade pupils. In addition to the elementary course in general business, an elective course in clerical training was occasionally offered as advanced work.

Early Junior Business Courses. The comparatively new courses in elementary or junior business, which fit so appropriately into the junior high school curriculum today, have had an interesting history. In 1919, Frederick G. Nichols, then Chief of the Commercial Education Service, Federal Board for Vocational Education, Washington, D.C., made a survey of junior commercial occupations in sixteen states.[3] His study showed that junior workers—those under seventeen years of age—were usually not employed as bookkeepers and stenographers, but rather were in less specialized positions demanding only elementary business and clerical training. Nichols therefore advocated the introduction of a course in junior clerical training. He believed that students who left school early to go to work would, with such training, be better prepared for the positions they ordinarily entered, while those who remained in school would be better fitted for more advanced business study. Although in some schools there were courses in junior business when Nichols made his survey, the publication of his study had considerable influence in stimulating introduction of such courses. The type of junior clerical training advocated by Nichols, however, was not retained very long in the curriculum of the secondary school.

[3] Federal Board for Vocational Education, *Survey of Junior Commercial Occupations*, Commercial Education Series 4, Bulletin 54 (Washington, D.C.: Government Printing Office, 1920).

One stage in the development of junior business courses was characterized by a tendency to imitate the general science courses of the junior high school. Just as the early courses in general science included some physics, chemistry, biology, and other science subjects, so the composite courses in junior business at first included a smattering of almost every subject in the business program. But the general business courses of this type did not appeal to pupils because their content was highly encyclopedic and poorly integrated. Even so, these early courses marked a definite forward step in the development of junior business courses.

Modern Courses in Junior Business. It is generally believed today that the objectives of courses in junior business should be:

1. To give pupils a basic understanding of business in America and the world today
2. To give pupils an understanding of how modern business services may be used and to help them become more skillful users of these services
3. To provide guidance with respect to business subjects and occupations
4. To serve as an introduction to other courses in business

It is being recognized increasingly that training for specific jobs cannot be offered in junior business courses. Therefore, these courses should be concerned with those business activities that are appropriate for everyone, regardless of his future vocation. They should have only general-use objectives, covering those phases of everyday business with which the great majority should be familiar for the wise management of their personal, family, and business affairs.

More than 400,000 students are enrolled in introduction to business courses today, mostly at the junior high school level. There is no doubt that among the business subjects as a group this type of course ranks in popularity with typewriting, bookkeeping, and shorthand. This is due in part to the fact that it is offered earlier in the school curriculum. The interest in the junior business course and the success which it has met suggest that it will continue as a part of the business offerings in the junior high school.

Offerings in Business. Because the courses in business are usually a part of the business education program in the senior high school, the course offerings at the junior high school level are not very extensive. More and more junior high schools, however, are offering courses in business as part of general education. The percentage of schools, among the 370 studied by the authors, which offer various required (R) and elective (E) courses in business is as follows:

		Two Semesters		One Semester	
		Percentage of Schools	Average Periods Weekly	Percentage of Schools	Average Periods Weekly
Seventh grade:					
Elem. business	(R)	1	2.0	1	5.0
Elem. business	(E)	1	5.0		
Jr. bus. training	(R)	1	2.0		
Eighth grade:					
Business education	(R)	2	5.0	1	4.0
Business education	(E)	7	4.2	1	5.0
Typing	(R)	1	3.0		
Typing	(E)	2	3.8		
General business	(E)	1	5.0	1	
Jr. bus. training	(R)	1	5.0		
Ninth grade:					
Business education	(R)	3	4.6		
Business education	(E)	26	4.8	1	
Jr. bus. training	(R)	1	5.0		
Jr. bus. training	(E)	8	5.0		
General business	(R)	2	4.8		
General business	(E)	7	4.8		
Bus. mathematics	(R)		4.0		
Bus. mathematics	(E)	3	5.0	1	5.0
Typing	(R)			1	5.0
Typing	(E)	8	4.7	1	4.0

Content of Junior Business Courses. Since the American teacher leans so heavily on textbooks for instructional materials, an analysis of textbooks provides a good method of summarizing the content of secondary school courses. Since World War II there has been a tendency to eliminate most, if not all, of the formal occupational material which was formerly so significant a part of the junior business course. Specialized instruction in the work of the billing clerk, the mail clerk, the messenger clerk, and the stock clerk, for example, has been practically eliminated from all recent editions. The following topics are among those being considered in more recent texts: What is business? Guidance in business education and toward business occupations; Banking, as it influences the student; Advertising, its use by the consumer and its importance for the business man; Methods of paying; Mailing and other means of communication; Traveling; Telephoning and telegraphing; Personal budgeting; and Filing in the home, school, and business.

The purpose of such topics is not to accumulate a mass of information, but rather to develop the ability to use the skill and knowledge that is learned. More important than facts is understanding of the opportunities and services of business to the entire community. More recent textbooks present junior business training as an integrated subject, though some of the texts still treat the subject as a mélange of bookkeeping, arithmetic, vocational guidance material, and a smattering of business practice. The writers of these texts evidently still feel that the subject is nothing more than a preliminary presentation of what is to come later in senior high school.

In a small number of schools, an effort is being made to present junior business training as a preview of business education in the senior high school. This means that junior business training is a series of try-outs. In some schools, for example, students are given six weeks of general clerical training, six weeks of sales training, and six weeks of guidance in the field of business. This procedure has not become typical. Moreover, when these children go to senior high school they must begin their learning all over again. If they do not go on with some of the business subjects in the senior high school, the try-out period in the junior high school appears to be of no value and consequently, except for some marginal guidance value, the effort is wasted.

The duplication of material in business with other subjects presents a serious problem for teachers of the junior business course. Many materials now taught in the ninth-grade social studies courses are also presented in the junior business course. This is especially unfortunate in those instances where overlapping is poorly coordinated. So many worth-while learning experiences can be provided in the junior business field that teachers of the social studies, arithmetic, home economics, and other subjects which include certain aspects of business should have no difficulty in effecting a satisfactory division of content among the various courses. Certainly, if the problem of duplication is intelligently studied by the teachers concerned, a satisfactory coordination of the various subjects related to junior business could be readily achieved.

It seems certain that the essential elements of junior business training will remain in the junior high school program of studies. The form is not, however, so certain. If the core curriculum is widely accepted in the junior high school, the subject matter of junior business may well become an integral part of the core offering. Some of the more technical learnings may be postponed until the senior high school years, when they would serve as a foundation for a program of basic business education for those interested in the subject vocationally. If general junior business is made a part of the core in the junior high school some or all of the core teachers should receive minimum business training in their teacher-preparation program.

Typewriting Instruction. Typewriting instruction in the junior high school is of special value because it fits into the work of so many other activities. Minimum skill in typewriting is easy to acquire and the opportunities for utilization in the junior high school are so numerous that it seems almost unfair to deprive the pupils of this opportunity. With skill in typewriting, junior high school students can integrate their work more effectively in English, journalism, history, and other subjects. The ability to use the typewriter facilitates the use of various forms of spirit and stencil duplication. It gives students an opportunity to become aware of public relations within the classroom, the school, and the community which the school serves.

11. Science [4]

Early Developments in Science Education. Until recently science teaching in the two or three grades prior to the secondary school level has been influenced directly by the secondary school curriculum and indirectly by college entrance examinations and requirements. Emphasis was usually placed upon pure science. This situation continued until lay people and educators realized that the science education in our public schools was contributing little of functional value to the public school youth for his postschool experiences in real life.

Within the academic context, during the last decade of the nineteenth century and the first two of the twentieth, science teaching included the offering of physiology and/or nature study (both with a human orientation) in grade seven. If physiology was not included in grade seven, it was usually offered in grade eight. On an elective basis, physical geography (with heavy emphasis on basic concepts of astronomy, geology, and meteorology) usually made up the science course in grade nine. Rarely were concepts of physics or chemistry included in junior high school science courses, since they were coveted by the senior high school science teachers and considered appropriate only at the senior high school level.

Later Developments in Science Education. In time, the character of physical geography in the ninth grade was gradually modified, until

[4] The section on science was prepared by Stanley B. Brown, Associate Professor of Education, University of Colorado; V. Ronald Nelson, Chairman of the Department of Physics and Mathematics, Augustana College, Sioux Falls, S.D.; and Erich Hopka, Assistant Professor of Chemistry, St. John's College, Winfield, Kan.

by 1915 general science had succeeded the narrow physical geography course. Concepts of the biological and chemical aspects of science as well as general physics appeared. In spite of the hesitancy of the college entrance boards to recognize the new ninth-grade general science course as college preparatory, by 1920 general science in the ninth grade was offered in most schools. However, because of the reluctance of the colleges to accept ninth-grade general science for college admission, considerable pressure was exerted to offer general science in either the seventh or eighth grade. As a result many public schools throughout the United States began to offer general science in the lower junior high school grades.

In the twenties and thirties, general science in the junior high schools came to be generally taught in either the seventh or eighth grade and sometimes in both grades. Although biological science was recommended by some educators for the ninth grade as a general biology course, the recommendation was not widely accepted. By 1930, general science as the orientation or major introductory course began to be accepted in junior high schools throughout the country. General science, as one of the basic subjects in the junior high schools, has persisted to the present time.

Present Philosophy of Science Education in the Junior High School. Students of education recognize the importance of a philosophy of education that lends direction to learning experiences. The following statement outlines the basic philosophy which underlies the program of science education in the junior high school as it is expressed by leading science educators and teachers.

1. *Science is a significant factor in our modern society and economy, of which the early adolescent is a part.* From the time he arises in the morning until he retires at night he cannot escape the impact of science. Therefore, science education is imperative, not only in college and the senior high school, but also in the junior high school. In fact, science education should be a vital part of the educational experiences of every child from the lower grades in the elementary school through the senior high school.

2. *Junior high school science should be functional.* Emphasis should not be primarily upon cultural values but upon practical values. Science education should provide boys and girls with information and skills which will help them solve problems at their own level which are of immediate concern to them.

3. *Science education should contribute toward the realization of the goals of education in a democracy.* Science education has fallen short of its objectives unless it helps boys and girls gain better control

of the fundamental processes of formulating and transmitting ideas, helps them become healthier individuals and better members of their families and their communities, and assists them in making better use of their leisure and working time.

4. *Pupils of junior high school age have characteristics which differentiate them from other age groups.* Usually this is a period of rapid physical growth accompanied by an accelerated development of motor skills and abilities. Children are born investigators and want to make discoveries for themselves. At this age, we find a widening interest in the group and the concerns of the group; there is usually an awakening to and an interest in ideals; and there is evidence of a beginning interest in the vocational activities of adults. The alert science teacher is aware of these characteristics and plans instruction accordingly.

5. *Each child has an individual pattern of learning, and provision should be made for it.* Research studies in learning readiness seem to indicate it is a waste of time and energy to attempt to present concepts before the learner is ready for them. On the other hand, if the attempts are made too late, there is much lost motion in unlearning that which has been acquired. Although the evidence concerning readiness for science concepts is far from complete, the effective science teacher may well be aware of its importance.

6. *A number of different learning experiences may be used to attain the same objective.* But the converse—namely, that a number of objectives may be attained by the same learning experience—also has a sound psychological basis. Thus it is possible to use science experiences to help pupils gain ability to solve problems in fields other than science, to acquire social competence, and to understand the elementary features of group dynamics. All of these abilities are desirable outcomes of any educational program.

7. *The development of interests, attitudes, and appreciations is an important part of science teaching.* This involves a two-fold process: first, there is understanding of a body of concepts; and second, this knowledge is then emotionalized so that it will carry over into action. Because interests, attitudes, and appreciations based upon sound information and supported by emotional drives do modify behavior toward desirable science outcomes, the science teacher considers them an important adjunct to science teaching.

8. *Pupil evaluation must go beyond testing for acquisition of facts and manipulative skills.* The whole child reacts to the total environment. Consequently, pupil measurement must take into account wider areas of evaluation, such as behavior modifications in group action and personal habits.

Offerings in Science. In many junior high schools, science is a required subject in one of the three grades. In some it is required in all three grades. The percentage of schools which offer science as an elective (E) or required (R) course in each of the three grades is as follows:

		Two Semesters		One Semester	
		Percentage of Schools	Average Periods Weekly	Percentage of Schools	Average Periods Weekly
Seventh grade:					
General science	(R)	47	3.9	21	4.7
General science	(E)	2	4.3	1	5.0
Health	(R)	4	2.1	1	
Conservation	(R)	1	5.0		
Eighth grade:					
General science	(R)	62	4.0	3	4.6
General science	(E)	2	4.5	1	5.0
Health	(R)	2	2.5	2	4.6
Health	(E)	1	5.0		
Nature study	(E)	1	5.0		
Ninth grade:					
General science	(R)	44	4.7	5	4.6
General science	(E)	39	5.1	4	5.0
Biology	(R)	3	5.0		
Agriculture	(R)	1	7.0		
Physiology	(E)	1	5.0		

Trends in Junior High School Science. A recognition of the expanding role of science in the lives of all Americans is forcing our schools to re-examine our entire science-education program. We are living in an environment so changed and dangerous as the result of scientific and technological discoveries and inventions that there is great and obvious need for a fuller understanding and appreciation of both content and method. Likewise, it becomes increasingly important that our youth attain a certain proficiency in the scientific approach to thinking, investigation, and study.

Change in the curriculum is always a slow process. Sometimes it is difficult to weigh trends within the field because of this slow adaptation to the needs of youth. Practices vary from community to community, and only after much trial and error are changes adopted. Even then, the acceptance of new practices is never universal. This fact makes it difficult to isolate permanent trends in education. The very nature of our effort to provide an education for all American youth has accented the functional approach. Consequently, certain trends in the teaching of science seem obvious enough when we carefully scan what is being done in many junior high schools. The more important trends in curriculum and methodology in junior high school science are towards the following:

1. A more functional approach to the teaching of science through:
    a) The replacement of nature study by a broader, more functional, and coherent program of science that includes more physical science
    b) A science program which is not just a watered-down mixture of high school biology, physics, and chemistry, but rather an exploration of the problems existing in the natural environment of early adolescents
    c) The kind of science program which is as applicable to the small junior high school as the large one, eliminating much of the more technical and more expensive laboratory work found in large schools
    d) Science texts which are less college preparatory and encyclopedic but are more functional in the everyday life of early adolescents
    e) Teaching less material but teaching it more thoroughly, instead of employing all the material provided in the text
    f) Greater use of actual pupil experiences, problems, and projects
    g) Use of a more practical laboratory manual whereby the learner is required to organize the facts before the desired answer is formulated, with less filling-in of blanks, and less experimentation on a cookbook basis

2. Integration of science in the total school program through:
    a) A continuous, integrated twelve-year program of science education planned for general-education objectives
    b) Offering integrated courses in science as a requirement in the ninth grade in order to reach as many pupils as possible before they leave school; for a great majority of junior and four-year high school pupils, the science courses constitute part of their terminal education
    c) Increased emphasis on science as an integral part of the school program—either as a separate course or in combination with social studies or some other areas
    d) Science experiences and units built around the solution of meaningful and socially significant problems, the solution of which involves materials from several subject-matter fields
    e) More cooperative planning, with administrators, teachers, and pupils working together to carry on an effective science program

3. Enrichment opportunities in science teaching through:
    a) Development of course outlines by school systems and publishers to insure a planned sequence of subject matter from the

kindergarten through senior high school, and even grade fourteen where that is possible

b) The determination of curricular content after community surveys have been made and an inventory compiled of those
phases of community life pertaining to science

c) The study of the application of scientific principles in the
home, on the farm, in the industries of the community, and
their use in relation to the health, safety, sanitation, transportation, and communication of the community

d) Science textbooks written by teams instead of individuals—
teams composed of a junior high school science teacher, a subject-matter specialist, and a science educator engaged in
teacher education

e) Greater utilization of community resources; for example,
studying the birds of Middletown instead of the exotic birds of
Pakistan

f) Seasonal organization of subject matter; for example, studying
the flora which are native to the community when they are
present in the community

g) Use of a wide range of materials and an extensive reading program—several texts, periodicals, newspapers, pamphlets, and
audio-visual materials

h) Organization of science clubs and science fairs as a means of
enriching the regular courses

4. Recognition of individual differences in the science program
through:

a) Fitting and adapting science offerings, methods, and content to
the needs, interests, and abilities of youth instead of the interest
of scientists or lay concepts of what youth should be taught in
the science program

b) Science courses designed for all youth—the slow learner as well
as the rapidly-maturing individual—rather than exclusively for
the student who plans to continue his study of science

c) Individualization of experiments on the basis of the student's
unique interests

5. The role of problem-solving and scientific attitudes in science
teaching through:

a) An increased emphasis on the importance of problem recognition, followed by individual and group usage of the basic steps
of the scientific method of thought and experimentation for
solution of those problems

b) Having the learner organize and structure the facts before basic
understandings and a critical analysis can be made and before
the desired answer is formulated

c) Inculcation of desirable scientific attitudes, such as objectivity,
a respect for the cause and effect sequence, open-mindedness,

freedom from superstitions, and changing one's opinion when additional or new evidence justifies it

d) Use of the laboratory as a method of instruction whenever it is appropriate and needed rather than on set days

6. Administrative considerations in the teaching of science through:
   a) Elimination of a double laboratory period
   b) Combination classroom and laboratory to replace use of different rooms and different days for classwork and laboratory
   c) The many fine public relations opportunities that carry over into the adolescent's everyday activities and family-community life as a result of his learnings in the science program

7. Communication and keeping abreast with current happenings in science through:
   a) More demonstration and lecture-demonstration, with less individual laboratory work
   b) A study of the most efficient techniques of demonstrating scientific laws and principles
   c) Textbooks utilizing a psychological, instead of a logical, arrangement of subject matter
   d) The concept of a changing curriculum and changing curricular materials to keep step with changing communities, changing young people, and changing knowledge
   e) More atomic energy materials in the various science courses to help youth meet the problems and challenges brought into being by the atomic-air age
   f) Use of prepared diagrams rather than detailed, artistic drawings made by pupils
   g) Identification of common misconceptions and superstitions frequently accepted by misguided youth

8. Democratic values in the science program through:
   a) Opportunities for the exercise of reason and intelligence in the many activities of students in the classroom, laboratory, field trip, or everyday life of each pupil
   b) Recognition of the sanctity and dignity of each pupil in the total school program; mutual respect versus an erroneous bias or prejudiced feelings
   c) Realization that through cooperative effort there is usually greater potential value and unity than through work on an individual basis
   d) Development of experiments by means of group cooperation on the part of the pupils
   e) Attention to objectives which lead to modification of behavior as well as the objective of the acquisition of facts
   f) Realization that there is no one best way, but that all methodology has a part to play in modern science education

Problems in Science Education. Because so much research has been done and so much progress has been made in science teaching during the last twenty-five years, it does not follow that there are no problems left. There will always be problems in science education. Although many research studies have been done, many more are possible. The following problems seem to be the most urgent ones in the junior high school at this time:

1. What do boys and girls of junior high school age really need to know in the field of science for effective living today?
2. How can these needs be best organized for effective instruction?
3. At which stage in the mental development of the pupils can the various science concepts be most advantageously assimilated? This problem is particularly pertinent in the field of nuclear energy, which contains so many concepts difficult to demonstrate.
4. Just how are science concepts learned?
5. How can scientific attitudes be taught most effectively?
6. How should junior high school science classrooms be designed for effective teaching?
7. What kind of laboratory activities would be most appropriate for early adolescents?
8. How can more effective science textbooks, especially for the seventh and eighth grades, be prepared?
9. What measuring devices should be constructed for the evaluation of the less tangible outcomes of science instruction?
10. What is a desirable preparatory program for teachers of junior high school science?

QUESTIONS AND EXERCISES

9. Music

1. List and be able to explain fully five important trends in music education in the junior high school.
2. What music instruction should there be in the junior high school in addition to bands, orchestras, glee clubs, and choral groups? Justify your proposal.
3. What can be done in the junior high school to identify and make special provision for the boy or girl who has unusual musical talent?
4. Should music be required of boys and girls who lack ability or are not interested in music? If they are required to take music, what kind of instruction should they have?
5. Should individual or small group instruction be given in voice, piano, wind instruments, and stringed instruments? Should this be free like other classwork? Should the school provide instruments?
6. Some junior high schools have band and orchestra practice daily, like the basic subjects. How frequently would you schedule these groups?
7. Should general music be required or elective in the ninth grade?

10. Business Education

1. What are the possible contributions of business education to the general aims of the junior high school?

2. What opportunity does Nichols believe should be afforded boys and girls in the junior high school "to secure exploratory experiences in the field of commerce"?

3. What justification is there, if any, for placing both, either, or neither economic citizenship and introduction to business in the junior high school?

4. To what extent is typing justified as a course or segment of a course in junior high school?

5. What has been the success of exploratory courses in business in the junior high school? Obtain the opinion of experienced teachers or use the *Business Education Index* for references.

6. What will be the effect of the core curriculum on junior business work in the junior high school? Explain your answer in detail and give references to other opinions.

7. A few junior high schools have typing required in the junior high schools. What advantages are there to this requirement? What objections?

8. Would you favor requiring junior business of all pupils in the ninth grade?

11. Science

1. What changes in the content and method in junior high school science have taken place during the past fifty years?

2. Be ready to give a short class report showing how the techniques mentioned by Heiss, Obourn, and Hoffman are an expression of the philosophy of science teaching as given in this chapter.

3. Be prepared to describe the techniques used by Smith in determining the content of junior high school science.

4. Why are there still so many unsolved problems in the field of junior high school science although so much research has been done in it?

5. What science work would you require in the junior high school? What elective work would you offer?

6. Which of these plans do you prefer: (a) to offer science daily for one semester, or (b) to offer science every other day for a year? Substantiate your answer.

7. Plan the room, equipment, and other physical facilities for science in each of the three junior high school grades.

Chapter 9

DIRECTING LEARNING ACTIVITIES

1. Various Approaches to Methods

Importance of Methods. In developing a program for a junior high school, it should be recognized that, no matter how important the over-all aspects of the program may be, it is what takes place in the classroom that really counts. It is at this point that the total program is translated into learning experiences for boys and girls. Regardless of how well the school may be organized or how satisfactorily the whole curriculum may be planned, the effectiveness of the program will depend largely upon the nature of the learning activities in the classroom.

This means in effect that teaching methods become of the utmost importance. How teachers plan their work, the participation of pupils in planning, the imagination and resourcefulness that is employed in developing learning activities, the working relationships between pupil and pupil and between teacher and pupil, the learning atmosphere which prevails, the practices employed for evaluating the progress of pupils, the variety of materials that are available for instructional purposes, and many other aspects of methods have a direct bearing on the effectiveness of the junior high school program. In other words, teachers should give serious consideration to the teaching methods which are most appropriate for a junior high school program. It is the purpose of this chapter to suggest some developments in methods which are of particular significance to a program of education for young adolescents.

Development of Subject-centered Units. Before the days of the junior high school, the program of education was quite clearly subject-centered. In fact, the first junior high schools were developed partly as a protest against this highly subject-centered program. It was only natural in a subject-centered program that a subject-centered approach to teaching in the classroom would prevail. At first this took the form of day-by-day planning and teaching, which was largely of the memorization and drill type. Very soon, however, the unit approach to planning and teaching was introduced into the American schools. The earliest units were, of course, subject-centered units.

The subject-centered unit was a tremendous improvement over day-by-day planning and teaching. With a skillful teacher, the subject-centered unit led to many desirable learning outcomes other than the mastery of fundamental skills and information. Significant understandings, the development of worth-while attitudes, problem-solving skills, and a better realization of the relationships between various subject areas were some of the desirable outcomes. Furthermore, the subject-centered unit tended to reduce somewhat the emphasis on drill and memorization, and to direct attention to the basic understandings in the subject involved.

Although the subject-centered unit was a decided improvement over day-by-day planning and teaching, it had some decided shortcomings. For instance, it was based on the assumption that there was a given body of subject matter to be mastered in the same way and in a given length of time by all pupils, regardless of their individual interests and abilities. We know now, of course, that this is impossible. The subject-centered unit is still used extensively in the junior high school, but in many schools it has given way to other approaches to teaching.

Activity-centered Units. The next development in teaching methods, occurring in the late 1920's and early 1930's, was the activity-centered approach. In this approach the planning and teaching were done in large blocks of time or units, much as in the subject-centered unit. However, the new approach placed much emphasis upon pupil participation and activity. That is, it was an implementation of the point of view that pupils learn best by *doing* things.

The activity-centered unit was usually developed around some major activity, project, or problem. Much subject matter was included in it, but it was developed around the activities in which pupils were to engage in order to gain mastery of certain basic skills, develop understandings in the subject, and acquire certain basic information. The activity-centered approach gives pupils an opportunity to do things that are of interest to them and that seem of most value to them; and it permits some cooperative group participation. The outline of the activity-centered unit, however, is usually largely preplanned by the teacher and is presented to the pupils as a desirable activity for them, the details of which they may assist materially in planning.

Like the subject-centered unit, the activity-centered unit is used extensively in the junior high school today, particularly in such subjects as the language arts, social studies, and general science. In some schools, teachers make use of both the subject-centered and the activity-centered units, employing the one which is most appropriate for the particular unit concerned.

Experience-centered Units. Many of the desirable features included in the subject-centered and activity-centered units are basic to the experience-centered approach to teaching. However, there is one basic difference. Whereas the subject-centered and activity-centered units are largely preplanned by the teacher and in turn are given to the pupils, experience-centered units are developed by the teacher and pupils together. Experience-centered teaching grows out of the basic interests and experiences which pupils in the class have had.

In the experience-centered unit, there is much subject-matter content and there are many different pupil activities. But both the subject matter and the activities assume importance because they are related, as much as is possible, to the experiences pupils have had. The pupils, with their interests and experiences, therefore, are in the very center of the planning and the direction of the activities in the experience-centered approach to teaching.

The experience-centered approach seems particularly appropriate in the junior high school. Certain functions of the junior high school can be implemented particularly well through experience-centered teaching. For instance, the experience-centered approach should provide the flexibility needed for exploratory activities; it should give pupils many socializing experiences; and it should make it easier to individualize instruction. Because of its appropriateness in the junior high school, particular attention will be given in this chapter to the experience-centered approach.

2. Implementing the Experience-centered Approach

Characteristics of the Experience-centered Approach. In beginning a discussion of the experience-centered approach to teaching, it might be helpful to present a summary of its basic characteristics. Some of these have already been given in the brief description in the preceding paragraph, but they will be included in this list to make it as complete as possible. The characteristics most prominent in the experience-centered approach are as follows:

1. The learning activities are developed from the interests and the previous experiences of the pupils.
2. The learning activities are planned by the teacher and pupils together rather than by the teacher alone.
3. The learning activities are adapted to the needs, interests, and abilities of individual pupils.

4. There is much provision for group activities, especially small-group activities.

5. There is much provision for pupils to explore their individual interests and abilities.

6. There is much provision for teaching the fundamentals, but with emphasis on doing so in a functional setting.

7. There is a variety of materials and equipment to aid in the development of learning activities.

8. The human relationships in the classroom are cooperative, friendly, informal, and democratic, with emphasis on consideration for one another rather than on obedience to authority.

Developing Activities Around Pupil Experiences. We have long recognized that we can teach pupils most effectively if we begin with something they already know, with some experience they have had, or with some present interest of theirs. This means the teacher must first know his pupils well—their backgrounds in school and out, their previous experiences, and their interests in various aspects of school and out-of-school life. Although some of this information is available in records in the office, much of it the teacher must obtain direct from his pupils. Some of it he may gather through such formal means as interviews with pupils, questionnaires, and autobiographies. Much of it, however, will develop from having pupils participate in planning learning activities.

The teacher needs to assume real leadership in ascertaining the previous experiences and present interests of pupils and in developing learning activities around them. If appropriate interests do not seem to be available, he can do much to develop them. In other words, the teacher should not be satisfied with the interests he finds among his pupils; he should exert every effort to help pupils find new interests, especially some that may be appropriate in his subject. If the teacher has skill in helping pupils develop such interests, he will indeed be more successful in employing the experience-centered approach to teaching.

Pupil Participation in Planning. It has already been mentioned that pupil participation in planning and carrying on class activities is basic to the experience-centered approach and is widely used in the core curriculum. If the teacher does all of the preplanning on his own, he has little opportunity to become aware of the interests and backgrounds of his pupils in the unit to be covered. It is only by giving them an opportunity to express their thinking with respect to a unit that the teacher becomes aware of the concerns of his pupils, that their interests in various types of activities are permitted to emerge, and that they and the teacher may come together in their thinking with respect to the content of the unit and the way it is to develop. Although pupil participation in planning is particularly appropriate in the experience-centered approach, teachers will find much of value in using it also in the subject-centered and activity-centered units.

Some teachers have the feeling that junior high school pupils are too young to participate in planning. That certainly is not the case. In fact, there is no age at which pupils are unable to make some contribution to the planning of learning activities. It is true, of course, that the more mature pupils, especially those who have had experience in planning, can make more of a contribution to the planning of learning activities. But with a group of pupils who have had little experience in cooperative teacher-pupil planning, it is essential that a start be made.

It is not appropriate to give here a detailed discussion on the techniques of teacher-pupil planning. The following suggestions are appropriate at the junior high school level:

1. *To employ cooperative planning very effectively, the teacher must be superior in his understanding of children and in the knowledge of his subject.* Cooperative teacher-pupil planning is much more difficult to do effectively than is the presentation of a teacher-prepared plan. The unfortunate results which occasionally attend teacher-pupil planning are more often due to inadequate skill and background on the part of the teacher than to weaknesses inherent in the technique itself.

2. *The teacher must preplan his work more carefully as a basis for cooperative teacher-pupil planning than if he were to impose his own plan on the class.* The teacher's plan should provide suggestions for the content, activities, and materials to be included in the unit, suggestions for organizing and carrying on the work, and a method of procedure for the cooperative planning of the unit itself. The teacher's plan, therefore, is largely a statement of suggestions of what *might* be done, rather than what *is* to be done.

3. *The teacher should stimulate and guide the planning of the pupils without imposing upon them a preconceived plan of his own.* Some critics say that, in cooperative planning, the teacher actually imposes his own plan upon the class but leads the pupils to believe that it is theirs. This, of course, could hardly be considered cooperative teacher-pupil planning. Furthermore, few junior high school pupils could long be deceived in that way. The teacher should, however, suggest ideas tentatively and should play a prominent part in evaluating, accepting, rejecting, modifying, and coordinating the suggestions of the pupils.

4. *The teacher should retain a strong position of leadership in the planning of all units and learning activities.* Certainly, there should never be the feeling that the pupils alone are to make the decisions. That was never intended in the thinking of the educators who suggested so strongly the values of pupil participation in planning.

5. *The teacher should not spend too much class time on cooperative planning.* That is one of the errors teachers frequently make in using the cooperative technique. Pupils may lose interest in the learning activity if too much time is spent on planning it. Furthermore, so much time may be devoted to the planning of a learning activity that too short a time remains to complete it satisfactorily. This situation can be avoided by planning the broad outlines of the activity cooperatively, but having the teacher determine the details. For that matter, in the cooperative planning of any learning activity or unit of work, much will be suggested by the teacher and accepted by the pupils because of the pupils' inadequate experience and background in the subject.

6. *The teacher should realize that the concept of cooperative planning does not apply equally well to all subjects or to all topics within a subject.* Its use is also limited by the grade level of the pupils, by their intelligence, and by their previous experience in cooperative planning. In a superior ninth-grade class in social studies, the content, the activities, and the organization of a unit may well be planned in large part by the teacher and pupils together. With the same group in algebra, cooperative teacher-pupil planning may lead to considerable waste of time, with no significant compensating factors. The teacher should recognize that cooperative planning in any subject should be employed only to the extent that it leads to the improvement of the total learning situation.

Individual Pupil Needs Are Met. In the subject-centered unit, the major concern is to meet individual differences in the mastery of skills, knowledge, and information. Meeting individual differences in subject matter was, of course, important in the past, and it continues to be important today. However, we are concerned today with meeting individual differences in many other ways than in subject-matter achievement alone. In both the activity-centered and the experience-centered approach to teaching, there is much concern for meeting the different interests pupils may have, for recognizing the different stages of personality and character development that we find in the junior high school, for satisfying their needs in leadership development, and for recognizing emotional problems of individuals. The experience-centered approach to teaching should be employed with complete awareness of its possibilities for effectively individualizing instruction.

One of the best ways of adapting the work to the individual in the junior high school is to give pupils much opportunity to participate in planning the work that is to be done. In fact, it is difficult to see how a teacher who does his preplanning alone can be very successful in ascertaining the interests of individual pupils. Only by giving his pupils an opportunity to express themselves with respect to a given unit of work can he find out what individual pupils would like to do. Cooperative teacher-pupil planning also enables the teacher to ascertain such personality characteristics as shyness, aggressiveness, reluctance to work with others, ability to work with others, interest in assuming leadership responsibilities, and many other personality and character qualities that should be of concern to the teacher. As these qualities come to the attention of the teacher, he is able to capitalize on them in finding activities that enable pupils to do what they like to do and, what may be of even more importance, to help them engage in activities that will be most helpful to them.

The informal organization of the experience-centered class also makes possible individualization of teaching in other ways. Small-group activities, for instance, are exceedingly helpful in finding an appropriate place in the learning situation for every child. Such activities help the shy child emerge, give the more aggressive pupil an opportunity to adapt his aggressiveness, and in other ways help pupils learn to work together. Furthermore, as part of such a group activity, pupils who are reluctant to appear alone in an oral activity before the class may be more willing to do so.

In the experience-centered class, there is also an opportunity to group pupils for various types of learning activities that involve the mastery of fundamental skills. Pupils may be grouped in terms of their reading abilities for more effective instruction in reading. The same may be done with such other skills as written expression, spelling, penmanship, and arithmetic. Such groups should not be rigid; rather they should be sufficiently flexible so that pupils may find themselves in different groups for instruction in different skills. Pupils should move from one group to another as their needs for special help change. Many educators prefer such informal grouping for instruction in the basic skills within the class to the highly regimented ability grouping between classes that has been so common in the past.

Group Activities Are Common. For some years, group activities involving the entire class have been used in certain junior high school subjects, such as English, social studies and science. Sometimes these activities were in the form of class discussions, but at other times they were dramatizations, panel discussions, debates, and many others. Such activities should be an important part of any class situation.

Recently, however, there has been much emphasis on small-group activities, a result no doubt, of the current emphasis on group dynamics, which is concerned with having all individuals participate in the activities of a group in so far as their ability permits. Obviously, if the class engages in many small-group activities, more individual pupils can participate. The small-group activities frequently merge into larger ones for the entire class.

By small-group activities we mean that the members of the class work in committees of three, five, or six pupils on various activities growing out of the unit being studied. The following suggestions may be made for carrying on small-group activities.

1. *The groups should not be highly organized, but should be rather informal.* Either the teacher or the group itself may select the leader. Certainly, after the group has had experience in working together, it is better to have the group select its own leader.

2. *The personnel of groups should ordinarily be changed from one learning activity to another or from unit to unit.* That is, it is not wise to have a group organization that continues for a semester or a year. If groups continue for an unduly long period, cliques may develop within the class.

3. *Each group must have clearly in mind the objective that it is to achieve.* Furthermore, it should know how that objective relates to the work of the class as a whole. The objective of a group should clearly relate to the objectives of the unit, and its work should make a real contribution to the progress of the unit for the entire class.

4. *Groups usually need some help in learning how to function together.* They must know the responsibility of members of the group, ways of proceeding efficiently with group activities, where and how to find materials, and how to bring their work to an effective conclusion.

5. *The groups should report occasionally on their progress to the class as a whole so that they may keep in touch with each other.* This is essential if the class is to continue to function as a well-unified group. Otherwise, one small group may go off on a tangent and waste much time.

6. *The groups need to know how to evaluate their progress.* They need to have someone occasionally suggest whether or not the group is functioning efficiently, whether it is proceeding as rapidly as it should, whether individual members are contributing to the maximum of their ability, and whether certain individuals may be

interfering with the progress of the group. One device is to have a member of the group act as an observer and occasionally give the group his reaction concerning the efficiency with which it is functioning.

7. *Groups need to be concerned with the problem of classroom atmosphere and order.* Teachers who fail to gain the cooperation of small groups in this respect may have too much noise and confusion for effective work. In that case, small-group activities may actually interfere with, rather than contribute to, the effectiveness of the total learning situation. The teacher must be sure that pupils are informed concerning their responsibility for a good working atmosphere, and he must continually be on the alert to prevent any abuse of it.

Importance of Teaching Basic Skills. One of the dangers in the experience-centered approach to teaching is that basic skills, such as reading, written expression, penmanship, and arithmetic may be neglected, because some of the instruction in these skills needs to be very precise, whereas the whole approach to experience-centered teaching is rather informal. In most respects, the informal and flexible aspects of experience-centered teaching are an advantage. With the teacher who lacks skill in this approach to teaching, however, the specific instruction necessary for the basic skills may be neglected.

Neglect of the basic skills is, of course, not desirable, nor is it an inevitable outcome of experience-centered teaching. In fact, just the opposite should be true. Where it is effectively carried on, the experience-centered approach should lead to much more functional instruction in the basic language skills than any other approach to teaching. The following suggestions should be helpful:

1. *The teacher should plan specific activities as a part of the total unit to provide instruction in the basic skills in his subject.* This does not mean that certain times need to be set aside for reading, spelling, or any other specific skill. It does mean, however, that the teacher thinks through the amount of time that should be devoted to effective drill on these skills and then sees to it that, in the total plan for a unit, such time is provided. If the teacher and the pupils plan their work some time ahead, the teacher should frequently suggest that on certain days it may be desirable to give attention to these skills.

2. *The teacher needs to be well informed concerning the best methods of teaching these skills.* One of the serious shortcomings of teachers of language arts in the junior high school today is that they are not adequately prepared in methods of teaching reading. Furthermore, some teachers also lack the subject-matter back-

ground to teach certain skills. That is sometimes true with grammar. The teacher of written and oral expression must obviously have a good command of grammar himself in order to be able to teach it effectively.

3. *The teacher needs to have available various types of materials for teaching the basic skills.* There needs to be a variety of reading materials to accommodate the pupils with reading skills at various levels. Drill material should also be available for work in written expression, spelling, and arithmetic. As with reading, there should be a sufficient variety of subject-matter materials to meet the needs of all pupils in the group.

4. *The teacher should give tests periodically which will measure the achievement of his group as compared with accepted norms and indicate the progress that his pupils are making.* It seems to be true that, in the schools where the experience-centered approach and the core curriculum have been introduced, testing programs are ordinarily more fully developed than in other schools. The results of testing programs should be used by the teacher as a guide to the amount of time that he needs to give to teaching the basic skills.

Appropriateness for Various Subjects. The experience-centered approach is especially appropriate for certain subjects, such as the language arts, social studies, general science, homemaking, and industrial arts. In these subjects the teachers may, indeed, go a long way toward developing the work of the class around the interests of the pupils, in having pupils participate in planning learning activities, in carrying on small-group activities, and in having pupils evaluate their own progress. In some other subjects, this may not be quite so appropriate.

It should be pointed out, however, that the point of view underlying experience-centered teaching may apply in one way or another to every subject in the junior high school curriculum. How, when, and where various aspects of experience-centered teaching are to be used should depend, of course, upon the judgment of the teacher. Its use will vary also with the experience of the teacher in the experience-centered approach, with the skill of the pupils in using this approach, and with the nature of the subject. For instance, in the social arithmetic work that is ordinarily taught in eighth-grade mathematics, much can be done to develop interesting units cooperatively with a group of pupils. That is not equally true with algebra in the ninth grade. Teachers should continually examine the work that they teach to see how the point of view underlying the experience-centered approach may best be implemented in their respective subjects.

3. DEMOCRATIC CLASSROOM RELATIONSHIPS

Meaning of Democratic Relationships. A generation ago, the emphasis on discipline in school was primarily on keeping children quiet. If there was complete silence from the moment the bell rang at the beginning of the period until dismissal, the teacher was believed to have a good disciplinary situation. Any movement about the classroom, any talking, or any other activity on the part of an individual or a group of pupils was possible only with the express permission of the teacher.

In recent years, we have changed out point of view somewhat about the type of situation that is most desirable in a junior high school classroom. We know, for instance, that the nature of the junior high school child of today is such that great tensions may be built up if he is in a repressed situation five or six hours every school day of the year. Furthermore, we feel satisfied today that, for certain types of learning experiences, the formal, regimented classroom of yesterday definitely interferes with, rather than contributes to, learning. It is believed by many educators that, to prepare junior high school pupils for democratic living, they should experience a democratic situation in all phases of the school program. This means a situation that is free from fear, punishment, repression, and unnecessary regimentation.

Some teachers and a few parents seem to believe that a democratic classroom situation is synonymous with noise and confusion. Nothing could be farther from the truth. Democracy in the classroom means that there is a spirit of friendship, cooperation, courtesy, and consideration toward others. Furthermore, the relationships between the pupils should always be such that effective learning can take place. With noise and confusion, that would obviously be impossible.

The type of classroom relationships should change, furthermore, with the nature of the learning situation. For instance, if a test is being given, there should ordinarily be complete quiet and order. If pupils are participating in a class discussion, each should speak only when recognized by the chairman. If there are committee activities, however, pupils need to work together in small groups and converse quietly enough so that they will not disturb others. Occasionally pupils may work cooperatively on a project that demands some physical movement about the room. Here, again, there should be consideration for pupils engaged in other types of activities.

A democratic classroom, therefore, is one in which pupils work in a friendly, courteous, and cooperative manner on a learning situation, and in which the nature of the classroom relationships are determined by what is most desirable for the particular learning activities concerned. This type of classroom situation is especially appropriate for the experience-centered approach to teaching.

The Teacher as a Classroom Leader. In the formal, regimented classroom the teacher's responsibility is clear and direct. He is there to maintain order and make rules for pupil conduct, and to reprimand or punish pupils who violate those rules. In a democratic classroom situation, the teacher's responsibility for discipline is not so simple or clearly defined. He must be a strong, democratic leader in the best sense of the term. Instead of merely making rules and giving orders, it is his responsibility to see that pupils learn how to work effectively together. Much of his time will be devoted to helping them see their responsibilities toward each other, to helping them understand what courtesy and consideration mean, and to teaching them to control their own desires for the benefit of the group as a whole.

Some pupils may not respond readily to democratic leadership from the teacher, usually because they have not had experience with such an approach to classroom relationships. The teacher must remember that, in any case, he must always begin with the pupils where they are. He may need to be somewhat of an authoritarian for a time, though to a progressively decreasing amount, because that is what the pupils have been accustomed to. But he should never forget that his responsibility lies in helping pupils get ready for cooperative, courteous, democratic living. This is, indeed, the great responsibility of the classroom teacher so far as pupil relationships are concerned in the junior high school today.

The Class Should Become a Group. If a satisfactory democratic relationship is to exist in the classroom, it is essential that the entire class take on the characteristics of a functioning group. This is most important when the experience-centered approach is being used, particularly in language arts, social studies, science, and similar subjects. In subjects like mathematics, where much of the work is of an individual nature, this is not so essential.

By "becoming a group," we mean that the pupils identify themselves with the group as a whole, rather than thinking of themselves only as individuals. They form loyalties to the group, they enjoy being identified with it, they have a strong feeling of "belongingness" toward it, and they are willing to cooperate with the other group members. There is no one procedure which can be prescribed for helping the class become a group. The following suggestions, however, might point in that direction.

1. *The teacher should study the arrangement of the furniture in the room to see what might be best for helping pupils function as a*

group. If the furniture is movable, it might be well to place it in a semicircle. Although this may not be appropriate for mathematics, it might be effective in classes where group discussions are common.

2. *The teacher should help pupils get to know each other during the first few days.* This means that pupils should know each others' names, and they should decide whether to call each other by their last names, first names, or nicknames.

3. *Teachers should help pupils become acquainted with each others' backgrounds early in the term.* Each pupil should be aware of the backgrounds, experiences, and interests of his classmates. He should know them not only as names but as individual people.

4. *The teacher should help pupils understand what is meant by effective group activity.* They should realize their responsibilities to the group as a whole, the satisfactions that come from functioning as a group, the common courtesies that members of the group extend to each other, and the position of the teacher as a leader in a democratic group.

5. *The teacher should help pupils gain experience in group procedures.* For instance, they need to know the responsibilities of the chairman, the responsibilities of members of the group to the chairman, how to set up an objective for a group activity, the importance of having each member contribute to achieving that objective, and how to bring any group activity to some satisfactory conclusion. The teacher may need to plan some activity early in the term which involves the group process. The sooner the class begins to function as a group on some common project, the more likely it is to develop unified group feelings.

6. *The teacher should also become a member of the group.* A number of things might be helpful in this respect. One is to remove the desk as a center of authority; the teacher may well assume a place in the circle with the rest of the group. There is always danger that the teacher will be such a strong member of the group that he will unintentionally and unconsciously dominate the thinking of the pupils.

7. *The teacher should maintain a strong position as a democratic leader of the group.* Much of the time he may well be in the background, but he is always ready to suggest ways to proceed effectively, to offer suggestions as to how some pupils may participate better, and to assume control if more democratic processes fail to function.

4. Teaching Aids and Materials

Use of Textbooks. In the experience-centered approach to teaching, it is obvious that a wide variety of instructional aids and materials is essential. This does not mean dispensing with a basic textbook.

Rather, it means that, regardless of the use of a basic textbook, emphasis should be placed on having available many different types of teaching aids and materials as a basis for a variety of learning activities that may be planned by teacher and pupils.

In place of a basic textbook, it is a common practice to have several sets of reference books in the classroom. In the social studies classroom there may be several sets of history books, geographies, books on economics and sociology, and reference books in civics and government. In some subjects, such as language arts, social studies, and science, it is highly desirable to have at least one encyclopedia in the classroom. If encyclopedias are made available to pupils in the classrooms, they tend to make much more of a contribution to learning activities than if they are kept only in a school library. Particularly where the experience-centered approach is used, it is highly desirable to have such basic reference materials available in every classroom.

In some subjects, such as mathematics, foreign languages, and other skill subjects, a basic textbook may be highly desirable. Even in those subjects, however, it is to be hoped that the classroom teacher will locate other instructional materials to meet the various needs, interests, and abilities of individual pupils. Furthermore, the teacher should consider the textbook as an aid, rather than as an end, to instruction. He should study the needs of his pupils and make use of the materials in the textbook, reference materials in the classroom, library materials, and any other instructional materials that are available in meeting those needs.

Employing Community Resources. Much has been said in recent years about the use of community resources as an aid to the instructional program in the junior high school. Actually, these resources are being used all too little in most schools at the present time. There are several reasons for this, among them a lack of understanding on the part of teachers of the manner in which these resources can be used, the difficulties encountered in arranging for their use, and lack of information concerning the various types of resources that are available in a given community. In the activity-centered and experience-centered approaches to teaching, community resources are exceedingly helpful.

The first step in the effective employment of community resources as an aid to instruction is to make a thorough survey of all of the resources available in the community which would be of help in the program of the school. This survey should be conducted cooperatively by all the teachers in school, so that there will not be duplication of effort. The survey should include every civic, labor, business, industrial, historical, and cultural agency in the community, and cooperation of leaders in these agencies should be sought. The resources revealed by such a survey should be arranged under appropriate headings; they should be printed or mimeographed; then they should be placed in the hands of all teachers concerned.

The school needs to have a definite policy concerning the use of community resources. There are always some dangers involved, such as the use of the schools for propaganda purposes by business, labor, or other agencies. Hence all resources need to be carefully reviewed to be sure that they have a real contribution to make to the instructional program of the school. The matter of cost also needs to be considered, particularly when pupils take field trips, when visitors are brought to the school, or when materials or speakers are obtained from local agencies. Certain practices need to be established with respect to field trips so that the pupils may be protected against unnecessary accident hazards. Particularly with pupils of junior high school age, it is essential that there be a well-formulated statement of policies concerning field trips.

Audio-Visual Materials Are Helpful. The use of audio-visual materials has become such a common practice today that it needs no justification. These materials are particularly appropriate in the junior high school because they appeal to almost every interest of young adolescents. Furthermore, the young adolescent frequently has a greater interest in things that can be seen or heard than he has in the printed page.

Although audio-visual materials are widely used, they are not always used with the most effectiveness. The following suggestions may be helpful.

1. *Audio-visual materials should be selected and their use planned in terms of the particular contribution they are to make to the objectives of the unit being studied.* These materials too often are presented to the class with no definite purpose in mind. Audio-visual materials may be used with particular effectiveness (a) to introduce or summarize a unit; (b) to stimulate pupil interest in classwork; (c) to present information not as readily available in other sources; (d) to clarify difficult material; and (e) to correlate learning experiences in school with real-life situations outside the school. The selection and use of these materials should be made with such purposes clearly in mind.

2. *Audio-visual materials should always be previewed by the teacher.* The preview is stressed especially because some teachers who use rented materials frequently neglect to preview them. This is particularly true with movies. Two purposes are served by the pre-

view: (a) it serves as a final check to be sure that the material is appropriate; and (b) it enables the teacher to plan more satisfactorily for introducing, for presenting, and for following up the material.

3. *The time for the presentation of the material should be well planned and economically used.* The writer not long ago observed the showing of a film which took only half the class period. The teacher then repeated the showing because he had nothing else planned. Such waste of time in the presentation of audio-visual materials is far too common. There also is frequent waste of time by the teacher who is inexperienced in the use of the equipment for audio-visual materials. When such materials are employed, considerable care should be exercised in planning the use of the equipment, the preparation of the class for the presentation, and the follow-up activities.

4. *The pupils should be prepared for the presentation of any audio-visual materials.* They should be given sufficient background to understand the material; they should see its relation to the unit being studied; they should know what to look for in the presentation; and, if possible, they should make some application of what they have learned.

5. *The amount of audio-visual material which is employed should not be disproportionate as compared with other types of instructional materials.* There is always the danger of "faddists" in the American schools—those who become too enthusiastic about something new. For instance, in a certain school motion pictures are shown in the history classes about once a week because the department head is enthusiastic about this type of material. It is doubtful that so much time for this type of instructional material can be justified.

6. *The teacher's plans for the use of audio-visual materials should be made weeks ahead.* If the materials are rented, planning ahead is necessary in order to reserve them for when they are needed. Advance planning is also desirable for the efficient use of equipment within the school and for the completion of satisfactory long-unit plans in which these materials are to be used.

Production of Audio-Visual Materials. In the junior high school, the production of audio-visual materials can be particularly effective as an aid to the instructional program. Production of these materials should, of course, be participated in by the pupils, but it needs to be carefully planned and supervised by the teacher. There is no limit to the variety of audio and visual materials that may be produced by junior high school groups. Only a few of them will be mentioned here.

Because of the emphasis that should be given to oral expression in the junior high school grades, the tape recorder can be used with particular effectiveness in various oral activities in almost every subject. In the English class, dramatizations, oral reports, class discussions, and other similar activities may be recorded. These recordings are particularly helpful for improving the vocabulary, pronunciation, diction and forcefulness of boys and girls. Similar oral activities may be recorded in science, social studies, health, home economics, foreign languages, and almost every other subject in the curriculum. Aside from the value of the tape recordings in improving the speech habits of pupils, they may provide tremendous motivation for various learning activities.

Pupils may also prepare slides for use in various learning activities. Unusual art talent is not necessary for the preparation of such materials. Simple slides that may contribute to the effectiveness of an oral presentation in history, civics, science, or English, may be produced by pupils without unrealistic demands upon imagination and artistic ability. Occasionally, pictures may be taken with a 35 mm. slide camera, film strips may be prepared, and movies may be made of appropriate class activities.

In some junior high schools, various audio-visual aids have been used effectively to prepare records of various extraclass activities. For instance, in one school a tape recording is made of every school assembly so that pupils a year later may have the advantage of hearing the manner in which previous assembly programs have been conducted. Sometimes films or slides are made of various pupil activities as a basis for orientation of freshmen, for discussions of school activities with parents, and for orientation activities with teachers new to the school. If pupils participate in the production of these materials, they may perform with greater enthusiasm and effectiveness. Furthermore, these materials may be helpful in improving similar activities in the future.

5. Helping Pupils Study

New Approach to Supervised Study. Not many years ago we heard much about supervised study in the junior high school. The thinking concerning supervised study was, however, based on an approach to teaching which is gradually disappearing from the junior high school classrooms. That was the assign-study-recite approach, consisting of an assignment given by the teacher, of a study period either in school or at home when pupils did the assignment, and of a recitation based on that study.

The early approach to supervised study fitted into this assign-study-recite procedure. It was designed to improve the effectiveness of the study phase of this cycle. In other words, supervised study was based on the assumption that pupils would be given an assignment, that they needed to study or prepare that assignment, and that a recitation of some kind would follow. It was the purpose of supervised study to have pupils do their assignment under the supervision of the teacher who gave it. Consequently, class periods in the junior high school were lengthened and the number of separate study halls was reduced so that pupils could do much of their work under the close supervision of the teacher who gave the assignments.

In recent years, however, there has been a tremendous change in the methods of teaching in the junior high school. Instead of the assign-study-recite approach, teacher and pupils are working as a team in planning, preparing, and conducting learning activities. In other words, the entire learning activity from the beginning to the end is cooperative, with pupils and teacher working together. Instead of an assignment which is followed by a study period, the learning activity from its inception to its completion is in large part a cooperative effort for the teacher and pupils.

The new approach to supervised study, therefore, is one which recognizes the needs of a cooperative learning activity in the junior high school classroom. It is one that emphasizes the need for having the teacher and pupils have time to work together in planning, preparing, and conducting learning activities. This approach to supervised study recognizes the importance of the teacher's help in the work that pupils are to do, but it emphasizes also the importance of having sufficient time for teacher and pupils to work together on an activity which they jointly select, plan, and carry through.

Use of the Library Is Changing. In the cooperative working situation which has just been discussed, there is also a need for a new approach to the use of the library. Traditionally, the library has been used much like a study hall, pupils being assigned there during study periods when they have library assignments to do. As teacher and pupils work together on learning activities, the library, in the traditional sense, is not particularly effective. Today it is thought to be more desirable for the teacher to take his class to the library and help pupils use the resources there for the learning activities. Consequently, the library is being used by entire class groups through prearrangement with the librarian. The new libraries are arranged so that entire class groups may be brought into a room or a section of the library and work together without disturbing other pupils who are there for individual work. Sometimes a wall separates the classroom corner from the rest of the library; in other cases the library is L-shaped with class groups using one section of it; in still others there is a room adjoining the library which is unassigned, and therefore may be used by class groups that need the resources of the library.

Frequently, pupil committees need to use the library. Many of the new junior high school libraries have several committee rooms for use by such small groups. Usually they have a glass partition so that the librarian may more readily supervise the work. Committees are sent to the library from their classes for these activities. Such opportunities for small pupil groups to use the resources of the library are indeed essential to the newer approaches to planning and carrying on learning activities which have been discussed in this chapter.

The junior high school library is also becoming the center for many instructional materials other than books, encyclopedias, and similar references. Audio and visual materials particularly are being placed in the library for pupil use. In some of the new schools, there are small listening and preview rooms adjoining the library where individual pupils or small groups may hear recordings, view film strips, examine slides, and preview other audio-visual materials that may be helpful in developing a learning activity. Like the conference room, these small listening and viewing rooms are usually separated from the library by a glass wall, so that the librarian may readily supervise the activities of pupils there.

It is also a common practice for library materials to be taken into the classroom. For instance, before work proceeds far with a new unit, the teacher explores the library to locate all the reference material possible. These materials are then assigned to his classroom for the time that the group works on that unit. In some schools this is carried out on a well-organized basis. In the Valley Regional High School, Deep River, Connecticut, a six-year secondary school, each room is provided with a movable bookcase which may be wheeled into the library for convenient transfer of library materials to the classroom. The use of library materials in the classroom is one more practice for employing effectively the cooperative approach to planning and carrying on classroom activities.

Study Halls Are Disappearing. The practice of having separate study halls was copied from the four-year high school at a time when the assign-study-recite approach to teaching predominated. In that approach the separate study hall was, of course, exceedingly appropriate.

It has been suggested previously that today we think of the learning situation in the junior high school as cooperatively planned and carried on by teacher and pupils. It is much more than a textbook assignment which needs to be read in preparation for a recitation in class. In the cooperative approach, the teacher and pupils think through the learning activity together, from the time that work on it is initiated until it is brought to completion. This approach to teaching demands that the teacher and his pupils spend much time together. It should be obvious that, for this approach, the separate study period under a different teacher has little value. That is as true in such skill subjects as mathematics and foreign languages as it is in language arts, social studies, and general science. It is certainly true in such subjects as homemaking, industrial arts, arts and crafts, and music. Although many junior high school educators today recognize the limited values of a separate study period, opinion is divided on the subject. Consequently, study halls continue to be used in a majority of the junior high schools.

It is true, however, that in a considerable number of junior high schools, separate study halls have been discontinued entirely. That is especially the case in schools that have adopted some type of a core curriculum, with several class periods being combined and taught by one teacher. Sometimes the class periods are lengthened to absorb the time pupils formerly spent in study halls. In the ninth grade, frequently, the program of pupils is enriched by having them take additional work. The Burbank Junior High School, Burbank, California, is a good example of this practice. There in the ninth grade, as well as in grades seven and eight, pupils have a full schedule of classes throughout the day. Most pupils have an elective subject, which meets daily throughout the week, such activities as student council, band, orchestra, the school newspaper, a school service club, or some similar activity.

Home Work Is a Problem. Educators continue to be divided in their opinion concerning the advisability of home work in the junior high school. Many educators are inclined to doubt its advisability in grade seven and possibly grade eight, but they are not so sure that home work should be discontinued in grade nine. The problem of home work is further complicated by the mixed attitude of parents on the subject. Some parents are strongly opposed to home work for pupils of junior high school age, but there are others who are just as critical of the school when home work is not given. A recent study by Byers shows, however, that home work continues to be given in most junior high schools.[1]   The percentage of schools which give various amounts of home work per day in each of the junior high school grades is as follows:

HOURS OF HOME WORK PER DAY

Grade	None	½-1	More Than One	No Reply
7	15%	65%	12%	8%
8	10%	62%	19%	9%
9	8%	45%	37%	10%

In studying the problem of home work, one should always remember that, in the junior high school, we are dealing with young adolescents, whose physical, emotional, and psychological development have direct bearing on this subject.   All too often the same arguments that are given for home work for older adolescents in the senior high school are applied also to the junior high school group.   It must be remembered, however, that we are concerned with junior high school, not senior high school pupils.

It is not just a matter of saying that there should or should not be home work in the junior high school.   Certainly the amount of home work should be decidedly limited.   In certain situations, and for certain purposes, home work may be desirable.   The following suggestions may be helpful in formulating a satisfactory policy concerning home work.

1. *The health of the young adolescent demands much relaxation, rest, and sleep.*   Boys and girls at this age level are undergoing certain physiological, emotional, and physical changes that require exercise outdoors, opportunities to relax, and at least nine to ten hours sleep every night.   The home work that is given in the junior high school should not be permitted to interfere with these needs. Certainly, the textbook type of study activity which taxes a pupil's eyes and which keeps him hunched over a book, is not appropriate outside school hours if a young adolescent has been exposed to much of it during the day.

2. *The ability of pupils to study independently with profit at this age is indeed limited.*   It is only the better student who can ordinarily do much work independently with profit.   Not much can be expected in the way of independent study from pupils in the lower half of the class.

3. *The situation in most homes is not conducive to satisfactory home study by pupils.*   Radio and television certainly are serious hindrances to a satisfactory home study situation.   Furthermore, in spite of smaller families, the new homes of today are relatively small and crowded.   There is usually no place where a child can

---

[1] Richard S. Byers, "Articulation in the Junior High School" (Unpublished doctoral thesis, University of Connecticut, Storrs, Conn.), p. 112.

go to study where he is free from interferences by the family. What is more, the home life of the child is so important that we should make no serious attempt to upset the usual situation in the home.

4. *The young adolescent today has many significant educational activities that occupy his time outside school hours.* For instance, there are Boy Scouts and Girl Scouts, High-Y, 4-H Clubs, church youth groups, and music lessons. A few junior high school pupils have out-of-school employment, such as selling newspapers and baby-sitting. It is usually recognized by both educators and parents that such activities have educational values for the young adolescent that are as significant as many of the learning activities in school. The school should therefore recognize that these activities exist and should not interfere with them unnecessarily.

5. *Certain types of learning activities that are begun in school may well be continued outside school hours.* Some drill activities on basic skills fall in this group, such as spelling, arithmetic, and English. Drill activities of this kind should begin in school so that the child understands clearly how it is to be done. These activities should continue only for a short period outside school hours. Even more appropriate, however, are the cooperative learning activities begun in school as a part of the experience-centered approach to teaching. If pupils play a significant part in planning these activities, they may well know how to proceed with them independently of the teacher. For instance, a group may take a field trip, interview some local person, work as a committee on some project, or engage in some creative activity either as individuals or as members of the group. A trip through the woods on Saturday afternoon to collect materials for a science class is another example of this type of out-of-school activity. Activities such as these need to be well planned in school so that the child knows how to proceed. Because they do not call for an intensive type of textbook activity, they are appropriate for young adolescents outside school hours. Furthermore, they can be done more effectively away from school than in the classroom.

Teaching Study Skills. The experience-centered approach to teaching requires many more study skills on the part of pupils than a subject-centered learning activity. Study skills which are used by pupils in the more forward-looking classrooms of today include the following: (1) how to use the textbook, (2) how to use the library, (3) how to use the dictionary, (4) how to use a newspaper, (5) how to prepare and use graphic materials, (6) how to take dictation, (7) how to take notes, (8) how to outline, (9) how to prepare written work, (10) how to solve problems, (11) how to prepare and present oral reports, (12) how to prepare and present debates, (13) how to prepare projects, (14) how to prepare assignments for class discussions, (15) how to memorize, (16) how to drill, (17) how to prepare for tests, (18) how to engage in committee and other small group work, (19) how to interview, (20) how to prepare panel discussions, (21) how to evaluate one's own progress, and (22) how to participate in planning a learning activity cooperatively with the teacher and other pupils.

Study skills such as these are not acquired incidentally. Pupils gain skill in such activities only if they are given help by the teacher. Some suggestions on study skills can be given in the homeroom or in special classes on how to study. The most appropriate place, however, seems to be the classroom in which these skills are actually used. For instance, library skills may well be taught at an appropriate time as part of the work in English, social studies, or general science. The library should, of course, play a key part in such instruction. Similarly, other skills suggested in the preceding paragraph should be taught in the appropriate subject at a time when a need for that skill appears. If such attention is given to study skills, junior high school pupils should be able to do their school work more effectively.

6. Conclusion

This summary of methods of directing learning activities in the junior high school is by no means complete. It presents only the most important developments in teaching methods. The experience-centered approach is by far the most significant of these developments. Although it is not as yet used extensively in the junior high schools, it has been gaining quite rapidly in influence and acceptance. We need to experiment with this approach and many others to develop the most effective teaching methods for the junior high school. Teaching methods are exceedingly important in the implementation of the basic philosophy of the junior high school.

Questions and Exercises

1. Describe in some detail each of the following approaches to teaching: (a) subject-centered, (b) activity-centered, and (c) experience-centered.
2. Select a subject, and explain in some detail how you might develop a unit of study in that subject employing one of the three approaches given in Question 1.
3. Select a unit of work in any subject and explain in some detail how you would plan that unit cooperatively with the pupils.
4. How would you help a class become a group? Be specific in your suggestions.

5. How would you develop democratic human relationships in the class-room? Be specific in your suggestions.

6. Explain how you can use the library most effectively as a source of learning materials in your subject.

7. What are the advantages of having separate study periods in the junior high school? What are the disadvantages? Which do you favor?

8. What should be the approach to home work in the junior high school? Substantiate your answer.

9. Develop a plan for teaching pupils how to study effectively for the subject you expect to teach. Be specific in this plan, showing the skills that need to be taught and how you expect to teach each one.

Chapter 10

MEETING INDIVIDUAL DIFFERENCES

Attention to the differing needs, interests, and abilities of individual pupils is as old as the junior high school itself. Almost every early writer on the subject stressed the meeting of individual differences as one of the major functions of the junior high school. But changes have taken place in our thinking with respect to the manner in which individual differences might be most effectively satisfied.

In the early junior high schools attention was given almost entirely to administrative practices that would make it possible to meet more effectively the individual differences among pupils. Such practices as homogeneous grouping, elective curriculums and courses, special classes for gifted and for slow-learning pupils, differentiated marking practices, and promotion by subject were emphasized. More recently, some educators have come to believe that, regardless of administrative arrangements, much of the individualization of teaching must be made through the materials and methods employed in the classroom. In other words, *it is as important, or more so, to work effectively with boys and girls in learning situations as it is to make administrative arrangements to care for the needs of the individual child.* In this chapter, both methods of teaching and administrative practices that provide for individual differences will be discussed.

1. KNOWING THE INDIVIDUAL PUPIL

Knowing the Pupils. The first step in employing effective methods of teaching for individualizing instruction is for the teacher to know much about his pupils. He must know each individual well—his psychological background, home background, previous achievement, interests, and any other information that may have a bearing on the child's work in school. Although the following list is by no means complete, it gives some indication of the types of information which every teacher should have about his pupils:

1. *Home and family backgrounds.* Should include information about the social-economic status of the family, language spoken in the

home, number of children, occupation of the father, and cultural background of the family.

2. *Psychological backgrounds.* Should include intelligence quotient, aptitudes for various school subjects, mental health, emotional adjustment, and relations with other pupils.

3. *Health and physical backgrounds.* Should include information about hearing, sight, posture, serious illness, and chronic disorders. In the last group, such disorders as epilepsy, diabetes, heart disease, and nervous difficulties are especially important.

4. *Educational and vocational interests.* Should include information about the child's interest in continuing in school, his probable educational goal after completing senior high school, and his present vocational interests.

5. *Cultural, social, recreational, and hobby interests.* Should include information about talent in music and art, reading interests, sports participation, creative hobbies, and participation in social activities.

6. *Out-of-school activities.* Should include information about the child's vacation activities, out-of-school employment, travel, and participation in civic and community organizations.

7. *Educational achievement and participation.* Should include information about previous marks, standard achievement test records, diagnostic test records, and participation in extraclass activities in school.

8. *Character, citizenship, and conduct.* Should include information about moral character, leadership qualities, participation in school service activities, and behavior in school.

9. *Social adjustment.* Should include information about relations with other pupils in school, ability to work cooperatively with others, ability to form friendships, and participation in school social functions.

Sources of Information About Pupils. Many sources of information about pupils are available to teachers. One of these is the records in the various school offices, including those of the principal, the guidance officer, and the nurse. In some schools, the information on these records is summarized and placed in the hands of all the teachers. Most often, however, the teacher is expected to come to the various offices and gather that information for his pupils. It is urgent that he do this early in the year, so that he may begin at once to use the information to meet the individual needs of pupils in his classes.

Another source of information is the pupil's previous teachers. The homeroom or core teacher is perhaps the best source of information because he should have had more contact with the pupil than others. It is well, however, for the present teacher of English to discuss the work of pupils with their previous teachers of English, and similarly for teachers of the other subjects. Although much of this may be done on an informal basis, in an occasional school arrangements are made for teachers of pupils for the current year to have conferences with previous teachers. In one school, a conference is arranged between sixth-grade teachers and the homeroom teachers of the incoming seventh-grade pupils, in order to give information to the junior high school teachers which cannot readily be placed on the school records.

The child's home is an important source of information about his backgrounds and interests. In some schools it is the practice to encourage teachers to visit the homes of pupils. In the junior high school, the homeroom teacher is the one who most commonly makes such visits, although teachers of home economics frequently do so too. Because it is difficult to visit the homes of all of their pupils, such visits are not often made by classroom teachers except in the case of pupils about whom they have some concern. Home visits should not be made only for the purpose of discussing problem cases with parents; they should be used early in the year as a means of gathering information concerning the interests and backgrounds of the child that may have a bearing on his work in school. Teachers also have an opportunity to meet parents in churches, civic organizations, and other community groups.

An excellent source of information about the pupil is the pupil himself. Early in the year, every teacher should use some devices for obtaining information about himself from the child. This is particularly important for two reasons: (1) certain interests and backgrounds of a child change so rapidly that information on the office records soon is out of date; and (2) each teacher may be interested in certain information that has a bearing on his own subject which may not be readily found in the office records. Devices used for this purpose include questionnaires, autobiographies, and interviews with the pupils. Particularly in the core classes where the number of pupils is fewer and the time permits, teachers have conferences early in the year with all pupils. Such conferences also serve another purpose; namely, they provide an avenue for establishing rapport between the teacher and the individual child.

Using Information About Pupils. Information about pupils may be used in a number of different ways by the teacher. For instance, information about sight and hearing may serve as a basis for seating pupils in the room, while other information may be used as a basis for guidance conferences. For the moment, however, we are concerned primarily with the uses the teachers may make of this information in meeting the needs, abilities, and interests of pupils in their classes through the teaching methods which they employ. A number of examples may serve to illustrate these uses.

Teachers of skill subjects such as the language arts, mathematics, and foreign languages need to have test information concerning the previous achievement of their pupils as a basis for individualized work. Sometimes this information may be used as a basis for arranging pupils in groups within a class and for selecting study and drill materials in these subjects. The interests of pupils are also of considerable value to the teacher for individualizing instruction. For instance, the teacher of English should know much about the interests of his pupils in hobbies, sports, music, and other cultural and recreational activities, as a basis for the oral and written work that they may do in his classes. The present vocational interests of pupils may also be capitalized upon for oral and written activities.

Information concerning the personal backgrounds of the child are of particular concern to the teacher as he tries to meet individual needs. The teacher should be informed about the child's willingness or reluctance to appear before a group in oral activities; he should know something about the reading materials which may be found in the child's home; and he should know about chronic disorders of his pupils which may have a bearing on the nature of their participation in class activities. As an example, a child who has a physical defect may be more reluctant to participate in an activity before the group than is true of other children. Similarly, the child who comes from a foreign-speaking family may have speech problems that should be given special attention by the teacher. In other words, almost every type of information about the child may give the teacher some indication of the class activities from which the child might profit most. It may also suggest a diplomatic approach to gain participation of the child in those activities.

2. METHODS OF TEACHING

Flexible Methods of Teaching. In individualizing instructional activities, it is particularly important that flexible methods of teaching be employed. There should be a variety of learning activities, so that pupils may find one or more that are particularly suited to their individual abilities, backgrounds, and interests. The number and nature of such activities will obviously vary from subject to subject and from unit to unit. In a literature unit, readings may be graduated according to various ability levels, projects may be suited to differing interests, and different types of oral and written activities may be provided. The spelling words may be so arranged that they include simple ones for the slow learners and more difficult ones for the rapid learners.

Furthermore, the approach that is used to teach spelling should give pupils of various ability levels an opportunity to move along at their own rate of speed. Similarly, in the mathematics class there should be drill materials that are appropriate for pupils who are at varying stages of mastery of the skills and problems concerned.

A second means of achieving flexibility in teaching methods is for the teacher to prepare plans which are always flexible in nature. In the older approach to planning, the teacher did all of his planning outside class by himself and brought it to the class in a form that was considered more or less final. Obviously such an approach to planning is too rigid and regimented to permit the flexibility that is desirable if pupil needs are to be met. All plans must be considered tentative, both at the beginning of a unit of work and also later on, so that adaptations and changes can be made to fit the needs and interests of various members of the group.

A third type of flexibility in methods is to use a sufficient variety of instructional material to reach all pupils. This means that there must be reading materials for all levels of reading ability and of a sufficient variety so that there are some which may reach the interests of all pupils. The same thing is true of audio-visual materials, community resources, pamphlet and other current materials, and various other teaching aids. In other words, the variety of teaching materials should recognize every level of ability and every type of interest that may be found in the group.

Unit Approach to Teaching. For many years the unit approach to planning and carrying on learning activities has been recognized as a desirable means of providing flexibility in the methods of teaching employed in the classroom. It is relatively easy to provide flexibility in methods through the unit approach partly because this is a long-term approach to learning and teaching. By planning learning activities several weeks ahead, it is easier for the teacher to make adaptations in learning activities, instructional materials, and methods of evaluation which are essential if the various pupil needs, interests, and abilities are to be met.

The fact that a teacher uses the unit approach does not necessarily mean that individualization of teaching will follow. For instance, a teacher may use a highly regimented preplanned subject-matter unit which has little more flexibility than day-by-day textbook teaching. The important thing is that the unit plan does make it easier to use a flexible approach to teaching which can more readily provide for individual differences. The following suggestions may be helpful in developing units to meet individual differences:

1. The teacher should be well informed concerning the various abilities, needs, and interests of pupils which may have a bearing on the unit which is to be planned.
2. The teacher should explore every possible source of instructional materials in order to gather a variety which will provide something for every pupil ability and interest.
3. The teacher should prepare as detailed a list as possible of various types of projects and activities which may be appropriate for pupils as they work on the unit.
4. The matter of tests, examinations, and informal means of evaluation should be studied for the unit in the light of the individual differences among the pupils.

Pupil Participation in Planning. The advantages of having pupils participate in planning a unit as a step toward individualizing instruction cannot be overemphasized. In fact, it is difficult to see how a teacher can be reasonably sure of meeting the interests of pupils without having them contribute their own ideas to the list of activities that are included in the unit. The teacher can become acquainted with interests of pupils primarily by giving them an opportunity to react to his suggestions for activities in the unit, by encouraging them to formulate suggestions of their own, and by deciding cooperatively with them upon the activities which may finally be included.

Pupils should not only participate in deciding upon learning activities, but they should also be encouraged to make suggestions about the instructional materials that may be appropriate. For instance, they may indicate resource people in the community whom they know and enjoy hearing; they may be familiar with various community agencies that have a contribution to make to the unit; they may have contacts through their parents with labor, industrial, and business agencies that have a bearing on the unit. In other ways, too, the broad contacts that pupils have in the community should make it possible for them to make a tremendous contribution to the list of instructional materials that are available. In such ways as these, individual differences may be met more effectively by having pupils participate in unit planning.

Grouping Within Classes. More and more in the junior high school, we are following a practice commonly employed in the elementary schools; namely, the grouping of pupils according to individual differences within classes. This grouping is usually on an informal basis as contrasted with the formal, regimented homogeneous grouping between sections. That is, the class works together much of the time as a total group, but the pupils may be grouped for instruction in such basic skills as reading and spelling.

The nature of these groups within classes is kept informal and flexible. Pupils may be placed in reading groups, but the composition of these groups is not necessarily rigid or in any sense permanent. For some reading activities, all pupils may actually work together as a total class group. For others, they may be kept in groups according to reading speed and comprehension, but with the pupils moved readily from group to group as their skills improve. In such flexible grouping within a class, the pupils do not become as clearly identified with a given group as when they are placed in different sections according to ability. At the same time, in the hands of a skillful teacher, the flexible approach to grouping within a class can be effective in meeting the abilities of individual pupils without the undesirable features that sometimes are associated with ability grouping in different sections.

It should be emphasized that merely placing pupils in different groups within a class does not, in itself, lead to better individualized instruction. The teacher must then locate instructional materials that are appropriate for the various ability levels; he must prepare appropriate drill materials; and he must vary the learning activities from one group to another. It is the adaptation of methods to the needs and abilities of the various groups that is important. The device of grouping itself is merely a means to an end.

Changed Emphasis on Remedial Instruction. In the last decade or so, our attitude concerning the purpose and place of remedial instruction in the junior high school has undergone some changes. There was a time when any pupil who was below so-called grade standards was considered to be in need of remedial instruction. Today we are placing more emphasis on a developmental, rather than a remedial, program in the basic skills. For instance, we feel now that an effective program of instruction in reading and arithmetic should bring pupils to a standard of work that is appropriate for their individual ability, rather than bringing all of them to a uniform grade standard. Pupils in the lowest fourth of the total group in ability may never be brought up to the grade median in the skill subjects unless other important aspects of the instructional program are neglected. Similarly, pupils who are above average in abilities should be expected to achieve much better than the accepted grade norms. The developmental approach emphasized today in teaching the basic skills suggests that all pupils should be brought to a standard of achievement which is appropriate for the abilities which they possess.

At the same time, there will always be some remedial problems. These will concern, however, primarily those youngsters who are not doing as well as their ability permits. For these pupils, some special instruction should be given to help them improve in the skills in which they are deficient. The following suggestions may be helpful in doing this:

1. Pupils who are not doing as well as they should may be identified through appropriate achievement tests.
2. A thorough study of pupils in need of remedial help should be made, including a complete case study of their psychological and emotional backgrounds, native talents and abilities, previous achievement in school, and out-of-school backgrounds.
3. A program of instruction should be provided, either in the regular classes or in special classes created for this purpose, to meet the needs of the individual pupils concerned. In some cases, individual and clinical help may be necessary. In others, the work may be carried on in class groups with other pupils. In any case, this instruction should be given only as long as it seems appropriate in helping the child remove his learning deficiencies.

3. HOMOGENEOUS GROUPING

Development of Homogeneous Grouping. In order to understand the various practices, the advantages, and the disadvantages of homogeneous grouping in the junior high school today, it may be helpful to know something about its development. Homogeneous grouping was one of the first administrative practices that was clearly associated with the junior high school. Like departmentalized teaching and promotion by subject, it early came to be considered one of the basic characteristics of the junior high school. There was a reason for the early interest in homogeneous grouping. As has already been mentioned, meeting individual differences was one of the purposes emphasized most strongly for the introduction of the junior high school. Homogeneous grouping seemed to provide a simple and easily administered plan for meeting individual differences.

Homogeneous grouping was introduced in the decade before 1920, when the entire program of the secondary school was clearly subject-centered. It seemed to provide an easy way of giving pupils the precise dosage of subject matter which they, with their differences in ability, would be able to master. The idea immediately appealed to junior high school educators over the country, with the result that many faculties became enthusiastic about the development of a plan for homogeneous grouping.

During the 1920's, the peak of interest in homogeneous grouping was reached. "How to group" was the subject for discussion at educational conferences, in the professional periodicals, in books on junior high school education, and in professional courses. Each school tried to outdo its neighbor in developing an unusual plan for homogeneous grouping. During this decade, few educators seriously questioned the advisability of such grouping, devoting most of their attention to the manner in which it should be carried on.

Obviously, such universal enthusiasm for any practice could not continue long unquestioned. Soon some educators began to doubt the advisability of homogeneous grouping, at least in the extremely rigid and regimented form in which it was practiced in many schools. The doubts about homogeneous grouping were increased during the 1930's with the appearance of several publications on the subject of mental hygiene in the schools. Principals and teachers began to feel more responsibility for the mental and emotional health of their pupils. Some educators suggested that homogeneous grouping, especially in the extreme form in which it was used in some schools, created pupil tensions that were in conflict with the practices desirable for good mental health. Consequently, some reaction set in against the practice of homogeneous grouping. To this day, however, such grouping continues to be used in one form or another in many junior high schools.

Purpose of Homogeneous Grouping. It might be well to give a definition for homogeneous grouping. *By homogeneous grouping is meant the arrangement of pupils into groups for instructional purposes in such a way that the members of any one group are reasonably alike in ability, interests, educational or vocational goals, or some other factor of importance to the learning situation.* The informal grouping which is practiced within a class, as is so commonly done for certain skills in the elementary school, is ordinarily not thought of as homogeneous grouping. Rather, homogeneous grouping means that pupils, on the basis of some criteria, are placed in different classes for instructional purposes.

The purpose of homogeneous grouping, obviously, is to make it easier to meet the various needs, interests, and abilities of individual pupils. Putting it another way, homogeneous grouping should make it easier for the teacher to individualize instruction. Through such grouping, an effort is made to reduce the range of differences in the needs, interests, and abilities of individual pupils which are ordinarily found within any one class group.

Types of Homogeneous Grouping. There are several types of homogeneous grouping in the junior high school. *The most common one is to group pupils according to their ability to do school work.* Where this plan is employed, pupils are arranged into class groups on the basis of such measures as the intelligence quotient, mental age, school marks, and estimates of pupil abilities prepared by the teachers. This plan for homogeneous grouping is easily administered and, in many schools, has proved very satisfactory, particularly in the so-called academic subjects.

A second plan for homogeneous grouping is based on the elective courses or curriculums in which pupils are enrolled. Pupils are grouped in terms of such curriculums as college preparatory, general, commercial, vocational, or homemaking. This plan is rather common in sections of the United States, such as New England, where the college-preparatory function of the high school is strong. Homogeneous grouping based on elective courses and curriculums, however, is not very appropriate in the junior high school. It has never been widely employed in the seventh and eighth grades; and, since specialization in the school program is being postponed more and more to the senior high school, this plan of grouping probably will be discontinued in the ninth grade as well.

A third plan of homogeneous grouping, quite prevalent in the elementary school, has not yet gained wide acceptance in the junior high school; namely, *the grouping of pupils according to reading ability.* Usually this plan gives some consideration to factors other than reading skills, such as the social and emotional adjustment of the child, but the primary criterion for grouping is the reading ability of pupils as measured by standardized tests.

There are distinct advantages in grouping pupils according to reading ability. First, at the junior high school level the pupil's reading ability, perhaps more than any other factor, determines his ability to do school work, especially in the academic subjects. Second, it is easier to adapt study materials to the various ability groups in terms of reading levels. And, third, pupils and parents alike are more willing to accept such a criterion for grouping without prejudice, because it does not seem to carry the same stigma as such criteria as marks or measures of intelligence.

Since by far the most common plan for homogeneous grouping is the one based on the ability of pupils to do school work, the discussion which follows will be concerned chiefly with that plan. Most of the research on the subject of homogeneous grouping has been concerned with those plans for grouping which are based on measures of pupil ability. Much of the thinking and the research on this subject may be applied, of course, to all types of homogeneous grouping.

Extent of Ability Grouping. Even though there may have been some reaction against the highly regimented plan of ability grouping so common two or three decades ago, ability grouping in one form or another continues to be widely practiced in the junior high school. Two studies made by the authors of grouping practices in the junior high school, the first in 1939 and the second in 1954, seem to indicate, however, that grouping may not be quite so popular as it has been in the past. For instance, in 1939 more than two-thirds of the schools all over the country to which checklists were sent had some form of grouping. In a similar checklist study in 1954, however, only half of the schools continue to have ability grouping in some form. The greatest decline seems to be in the practice of having classes *in all subjects* grouped according to ability. The data presented in the following table indicate the percentages of junior high schools employing various grouping practices in 1939 and in 1954.

Grouping Practices	1939	1954
Classes in some subjects according to ability	36%	31%
Classes in all subjects according to ability	22%	11%
Classes according to ability with different groupings for different subjects	11%	8%
Groups within classes according to ability	14%	16%
Classes arranged without reference to ability	30%	49%

The placing of pupils in remedial classes, however, continues to grow as a grouping practice. Two-thirds of the schools in the 1954 study have such classes. Most of them are in reading, but a fairly large number of schools also have remedial classes in arithmetic. Remedial classes are somewhat different from ability grouping in the usual sense, because presumably pupils are placed in such classes in terms of a present deficiency in a subject or skill but may be returned to the regular classes when that deficiency has been removed.

Desirability of Ability Grouping. The desirability of ability grouping has been argued vigorously pro and con since it was first introduced into the secondary schools several decades ago. Even among the schools that employ this practice, there is little agreement regarding its desirability. As far back as 1932, when a study of ability grouping was made as a part of the National Survey of Secondary Education, only a third of the junior high schools where ability grouping was employed felt that it met with "unusual success." [1]

---

[1] Roy O. Billett, *Provision for Individual Differences, Marking and Promotion*, National Survey of Secondary Education, Monograph No. 13, United States Office of Education Bulletin No. 17 (Washington, D.C.: Government Printing Office, 1932), p. 48.

Controversy over the desirability of ability grouping has centered particularly around two issues: *first, does it have an undesirable effect on the mental and emotional health of the pupils; and, second, does it result in a more effective learning situation?* Disagreement has been especially heated with respect to the first issue. The opponents of ability grouping have contended that it places a definite "label" on pupils in terms of mental ability; that it develops attitudes of superiority on the part of the bright pupils, while it unduly discourages the slow; that it leads to the development of cliques and castes in school; and that it places undue emphasis on scholastic ability as compared with other qualities that are desirable or essential for happiness and success in life.

On the other hand, the proponents of ability grouping hold that the effect on pupil attitudes is far more detrimental if superior, average, and dull pupils are placed in competition with each other in the same groups. They contend that the superior pupils develop undesirable attitudes toward others in their classes who do not perform well in their work; that slow pupils become discouraged when their performance fails to measure up to that of the better pupils; and that slow pupils hesitate to participate in the presence of the bright pupils.

Conclusions from Studies. The controversy regarding ability grouping has led to numerous studies of various aspects of the problem. Most of these studies were made some years ago and tend to emphasize the achievement of pupils, particularly in the subject-matter skills. They lead to the following conclusions.

1. It is possible to group pupils for instructional purposes so that classes are more similar in ability in a given subject or group of subjects than they would otherwise be, but it is not possible to arrange pupils into groups which are completely homogeneous.
2. Achievement is slightly higher in homogeneous than in heterogeneous groups. Homogeneous grouping appears to be most effective with pupils who are below average, next with average pupils, and least with pupils who are above average. But the evidence regarding the effect of grouping on achievement is not at all conclusive.
3. Following the introduction of ability grouping in a school, there has usually been a reduction in the percentage of failures.

Some early studies were also made regarding the effect of ability grouping on the mental health of the child. The evidence on this point, however, is meager and inconclusive. The studies tend to show that the effects of ability grouping upon slow children probably are no more harmful than placing them in classes where they have little chance to equal the achievement of the other pupils. The experience of educators with ability grouping, however, leads many to the conclusion that certainly in some cases the attitudes of both bright and slow-learning pupils have been adversely affected by ability grouping.

Effective Practices in Ability Grouping. Because ability grouping is used so widely in the junior high school, it seems appropriate to give some suggestions concerning the practices which have been found most desirable. Whether one approves of ability grouping or not, it certainly seems to be true that *its effectiveness depends in large part upon the manner in which it is administered and employed.* The studies of ability grouping, as well as the experience of teachers and administrators, substantiate this general conclusion. It should be emphasized also that, from the standpoint of individualizing instruction, ability grouping in and of itself has little merit. *The important thing is what teachers do to individualize instruction within the various groups, once they are arranged according to pupil ability levels.* In other words, it is the *method* of teaching employed in the classroom which is of most importance, not the particular grouping device.

On the basis of studies and experience, it is suggested that ability grouping is likely to prove most satisfactory when practices such as the following are employed:

1. Pupils should be grouped separately for each subject rather than be placed in the same groups for all subjects. If it is not feasible to arrange different groups in all subjects, at least there should be different groups for the so-called academic as compared with the nonacademic subjects.
2. A combination of several criteria is better as a basis for grouping pupils than one criterion alone. The criteria that have been shown to be particularly satisfactory are the intelligence quotient or mental age, school marks, and ratings of pupils by their teachers.
3. The social adjustment of the individual pupil should be given serious consideration in the arrangement of ability groups. A child who is unhappy because of the group in which he is placed may lose far more than he will gain by being placed with pupils of his own ability level.
4. There is little advantage in arranging pupils into more than three broad ability groupings—above average, average, and below average, with a considerable majority in average groups.
5. The personnel of the various groups should not be changed too frequently because pupils so often encounter difficulties when they shift from group to group. Preferably, groups should be re-

arranged only at the beginning of a school term. However, it should be possible at any time during the term to shift pupils who are seriously misplaced.

6. Teachers should modify their teaching plans for each of the various ability groups. This adaptation should be made in subject content, study materials, and instructional methods. The nature of the work, as well as the amount to be covered, should be modified from group to group.

7. Teachers should individualize the work within each ability group as well as differentiate it for the different groups. This is essential because no group is ever completely homogeneous in abilities, needs, and interests.

Practices Which Avoid Undesirable Pupil Attitudes. Experience with ability grouping has demonstrated some basis for the charge that it leads to the development of undesirable pupil attitudes. Some grouping practices accentuate this problem while others tend to relieve it. For instance, in some schools far too much attention is focused on ability grouping in the thinking of both teachers and pupils. Frequently this is due to such practices as the use of symbols to designate the ability level of groups, careless remarks by teachers concerning the abilities of pupils in certain groups, and similar practices which tend to "label" pupils both in their own thinking and in that of their classmates. Practices such as the following are suggested to avoid the development of undesirable pupil attitudes as a result of ability grouping.

1. *Pupils preferably should be grouped heterogeneously in some places in the school program to avoid being identified with a certain ability level.* This is especially desirable in schools where the pupils are placed in the same ability groups for most or all of their courses. For instance, heterogeneous grouping may be employed in the home room.

2. *Letters, numbers, or other symbols should not be used to designate the ability levels of the various groups because they tend to "label" the group and all its members in the eyes of both pupils and teachers.* If symbols are necessary in the office for administrative purposes, they should never be placed on pupils' program cards, class schedules, or other items that reach the pupil, nor should such symbols be used by teachers in the presence of the pupils.

3. *Teachers should avoid making any reference in the presence of pupils to the ability level of the various groups.* This is fully as important with the high as with the low groups. Thoughtless remarks by teachers who become impatient with the slow groups are all too common.

4. *Pupils should be shifted from one ability group to another at a time and in a manner that does not attract too much attention.* For instance, changes should preferably be made at the beginning of a school term when there are ordinarily many shifts in the personnel of the various groups for reasons other than ability. Exceptions to this rule can be made for pupils who are seriously misplaced, either in terms of ability or social adjustment.

5. *Pupils should never be shifted from one group to another as a reward or punishment, either for achievement or conduct.* This practice tends to emphasize any stigma that may be attached to the low groups. Furthermore, it tends to make the various groups less homogeneous so far as the learning abilities of pupils are concerned. There is no justification for this practice.

Desirable Approach to Ability Grouping. Up to this point, the present discussion of grouping has centered largely around the current thinking concerning it and the ways in which it might be employed effectively in those schools which have it. Because of the controversy that persists concerning its desirability, the authors would like to state their own position with respect to ability grouping.

There is little question in the mind of the authors that the highly regimented form of ability grouping so common two or three decades ago, but still practiced in many junior high schools, is not desirable. It seems to make a fetish of the device of grouping rather than emphasizing the purposes that it is designed to serve. At the same time, those educators who insist that ability grouping in no form should be employed in the junior high school also seem to be taking an extreme position. It is true that the informal grouping practices within a class in the elementary school seem to work satisfactorily there. It may also be true, however, that in the junior high school the arrangement of pupils in groups according to ability at times and for certain purposes may prove desirable.

It does not seem appropriate, therefore, to make a sweeping conclusion that one is for or against ability grouping. Rather, it is a matter of developing a sound approach to grouping practices. The following approach is suggested.

1. *The prevailing social situation in the school should be a normal one, with pupils of all abilities, interests, and backgrounds having many contacts with each other.* This approach certainly means that any evidence of ability grouping in the homeroom, in assemblies, clubs, student council, and other extraclass activities is inappropriate. Furthermore, it suggests that in most classes and most subjects ability grouping should not be employed. In a normal social situation, pupils have sufficiently free social contact

with each other so that they may make their own friends and develop their own social acquaintances without the interference of a system imposed by the school.

2. *It seems true, however, that in certain situations and for certain purposes ability grouping may be desirable.* These situations vary from school to school, both because of the nature of the student body and the skills of the teachers in individualizing instruction within heterogeneous groups. Consequently, one cannot list certain subjects in which ability grouping would be desirable in every school. Some examples, however, may be given of situations in which ability grouping may be particularly appropriate. For instance, in ninth-grade mathematics it is usually desirable to group pupils according to ability for algebra, general mathematics, business mathematics, and other mathematics classes. In reading and the other language arts, it is also sometimes much easier to meet the individual needs of pupils by placing them in groups according to their abilities in these subjects. Similarly, ability grouping may be used appropriately in a music organization, sports activities, and other activities where special talents, skills, and backgrounds are required. In any case, however, such grouping should be employed in terms of the pupils' needs in a given subject or activity rather than in terms of some over-all criteria which are applied in blanket form to the entire school program.

3. *Ability grouping serves less purpose in core classes, common learnings classes, and other class arrangements in which pupils take several subjects and spend several periods with one teacher.* As in the elementary school, the core class makes it possible for the teacher to do informal grouping within a class, and thereby satisfactorily meet the needs of pupils in the various subject areas. It may be true, also, that the teachers in these classes have developed more skill in working with pupils in small groups. Certainly, the core teacher finds it easier to become well acquainted with the needs, interests, and abilities of his pupils. Consequently, the core classes make it possible for teachers to meet individual differences more easily than in other classes.

4. *The methods of teaching that are used should receive more emphasis in individualizing instruction than such administrative practices as ability grouping.* This has been the emphasis for years in the elementary school. In the secondary school, however, we have devoted much of our energy to developing administrative devices for meeting the different needs, interests, and abilities of pupils. Experience has shown that it cannot be done primarily in that way. *It is time to give more attention to the ways in which teachers should work with pupils in the classroom as a means of effectively meeting the individual differences among those pupils.* Until that is done, we cannot expect to achieve satisfactorily this function of the junior high school.

4. Provision for Gifted Pupils

Pupils Who Need Unusual Experiences. There are pupils who differ so markedly from the average child in abilities, needs, and interests that it is difficult to provide adequately for their education through the usual methods for individualizing instruction. Some of these pupils, such as the blind, the deaf, the crippled, and the feeble-minded, are ordinarily placed in special schools or in special classes where suitable learning experiences can best be provided for them. There are at least two groups of exceptional children, however, who are kept in the regular schools, where special provision must be made to meet their needs. These pupils are the intellectually gifted and the slow learners. In any adequate program for individualizing instruction these two groups of pupils must be given special consideration.

Neglect of the Gifted Child. The child with decidedly superior ability is indeed the forgotten child in the secondary school of today. No other group of exceptional children is similarly neglected. For the mentally retarded pupil, there are opportunity rooms, special teachers and courses, and study materials suited to his interests and abilities. For the blind, the feeble-minded, and the deaf, there are special classes or separate schools. Even the truant and the chronic trouble-maker are granted special consideration in the instructional program of many schools. But the occasional child who has outstanding intellectual ability is usually given an educational experience that differs little, if at all, from that of his less talented fellows. The late Professor Leta S. Hollingworth of Teachers College, Columbia University, who devoted many years to the study of gifted children, some time ago summarized the situation in the schools with respect to these children as follows:

> Children testing at or above 140 I. Q. are unrecognized by the school, are unprovided for in mass education, are functioning far below their mental level in the elementary school, yet are maintaining themselves scholastically and socially without giving much trouble to either school or society. They earn high "marks" without effort and waste one-half or more of their time during the school day either in idleness or in the performance of routine tasks and errands, under the general concept of "helping the teacher." [2]

Strangely enough, the exceptional qualities possessed by the gifted child are the very reason for his being overlooked. The mentally retarded child, the truant, the blind, and the deaf—all of them have

[2] National Society for the Study of Education, *Intelligence: Its Nature and Nurture,* Part I (Thirty-Ninth Yearbook) (Bloomington, Ill.: Public School Publishing Co., 1940), p. 66. Quoted by permission of the Society.

characteristics which soon bring them to the attention of the teacher. But the ability possessed by the gifted child enables him to do so well at school that he apparently presents no peculiar problem. *There are, consequently, two important things that should be included in an educational program for the gifted child: (1) a well-developed plan for locating those pupils who are so gifted that they need special attention in school, and (2) an organized program of learning experiences which are a real challenge to the superior abilities of these pupils.*

Characteristics of the Gifted Pupils. Although it is difficult to define precisely the nature of the gifted child, there are some characteristics which he is generally considered to possess. His most distinguishing characteristic, according to both popular and authoritative belief, is superior intelligence. Terman and Burks, for instance, state that those children with an I. Q. of 130 to 140 or more "are sufficiently unlike average children to need special educational opportunities."[3] In the Cleveland schools, pupils with an I. Q. of 120 or more are eligible for special classes for gifted pupils.[4] The practice in Baltimore is to examine the records of all pupils with an I. Q. of 110 or more, in the belief that many of them may have special abilities which justify giving them an enriched program.[5] Although there is not complete agreement by authorities concerning the precise dividing line between the intelligence of gifted and nongifted children, it may be suggested that all children in the junior high school with an I. Q. of 125 to 130 or more should be studied to locate those who should have educational opportunities different from those of the average child.

Contrary to popular belief, the gifted pupil is also superior in qualities other than intelligence. Instead of being small and puny, socially maladjusted, and of a nervous temperament, intellectually gifted children, on the average, are slightly superior in these respects. More specifically, studies of the characteristics of intellectually gifted children show that, as a group, they are above average in height, weight, and other physical health; they are superior in character qualities, personality traits, and social intelligence; and they are more likely than average children to become leaders in school activities.[6] Though it may not be important from an educational standpoint, there is even

[3] Carl Murchison, ed., *Handbook of Child Psychology* (2d ed.; Worcester, Mass.: Clark University Press, 1933), p. 774.

[4] Merle R. Sumption, *Three Hundred Gifted Children* (New York: World Book Co., 1941), p. 48.

[5] Charles F. Willis, "Aims For the Education of Gifted Children in the Elementary School," *Baltimore Bulletin of Education*, XVIII (September-October, 1940), 3.

[6] National Society for the Study of Education, *Intelligence: Its Nature and Nurture*, Part I (Thirty-Ninth Yearbook) (Bloomington, Ill.: Public School Publishing Co., 1940), pp. 221-27.

some evidence from at least one study that gifted children are more attractive in appearance than intellectually average children.[7] It is exceedingly important that all these superior qualities be taken into consideration in planning an educational program for gifted pupils.

Practices for Meeting Needs of Gifted Pupils. A number of practices are employed in the junior high schools for meeting the needs of gifted or decidedly superior pupils. In the survey of 370 schools by the authors, the following practices were reported from the percentage of schools indicated:

Given special opportunities or enriched experiences in regular classes	35%
Given special responsibilities in extraclass activities	23%
Given special responsibilities in regular classes	20%
Placed in special classes for decidedly superior pupils	13%
Given no special attention	7%
Other practices	2%

Acceleration of Gifted Pupils. The oldest plan for modifying the school program to meet the needs of gifted pupils is to accelerate their progress through school. Acceleration is based in part on the assumption that there is a more or less fixed body of subject matter to be mastered at each grade level, and that, since the gifted child learns more readily than the average child, he should proceed more rapidly with the mastery of that subject matter and the completion of the school program.

Three plans for acceleration have been rather widely employed in the junior high school: (1) to have gifted pupils carry extra courses; (2) to have them take the usual number of courses, but to complete those courses more rapidly; and (3) to organize a special curriculum, open only to gifted pupils, which provides for accelerated progress. The first plan is the simplest to administer because it involves little or no reorganization of the program of the school. Under this plan, the gifted pupil takes the same courses as the average pupil, but he carries more than the prescribed number of courses at one time. Consequently, he completes the total curriculum more rapidly than his less able classmates.

The second plan, to have gifted pupils take the usual courses but complete them more rapidly, and thus go through school in less time, requires some administrative adjustments, but it involves no serious modification of the curriculum itself. Like the first plan, it assumes that the gifted child should study the same things as the average child,

---

[7] *Ibid.*, p. 222

but that he should master those things more rapidly and study them at an earlier age.

The third plan for acceleration—the organization of a special curriculum—recognizes some differences in the educational needs of gifted pupils other than the length of time they should take to complete the school program. Where this plan is employed, a special curriculum is usually developed which provides for the adaptation of both subject content and teaching method. But, like the other plans, the primary purpose of the special curriculum is to enable the gifted pupil to accelerate his progress through school.

The special-curriculum plan has been introduced particularly in the large cities where there is a sufficiently large number of gifted pupils to justify such a curriculum and a special staff trained for this work. Baltimore, Maryland, for instance, has had a special curriculum since 1902 whereby superior pupils are able to complete in two years the equivalent of seventh-, eighth-, and ninth-grade work.[8] In Baltimore, pupils selected for this program are sent to a special school where, under the direction of specially trained teachers, they participate in a program developed primarily to suit the needs, interests, and abilities of intellectually superior children.

In the junior high schools of New York City, pupils with I. Q.'s of 130 or more and sufficient maturity, are placed in Special Progress Classes where they pursue a special curriculum. The pupils in these classes may complete the work of the three junior high school grades in two years. Moreover, there is every encouragement for teachers of these classes to adapt the curriculum to the needs and abilities of the pupils, with the result that opportunities for an enriched program are combined with acceleration. In New York, the pupils in the Special Progress Classes continue in the regular schools, and have a part in the life of the school much like other pupils.

Enrichment for Gifted Pupils. The objection by some educators to acceleration as a means of meeting the needs of gifted pupils has resulted in the introduction of another practice for this purpose: namely, *the development of a program of enriched learning experiences for gifted pupils through adaptation of the usual content, materials, and methods of instruction, but with no reduction in the time required to complete the program.* Like the accelerated program, the enriched curriculum is based on the assumption that the needs of the intellectually gifted child are different from those of his less talented fellows. There is a fundamental difference, however, between these

[8] Florence R. Lane, "Acceleration in the Junior High School—Past and Present," *Baltimore Bulletin of Education*, XVIII (September-October, 1940), 32-33.

two approaches to the problem of adapting the school program to the needs of gifted pupils. The accelerated program, for instance, is concerned primarily with hurrying the gifted child through the school program because he can learn more rapidly than the average child. *The enriched curriculum, however, is based on the assumption that the nature of his learning experiences, rather than the speed with which he completes them, is of paramount importance to the educational growth of the gifted child.* Consequently, in the enriched program, emphasis is placed on providing learning experiences which are suited to the interests, the needs, and the superior abilities of the gifted child.

There are numerous ways of enriching the school program for the gifted child. The more common ones may be summarized as follows:

1. Enrichment through a special curriculum taught to gifted children in segregated groups
2. Enrichment through adaptation of the instructional program within the regular classes
3. Enrichment through special activities and responsibilities for gifted children in the homeroom, the administration of the school, and extraclass activities

Enrichment in Special Classes. The first of these plans—a special curriculum taught in special classes—is perhaps the most effective arrangement for providing an enriched program for gifted children. In the special class, the teacher has more freedom to develop learning experiences that are suited to the peculiar needs, interests, and abilities of these pupils. The chief difficulty with special classes is the fact that they are ordinarily inadvisable except in large communities and large schools. If we assume that approximately 1 to 2 per cent of the pupils are sufficiently superior to be placed in such classes, it is ordinarily not feasible to organize them in schools with an enrollment of less than 1,200 to 1,500 pupils.

The Major Work Program in Cleveland, first introduced in the elementary schools in 1921, and later extended to the junior and senior high schools, is an example of an enriched program offered in special classes.[9] In the Cleveland program, pupils with an I. Q. of 120 or more may be segregated in classes under specially trained teachers. In the Major Work classes, the pupils are given a greater variety of activities, more challenging learning situations, and a reduced amount of drill and memory work. Not only are the teaching methods and subject content in these classes adapted to the abilities and needs of the

[9] Sumption, *op. cit.*, chap. ii.

pupils, but there is also considerable modification in the instructional materials, the type of classroom equipment and furniture, and the organization and arrangement of the classroom. The Cleveland plan has been very satisfactory as a means of meeting the needs, abilities, and interests of the gifted child.

One serious objection to special classes for gifted pupils is that they may set the pupils apart from the rest of the school. If that occurs, it is indeed unfortunate both for the social situation in the school as a whole and for the relationship of the gifted pupils with their fellows. The gifted pupils in later life will not be entirely segregated from the rest of society. In fact, if they are to use their talents effectively in the professions, business, government, and industry, they must understand, appreciate, and work with people of a variety of backgrounds and ability levels. *Every effort should therefore be made to see that some of the activities of pupils in the special classes are well integrated with the life of the school as a whole.* One plan is to place these pupils in heterogeneous homeroom groups and have them take some of their subjects in the regular classes. Certainly, in the extraclass activities of the school, the gifted pupils should participate according to their interests and talents with all other pupils. Some of the dangers of special classes for gifted pupils can be avoided if adequate precautions are taken.

Enrichment in Regular Classes. Although enrichment is more easily provided in special classes, some adaptation to the needs of gifted pupils also can be made in the work of the regular classes. The more common practices for this purpose include special projects, additional readings, leadership responsibilities in group projects, and responsibility for certain matters of classroom administration and routine.

In the regular classes, teachers frequently challenge the talents of superior and gifted pupils by urging them to engage in optional activities that are beyond the minimum assignments demanded of all pupils. These activities usually consist of additional readings, extra problems, more exercises, or special projects. *It is important to realize, however, that additional work does not necessarily constitute enrichment.* In fact, if it is more work of the same kind, it may actually prove a waste of time for the gifted child. The child who learns quickly needs less, rather than more, activities of the type demanded of his slower-learning classmates. *Supplementary learning activities assigned to the gifted child should be of such a type as to present a challenge to his superior abilities which is not possible in the regular work of the class.*

The monitorial plan is still used occasionally in a limited form to keep superior and gifted children busy in regular classes. Under this plan, the gifted pupil assists the slow-learning ones with their work. Although there may be justification for this practice in some i stances, it should not be employed under the guise of enrichment. Tl is practice no doubt is of help to the teacher and the slow-learning pupils, but more often than not it contributes little to the educational growth of the gifted child.

Enrichment Through Extraclass Activities. In most junior high schools, the program of pupil activities outside the classroom offers splendid opportunities for enriching the learning experiences of the gifted child. These responsibilities may take many different forms. The gifted child may assume administrative responsibilities in the homeroom, the cafeteria, the library, or the offices of supervisory and administrative officials; he may participate in more extraclass activities than other pupils; or he may assume some responsibility for leadership in the planning of those activities.

There is the danger, however, that gifted pupils will be exploited and their time wasted by giving them minor responsibilities which constitute little more than "busy work." Whatever extraclass responsibilities are employed for enrichment should be such that they will challenge the superior talents of gifted pupils and make a significant contribution to their educational growth and development.

Instructional Methods for Gifted Children. The learning experiences for this group can be greatly enriched through the use of appropriate teaching devices, techniques, and methods. Not only *where* and *what* they are taught, but *how* they are taught should be considered in developing a program for the gifted pupils.

Instructional methods and techniques which are especially appropriate for gifted pupils are those which emphasize: (1) pupil participation in planning learning activities; (2) pupil leadership in carrying on these activities; (3) creative work by the pupils; (4) freedom for pupils to select individual projects; (5) a variety of instructional materials; (6) problems and projects demanding abstract and critical thinking; (7) individual and group oral activities; (8) a minimum of repetition and drill work; (9) freedom from unnecessary administrative restrictions; and (10) pupil leadership and responsibility in organizing the class and in discharging classroom routine. A learning situation with these characteristics, under the supervision of an intelligent, resourceful, and stimulating teacher, should prove challenging to the superior abilities and the peculiar interests and needs of the gifted child.

The Gifted Child in Medium-Sized and Small Schools. In communities that are sufficiently large to provide special classes for gifted children, the needs of these pupils are not likely to be overlooked by an alert administrative and supervisory staff. That is not true, however, in medium-sized and small school systems. In these systems there may be such a small number of gifted children that they will be entirely overlooked. The administrative and supervisory authorities in medium-sized and small systems must, therefore, have a definite plan for locating gifted children and for meeting their peculiar needs. The following suggestions may be helpful for developing such a plan.

1. *A teacher or a faculty committee should be assigned the responsibility of locating gifted children and planning activities to meet their needs.* It is desirable for the teacher or some member of the committee to have special preparation for this work.

2. *The special teacher or committee should study carefully all pupils in school to locate those who may be considered to be intellectually gifted.* The I. Q. or M. A. is probably the first criterion that should be used for this purpose. But there are others, including previous achievement in school, teachers' estimates of the pupils' abilities, information on personality and character qualities, and evaluations of the pupils' mental and physical health.

3. *The special teacher or committee should prepare an individual program of enrichment for each gifted child.* These programs should be developed after discussions with the principal, counselors, nurse, school or family physician, classroom teachers, and parents. Provisions such as the following may be included in the various programs for gifted children: (a) arrangements for carrying extra courses; (b) special work within the regular classes; (c) special responsibilities in the homeroom; (d) more participation in extraclass activities than for average children; (e) responsibilities in administration of the school; and (f) individual help outside regular classes.

4. *The special teacher or committee should be responsible for implementing each special program and for planning adequate follow-up activities.* This should include assistance to the various teachers in planning special learning activities, a periodic evaluation of each pupil's progress, occasional consultation with the child's parents, frequent study of his social, personality, and character development, and periodic health examinations.

5. *The special program for each gifted child should be revised periodically.* This should be done probably once a semester for the main features of the plan, oftener for the details.

It cannot be overemphasized that the utmost care should be taken by the teachers responsible for planning these special programs. Spectacular programs certainly should be avoided. Furthermore, it would be unfortunate indeed if too much attention, both on the part of the pupils and the faculty, were directed toward the gifted children and their special educational activities. Both teachers and parents must realize that, in planning and carrying on these programs, the best interests of the child should be the primary consideration.

5. PROVISION FOR THE MENTALLY RETARDED CHILD

Problem of the Mentally Retarded Child. Whereas, until recent years, the gifted child has been almost forgotten in the educational program of the school, just the opposite has been true of the mentally retarded child. Since the beginning of organized education, in one way or another, he has been the object of special attention. In the earliest schools, this attention often took the form of punishment for not "knowing his lessons," with the dunce cap, detention during recess or after school, or even a whipping being used to stimulate the child's learning. Although the means of meeting his peculiar needs have changed considerably since this early period of American education, the mentally retarded child has continued to the present time to be an object of special consideration and attention.

It is generally conceded by authorities on the subject that about 2 per cent of the school population "have definite mental limitations which are so extreme that their failure to succeed in school with average children is conspicuous." [10] A few authorities would place the proportion somewhat higher. If we accept the 2 per cent figure, the mentally retarded group will not be particularly large in any one school. But for the nation as a whole, these children constitute a sufficiently large group to be of serious concern to both educator and layman.

Many children of low intelligence, of course, will not reach the junior high school. Some will be sent to special institutions; others will be retained in the special rooms at the elementary school level or will be sent to special intermediate schools; while some will have reached the compulsory attendance age limit or have withdrawn from school for various reasons. Consequently, the proportion of the junior high school population which is so mentally retarded as to need special education may be smaller than in the elementary school. Nevertheless, these pupils constitute a sufficiently difficult educational problem to deserve special consideration in the junior high school program.

Intelligence of Mentally Retarded Pupils. Low mental ability is obviously the most distinguishing characteristic of the mentally re-

---

[10] Christine P. Ingram, *Education of the Slow-Learning Child* (New York: The Ronald Press Co., 1953), p. 5.

tarded child. Authoritative opinion, as well as administrative practice, tends to place children with I. Q.'s between 50 and 75 or 80 in the mentally retarded groups. Professor Arch O. Heck, of Ohio State University, who has made a nationwide survey of special classes for mentally retarded children, states that, although practice varies, those with I. Q.'s from 50 to 70 or 80 are usually admitted to the special classes.[11] Another student of the problem, Christine P. Ingram, suggests that children with I. Q.'s from 50 to 75 are sufficiently handicapped to require special provision in the schools. "The majority of these pupils at fifteen and sixteen years of age will not have succeeded beyond minimum third-, fourth-, or fifth-grade standards when measured in terms of grade achievement."[12]

Few pupils with I. Q.'s below 60 or 65 will reach the junior high school. Consequently, the mentally retarded group in the junior high school will consist primarily of children with I. Q.'s from 60 to 75 or 80. *It is recommended, therefore, that all children in the junior high school with I. Q.'s below 80 be examined to locate those who need a special program of education which is different from that for normal children.*

Other Characteristics of the Mentally Retarded Child. There are many factors other than intelligence which have an influence on the child's ability to learn. These other factors not only have a bearing on the type of educational experiences which should be offered the mentally retarded child, but they must also be considered in deciding which children, especially among those with I. Q.'s from 70 to 80, should be segregated for special education. While many of these pupils can succeed in classes with normal children, there are others who need special educational opportunities because of such factors as immature physical development, sensory defects, emotional instability, irregular school attendance, repeated failure in the grades, or an extremely adverse home environment.

Mentally retarded children as a group fall below the averages for normal children in such characteristics as height and weight, motor ability, and social development. There is, however, a great deal of overlapping in physical development between the two groups, many of the mentally retarded equaling or exceeding the norms for normal children. These group differences in physical characteristics, as well as the variations among pupils within the group, must be taken into consideration in planning educational activities for mentally retarded pupils.

[11] Arch O. Heck, *The Education of Exceptional Children* (New York: McGraw-Hill Book Co., Inc., 1940), p. 358.
[12] Ingram, *op. cit.*, p. 6.

Educational Needs of the Mentally Retarded Child. There is a serious lack of understanding on the part of both teachers and laymen of the educational needs of the mentally retarded child. The common belief is that an educational program for these children should be confined largely to those school subjects which emphasize two types of things: (1) the basic skills and knowledge, and (2) manual activities. Such a program, however, is as inadequate for the mentally retarded as it would be for normal children.

The adult life of many mentally retarded persons actually will not differ greatly from that of their mentally normal fellows. They will necessarily engage in most of the activities common to the average citizen. The mentally retarded adult probably will earn his own living; he will be expected to conform to the customs and to obey the laws of his community; he may participate in a limited way in the affairs of his community; he may be permitted to vote in local, state, and national elections; he will have leisure hours like the normal adult; and he may even marry, establish a home, and raise a family. It is true, of course, that his participation in such activities may be restricted in some instances by state laws, as well as by lack of interest and low mental ability. But the fact remains that many mentally retarded persons will and should live much like normal adults in their community. These prospective adult activities of the mentally retarded person, as well as his intellectual, physical, social, and personal characteristics, therefore should guide those who are developing a curriculum to meet the needs of such a group of children.

Methods of Instruction for the Mentally Retarded Child. The way in which the mentally retarded child learns is sufficiently different from that of the normal child to necessitate considerable adaptation in classroom methods. As compared with the normal child, the mentally retarded pupil learns at a slower pace, his span of attention is shorter, he loses interest more quickly, he works more readily with concrete things than abstract ideas, and his level of achievement is low. The instructional methods which are employed must take these characteristics into consideration.

Teachers who lack an understanding of the mentally retarded child frequently overemphasize drill and memory work with these pupils. This is indeed a mistake. Although these children may need more drill on fundamentals than those of normal intelligence, they should also engage in a variety of classroom activities much like normal children. The following suggestions may serve as a guide to the teacher in the adaptation of classroom methods for mentally retarded children.

1. There should be frequent drill on basic knowledge and skills, but the drill periods should be relatively short.
2. There should be group activities to develop desirable social qualities, but these activities should be simple and relatively brief.
3. There should be emphasis on concrete—audio-visual—rather than verbal and abstract, learning activities.
4. There should be emphasis on oral, rather than written, learning activities.
5. There should be emphasis on manual activities that will develop muscular coordination and motor skills.
6. There should be emphasis on individual help to pupils.
7. There should be little homework or other learning activities that are not carried out under the immediate supervision of the teacher.
8. There should be careful study by the teacher of the characteristics and the needs of each individual child.

Special Classes for the Mentally Retarded. For years, specialists in the education of mentally retarded children have advocated the provision of special classes or schools for these pupils. The chief advantage of this plan is obvious; namely, *an educational program which is well suited to the needs, interests, and abilities of the mentally retarded child can be provided more effectively in segregated classes than in the regular classes with normal children.* The effectiveness of special classes and schools for the mentally retarded has been amply shown through years of experience with such classes in cities in all sections of the United States.

One difficulty with special classes for the mentally retarded pupils is that they set these pupils apart from the other pupils in school. Every effort should be made to avoid this situation. *Whether they are in special classes or not, the mentally retarded pupils should feel that they are an integral part of the total life and program of the school.* This may be done in a number of ways. The mentally retarded pupils may be placed in the regular home rooms and in regular classes in some subjects. Certainly, they should have a part in extra-class activities in so far as their limited interests and abilities permit. In most instances such participation may be of a rather passive nature, such as attendance at assemblies and membership in some clubs. A special designation for classes for the mentally retarded should be avoided. In other words, a concerted effort should be made to avoid attracting undue attention to the special classes and to help the mentally retarded pupils have a feeling of belonging to the school community.

Some indication of the extent to which special classes are provided for decidedly slow-learning or mentally retarded pupils in the junior high school is given by the results of the survey of 370 schools by the authors, with the percentage of schools having the practices indicated:

Given special help in regular classes 48%
Placed in special classes 45%
Other practices 4%
Given no special attention 3%

The Mentally Retarded Child in Small Schools. In small communities, it is probably best to send children of low intelligence to special public or private institutions. There will be some mentally retarded children, however, who for various reasons had best be retained in their home communities. Furthermore, in many states the special institutions cannot accommodate all the mentally retarded children for whom application is made. For these children, some provision must ordinarily be made in the public schools.

In schools with homogeneous grouping, certain mentally retarded children can be placed in the low groups where they can be given individual work. The teachers who have such pupils, however, must be thoroughly informed regarding their abilities and the type of learning activities most appropriate for them.

Another plan which is feasible in the small school is to retain the mentally retarded pupils in the regular classes in nonacademic subjects like music, art, industrial arts, home economics, and physical education, but segregate them for the academic subjects, especially for English and mathematics. Since it is in the academic subjects that the mentally retarded child usually has most difficulty, this plan provides much of the advantage of the segregated program without great cost.

6. Adapting Administrative Practices for Individual Differences

Meeting Individual Differences Through Elective Courses. In the early junior high schools, the practice of offering elective courses and curriculums was widely used as a means of meeting the individual needs, abilities, and interests of pupils. It was only natural that this practice should be introduced, because it prevailed in the four-year high school at that time. Some years of experience with elective courses, however, have led junior high school educators to believe that the practice is not so appropriate in the junior high school as in the senior high school. Consequently, there has been less emphasis on elective courses in the junior high school than was true at certain times in the past. *Instead, it is believed today that individual differences among boys and girls should be met within the framework of one* *common basic program, rather than through the provision of differ-entiated curriculums and courses.*

It is true, of course, that elective courses are still offered in the junior high school. In the seventh and eighth grades these are confined in some schools primarily to such offerings as the music organizations and certain extraclass activities. In the seventh grade it appears to be the exception rather than the rule to offer elective courses. A few schools offer electives in the eighth grade. In the ninth grade, the practice with respect to elective courses in most schools is much the same as it has been for many years. That is, most pupils are offered one or two electives much as in the ninth grade of the four-year high school.

It is true, however, that many junior high school educators believe that even in the ninth grade an extensive offering of elective courses is neither necessary nor desirable. More and more, the program in the ninth grade is being developed like that in the seventh and eighth, with a basic curriculum being required of all pupils. At the present time, however, this is the practice in only a small number of junior high schools.

Adaptation of Marks and Progress Reports. Perhaps no other practices in the junior high school have interfered more with meeting individual differences effectively than those of examinations, marks, and pupil-progress reports. No matter how much a teacher may try to adapt the work in his classes to the needs and abilities of individual pupils, the effectiveness of his efforts is largely lost when the time comes to give examinations, to give marks, and to issue report cards. Obviously, it is impossible to have the individual pupil engage in learning activities adapted to his level of ability and then, at the end of a marking period, evaluate his work and mark him on the basis of a uniform standard that applies equally to all pupils. Regardless of what other effect traditional marks and report cards may have had, they have certainly served to defeat most of our efforts at individualizing instruction in the junior high school.

In recent years, no subject has been studied more than that of marks and pupil-progress reports. Educators, teachers, and parents recognize that some way must be found of meeting individual differences in the evaluation, marking, and reporting practices, as well as in methods of teaching. Some schools are already doing that. In many schools today, marks and pupil-progress reports are based on the individual potentialities of pupils, rather than on one uniform standard that is applied to the entire class. Much more experimentation needs to be done, however, before we can feel completely satisfied that the new approaches to evaluation, marking, and reporting pupil progress give sufficient recognition to individual differences.[13]

Promotion by Subject. One of the basic characteristics common to the early junior high school was promotion by subjects. It was believed that this would be one way of more effectively meeting individual differences. In the ninth grade, promotion by subject still continues to be the prevailing practice, but in the seventh and eighth grades it has been discontinued in many schools, at least in the rigid and formal manner that once pertained. In most junior high schools today, promotions are made on the basis of what seems to be best for the individual child. In other words, a child may proceed with his grade in all subjects, or he may be retained in certain ones and not in others. The needs of the individual child, rather than a grade standard in each subject, become a major criterion for making decisions about the promotion of pupils.

7. Conclusion

Administrative practices seem to have dominated this discussion of individualization of instruction. Yet it is the methods of teaching which are today receiving the most emphasis in the thinking of educators as they approach the problem of meeting individual differences. We must find ways of working effectively with individual children, in terms of their needs, interests, and abilities. Administrative devices are merely an aid in making that possible. Methods of working effectively with individual pupils in the classroom are at present the chief approach to meeting individual differences.

Questions and Exercises

1. In what respects do junior high school pupils differ from one another? List them.
2. How can you obtain information about the characteristics of individual pupils in the school?
3. What are the arguments for and against promotion by subjects?
4. What is present thinking regarding elective courses and curriculums in the three junior high school grades? What is your own point of view? Substantiate it.
5. Evaluate each of the principal arguments for and against ability grouping.
6. What influence have the literature and thinking on mental health had on ability grouping?

[13] A more detailed discussion of new approaches to marking and reporting pupil progress is presented in Chapter 14.

7. Evaluate the point of view of the authors concerning ability grouping.

8. What methods of teaching are especially appropriate for the gifted pupils? For the mentally retarded?

9. What are the arguments for and against acceleration of gifted pupils? Enrichment?

10. Select any subject, and show how you could provide enrichment in that subject for the gifted pupils.

Part III
GUIDANCE AND EXTRACLASS ACTIVITIES

Chapter 11

THE GUIDANCE PROGRAM

1. Basic Philosophy

Concepts Basic to a Guidance Program. Significant concepts which should form the basis for any well-organized program of guidance in the junior high school include the following:

1. *Guidance is not something new.* Parents and other relatives, the clergy, and social workers, as well as teachers, for generations have rendered valuable guidance service to young people. The modern guidance movement is largely an extension of these services, but it is based on a greater recognition of their importance and on a more scientific and determined approach to the problem.

2. *Guidance is much broader and far more important than vocational guidance alone.* It also includes health, educational, social, civic, leisure, and recreational guidance, and guidance concerning personal problems in such areas as mental health, religion, sex, finances, and family relationships.

3. *Guidance is as legitimate an educational activity as the study of English, mathematics, and social studies.* Any pupil experience must be considered educationally worth while to the extent that it influences pupil growth toward desirable educational goals. This is ordinarily accomplished by stimulating pupil acquisition of information, ideals, attitudes, skills, understandings, and interests which result in behavior desirable for the individual and for society.

4. *Guidance does not consist primarily of making decisions for young people, or of encouraging them to make decisions of their own immediately.* Rather, it is assistance to young people (a) in studying their own problems, (b) in discovering and exploring potential interests and capacities, (c) in getting information about opportunities for further education, (d) in becoming familiar with the opportunities, activities, demands, and rewards of various vocations, and (e) in developing desirable personality and social qualities.

5. *Guidance may be either individual-conference or group guidance.* The individual conference is, of course, more appropriate in situations where the problem is a personal one. Group guidance is carried on in homerooms, class groups, assemblies, etc.

237

6. *Guidance is not confined to counseling alone, but is carried on in many other ways and through many channels.* Guidance may be provided through (a) the older subjects in the curriculum, (b) new subjects with special guidance purposes, such as occupations and vocational civics, (c) exploratory courses, such as junior business training and industrial arts, (d) homeroom or core-group activities, (e) individual counseling, (f) assemblies, clubs, and other extraclass activities, and (g) field trips.

7. *Guidance cannot be confined to a few specialists, but must be carried on by the entire professional staff.* The participation of each staff member must be limited by his training, experience, interests, and personal qualities. But in a well-planned guidance program every teacher should render some guidance service, while those who are specialists through background and training should serve as leaders in directing the program, in gathering and analyzing information about individual pupils, and in the more difficult problems of counseling.

8. *Guidance should be careful to avoid influencing pupil decisions through distorted, overemphasized, or incomplete information.* Many attempts at guidance are based on methods and information which are so unreliable that they border on quackery or professional malpractice. Examples of ill-considered guidance practices are: (a) misunderstanding by teachers regarding the values of the subjects they teach; (b) misinformation about college-entrance requirements; (c) advice to pupils about going to college without careful consideration of some of the important factors involved; (d) misinformation about various vocations, not only by teachers, but also by representatives of the professions, business, and labor; (e) misinterpretation of test results and other pupil data; (f) attempts by counselors to give pupils answers in cases where there is no answer and in cases where the pupil should think through his own answer; (g) encouraging pupils to make premature and ill-considered decisions; and (h) the use of so-called guidance services of the racket variety, frequently provided on a fee basis by individuals, commercial organizations, and representatives of some educational institutions.

9. *Guidance is sufficiently important so that the school should be organized and administered with the guidance function prominently in the foreground.* Teachers should be selected in terms of their competence in guidance, as indicated by training, experience, and personal qualities; guidance responsibilities should be considered in arranging the teacher's load; school records should be expanded, organized, and simplified for guidance purposes; ample time should be allowed in the school program for guidance activities; and opportunities for the in-

service improvement of teachers for guidance activities should be made available.

10. *Guidance must be based upon and make use of all appropriate resources in the community, directed and integrated through the program of the school.* This should include the use of such physical resources as civic agencies, higher educational institutions, and business and industrial firms and the use of human resources such as parents, ministers, priests, youth organizations of various types, civic leaders, professional men and women, and representatives of labor, business, and industry.

11. *Guidance should be based on a variety of data about the individual pupil.* A serious danger in rendering guidance service is that teachers, counselors, and others may answer questions for pupils or assist them in finding answers to their questions without adequate information about the pupils. This unfortunate practice is unwittingly participated in by many teachers who do not realize what data are necessary as the basis for intelligent decisions. Fortunately, the amount and variety of pupil data which are available in the junior high schools have increased greatly in recent years.

2. Educational Guidance

Types of Orientation Activities. Some orientation to the junior high school may be provided before pupils leave the elementary school. In the study by Byers, it was found that certain practices are used to help inform sixth-grade pupils about the program of the junior high school, in the percentage of schools indicated: [1]

Sixth-grade pupils visit the junior high school	68%
Principal meets with sixth-grade pupils	46%
Handbooks are given sixth-grade pupils	45%
Junior high school pupils meet with sixth-grade pupils	24%
Junior high school teachers meet with sixth-grade pupils	19%

As an example of good practice in this respect, the Manhattanville Junior High School of New York City has a program for orienting sixth-grade pupils in the spring before they enter the junior high school. Included in that program are: (1) the showing of 35 mm. color slides of activities in the Manhattanville Junior High School; (2) visits to the junior high school by sixth-grade pupils and their teachers; (3) an open-house evening for the parents, including a ques-

[1] Richard S. Byers, "Articulation in the Junior High School" (Unpublished doctoral thesis, University of Connecticut, Storrs, Conn., 1955), p. 117.

tion-and-answer period, tour of the building, and refreshments; and (4) a booklet, "Welcome to Manhattanville," distributed to the entering pupils.

In the Lincoln Junior High School, Santa Monica, California, a program for the orientation of entering seventh-grade pupils includes a visit to the elementary schools by the junior high school principal, attendance of sixth-grade pupils at an orientation assembly in the junior high school, and visits by parents to the junior high school to meet the teachers and to receive information about the junior high school. Each incoming pupil is assigned a "big brother" who helps him get acquainted.

Orientation to a New School. The school has a responsibility for helping new pupils become readily adjusted to its customs, traditions, activities, policies, and regulations. More specifically, orientation activities should be provided with respect to the following: (1) the customs and traditions of the school—its history, songs and yells, special sports events, and honors and awards; (2) extraclass activities—assemblies, clubs, music organizations, social functions, athletics, student government organizations, pupil publications, and speech groups; (3) certain administrative policies—the marking system, use of textbooks and equipment, bases for promotions and failures, use of the library, participation in extraclass activities, the cafeteria, transportation, home work, and final examinations; and (4) rules and regulations—school hours, reasons for leaving classes or the building, absence and tardiness, changes in pupil programs, use of automobiles and bicycles, payment of fees and fines, mutilation of school property, corridor conduct, transfer or withdrawal from school, library rules, make-up work for absence, responsibility for valuables, and fire drills. These are a few of the things which bewilder new pupils and in which they should be oriented as a basis for ready adjustment to the new school.

The most popular avenue for orientation activities is the homeroom. In many schools much of the first semester in homerooms for new pupils is devoted to orientation. Other avenues for orientation activities are assemblies, printed or mimeographed materials, guidance handbooks, and orientation classes. In many schools, the first few weeks in the seventh-grade social studies class are devoted to orientation.

Orientation activities frequently emphasize the educational program and the administrative organization of the school but neglect to help new pupils become acquainted with older pupils and the faculty. It is doubtful whether any pupil will feel completely at home in a new school environment until he knows the faculty and prominent older pupils at least by name, and has formed new friendships among his own classmates. Practices which are employed in some junior high schools to help new pupils get acquainted include: (1) introducing teachers and pupil leaders at assemblies; (2) the assignment of older pupils to help the newcomers get acquainted; and (3) parties given for new pupils.

Orientation Units. In some junior high schools a series of ten or twelve lessons has been planned for the first month of school for incoming seventh-grade pupils. Typical of these lessons are the following from the Thomas Junior High School, Philadelphia, Pennsylvania:

Lesson I: The school day, building orientation, and more important rules. Information about the opening of school, the length of periods, the schedule bells, assemblies, and lunch period; explanation of the roster card; plan of building; the numbering and location of rooms; lunch rules; excuses for absence and tardiness; books and material for classes.

Lesson II: Traffic regulations. Need for; standards and ideals; rules.

Lesson III: Student material, equipment. Lesson book: specifications; how kept; other equipment for all classes; care and arrangement of books and material.

Lesson IV: Personal appearance. Cleanliness; neatness; clothes; conventions; posture.

Lesson V: Lunchroom ethics. Standards and ideals; regulations; after lunch.

Lesson VI: Group meeting. Parliamentary procedure; order of business and parliamentary form; the school bank.

Lesson VII: Aims, purposes, and functions of the junior high school. The curriculum; special aims and functions.

Lesson VIII: Home study. Proper environment; rules for effective study.

Lesson IX: Attendance. Meaning and importance; state laws; proper excuses; details of routine.

Lesson X: Punctuality. Importance in business world; school punctuality.

Lesson XI: Student organizations. School government; student agencies for government; activities and duty.

Lesson XII: Ethics of the auditorium. Advantages of auditorium privileges; means of entrance, seating, and exit; behavior.

Much of the time spent on such lessons should be given over to discussion by pupils. Attempts are made to lead them to form the desired attitudes as well as to develop and acquire useful information. A collection of supplementary reading material should be made available for voluntary reading and special reports. Such a series of lessons might well be substituted in the junior high school for instruction in some seventh-grade subjects for two or three weeks.

Orienting Parents of Entering Pupils. Parents need orientation to a new school as much as their children do. If the parents are well informed, they can do much to help pupils become readily adjusted to the program and the practices of the junior high school. Byers found that the importance of orienting the parents of entering seventh-grade pupils is recognized in many junior high schools, the following practices being employed in the percentage of schools indicated: [2]

Parents visit the school	80%
Parents meet to discuss the school program	49%
Materials are sent to parents	48%
Information appears in the newspapers	27%

Getting Acquainted with Entering Pupils. It is fully as important for teachers to get acquainted with entering pupils as it is for the pupils to become oriented to the school. Some things may be done to get acquainted with pupils before they enter, while other activities may help accumulate information about them after they arrive. In many junior high schools, information is obtained about pupils from the elementary school through the cumulative records, summaries of information about the personality, character, and citizenship qualities of pupils, and meetings of sixth- and seventh-grade teachers to discuss the backgrounds of entering seventh-grade pupils.

In the junior high school, numerous practices are used to accumulate information about pupils on a continuing basis. For instance, many types of information are recorded from time to time on the cumulative records; interest inventories are administered to pupils; homeroom teachers and counselors have periodic conferences with pupils; information of an anecdotal nature is accumulated; and pupils are asked to prepare autobiographies. Such information about pupils who are new in the school should prove exceedingly helpful to teachers and counselors in guidance activities.

Pupil Decisions Regarding Education. Pupils can be prepared in the junior high school for many important decisions and adjustments which they must make relative to their present and future educational activities. These decisions and adjustments include such matters as how long to continue in school, the choice of elective curriculums and courses, the choice of extraclass activities, adjustment to the rules, customs, and administrative policies and practices of the school, and success in school. The educational guidance activities carried on in

[2] Byers, *op. cit.*, p. 122.

the junior high school to meet these problems may be grouped into two broad categories: (1) those which help pupils plan their program of courses, curriculums, and extraclass activities, and (2) those which help them succeed in the educational activities which they decide to undertake.

Guidance in Planning Educational Programs. In the past, the choice of elective curriculums and courses has, in most schools, been a hand-to-mouth process, hurriedly done once each semester on the basis of little study or knowledge of the factors concerned. Not only have pupils been given little training in planning an educational program, but the advice of teachers in the choice of electives has frequently been based on tradition, hearsay, or a bias in favor of the subjects they teach. Therefore, in the past the selection of and registration for certain curriculums and courses has actually been more of an administrative than a guidance activity.

In most junior high schools today, the planning of a pupil's educational program is considered an important matter, undertaken in a serious and systematic manner, and based upon reliable information and extensive study. Frequently the eighth- or ninth-grade pupil outlines a tentative program several years ahead which he records in "My Educational Plan Book." This plan ordinarily includes the pupil's tentative decisions and choices regarding his vocational future, plans for the continuation of his education in senior high school and college, and choices of elective curriculums and courses in the senior high school.

The preparation of such an educational plan is, in itself, an exceedingly worth-while experience for the pupil. It is usually an outgrowth of discussions in homerooms and assemblies, conferences with parents, and interviews with the pupil's homeroom adviser and the school counselor. In advising the individual pupil, all available information regarding him is drawn upon by the school faculty—information obtained from school records, from observation of the pupil and his work, and from pupil-teacher conferences. After much careful study, a plan for his educational work is finally developed by the pupil. It is recognized by the pupil, the parent, and the school that the plan is purely tentative and should be subject to periodic re-examination and revision.

It is believed by most educators today, as well as by pupils and parents, that extraclass activities are almost as important in the educational program as class activities. If this point of view is accepted, the faculty must recognize a responsibility for stimulating and advising pupils with respect to participation in those activities. That is, in fact, the policy in many junior high schools today. Not only are pupils informed about extraclass activities in the junior high school, but frequently they also learn about such activities which will be available later in the senior high school.

There are numerous procedures and avenues for assisting pupils with the choice of courses and extraclass activities. Information regarding elective courses and extraclass activities is given pupils through such avenues as the homeroom, assemblies, printed or mimeographed materials, guidance handbooks, and special orientation classes.

In addition to background information which pupils should have concerning elective courses and activities, they should be given individual help in planning their educational programs in the junior high school. Such guidance is usually given through individual conferences with the homeroom adviser. The school counselor also gives individual help, especially to pupils who have problems that are too difficult for the homeroom adviser.

Guidance Concerning Pupil's Educational Future. Much of the educational guidance in the junior high school should be directed toward helping pupils plan their educational activities for senior high school and college. Pupils should be given or have made available to them information about educational opportunities beyond the junior high school, they should discover and try out their educational aptitudes and interests, and they should become familiar with the programs of the senior high school they expect to enter. Junior high school pupils should make such a study of future educational opportunities by means of homeroom discussion, assemblies, vocations or occupational civics courses, and pupil handbooks. In a few schools, orientation classes serve as a means of helping pupils study opportunities for further education. Guidance activities such as these stimulate pupil interest in further schooling and encourage adequate planning for senior high school and college.

The procedures employed to give information to junior high school pupils concerning the courses, activities, and organization of the senior high school include talks by principals, counselors, and teachers of both senior and junior high schools, homeroom discussions, mimeographed bulletins, guidance handbooks, and special orientation classes.

It is not easy to help pupils discover and try out educational aptitudes and interests. If the junior high school is to fulfill the exploratory and guidance functions, some try-out experiences should be provided. Most schools offer exploratory courses for this purpose, such as junior business, general science, general mathematics, general language, and industrial arts. Recently, some educators have come to doubt the exploratory value of such courses. Properly taught, however, they should be of some help to pupils in discovering and trying out their educational aptitudes and interests.

Guidance Based on Educational Diagnosis. Another area of educational guidance is that related to assisting pupils to improve their achievement in school. Practices commonly employed to discover the causes for discrepancy between a pupil's capacity to learn and his actual achievement include:

1. Diagnostic testing to ascertain the specific locus of a pupil's learning difficulties
2. Examination of the pupil's past school record to discover areas of incapacity, interests, and character traits which may have a bearing on scholastic achievement
3. Consideration of all available data on individual pupils which might throw light on emotional problems related to achievement
4. Conferences with pupils and parents to discover physiological or psychological causes of low achievement, such as ill health, defects in hearing and sight, discouragement, and antagonism toward teachers
5. Search for possible sources of interference with satisfactory achievement—excessive outside work, time spent with radio or television programs, insufficient sleep, poor study conditions at home, or inability to purchase school supplies
6. Conferences with a pupil's classmates to discover information relative to various factors that affect achievement

Preparing Teachers for Educational Guidance. The greatest burden for educational guidance falls upon the individual teachers. Even in schools with a part- or full-time counselor, most of the educational guidance activities are carried on by homeroom and classroom teachers. It is essential, therefore, that teachers be prepared for their participation in the educational guidance program.

Before teachers can assist pupils in the choice of elective courses and the planning of their educational programs, they must be thoroughly familiar with the curriculums and courses of the junior and senior high schools. In most schools, definite measures are taken to provide teachers with this information through (1) printed or mimeographed summaries of elective courses issued to teachers, (2) study by the teachers of courses of study, and (3) discussions at faculty meetings of elective curriculums and courses.

By the beginning of the ninth grade, pupils who intend to go to college must plan their high school program for college entrance.

The junior high school teacher, therefore, is in a crucial position for advising pupils with respect to planning for college. As a basis for intelligent guidance in this matter, teachers must be informed about those college-entrance requirements which are related to junior and senior high school work. Some junior high schools make this information available to teachers by providing a file of college catalogs, by issuing summaries of college-entrance requirements, and by discussing the subject in faculty meetings.

In order to advise pupils regarding elective courses, teachers should have some understanding of the aptitudes, abilities, and personal qualities which are desirable for success in those courses. In some junior high schools this matter is studied in faculty meetings before teachers advise pupils regarding their elective choices. In others, information is prepared by guidance directors or counselors and issued to teachers in special bulletins and teachers' handbooks. In many schools, however, the teachers are given little or no help in this matter.

3. Vocational Guidance

Reduced Emphasis on Vocational Guidance. In the first quarter of this century, when jobs for youth were plentiful and the great mass left school for work between the ages of thirteen and sixteen, it seemed important in the junior high school to help boys and girls choose a life's vocation. Various types of vocational guidance activities therefore were introduced into the junior high school very early in its history.

But the need for vocational guidance at the junior high school level has changed greatly. Because of child labor laws, compulsory school attendance laws, labor union regulations, higher wages for family heads, a more attractive secondary school program, and numerous other influences, boys and girls increasingly remain in school beyond the junior high school grades. As a result, the senior, rather than the junior, high school has become the appropriate place for the major emphasis on vocational choices.

In a great majority of junior high schools today there are, nevertheless, many vocational guidance activities, but they are directed largely toward providing pupils with an informational background for making future, rather than immediate, vocational choices. For example, in the junior high school today most emphasis is placed on (1) exploring vocational interests through try-out and study, (2) acquiring a background of vocational information, (3) learning the importance of careful thought and study before making vocational decisions, and (4) learning what is important to consider in thinking about a choice of vocation. *The definite choice of a vocation, however, is postponed to the senior high school.*

Vocational Information as a Basis for Guidance. In the 1920's and 1930's, many junior high schools offered a course in vocational information under the title of "vocations," "occupations," or "vocational civics." In recent years, however, the number of schools offering such a course has decreased. The purpose of the vocations courses, which are usually taught for one semester in either the eighth or ninth grade, is to stimulate pupil interest in various vocations, point out the importance of making careful vocational decisions, and provide an informational background for future vocational choices.

One of the most serious difficulties with the occupations course is that of finding teachers who are qualified for this work by training, experience, and personal qualities. Teachers of the vocational subjects, such as business and industrial arts, are frequently assigned to this course, but experience has shown that they are little if any better qualified than teachers of the academic subjects. It cannot be stressed too strongly that teachers of the occupations courses need special preparation and experience if these courses are to be taught effectively.

Other Avenues of Vocational Information. In the junior high school, the courses in occupations are not the only avenue for the study of vocational information. Other courses in the curriculum, especially social studies, English, commercial, industrial arts, and home economics, may be used to inform pupils about the opportunities, requirements, and activities of various occupations. As a basis for oral and written work in these courses, pupils frequently investigate vocations in which they are interested; they interview professional, business, civic, and labor leaders; they go on field trips to industrial and commercial establishments. Inviting professional, industrial, and labor leaders to address classes has rarely proved to be of great value for this purpose. In the hands of a resourceful teacher, practically every subject in the curriculum presents some important opportunities for the study of occupational information.

Pupils receive an informational background for making vocational decisions in many phases of the school program other than the regular classes. The most common channels for obtaining this background include the following: (1) pupil-teacher conferences, (2) homeroom discussions, (3) talks by persons from various vocations, (4) special orientation classes, (5) guidance and pupil handbooks, and (6) printed and mimeographed bulletins.

Vocational Guidance Through Counseling. Although it is the practice today for pupils to postpone making vocational choices until they reach the senior high school, there is need for the services of a trained vocational counselor. There are some pupils who expect to leave school during or soon after their junior high school work. Then, too, there are many boys and girls in the eighth and ninth grades who should make tentative vocational choices preliminary to planning their high school programs. Such cases call for the services of a person who has had more training in vocational guidance than most teachers.

The vocational counselor should be familiar with the activities and opportunities of the more common vocations and the sources of occupational information. He should have training in techniques for obtaining and interpreting data about individual pupils through such devices as intelligence and aptitude tests, achievement marks, vocational histories, records of information on socioeconomic status and home backgrounds, and adjustment and interest questionnaires. Finally, he should be a keen analyst of human nature, a skillful interviewer, and a capable diagnostician.

Need for Health Guidance. In the modern junior high school, it is recognized that the school's responsibility for the welfare of the child's health is not adequately discharged either by courses in physiology, hygiene, and health, or by a program of physical education and athletics. In addition to the work offered in such courses, definite measures should be taken to build good health habits and to guide boys and girls toward more healthful living. The informational background for desirable health habits can be given in the various health courses, but to develop good health habits this informational background must be supplemented by individual and group activities of a guidance nature.

The concept of health has been extended in recent years so as to include mental as well as physical health. Mental health should not be thought of as totally distinct from the child's physical health. Indeed, mental and physical problems are closely related, one usually having a rather direct bearing on the other. But frequently the causes underlying mental and emotional instability are different from those leading to physical ill health, and therefore may require different treatment. Both mental and physical health, therefore, need attention in the guidance program of the junior high school.

Practices in Physical Health Guidance. The activities in physical health guidance should be directed toward two purposes: (1) the discovery and treatment of physical ailments and defects among pupils, and (2) helping pupils acquire sound health habits and practices as a basis for continued good health. Facilities and staff should be provided to achieve these purposes. There should be periodic and thorough physical examinations, measures for the correction of physical defects and ailments, suggestions to teachers for meeting the needs of individual pupils, and follow-up activities with pupils and their parents. The child, his teachers, and his parents should be informed by the school officials regarding any present ailments and defects; they should agree on measures to improve the child's health, and they should have frequent conferences to assure cooperation in any corrective treatment.

In the past, health guidance in many schools has been confined largely to the correction or improvement of health ailments and defects, but some activities are being introduced which emphasize the maintenance of good health, rather than the improvement of poor health. Problems of nutrition, relaxation, sleep, cleanliness, exercise, and posture, figure prominently in these activities. In many schools these problems receive only incidental consideration, as in athletics, physical education, science, and home economics. But the subject of desirable health habits is being emphasized more and more through organized activities in the homeroom, clubs, and assemblies, as well as in the health and hygiene classes.

A program of physical health guidance demands not only a staff of teachers with a sympathetic interest and some training in health problems, but it needs a group of competent specialists, such as nurses, physicians, and dentists. In most school systems today there is either a part-time or full-time nurse. Outside the large cities, relatively few schools have a physician who is readily available to assist in health guidance. In small communities, the usual practice is to retain a school physician on a part-time basis, with his duties limited to giving physical examinations and assisting in emergency situations. This part-time help is not adequate for effective health guidance. Until a staff of health specialists is available, it will be impossible to offer adequate health guidance opportunities in the junior high school.

The percentage of junior high schools providing certain types of health services as reported by Fennell from his study of 224 schools is: [3]

Eye examinations	89%
Auditory examinations	85%
Physical examinations	74%
Dental examinations	64%
Chest X-rays	57%
Heart examinations	46%
Sodium fluoride treatments	13%

[3] Edward Glenn Fennell, *An Analysis of Programs of Outstanding Junior High Schools in the United States* (Unpublished doctoral dissertation, Cornell University, Ithaca, N. Y., 1953), p. 115.

Guidance with Respect to Sex Problems. A great deal has been written in recent years about sex education in the secondary school. This interest has developed from the fact that many of the emotional and social maladjustments among pupils in early adolescence are related to sex problems. As yet, little is done in most junior high schools to help pupils *avoid* maladjustments that are related to sex, although in most schools they are assisted in meeting such problems once they arise.

There are important factors that prevent a satisfactory program of guidance with respect to sex problems in the junior high school; and until these difficulties are solved, there is not likely to be much progress in this matter. The more significant factors that impede satisfactory guidance in sex matters include:

1. Lack of understanding on the part of junior high school teachers of the physiological and emotional problems related to sex among early adolescents
2. Lack of specialists who understand such problems, especially in small schools and communities and in areas with limited funds for education
3. Lack of agreement among educators on the sex matters suitable for discussion in school, the places in the school program where they might best be treated, and the methods of presenting and discussing them with pupils
4. Lack of encouragement or approval from parents regarding the discussion of sex problems in school

Practices in Mental Health Guidance. For some time, the period of early adolescence has been recognized as one of considerable emotional stress and strain. The rapid physical growth of the child, the coming of physiological maturity, the breaking away from family domination, and numerous other factors at this age lead to complex problems of mental, emotional, and social adjustment. Some of the instructional practices of the school—marks, discipline, report cards, home work, and pressure for achievement—have actually intensified these problems for some children. In a majority of the junior high schools, a program of mental health guidance is now provided to relieve these problems of emotional adjustment.

Guidance for mental health must be concerned with two types of problems: (1) the prevention of serious maladjustments, and (2) the relieving of cases of maladjustment once they arise. For the prevention of maladjustments, planned activities of various kinds are carried on in the homerooms, assemblies, and physical education and home economics classes. These activities are intended to accomplish results such as the following:

1. To help pupils appreciate the importance of mental and emotional stability
2. To help pupils understand how they can exert themselves to make such adjustments
3. To inform pupils regarding the influence of sleep, recreation, exercise, and other personal habits on mental and emotional stability
4. To develop desirable attitudes toward marks for achievement, examinations, home work, discipline, and other school practices that frequently lead to mental and emotional problems
5. To develop wholesome pupil attitudes toward and relationships with the opposite sex
6. To develop wholesome pupil attitudes toward and relationships with other members of the family, the school, and other groups
7. To inform pupils regarding problems of physical and physiological growth that are peculiar to the adolescent

Preparation of Teachers for Mental Health Guidance. Progress in developing guidance activities related to mental health has been limited by the difficulty which the school staff encounters in locating, diagnosing, and solving cases of maladjustment. It is relatively easy to locate and diagnose hearing difficulties, poor eyesight, weak lungs, and other physical ailments and defects, but it is a far different matter to locate cases of mental, emotional, and social maladjustment among pupils. The problem of mental health guidance is complicated still further by the fact that much of the responsibility for locating cases of maladjustment lies with the individual teacher. This is true not only because many schools are too small to afford specialists in mental health problems, but also because the teacher, through his intimate contact with pupils, is in the best position to observe individual problems of adjustment in their early stages. *It is important, therefore, that the individual teacher have an adequate understanding of mental hygiene, the psychology of adolescence, and problems of mental, emotional, and social adjustment.* Many teachers lack such preparation.

In many junior high schools, however, definite activities are carried on to prepare teachers for mental health guidance. In some schools, problems of emotionally maladjusted pupils are studied at faculty meetings, professional books on the subject are available in a faculty library, or bulletins on the subject may be prepared for teachers by the school psychologist or psychiatrist. Many school systems also have specialists to assist teachers in studying mental health problems, such as health nurses, physicians, trained counselors, psychologists, and psychiatrists.

As a basis for their part in mental health guidance, teachers obviously need much more preparation in the field of mental hygiene and related problems. They should have some training in this area as part of their pre-service professional education. In addition, every encouragement should be given teachers in service to study further in the field of mental hygiene through summer and extension work, professional reading, and group faculty study. Extensive study of mental and emotional problems by prospective and in-service teachers is essential to meet the demands of mental health guidance.

If adequate help is to be given pupils in mental health, qualified specialists need to be provided. At present the nurse, the physician, and the counselor usually assume this responsibility. However, psychologists and psychiatrists are also needed. Study of 370 junior high schools by the authors indicates that such specialists are being increasingly provided, 38 per cent of the schools having the services of a psychologist available, and 19 per cent having access to a psychiatrist.

4. Guidance in Other Areas

Social and Civic Guidance. A program of social and civic guidance is especially important in the secondary school because many conflicts and maladjustments among pupils are brought into relief by the social and civic life of the school. Problems that frequently arise in such activities of the school include those related to boy-girl relationships, the socioeconomic status of the pupil, the pupil's appearance and dress, individual and group discipline, and certain moral issues. Because of these problems, the junior high school staff should be alert to the opportunities afforded in the social and civic life of the school for carrying on an effective program of social and civic guidance. The homeroom, assemblies, clubs, athletics, and social activities are particularly appropriate channels for guidance of this type.

Need for Recreational Guidance. It is needless to review in detail the changes in American life during the past century which have intensified problems of leisure and recreation. A summary of the more important changes should impress one with the need for educating youth for leisure and recreational pursuits. These include:

1. An increase in leisure time for youth in both urban and rural communities, resulting primarily from the passing of chores at home, the decline in opportunities for vocational employment, and the decrease in working hours
2. An increase in urbanization of our population resulting in sophistication of youth, gang life among young people, commercialized vice, and a growing looseness in the inhibitions and ties of the home, church, and community

3. The passing of leisure activities from the home and its immediate neighborhood to places and localities some distance from the home
4. The stupendous development of commercialized amusements, both of desirable and undesirable types, resulting in increased cost of leisure activities and leading to certain moral problems

These are a few of the problems that have created a great need for guidance of youth in the development of wholesome interests for leisure. The situation is especially acute in the junior high school because, at this age, pupils extend their circle of friends, develop interests in leisure activities that include the opposite sex, and desire freedom from domination by the family in the choice of their recreational activities.

Practices in Recreational Guidance. In the junior high school today, there is not only preparation for participating in activities for leisure, but there is also guidance in the choice of activities for leisure time—in sports and games, dramatics, reading, music, art, dancing and other social pastimes, hobbies, radio, television, and movies. There is hardly any phase of the school program which does not have some activities appropriate for recreational guidance.

Some leisure-time activities, such as reading and music, have received attention in the school program for a good many years. Recently, many other leisure-time activities are also being introduced into the school program. One of the most interesting recent developments in leisure-time activities is the attention being given to hobbies. The most popular avenue for developing hobbies in the junior high school is the club program. Hobbies also receive attention in industrial arts, home economics, and English classes. A few schools even have special hobby classes.

The increased attendance at movies and the rapid introduction of the radio and television into practically every American home have forced the school to assume some responsibility for developing wholesome interests in these leisure-time activities. Many schools have activities in English classes with movie appreciation as an objective. Activities for guidance of pupils in movie appreciation are presented also in homerooms, assemblies, auditorium activities, and movie clubs. Not a great deal of attention is given to developing appreciation of better radio and television programs, although in a few schools there are some activities for this purpose in English and music classes and in radio and television clubs.

For a generation, the secondary school has given some recognition to participation in sports as a wholesome recreational activity. But the average American adult is more often a sports spectator than a participant. Furthermore, the more popular American sports—football, basketball, and baseball—are too strenuous for most people a few years after they leave the secondary school or college. Because of this, there has been a growing recognition in the secondary school that boys and girls should be helped to enjoy the more common sports as spectators as well as participants. Consequently, most junior high schools today have some activities for teaching pupils about sports as a basis for more enjoyable spectatorship. Topics included in such a study are the history of various sports, outstanding teams and players, and rules of the game. The sports-study club, found in many schools, is one of the most effective and popular activities for this purpose. Other activities include talks and discussions in homerooms, assemblies, physical education classes, pupil handbooks, and the school paper.

Personal Guidance. In addition to the types of guidance problems already discussed in this chapter, junior high school pupils present others which are difficult to classify. These include financial difficulties, religious conflicts, worries about personal appearance, sex problems, unpopularity with classmates, difficult family relationships, and lack of friends. Because of their purely individual and personal nature these may be called personal guidance problems. The following cases are examples of such problems:

Frederick, twelve, an only child, is small for his age, young for his grade, and has been pampered and spoiled at home. As a result, he is not very cooperative in activities at school. He does not adjust well to a group situation where his own wishes must be submerged to those of the group. When he is admonished by the teacher or crossed by other pupils, he cries easily.

Harold, fourteen, has been slow to develop in some respects; although tall, he has a high-pitched, childish voice and is physiologically underdeveloped. He suffers from a feeling of inferiority.

Hazel, fourteen, is very discouraged because she cannot afford to dress and appear as well as other girls. She would like to work part time after school or Saturdays, but is unable to find such employment. She is afraid she must withdraw from school upon reaching 16, the compulsory attendance age limit.

Edwin, twelve, grade eight, has an I.Q. of 135, but is under-age and physically small for his grade, though slightly large for his age; he is seriously concerned about not being able to participate in athletics and engage in other activities normal for his grade.

Dora, thirteen, is emotionally upset a considerable part of the time because of mistreatment and lack of affection from a stepmother. At school she seeks sympathy and also the affection she does not receive at home. Her emotional condition apparently is affecting her physical health, as well as her personality development.

Mary, fourteen, wants to attend school parties and similar functions at the homes of friends, but her parents refuse to let her go out in the evening because they feel that, regardless of the supervision that may be provided, girls of her age should not be out after supper. She is developing a hostile attitude toward her parents and a feeling of social inferiority in school.

Jack, fifteen, does poor school work partly because of bad eyesight. But he continually "loses" the glasses provided for him by the school because the boys call him "grandpa" when he wears them. He is more concerned about the approval of his friends than the danger of failing his grade.

Margaret, thirteen, is fat, her eyes are slightly crossed, and she has a large birthmark on her face. Both boys and girls either pity or shun her. She has no real friends. She knows that her vocational opportunities after leaving school are very limited. "Why should I live?"

For many problems such as these the school can provide no solution. But, through guidance, it may be able to check the damage that is being done to the child's personality. Most of all, these youngsters need an interested and sympathetic listener. Many of them find it difficult to discuss their problems with their parents or fellow youth. The teacher or school counselor frequently is a more appropriate person to hear their troubles and to discount the importance which the emotionally upset child may attach to them. In some instances, the conditions which have produced the child's problem may be remedied. But if the school does no more than to provide sympathetic persons to hear the pupil's problems, it may still have rendered him a valuable service.

In every school there should be staff members who are qualified through training, experience, and personality to help pupils with these personal problems. Every child should have at least one teacher in whom he has complete confidence. In the junior high school, more than at any other level, the number and the seriousness of personal problems among pupils makes it exceedingly important that there be adequate provision for personal guidance.

5. Information About Pupils as a Basis for Guidance

Importance of Data About Pupils. Two types of guidance philosophy and practice are unsound and may hinder the effectiveness of the guidance program. One of these—sometimes called the "Pollyanna" philosophy—holds that all that is necessary for effective guidance is a person with a good personality and the desire to do good. Adherents of the "Pollyanna" philosophy of guidance not only consider scientific data about pupils as unnecessary, but some believe that tests and other scientific instruments are little more than pseudo-scientific gadgets.

A second point of view, fully as fallacious as the "Pollyanna" attitude, is that "you do it with mirrors" through tests and test scores. The test enthusiasts believe that test data provide the answers for all guidance problems—the occupation for which one is best suited, probable success in various elective courses, whether or not one should go to college, and similar problems. Actually, this perverted use of test results is hardly more effective in guidance than crystal-gazing or phrenology. Yet many teachers, counselors, school administrators, and college teachers of psychology and guidance deceive themselves and their associates into believing that this is sound guidance practice.

Those who aspire to give effective guidance should avoid both of these extremes. It is true that, for some guidance problems, a sympathetic attitude on the part of the counselor and a certain amount of common sense are sufficient. But for many problems, considerable objective data about pupils are essential. It is important, therefore, that the teacher and the counselor be prepared to gather, interpret, and use objective data about individual pupils as a basis for effective guidance.

It is unfortunate that, in many schools, available data about pupils are not used for guidance purposes as much as is desirable because they are not readily accessible to the teachers. If it is to be of the most value in guidance, information about individual pupils should be in the hands of those teachers who are likely to use it. In many schools, however, there is a tendency to keep these data exclusively in the office of the principal or counselor. Consequently, it may not be convenient for the teacher to obtain this information at the moment when he most needs it.

It cannot be emphasized too strongly that homeroom teachers, especially, should have convenient access to all data about pupils assigned to them. The most satisfactory practice is to place in their hands duplicates of the pupil records which are in the central office. Classroom teachers, however, also have sufficient guidance responsibilities to justify giving them considerable information about individual pupils. It would be difficult to provide them also with duplicates of these records. In some schools, a summary of the more significant pupil data is given to teachers for all pupils who are in their classes, with the suggestion that they consult the office records frequently for further information. Another plan is to place either duplicates or summaries of these records in a teachers' office where they are readily available to all staff members. *Whatever plan is employed for this purpose, it is essential to the success of the guidance program that all information about pupils be readily available to the homeroom and classroom teachers.*

Methods of Obtaining Data About Pupils. Among the more satisfactory devices and procedures for obtaining information about pupils as a basis for guidance are: (1) an analysis of achievement and other records ordinarily maintained in the principal's or counselor's office; (2) the use of mental, achievement, and prognostic tests; (3) questionnaires submitted to pupils, parents, and other appropriate persons; (4) conferences with pupils and parents; (5) visits to the pupils' homes; and (6) reports by teachers. The procedures must necessarily be selected in terms of the information that is desired.

Much information can be obtained from the pupil himself through questionnaires and conferences. Information about participation in extraclass activities, out-of-school activities, and vacation and part-time employment may readily be obtained in this way. The teachers themselves are another source of pupil data which is frequently neglected, particularly in the large school. The anecdotal record, which has received so much emphasis recently, is one way of accumulating for guidance purposes some of the valuable information teachers have concerning their pupils. These procedures and many others may be employed to advantage for obtaining information and data about individual pupils as a basis for an effective guidance program.

Training in Interpretation and Use of Pupil Data. It is essential to the success of the guidance program that teachers receive both pre-service and in-service training in the interpretation and use of data about pupils. Pre-service training should include professional study in the colleges and universities. This must be supplemented, however, by training through various channels as teachers in service engage in guidance activities with junior high school pupils. Placing recent books on tests and measurements in a faculty library, issuing bulletins from the counselor's office, study of this subject at faculty meetings, and conferences between the counselor and teachers who are inexperienced in guidance are useful ways of helping teachers learn to use data about pupils.

6. Avenues of Guidance Service

Guidance Through Homerooms and Core Rooms. The homeroom provides a splendid avenue for both individual and group guidance. Its effectiveness for guidance lies primarily in the fact that it permits an informal pupil-teacher relationship not so readily possible in the more formal atmosphere of the classroom. In the homeroom, the pupil is encouraged to express his own views, to challenge the opinions of his fellows, and to discuss personal problems frankly with the teacher. This informal atmosphere makes the homeroom the key place in the entire guidance program.

The spread of the core plan in the junior high school has resulted in a considerable increase in both individual and group guidance. The core teacher usually has only two groups of pupils, and consequently is able to know individual pupils much better than the teacher who has four or five different groups. This has made it easier for the core teacher to carry on effective guidance activities.

In schools with a core program, it is a common practice to combine the homeroom with the core groups. In some schools, as at the Weeks Junior High School, Newton, Massachusetts, additional time is provided for the homeroom activities. In others, these activities are combined with English and social studies. In any case, the homeroom activities are closely integrated with the language arts and social studies work of the core classes. In fact, this integration of the homeroom with the work of the core classes is a step toward bringing the homeroom more closely into the educational program of the school.

Guidance Through the Curriculum. The curriculum should be so developed that it may serve as an effective channel for guidance. Some courses should be introduced primarily to provide opportunities for pupils to explore their interests and capacities—such courses as industrial arts, music, junior business training, and general science. Furthermore, every subject in the curriculum should be so taught that pupils may not only explore their interests and capacities, but also that they may acquire a background of information which may be useful in making future educational and vocational decisions.

A specific course in the curriculum, designed primarily to give information as a basis for guidance, is the occupations or vocations course. In this course the pupil is informed about the relative demand and supply of the various vocations, economic and other rewards, nature of the work, tenure, suitability at various ages, seasonal influences, social prestige, hazards to health and safety, required training or experience, personality and character traits desirable for success, and similar information.

Guidance Through School Publications. Other useful channels for giving pupils information as a basis for guidance—particularly educational guidance—are the various school publications, such as the school paper and the pupil handbook. Through the school paper, pupils can be informed about various phases of school life—elective curriculums and courses, extraclass activities, the history, traditions, and regulations of the school, and changes in the policies and educational program of the school. The editorial columns of the school paper may also serve as means of influencing pupil opinion, developing school spirit and morale, and developing desirable social attitudes and ideals. In these ways and in others, the school paper provides a convenient channel for disseminating information which may be useful as a basis for guidance.

The pupil handbook, more than any other school publication, has guidance as its prime purpose, especially educational guidance. A copy of the handbook ordinarily is given to every pupil. In the seventh grade, it frequently serves as a basic reference for orientation activities in the homeroom. It is also used as a basis for guidance in the eighth and ninth grades. Like the school paper, the handbook has become increasingly an all-pupil publication. In some schools, the handbook is prepared by such pupil groups as the student council, a citizenship club, or an English class. Pupil preparation of the handbook should increase its guidance value because the material is likely to be presented from the pupils' point of view.

Guidance Through Extraclass Activities. Assemblies, clubs, social functions, athletic teams, speech groups, and other extraclass activities provide splendid opportunities for guidance. Many of these activities, such as speech groups, clubs, and music organizations, permit pupils to explore and try out both present and potential interests and capacities. Information that is of value for educational, vocational, and recreational guidance may also be conveyed to pupils through these activities. Then, too, because of the intimate teacher-pupil relationships which usually develop in extraclass activities, many casual opportunities appropriate for guidance present themselves.

As a basis for effective guidance, the program of extraclass activities should be sufficiently broad to provide for the needs of every pupil. There should be clubs that appeal to every interest, speech activities for all interested pupils, competitive sports for pupils of every ability, and broad offerings in music, dramatics, hobbies, and journalism. Furthermore, it would be desirable for every pupil to explore different capacities and interests through participation in many different activities during the years he spends in the junior and senior high school.

The school assembly constitutes a widely used channel for guidance in the junior high school. For social and civic guidance, assemblies are a means of developing high ideals, desirable attitudes, and an understanding and acceptance of recognized social customs. For educational guidance, the assembly is of value for giving information about courses and activities, for orientation of new pupils in the history, traditions, and policies of the school, and for developing wholesome school spirit and morale.

Every phase of the extraclass program of the school provides some opportunities for effective guidance activities. Clubs, assemblies, sports, school publications, speech activities, social functions, and pupil participation in management and government—all have their place in the guidance program.

Individual Guidance Conferences. Many guidance problems are of such an individual nature that they demand attention to the individual pupil impossible in group activities. The most valuable means of individual guidance is the conference between the teacher, or counselor, and the pupil. It is important, therefore, to make ample provision for such conferences. In most schools, however, there is no clear-cut policy or organized plan for individual conferences with pupils. The individual conference is commonly an incidental affair which is squeezed into the school program more or less as convenience permits. In many schools, individual conferences are reserved largely for pupils with serious guidance problems, thus raising some suspicion in the minds of pupils about this valuable channel for guidance. A policy of encouraging individual conferences with pupils is important to the success of the guidance program.

Individual Conferences with Guidance Specialists. Like the homeroom teacher, the guidance specialists in a school do not find it easy to arrange individual conferences with pupils. Their problem is complicated by the fact that there may be several hundred pupils for every specialist. With such a pupil load, the specialists devote their attention primarily to those pupils who are considered problem cases. This situation tends to discourage pupils from seeking individual conferences with the guidance specialist. Furthermore, if such conferences are arranged, the specialist may lack the time for follow-up conferences to become fully acquainted with the individual pupil and his peculiar problems.

In every school, some measures should be taken to encourage all pupils to seek the services of the guidance specialists. The homeroom is perhaps the most appropriate place for this purpose. In the homeroom, pupils should be informed of the services offered by the various specialists, they should learn what problems might well be taken to the specialists, and they should be assisted by the teacher in arranging for such individual conferences. Information concerning the services of the guidance specialists should also be presented in the pupil handbook, the school paper, and other publications. Finally, the specialists should meet pupils in assemblies and in small group conferences. With contacts such as these, the pupil should be more receptive to individual conferences with the various guidance specialists in his school.

7. Conclusion

The concept of guidance in the junior high school has undergone considerable change in recent years. With pupils continuing to go to school longer, vocational guidance is being postponed largely until the senior high school. In the junior high school, more attention is being given to the emotional, health, educational, social, and character problems of early adolescents. Most of the progress, however, has been made in providing qualified staff for guidance. Many more schools today have psychologists, psychiatrists, guidance directors, and other specialists as compared with a decade or two ago. Furthermore, homeroom and classroom teachers are better prepared to participate in guidance activities. The improvement in the qualifications of the staff for guidance should lead to more effective guidance activities in the junior high school.

Questions and Exercises

1. What types of guidance services are most important for youth of junior high school age?

2. List six types of guidance services and under each give the more important services that can be rendered in the junior high school.

3. What responsibility for guidance should be assumed by each of the following: (a) principal, (b) dean of boys or dean of girls, (c) nurse, (d) physician, (e) coach, (f) homeroom teacher, and (g) classroom teacher?

4. Some educators believe that the homeroom and classroom teachers must assume the major responsibility for guidance in the junior high school, while others feel that this should be assumed by the guidance specialists. Give your point of view, substantiating it fully.

5. What are some guidance activities that may be taken care of better through group guidance than through individual guidance? Make a list of such activities.

6. Prepare a plan for helping incoming junior high school pupils become oriented and assimilated in a new school.

7. Prepare a plan for assisting junior high school pupils to get ready for senior high school life.

8. Make a list of all the types of information about junior high school pupils which would be desirable for a superior guidance service. After each one, state where you would get the information and for what type or types of guidance it is most useful.

9. Prepare a list of important suggestions on counseling which would be helpful to teachers lacking experience in guidance.

10. What should be the principal responsibilities of a head counselor in a junior high school? What kinds of training and experience should he have had? Be specific.

11. What are the various ways of discovering the vocational, educational, and recreational interests of junior high school pupils?

12. Write out a real or imaginary case history for a junior high school problem case. Tell what a counselor should do to try to help the individual.

13. Are discipline problems guidance problems? Explain.

14. Explain quite fully how one of the following subjects can serve as an avenue for guidance: English, social studies, junior business, Latin, or industrial arts.

Chapter 12

THE HOMEROOM

1. Functions of the Homeroom

The general objectives of the homeroom correspond to those for other phases of the educational program of the junior high school, but there are also specific functions which it is generally believed that the homeroom should serve in reaching those objectives. The generally recognized functions of the homeroom include:

1. To facilitate certain aspects of the administration of the school
2. To supplement the curriculum
3. To promote pupil participation in extraclass activities
4. To provide facilities and opportunities for guidance
5. To provide opportunities for developing desirable social, personality, and character qualities among pupils
6. To assist in the development of desirable pupil attitudes toward the school and its program
7. To personalize the contacts of the pupil with the administrative and educational activities of the school

Administrative responsibilities of the homeroom generally include the following.

1. To make administrative announcements and convey necessary information to pupils and parents
2. To discuss and explain administrative policies and practices
3. To check and record pupil attendance and tardiness, to promote better attendance, and to reduce tardiness
4. To distribute and collect pupil report cards, to interpret marks, and to discuss the significance of scholastic achievement
5. To promote attendance at various extraclass activities and to conduct ticket sales for them
6. To receive deposits and administer other details of the school savings bank
7. To check on the health of pupils and administer certain details of the health program, particularly those matters dealing with the prevention and control of contagious diseases

263

8. To take care of the details of registering pupils for courses, curriculums, and extraclass activities
9. To provide an agency in school for certain civic and charitable activities of the community in which the school may cooperate

Contributions to the Curriculum. There is much that young people should learn which cannot readily be introduced into the school program, either as new courses or as additions or modifications to courses now in the curriculum. Examples of such areas are: good manners, personality and character problems, parliamentary procedure, study habits, and problems of safety and accident prevention. For a number of reasons, it is difficult to introduce such topics into the regular courses.

The homeroom is a logical place for introducing such topics. The informal teacher-pupil and pupil-pupil relationships make it possible to study with considerable effectiveness such topics as good manners, character qualities, and personality problems. Furthermore, as compared with the regular courses, it is much easier to introduce these topics in the homeroom as need arises during the school year. In fact, in some schools the homeroom period is already overcrowded with materials for study because so many topics have been introduced there more appropriately than elsewhere in the school program.

Contributions to Extraclass Activities. Two significant contributions can be made by the homeroom to the extraclass program of the school. First, the homeroom may be used as an avenue for stimulating pupil interest in such activities as clubs, assemblies, athletic teams, and music organizations. In fact, the chief contact that pupils have with such activities is normally through the homeroom. In the homeroom, pupils are informed about the type of activities available; they learn the values of those activities; they are assisted in selecting activities in which they might be interested and might succeed; and frequently they are registered for the activities of their choice by the homeroom adviser.

The homeroom also contributes to the extraclass program by serving as a place for carrying on many pupil activities. For instance, homeroom groups frequently engage in the following activities: (1) they organize and present assembly programs, (2) they serve as the basic units for the pupil government of the school, (3) they provide teams for intramural competition in debate, athletics, etc., (4) they sometimes take turns in publishing the school paper, (5) they form competitive units in school campaigns and drives of various kinds, and (6) they may have their own programs of music, debates, and homeroom paper.

Contributions to Group Guidance. In many junior high schools, the homeroom has become the center for the entire guidance program, including both individual and group guidance. The informality and freedom of discussion possible in the homeroom make it an appropriate place for the study of those guidance problems which may be discussed with pupils in a group. Topics such as the following are frequently studied in the homeroom through group-guidance activities: (1) the planning of one's educational program, (2) vocational opportunities and choices, (3) good manners, (4) boy-girl relationships, (5) problems related to education beyond high school, (6) continuation in school beyond junior high school, (7) character problems, (8) problems of mental and physical health, (9) getting and holding a job, and (10) problems of accident prevention and safety.

Contributions to Individual Guidance. The homeroom adviser can provide valuable individual as well as group guidance. *In fact one of the chief purposes of the homeroom is to provide a place in the school program where such intimate and personal relations may be developed between teacher and pupil that effective individual guidance can take place.* Obviously, the amount of individual guidance that can be carried on in the homeroom depends upon the preparation, experience, and personal qualifications of the homeroom adviser. Certain other factors, however, also are of importance in determining the amount of individual guidance that can be carried on in the homeroom. These factors include the amount of information concerning their pupils which is available to homeroom advisers, the amount of school time allowed for individual conferences, the rooms available for such conferences, and the amount of time advisers are given for planning and carrying on individual-guidance activities. Unfortunately, in many junior high schools today, conditions do not obtain that are conducive to effective individual guidance in the homeroom. It would, of course, be extremely unwise for the homeroom adviser to assume responsibilities for individual guidance which he is not able to discharge effectively.

As a basis for effective individual guidance, the homeroom adviser should do everything in his power to establish satisfactory relationships with each of his pupils. To his homeroom pupils, he should be more than just another teacher. There should exist between them a friendly, intimate relationship which encourages the pupil to discuss frankly his most intimate problems. It is not easy for the adviser to establish such a relationship. It means, first of all, that the adviser has a sincere interest in his pupils, that he enjoys seeing them and visiting with them, that he is interested in their successes and failures, and that he will listen to their problems with sympathy and understanding. Furthermore, the adviser should know his pupils well, continually learning more about them—their interests in school, their home and out-of-school backgrounds and interests, their abilities and limitations, their educational and personal problems, and their hopes and ambitions. Finally, the adviser should have a sincere feeling of responsibility for his pupils—the feeling that their successes are, in a sense, his successes, and their failures, his failures. With such an interest in and understanding of his pupils, the homeroom adviser may well establish a sound basis for effective individual guidance.

In schools with a staff of guidance specialists, it is important that the guidance responsibilities of the homeroom teacher be clearly defined. Furthermore, there should be an intelligent and cordial working relationship between the technical staff and the homeroom teacher. The more technical guidance problems obviously should be left to the specialist. Usually, the technical staff is also responsible for the gathering of information about pupils, for the organization and direction of the guidance program as a whole, and for the training of teachers in the theory and techniques of guidance.

Contributions to Social and Character Education. Activities for developing social and character qualities are really guidance activities. But ordinarily they form such a prominent part of the homeroom activities that they deserve special consideration. In fact, in many schools a major portion of the homeroom program is devoted to a study of topics in the area of social, personality, and character development such as (1) good manners, (2) conduct at school parties and other social functions, (3) the forming of friendships, (4) relations with members of the family group, (5) problems of appearance and dress, (6) control of one's emotions, (7) school-citizenship attitudes, (8) leadership skills and qualities, and (9) good sportsmanship.

But the homeroom is more than a place for the study and discussion of social, personality, and character problems. It is also a laboratory where habits and skills in this area can be developed by pupils through active participation and practice. For instance, the homeroom provides laboratory opportunities for the following purposes: (1) for developing leadership skills through such activities as the election of homeroom officers and the planning and direction of homeroom activities, (2) for practice in good manners through social functions and other homeroom projects and activities, and (3) for the development of poise and ease before one's fellows through various activities. Opportunities such as these for developing attitudes and skills through actual experience in lifelike situations are some of the significant contributions of the homeroom to the educational program of the junior high school.

Contributions to Desirable Parent-Teacher-Pupil Relationships. Desirable attitudes on the part of both parents and pupils toward the program of the school, toward the teachers and other staff members, and toward various school policies and practices, grow naturally from a better understanding of the school. In many schools, it is considered the responsibility of the homeroom adviser to bring about such an understanding through activities like the following:

1. Visiting the homes of the homeroom pupils early in the school year
2. Inviting parents to visit school when their child is participating in some special activity in the homeroom, in an assembly, at a school party, or in some other extraclass activity
3. Keeping in touch with the parents when their child is having some difficulty or problem of an educational, disciplinary, health, emotional, or other nature
4. Informing the parents of any unusual activities or successes of their child, such as being on the honor roll or success in an extraclass activity
5. Keeping parents informed concerning changes in school policies and regulations through bulletins sent home with the child or through direct communication
6. Organizing the parents of the pupils in each homeroom as a sponsoring group. These groups of parents may be of valuable assistance in encouraging homeroom solidarity, in planning and in helping chaperon social events of the homeroom group, and in discussing policies in such matters as homework, hours of out-of-school social life, dress, etc.

2. THE ORGANIZATION OF THE HOMEROOM

Length and Frequency of Homeroom Periods. The desirable length and number of homeroom periods for any school depends upon a number of factors, including the following: (1) how well problems ordinarily studied in the homeroom are already being covered in the regular classes; (2) how well the materials and activities for the homeroom have been organized and developed; (3) how experienced and skillful the teachers are in planning and conducting homeroom activities; (4) how experienced and interested the pupils are in homeroom activities; and (5) the experience of the sponsors with the homeroom programs. These factors should be carefully examined before the precise nature of the homeroom period for any school is determined,

Authorities generally agree that the brief period at the beginning of the day is not a homeroom period in the real sense of the term. It is not long enough nor does it come at an appropriate time in the day for the kind of activities commonly carried on in the homeroom. It is suitable only as an administrative period for discharging certain essential routine duties, and probably should not be called a homeroom. The homeroom period, as that term is generally used, refers to a period of sufficient length to carry on the various functions outlined in the preceding section of this chapter.

In general, a short homeroom period—that is, one of less than 20 minutes or so—has not proved satisfactory. Such a short period does not permit a thorough program of well-conducted pupil activities which are desired for an effective homeroom program. The trend at present, therefore, is toward a longer homeroom period. In some schools, a regular class period is assigned to the homeroom, usually from 40 to 55 minutes in length. But, at the junior high school level, a period longer than 40 minutes may prove as unsatisfactory as a short one. That is particularly true in schools where the homeroom period is new and teachers are inexperienced in carrying on homeroom activities.

A plan for the homeroom period which has been popular, particularly in the junior high school, is to set aside a daily period of 30 to 45 minutes for various types of extraclass activities. Under this plan, one period weekly may be assigned to assemblies, another to clubs, and the others to homeroom activities. An activity period such as this should provide ample time for carrying on homeroom and other extraclass activities in a well-planned manner.

In the study by the authors of practices in 370 junior high schools, the percentages which have various numbers of homeroom periods per week are as follows:

Periods	Schools
1	19%
2	7%
3	4%
4	4%
5	60%
More than 5	6%

There is much variation in the length of the homeroom periods, in the 370 schools surveyed, with quite a few 10 minutes or less in length, and others 100 or more minutes long. The median length is 32 minutes. In the schools with exceptionally long periods, the homeroom is combined with subject classes, as in the core groups. The length of the homeroom period is as follows, with the percentage of schools indicated:

Minutes	Schools
1-10	13%
11-20	23%
21-30	28%
31-40	13%
41-50	17%
More than 50	6%

Time for Homeroom Period. Practice varies considerably among various schools concerning the time of day that is assigned to the homeroom. In some schools, considerable thought has been given to the reorganization of the daily schedule to provide a suitable time for the homeroom period. In others, it has been squeezed into a crowded schedule wherever it would least interfere with the regular classes.

The last period in the day is not a favorable time for the homeroom period. Pupils may be too tired late in the day to participate with enthusiasm in the type of activities that are carried on. Then, too, both teachers and pupils may consider the homeroom period an afterthought in the school program if it comes at the end of the day. According to the principal of one school which had this plan, parents frequently asked that pupils be excused during the homeroom period to work, to run errands, and for other unimportant reasons. This is not likely to be true, however, once the homeroom period is accepted as an important part of the school program.

The most favorable time for the homeroom period is probably the middle of the morning or early in the afternoon. At that time, pupils are usually sufficiently alert to be interested in activities like those carried on in the homeroom. Furthermore, it provides an appropriate break for the pupils in their schedule of classes.

Composition of the Homeroom Group. It is by far the most common practice to arrange pupils in homeroom groups heterogeneously, two-thirds of the junior high schools in the study by the authors having this plan. In only about 10 per cent of the schools is the membership in homerooms based on some plan of ability grouping. Since the homeroom should provide a normal social situation, it is indeed difficult to defend pupil ability as a criterion for arranging homeroom groups.

A few schools have reported satisfactory results with homeroom groups composed of pupils of different grades. Some principals suggest that the presence of some older pupils in each homeroom group provides better leadership, furnishes resource persons for the orientation of new pupils, improves disciplinary situations, and provides for the gradual introduction of junior high school pupils to positions of leadership.

The principals of some schools, however, feel there are certain disadvantages in having pupils from all three grades in the same homeroom. They suggest that the seventh-grade pupils are likely to be deprived of leadership experiences by the older pupils; that the interests of pupils differ from one grade to another; and that the problems to be studied in the homeroom are different for different grades. Because of these objections, the plan of having pupils from all these grades in the same homeroom has been discontinued in some schools.

Permanence of Homeroom Groupings. Both theory and practice are divided on the question of maintaining homeroom groupings intact during the junior high school careers of the pupils. There are definite advantages for maintaining the same groupings for several years, largely because of the friendships, the working relationships, and the loyalty and school spirit which can be developed. Especially in large schools and communities, where it is difficult to find intimate companionship, this practice may encourage the formation of friendships that will continue into senior high school and later life. It also permits an adviser to continue with the same pupils for several years. It is true, however, that the experience of making new friendships and the values that may be derived from the ideas of other pupils are strong arguments in favor of rearranging the composition of homeroom groups from year to year.

Retention of Advisers. Practice varies also with respect to retaining the same homeroom adviser for several years. The advantages of retaining the adviser are as follows: (1) the adviser develops a deeper interest in the welfare of his pupils, (2) he learns to know them much more intimately, and (3) he is able to follow through from year to year in helping pupils improve themselves and in correcting serious individual problems. Strong arguments can be advanced, however, in favor of changing homeroom advisers, among them the following: (1) some teachers work better with children of one age than another, (2) teachers may become specialists in the guidance problems of a certain grade, (3) pupils gain from contacts with different teachers, (4) teacher-pupil relations over a period of years may become too informal to retain the best disciplinary control over the group, and (5) inexperienced teachers do better with a new homeroom group.

3. Pupil Officers and Committees

Pupil Officers for the Homeroom. In the junior high school, it is customary to organize the homeroom with pupil officers and committees who assume the responsibility for planning and carrying on various activities. The officers usually include a president, vice-president, secretary, and treasurer, and, in some schools, representatives on the student council and other all-school boards and committees. There should be a definite statement of the responsibilities and duties of the various officers so that well-qualified pupils may be elected. The principal duties of these officers include the following:

President: presides at business meetings and takes charge in the absence of the teacher; sees that committees become active and discharge their responsibilities; and exercises general leadership.

Vice-President: substitutes for the president in his absence; assists the president in supervising the work of committees, seeing that they function; and may serve as chairman of an important committee.

Secretary: keeps minutes of each meeting; records attendance and absence; keeps records of homeroom activities; files written reports of committees and records the essence of oral reports; and carries on whatever correspondence may be necessary for the homeroom.

Treasurer: under the supervision of the homeroom adviser, collects money for homeroom purposes from the members; keeps a careful and accurate financial record; makes financial reports when called upon; and pays debts incurred by the homeroom.

In addition to these officers, in many schools there are student council representatives who represent the homeroom at meetings of the student council and take part in the discussions of the council. These representatives are active along the lines suggested in discussions of the homeroom group. They report to the members of the homeroom group on the activities of the council and serve on committees of the student council.

In most schools there is an executive committee of the homeroom made up of the officers and the teacher. The president is the presiding officer of this committee, while the homeroom adviser is the resource person.

Homeroom Committees. Many homerooms have found it desirable to have several standing committees elected twice a year, if not oftener. Among the committees most commonly found are the following:

1. *Citizenship committee:* to exercise leadership in developing policy and student morale in connection with standards of behavior and good

citizenship, and to encourage the participation and cooperation of all the homeroom members in the activities of the group.

2. *Social committee:* to make plans and to offer suggestions for the social life of the group, making recommendations to the teacher and the executive committee; to assume some responsibility for the planning and management of social affairs of the group; and to act as ushers and guides for visitors.

3. *Program committee:* In some schools the executive committee acts as a program committee, while in others there is a special program committee. In some schools there is a prepared outline of topics for each grade, which serves as a guide for the program committee.

In some schools there are other standing committees. In almost every school situations arise for the appointment of special or temporary committees to serve a particular purpose. These are usually appointed by the president and the homeroom sponsor. It is clear that there should not be too many committees, some of them having no particular function and not being active. That is not good civic training.

Election of Homeroom Officers. An excellent opportunity for citizenship education is provided by the periodic election of homeroom officers. These elections should be well organized and should approximate as nearly as possible a real-life citizenship situation. The following suggestions may be helpful in accomplishing that purpose:

1. The election should be well planned in advance by the executive committee or a special election committee.
2. Ample time should be allowed in the homeroom to carry on an election.
3. A day or two should elapse between the nomination of candidates and the election itself to permit pupils to study the qualifications of the candidates.
4. Pupils should understand the duties and responsibilities of the various officers and the types of persons who can best meet them.
5. A well-controlled, simple election campaign is a splendid means of presenting the qualifications of the candidates to the homeroom group.
6. Suitable safeguards should be set up to assure fairness in the conduct of the election, the counting of the ballots, and other details of the election.

Since the holding of a homeroom office is a worth-while educational experience, it should be offered to as many pupils as possible. Consequently, the term of office should not be long. For homerooms of about 30 pupils, from six to nine weeks is a satisfactory term of office. Furthermore, soon after election, the officers should be given some training for the duties and responsibilities they are to assume. Activities such as these are essential if the holding of homeroom offices is to be the most effective learning experience.

4. The Homeroom Adviser

Selection of Homeroom Advisers. In most schools, the pupil-teacher ratio is so high that practically all teachers must serve as homeroom advisers. This is indeed unfortunate because some teachers are not qualified, either by interest or ability, to serve effectively in this capacity. The problem, therefore, is not which teachers should be designated as homeroom advisers, but rather to which homerooms the teachers should be assigned. This responsibility usually falls upon the principal, the director of guidance, or a faculty committee. The following factors should be considered in making these assignments:

1. *The preferences of the teacher.* For instance, some teachers prefer homeroom groups in one grade to those of another. Furthermore, the teacher's preference for a specific homeroom group within a grade should be given some consideration.
2. *The experience of the teacher.* For example, a beginning teacher or one inexperienced in homeroom work should not be assigned to a group that is known to be difficult to manage. Unfortunately, the poorer groups are frequently assigned to the incoming teacher. This is indeed poor school administration. Those teachers with the most experience and training should be assigned to the most difficult homeroom groups.
3. *The teacher's total load.* The large homerooms or those which, in other ways, require the most time should be given to teachers who do not have a heavy load of class and extraclass activities.
4. *The teacher's previous homeroom assignments.* The difficult homerooms should not be given, year after year, to the same teachers. It is best for the morale of the staff if there is some rotation in the assignment of difficult groups.
5. *The teacher's grade assignment for classwork.* In some schools, teachers have homerooms in the same grades in which they teach. This plan enables the homeroom adviser to become more thoroughly acquainted with his pupils.

Preparation of the Homeroom Adviser. The adviser should have a sympathetic interest in the problems of junior high school youth; he should possess personal qualities that appeal to boys and girls; he should have preparation in the philosophy, organization, and methods of the homeroom; and he should have previous experience in teaching junior high school youth.

The administrative staff of the junior high school, however, should not be satisfied with the previous training and experience of teachers in homeroom work. A program of improvement in homeroom techniques should be part of the supervisory activities in every school. Activities which should be helpful for this purpose include: (1) faculty meetings devoted to the subject; (2) books on the homeroom in a faculty library; (3) bulletins on homeroom activities prepared by a director of guidance or a faculty committee; (4) visits to other homerooms; and (5) demonstration activities presented by competent homeroom advisers.

The beginning teacher, particularly, presents a problem of training for homeroom responsibilities. In large schools with a low teacher turnover, it is sometimes possible to avoid homeroom assignments for the beginning teacher. If it can be arranged, he should be assigned as an assistant for a year or two to a competent and experienced homeroom adviser. This policy also is helpful in relieving some homeroom advisers who have a heavy total teaching load. In small schools or schools with a high teacher turnover, the beginning teacher usually must be assigned a homeroom. In such cases, special attention should be given to helping the teacher become skilled in homeroom techniques.

Home Visitation and Contacts. It is recognized today that mutual respect and understanding between teachers and parents is fundamental to a satisfactory learning situation for the child. Consequently, activities that lead to closer cooperation between home and school are being emphasized increasingly in the junior high school. These activities are designed to give the teacher a more complete understanding of the child's background, to provide information regarding his out-of-school activities and interests, to help avoid misunderstandings and friction between the home and the school, and to encourage cooperation between the school and the home in helping the pupil with various educational and personal problems.

In order to establish such relations with the home, the homeroom advisers in many schools are encouraged to visit the homes of their pupils early in the school year. Frequently, these visits are arranged through the child, with the suggestion that the teacher would be pleased to have him present when he calls. When this visit is made, the teacher should not give the impression that he is studying the home or that he is reporting on the conduct or work of the pupil at school. In fact, it may be best if the pupil and his work in school are not discussed at all. Rather, the purpose of the visit should be to give the teacher an opportunity to become acquainted with the parents.

The homeroom teacher should not confine his contacts with parents to home visits. Useful contacts can also be made through the churches, service and civic organizations, the P.T.A., and other community organizations and activities. Formal contacts between the school and the home concerning specific problems are also maintained through the homeroom adviser, including reports of pupil progress, statements on school policy, invitations to school functions, and publications on various aspects of the school program. Usually, such contacts as these are maintained through the pupils, who take the materials home. But the homeroom adviser is responsible for making such contacts as effective and favorable as possible.

Pupil Data for the Adviser. As a basis for effective adviser-pupil relationships, it is essential that the homeroom adviser have complete and detailed information about all of his pupils. He should have information about them as follows: (1) intelligence test results, (2) past and present achievement in school, (3) participation in extraclass activities, (4) vocational, avocational, and educational interests, (5) physical and mental health, (6) home and family backgrounds, (7) character and personality qualities, (8) citizenship qualities, and (9) vacation and part-time employment. Information such as this is available in many schools but is usually kept in a central office where it is not readily accessible to the homeroom advisers. *It is essential that homeroom advisers have such information about their pupils conveniently available at all times.* This means that the advisers should have duplicates of pupil records or summaries of the important information on those records.

According to the survey by the authors, homeroom teachers are given copies of cumulative records in approximately 10 per cent of the schools. In quite a few schools, they are given records of the interests of pupils, mental test results, pupil participation in school activities, and out-of-school activities and employment. The most common practice, however, is to keep these records in a central office where teachers may examine them. If this information is to be extensively used, it is essential that at least summaries be actually in the hands of the homeroom teachers.

The homeroom adviser also can play an important part in accumulating information about pupils. The type of information ordinarily placed in the anecdotal records, for instance, can be obtained most easily by the homeroom adviser. This includes information about the pupil's personal problems, successes and failures in school activities, maladjustments, and interests. Periodically, the adviser can also prepare descriptive statements about the character and personality qualities of the child. But usually the responsibility of the adviser for pupil records extends far beyond the accumulation of anecdotal items. In fact, much of the pupil data required by the counselors, the principal, and others, can be obtained only through the homeroom adviser. Such data include information about the pupils' home backgrounds, interests, out-of-school activities, and participation in extraclass activities.

Teaching Load for Homeroom Advisers. At first, when the homeroom imposed only a few administrative duties, this added responsibility made little difference in the teacher's total load. But, as the homeroom program expanded, the adviser's responsibilities for guidance, administrative matters, and various homeroom activities have increased considerably. Today, in schools with a well-developed homeroom program, the adviser has homeroom responsibilities which are sufficiently burdensome so that they can no longer be absorbed by teachers already overloaded with other professional responsibilities. It is becoming an increasing practice not to assign junior high school teachers more than five classes a day, plus a homeroom and perhaps a club or other activity.

In schools where the homeroom is part of the core classes, this problem is usually resolved by having it become a part of the homeroom teacher's class load. Consequently, the core teacher does not carry the homeroom as an additional activity. Even for the core teacher, however, the homeroom responsibilities may be heavier than other teaching responsibilities.

Some things can be done to lighten the burden of the homeroom adviser, such as the following:

1. *Outlines of activities and materials for the homerooms can be prepared by a director of guidance or a faculty committee.* This would reduce the time which the homeroom adviser ordinarily devotes to planning activities for the homeroom. Furthermore, it would probably lead to more effective homeroom activities.

2. *Many records and reports now prepared by the homeroom adviser can be assigned to clerks in a central office.* Attendance records, the recording of marks, periodic reports on attendance and achievement, guidance records, and other pupil-data records are of this type. Not only can much time be saved for the homeroom adviser by relieving him of such duties, but frequently this work can be done with more efficiency and accuracy in a central office.

3. *More clerical help can be provided.* Clerks can do more accurately such things as checking standard tests, scoring objective tests prepared by the teacher, recording marks for teachers, keeping rec-

ords of books and supplies, and similar duties. Teachers also need stenographic help with the typing or mimeographing of tests and unit outlines, and for correspondence with parents, book publishers, and others. Such relief from administrative details related to classroom work would give teachers more time to devote to homeroom responsibilities.

4. *Guidance specialists should be provided to assist homeroom advisers with difficult guidance problems.* The employment of such specialists is desirable, of course, to provide expert help in guidance. Such help is essential also to relieve otherwise overburdened homeroom advisers.

5. Planning the Homeroom Program

Method of Planning the Program. Several different points of view are held by educators concerning the procedure for planning the program of homeroom activities. The more common ones are:

1. *The activities may be selected and developed by the adviser and pupils within each individual homeroom.* The activities developed under this plan are likely to meet the interests and needs of the homeroom pupils. There are three objections to this plan: (a) there may be needless repetition of some topics and omission of others because each homeroom develops its own program year by year, (b) it is time-consuming for the advisers and pupils in the various homerooms to prepare such programs, and (c) such planning demands advisers who are unusually competent in homeroom work. Consequently, there is the danger under this plan that the homeroom program will be poorly organized, and that teachers and pupils will lose interest in it.

2. *The activities may be selected and developed by a faculty committee working under the direction of the principal or director of guidance.* Usually, the manner in which the activities are carried on is left to the discretion of the individual homeroom group, but the content of those activities is prescribed in the outline issued from the central authority. The freedom of the individual group to select its own topics and activities is definitely limited under this plan. It does, however, give some assurance that there will be something worth while for the homeroom to do at every session.

3. *A suggested outline of activities may be developed by the director of guidance, the principal, or a faculty committee, but with each individual homeroom having considerable freedom to select and develop its own activities.* The outline of activities issued to the homerooms is, therefore, largely a statement of suggestions which may be modified and adapted as the individual group thinks best. This plan

provides something definite for the inexperienced, the unresourceful, or the busy homeroom adviser. It avoids the uncertainties which accompany the policy of having each homeroom plan its own program of activities, and yet it allows the experienced and resourceful teacher ample freedom to meet the needs of his group. This policy with respect to planning the program of homeroom activities is, no doubt, most in harmony with our present-day philosophy concerning the homeroom.

Types of Activities for the Homeroom. The different topics and activities which may be included in the homeroom program are indeed endless. They are drawn from almost every area of pupil interest and activity. These topics and activities may be grouped as follows:

1. *Activities that grow out of the organization and conduct of the homeroom itself,* such as (a) the election of homeroom officers, (b) the training of homeroom officers, (c) the arrangement of bulletin-board displays, (d) the decoration of the homeroom for various seasons, like Thanksgiving and Christmas, (e) the training of attendance officers and other pupil assistants, (f) social activities of the homeroom, and (g) the study of parliamentary procedure for homeroom meetings.

2. *Activities that grow out of the school program as a whole,* such as (a) the election of all-school officers—student-council members, yell leaders, song leaders, traffic assistants, and cafeteria monitors, (b) the sale of tickets for various extraclass activities, (c) the presentation and discussion of all-school activities—clubs, athletics, social affairs, pupil publications, and pupil government, and (d) the presentation of school policies, rules, and regulations.

3. *Activities of a guidance nature,* such as (a) orientation to the school, (b) planning one's school program, (c) how to study, (d) personality development, (e) school citizenship, (f) vocational decisions, (g) good manners, (h) good grooming, and (i) getting along with others.

4. *Activities of a service nature,* such as (a) school clean-up campaigns, (b) Christmas boxes for the needy, (c) Junior Red Cross activities, (d) presentation of assembly programs, (e) writing school songs and yells, (f) writing a school citizenship code or creed, and (g) assisting with school or civic improvement campaigns and drives.

5. *Activities of a miscellaneous nature,* such as (a) patriotic programs on appropriate days, (b) programs for Christmas, Thanksgiving, and other special occasions, (c) movie appreciation, (d) radio appreciation, (e) developing hobbies, (f) study of great Americans, and numerous other topics and activities.

Organization of Homeroom Programs. The outline of homeroom activities should be prepared as carefully as any other phase of the instructional program. From sad experience the principal and homeroom advisers have learned the value of a grade-by-grade plan to provide balance and to prevent repetition and duplication. The most common cause of the failure of homerooms has been the lack of advance planning of this type.

One way of organizing homeroom activities is to have a basic theme at each grade level or for each semester, around which the activities for that grade or semester are developed. Another plan is to have the homeroom activities organized in units, much like a course of study. The units ordinarily serve as the basis for several weeks' work, usually with four to eight units for a school year. Frequently, the units are developed around a central theme for the semester or school year. Whatever plan of organization is employed, the activities should be so arranged for the three junior high school grades that as a whole they form a well-developed educational program.

Selected Homeroom Programs. More and more schools are developing carefully outlined programs of homeroom activities. Several selected outlines of such programs are presented here.

The following are topics selected from the Muscatine, Iowa, Junior High School outline on eighth-grade orientation:

1. Purpose and ideas of homeroom
2. "Get acquainted"
3. Responsibilities of a junior high student
4. Good study habits
5. How to take tests
6. Good manners
7. Your health
8. Sportsmanship
9. Personality and character traits
10. Education or a job

In the New York City junior high schools, some topics for group guidance are the same for all grades, but with a different approach or emphasis in each grade. For example, the discussion of a junior high school code in the seventh grade includes these topics: "Why we need a code," "What groups of people have codes?" and "The honor pledge in the New York junior high schools and what it means." In the eighth grade the discussion of the junior high school code centers in questions such as these: "To what extent is the class living up to the junior high school code?" "To what extent am I as an individual living up to the code?" and "What can I do and what can my class do to improve the carrying out of the ideas of the code?" In the ninth grade, the discussion might be on these questions: "How has the junior high school helped me to be a better citizen?" and "In what way has the code become a part of my thinking and acting?" "Does it carry over after I leave high school?" Other basic topics for every grade are: Wise Use of Leisure Time; The Importance of Planning; Exploration: How to Develop Good Work Habits; Taking Stock, or Self-Evaluation; Unity Through Understanding or Human Relationships. In addition, the New York schools have topics for each grade: [1]

SEVENTH GRADE—FIRST HALF

Orientation

Topic 1: In what particulars is my new junior high school different from my elementary school?

Topic 2: What are the rules and regulations which I must carry out in my new school?

Topic 3: How can I learn to discover and overcome any defects or weak spots I may have?

Topic 4: How can I participate in extracurricular activities?

Topic 5: Summary and evaluation: What have I gained from group guidance during the first half of seventh grade?

SEVENTH GRADE—SECOND HALF

Living, Working, and Playing Together

Topic 1: Can I get along with people in school: My teachers, my classmates, my schoolmates?

Topic 2: Am I a desirable member of my community: In business places, in places of amusement, in public conveyances, on streets?

Topic 3: Do I add to or detract from the happiness in my home?

Topic 4: Am I the kind of person who is building toward success?

Topic 5: Do I realize that a permanent record is kept of what I achieve and of what I am?

Topic 6: Summary and evaluation: What have I gained from group guidance during the second half of seventh grade?

EIGHTH GRADE—FIRST HALF

Exploration and Evaluation of Subjects, Activities and Opportunities for Service

Topic 1: How can I explore and evaluate school subjects?

Topic 2: How can I explore and evaluate other school activities?

Topic 3: Of what value to me or others are the varied ways of preparing for and taking part in school and class activities?

[1] Quoted with permission from *Manual of Procedures in Individual and Group Guidance in Junior High Schools* (New York: Board of Education, 1952).

Topic 4: How can I explore and evaluate out-of-school activities?
Topic 5: Summary and evaluation: What have I gained from group guidance during the first half of eighth grade?

EIGHTH GRADE—SECOND HALF
Self-Evaluation and Self-Discovery

Topic 1: What must I know about myself?
Topic 2: Why, what, how, and when must I plan?
Topic 3: What are my interests?
Topic 4: What does my present record reveal about me?
Topic 5: How may I improve?
Topic 6: Summary and evaluation: What have I gained from group guidance during the second half of eighth grade?

NINTH GRADE—FIRST HALF
Educational and Vocational Planning

Topic 1: What is included in making a wise educational plan?
Topic 2: How can I get a bird's-eye view of possible courses and the careers to which they lead?
Topic 3: How do I measure up to the qualifications of those occupations I am considering?
Topic 4: Do I have enough information and advice to decide now on a tentative choice of course and career?
Topic 5: Summary and evaluation: What have I gained from group guidance during the first half of ninth grade?

NINTH GRADE—SECOND HALF
Looking Ahead

Topic 1: Am I planning wisely for my educational and vocational future?
Topic 2: What must I do in this grade to carry out my plan?
Topic 3: How can I get the most out of high school?
Topic 4: What should I know about my plans beyond high school?
Topic 5: What kind of a person am I now?
Topic 6: Summary and evaluation: What have I gained from guidance during the second half of ninth grade?

6. HOMEROOM PROCEDURES

Basic Principles for Homeroom Operation. There are certain basic principles which underlie the methods for planning and carrying on effective homeroom activities. The important ones follow:

1. Homeroom activities should be planned in their broad outlines a semester or a year in advance.

2. Homeroom activities should be planned in terms of worth-while educational objectives which are understood and accepted by both the adviser and the pupils.
3. Homeroom activities should provide for much pupil participation in selecting, planning, and directing those activities.
4. Homeroom activities should be selected and planned in terms of the interests and needs of the particular group of pupils concerned.
5. Homeroom activities which consist of "sermons" by the teacher and other teacher-centered activities should be employed sparingly, and then only for those problems which do not lend themselves readily to a pupil-centered approach.
6. Homeroom activities should be brought to a conclusion at a time when pupil interest is still at a high level.
7. Homeroom activities should be conducted in an informal, friendly manner which encourages pupils to express themselves freely and frankly on any topic or problem that is being studied.
8. Homeroom activities should be evaluated from time to time by the pupils and advisers of each group to improve the choice of activities and the methods for carrying on those activities.

Pupil Participation in the Homeroom. The very essence of good homeroom methods can be expressed in two words—pupil participation. More than anything else, the success of the homeroom will be determined by the effectiveness with which pupils participate in the selecting, planning, directing, and carrying on of the homeroom activities. It is important, therefore, that the homeroom adviser should understand how to encourage effective pupil participation. The following suggestions may be helpful:

1. Pupil planning committee to work with the adviser to plan the semester's or year's outline of homeroom activities
2. Opportunity for members of the homeroom group to suggest activities for the semester or year ahead to the pupil planning committee and the adviser
3. Definite pupil assignments made by the pupil officers or a pupil committee for the planning and presentation of the various homeroom activities
4. An effort to distribute among all members of the homeroom group the responsibility for planning and presenting the activities of the group
5. Opportunities for pupils to engage in creative activities that are related to the homeroom program, such as writing skits, drawing cartoons for the bulletin board, and making posters to advertise the various activities
6. Evaluation of the outcomes of the various activities, either by individual pupils or by pupil committees appointed for the purpose

Questions and Exercises

1. Be able to explain and give examples of the functions of the homeroom.

2. Be able to tell how you would organize the pupils in the homeroom of a junior high school for the purpose of carrying on effective homeroom activities.

3. For each grade of the junior high school, make a list of topics which would constitute a good program of homeroom activities.

4. Assume that you have a seventh-grade homeroom. Prepare a program of homeroom activities for the first two weeks of school which will help the pupils become oriented to the new school.

5. Outline in some detail the administrative responsibility for the school as a whole which can be taken care of through the homeroom. How would you have pupils assist with these administrative responsibilities?

6. How can the homeroom contribute toward developing better school morale and spirit? Be specific and detailed in your answer.

7. What data should the homeroom teacher have about each pupil in the group? How can he obtain that information?

8. Prepare a questionnaire which you would submit to pupils during the first week of school to obtain information about them which will be helpful to you as homeroom adviser.

9. Prepare a statement of suggestions for the methods you would employ to carry on homeroom activities. How do the methods and procedures appropriate for the homeroom differ from those of the classroom?

10. How can the homeroom contribute to each of the following types of extraclass activities: (a) assemblies, (b) clubs, (c) pupil government, (d) social activities, (e) athletics, and (f) school paper?

11. Should a homeroom group have the same adviser for the three years in the junior high school, or should the adviser be changed each year?

12. Suggest several topics for homeroom discussions and activities not mentioned in this chapter.

Chapter 13

EXTRACLASS ACTIVITIES

1. Principles Basic to the Program

Basic Points of View. Extraclass activities are not the frills of an otherwise essential educational program. Neither are they recreational activities to provide relaxation from the "work" of the school. Rather, these activities have a place in the program of the school primarily because they provide learning experiences important to the educational growth of the child. The dominant purpose of the extraclass program may therefore be stated as follows: *It should provide certain significant learning experiences for the child which cannot be offered as effectively elsewhere in the educational program of the school.* With that essential purpose in mind, the following principles are suggested for the program of extraclass activities in the junior high school:

1. The activities should be planned and carried on in terms of well-formulated and accepted educational objectives.
2. There should be a sufficient variety of activities to meet the individual abilities, needs, and interests of every child in school.
3. The activities should be offered, as far as possible, during school hours and in the school building or on the school grounds.
4. Participation in the various activities should be possible at little or no direct expense to the individual pupil.
5. Participation in the various activities should not be contingent upon the pupil's achievement or conduct in other phases of the school program.
6. Competitive activities should be conducted largely or entirely on an intramural rather than an interscholastic basis.
7. Audience activities, such as athletics, music, and dramatics, should be planned and conducted primarily for their contribution to the educational development of the students rather than the entertainment of an adult audience.
8. The extraclass program should be closely integrated and articulated with all other phases of the educational program of the school.

Contribution to Educational Objectives. The program of extra-class activities should be carefully planned and organized in terms of recognized educational objectives. This means, first, that in every school there should be clearly formulated objectives for the various extraclass activities; and, second, that the faculty sponsors of the various activities should plan them definitely in terms of the objectives.

The formulation of objectives for extraclass activities in the junior high school is not so common a practice as might be wished. Of course, the mere existence of such a statement of objectives does not insure that teachers will keep them in mind in planning extraclass activities. It is the responsibility of the principal, the director of activities, or some other supervisory authority, to help teachers keep it in mind and to plan activities in harmony with it. Suggestions for planning extraclass activities may be given teachers in faculty meetings, individual conferences, and teachers' bulletins, handbooks, and similar publications.

The rapid expansion of the extraclass program in recent years has created considerable concern among some educators lest the "essentials" of the educational program be neglected by some pupils. In many schools it is, indeed, a serious danger. The contention that much of the time devoted to extraclass activities might better be spent in other ways is not necessarily directed at an extraclass program as such, but, rather, at the purposeless, haphazard, and loosely planned manner in which that program is frequently carried on. The formulation of worth-while objectives for all activities in the extraclass program is an essential first step toward increasing its effectiveness.

Extraclass Activities for Every Child. So long as the view persisted that these activities were "extra," that they were outside and in addition to the curricular program of the school, participation was confined largely to pupils with special talents. Most schools had a varsity team in football, basketball, baseball, and track for the boys with talent in athletics, an all-school debating team for those with exceptional ability in public speaking, an occasional major dramatics production for those who were gifted in dramatics, and music activities for those with musical talent. In large schools, such a program served only a small proportion of the pupils. Frequently, the child who would profit most from participation in such activities was crowded out by the more talented pupils.

Particularly in the junior high school, the point of view concerning participation in the extraclass program has changed considerably. Today, it is felt that every child who can profit from these activities should participate in them. For instance, there should be several teams for every sport—enough to meet the needs of every interested and physically able child. Similarly, such activities as debating, dramatics, and music should be sufficiently broad and varied to provide a place for all the pupils who desire to participate. If extraclass activities are to be truly educational, every child in school should have the privilege of participating in them.

School Time for Extraclass Activities. There are a number of factors, other than a broad offering of activities, which affect pupil participation in the extraclass program. One of these is the time when the activities take place. Because of after-school jobs, bus transportation, and other out-of-school interferences, many pupils are excluded from activities that take place after school. Furthermore, pupils are too tired mentally after school hours to be enthusiastic about activities which require mental effort of a type similar to that of the regular classroom work. This is true especially of such activities as speech, dramatics, journalism, and certain clubs.

In the junior high school, the present tendency is to have most of the extraclass activities during school hours. In an increasing number of schools an activities period, either daily or several times weekly, is provided for this purpose. An excellent plan is to have one period daily, with different days set aside for clubs, for assemblies, and for homeroom activities.

Some activities, however, cannot be carried on satisfactorily during an activities period. The sports program, for instance, demands so much time that, in most schools, it is still an after-school activity. Certain music groups, such as glee club, band, and orchestra, also require more time than the activities period ordinarily allows. But music, like most other activities, is being included more and more in the regular school program. In many schools, the various music groups are assigned several full class periods weekly on a basis similar to that for the regular courses. At present, athletics is the only extraclass activity in the junior high school which persists widely on an after-school basis.

Cost of Extraclass Activities to Pupils. An important factor in limiting participation in extraclass activities is the expense to the individual child, especially in such activities as athletics and instrumental music, in which the cost of equipment is high. Then, too, in some schools, fees are charged for instrumental music lessons, which must precede or parallel the pupil's participation in the band or orchestra. Other expenses usually paid by the pupil include club dues, cost of pins and insignia, admission fees for parties, and subscription fees for the school paper, yearbook, and other publications. So long as these activities are expensive for the individual pupil, many will be deprived of this type of educational experience.

The present tendency is to keep down the cost of these activities for the individual child. Athletic equipment, music instruments, and similar items are being issued to pupils increasingly on the same basis as textbooks. Music instruments are provided in some schools by P.T.A. groups and service clubs. In many schools, fees for club membership, assembly programs, school parties, and athletic games, are limited to a purely nominal sum or are eliminated entirely. Club pins and other insignia purchased by the pupils are being discouraged.

This reduction in fees and dues creates a problem of financing the extraclass program. In some schools a season ticket, sold at a low cost, covers admissions to athletic games, concerts, speech and dramatic programs, and school parties. Frequently, subscriptions to school publications are also included in these tickets. In an occasional school, the entire extraclass program is financed by an appropriation in the regular school budget. Still another plan is to make the various activities largely self-supporting, but to avoid excessive costs to the pupils by a definite policy limiting the amount that may be charged for dues, pins, insignia, and similar items. Regardless of the plan that is employed, it is imperative that the cost of extraclass activities be kept to a minimum.

Achievement Prerequisites for Participation. It is traditional practice in the secondary school to insist upon minimum standards of academic achievement as a prerequisite for participation in some pupil activities. Such prerequisites were introduced primarily to eliminate abuses in interscholastic competition, especially in athletics. But the early point of view that extraclass activities were an educational luxury, and therefore should be a reward for the conscientious pupil, encouraged the application of scholastic prerequisites to activities other than athletics.

Scholarship prerequisites for participation in extraclass activities have not been so common in the junior as in the four-year and senior high schools. Even so, in the majority of junior high schools included in the survey by the authors, certain standards of achievement are a prerequisite for participation in some extraclass activities. Some scholarship prerequisite is found to exist in about one-third of the schools for participation in athletics and about one-third for being a member of the student council or holding an elective pupil office. In about one-third of the schools there is no scholarship prerequisite for participation in any activity.

Although scholarship prerequisites may be desirable in senior high school and college, it is difficult to justify them in the junior high school. There really is little logic in depriving a pupil of one educational experience just because he has failed to succeed in another. Yet that is precisely what happens when participation in athletics, speech, music, and similar activities is limited to those pupils who do well in such studies as English, Latin, and algebra. In schools where scholarship prerequisites are employed, the faculty would do well to re-examine this practice in the light of current thinking with respect to the educational values of extraclass activities.

Desirability of Intramural Competition. In recent years serious difficulties with interscholastic competition in the secondary school have caused educators to develop intramural teams and competition. Considered especially appropriate in the junior high school, the advantages of intramural competition at this level are:

1. It is easier to offer a broad program of activities to meet the various needs, interests, and abilities of all pupils.
2. It avoids the publicity for individual pupils which is so much a part of interscholastic activities.
3. It avoids the extreme public pressure for winning teams which frequently attends interscholastic competition.
4. It does not present the problem of supervising pupils on trips as with interscholastic activities.
5. It avoids the commercialized aspects of interscholastic competition.

Fortunately, there has never been as much public pressure for the introduction of interscholastic activities in the junior high school as at higher levels. Junior high school authorities, therefore, have been largely free to organize extraclass activities in terms of educational, rather than public relations, values. Although at present there is some interscholastic competition, chiefly in athletics, at the junior high school level, both educational thinking and practice tend distinctly toward intramural activities in the junior high school.

Attitude Toward Audience Activities. Certain undesirable practices are frequently incident to audience activities in the secondary school. These practices result chiefly from the desire of an overly ambitious faculty sponsor to present an impressive performance. This is true, not only in athletics, but also in music, dramatics, and speech activities. Unfortunately, an impressive performance is frequently given at the expense of the health and school work of the participants. Undesirable practices that may result from an overemphasis on the achievement of an outstanding performance are:

1. Participation by a few talented pupils is stressed at the expense of those less capable.
2. Demands for practice are made on the time and energy of the pupils, to the detriment of their health and other school work.
3. Sponsors may assist pupils with debate speeches, articles in school publications, and similar activities, to an extent which is questionable from both an ethical and an educational standpoint.

In the junior high school, the trend has been away from such an overemphasis on giving an outstanding performance in audience activities. The present point of view concerning such activities emphasizes the welfare of the pupils rather than the approval of the audience. The educational growth of the child, rather than impressing the audience, should receive first consideration in all extraclass activities.

Extraclass Activities in Six-Year High Schools. One of the weaknesses of the six-year high schools has been the tendency to minimize the importance of extraclass activities for the junior high school grades. There is a temptation to put most of the emphasis on developing the "varsity" teams, whose members are drawn primarily from the senior high school grades. Indeed, in many six-year schools there are no separate junior high school teams and sports activities. Furthermore, in many of the schools which have junior high school teams, the time provided for the use of the gymnasium and other facilities is totally inadequate. Frequently such facilities are available to junior high school groups only when they are not wanted by senior high school teams.

Obviously this is a situation which needs to be corrected. Sports activities can be justified only as part of the basic educational program. In that sense, they are as important at the junior as at the senior high school level. Provision for athletic teams, for competent faculty sponsors, and for the use of the gymnasium and athletic fields therefore needs to be made for the junior as well as the senior high school grades. The administrator and faculty in a six-year high school should take steps to provide such a program of athletics for the junior high school pupils.

The situation with respect to athletics for junior high school pupils in the six-year high school pertains also to other extraclass activities. The officers of the student council are usually senior high school pupils, the members of the orchestra and band most often come from the upper grades, and the participants in assembly programs are predominantly older pupils. Because of the superior skills and experience of the senior high school pupils, it is easy to see how this might occur. At the same time, the younger pupils are deprived of significant educational experiences. There should be many separate assemblies for the junior high school grades; there should be opportunities for junior high school pupils to hold some student council offices; clubs should be established especially for the junior high school group; and in other ways specific provision should be made for pupils from the lower grades of the six-year high school to have a prominent part in extra-class activities.

Integration with Other Aspects of the School Program. The idea of integrating the extraclass activities with the other aspects of the educational program is not at all new, for it was basic to the thinking underlying the first junior high schools. Furthermore, much progress has been made in effecting this integration. An early step was the introduction of an activities period which provided time in the daily schedule for many activities, especially for clubs, assemblies, and school service organizations. Then, too, in many schools the music activities, such as band, orchestra, and glee club, are placed in the daily schedule like any subject.

In recent years, however, some junior high schools have made even more progress toward integrating extraclass activities with the rest of the educational program. Especially in California junior high schools, the student council is scheduled daily or several times weekly, becoming in effect one of the elective courses for the council members. In some schools, clubs have been decreased in number, with more time being devoted to each. Frequently, the clubs are placed on the same schedule as any subject.

Then, too, much is being done today on an informal basis to bring about better integration between extraclass activities and the curriculum. The language arts classes prepare pupils for participation in the student council, assemblies, and student offices. Classes in art, music, home economics, and industrial arts also contribute much to various extraclass activities. Such correlation of extraclass activities with the curriculum has been extended considerably in recent years. This development is exceedingly desirable, and it should be given every encouragement.

2. Club Activities

Growth of Club Activities. In the junior high school, club activities have developed much more rapidly than most of the other extraclass activities. One reason for this extensive growth of clubs is the fact that they contribute so well to the realization of certain functions of the junior high school, especially the functions of exploration, differentiation, and socialization. Then, too, club activities can be adapted readily to the principles for extraclass activities in the junior high school outlined earlier in this chapter. Factors such as these have made club activities a significant part of the extraclass program in the junior high school.

Objectives of Club Activities. It was suggested earlier in this chapter that all phases of the extraclass program should contribute to the educational objectives of the school. Furthermore, it was urged that immediate objectives be formulated for the various extraclass activities. For club activities in the junior high school, the following objectives should be kept in mind and activities should be planned so as to make maximum contributions to them:

1. To assist pupils in developing qualities of leadership and follower-ship for later responsibilities as citizens
2. To help pupils explore and extend their present and potential educational and vocational interests and aptitudes
3. To help pupils acquire interests in hobbies and other worth-while leisure-time pursuits
4. To stimulate interest in, and to vitalize, other educational activities in the school program
5. To assist pupils to satisfy the urge to be active and creative, and to accomplish worth-while things
6. To help pupils acquire certain personal and character qualities, such as self-confidence, poise, initiative, resourcefulness, mental courage, cooperativeness, courtesy, and self-control

Meeting Pupil Interests in Club Activities. There is really no limit to the number of different interests in club activities that may be found among a typical group of junior high school pupils. In such a group, some pupils will be interested in hobbies, like stamp-collecting, marionette-making, soap-carving, cartooning, knitting, model-airplane building, and candy-making. Others will prefer citizenship and school-service clubs, like library assistants, traffic squad, and song-leaders. Still others will favor such curricular clubs as English, Latin, journalism, and history. It is not easy to provide a sufficient number and variety of clubs to satisfy this wide range of interests. Neverthe-less, that is the ideal which every school should strive to attain.

The first step toward providing a variety of club activities is to ascertain the interests and preferences of the pupils concerned. This cannot be done simply by asking pupils what clubs they prefer, since that would limit the club program to those activities with which the pupils have had some contact. Although the club program should permit pupils to explore and develop present interests, it should also direct their present interests into new channels. A careful inventory should therefore be made of both present and potential interests among the pupils concerned.

Various practices are employed in preparing a list of the club interests of pupils. The most common plan is for the teachers to prepare a list of clubs on the basis of their previous experience with junior high school pupils. The list of suggested clubs may then be submitted to the pupils through the homeroom, assemblies, pupil handbooks, individual conferences, the school newspaper, and the regular classes. Pupils should be urged to add other clubs to the original list, if their interests are not satisfied. Usually, the pupils are asked to indicate their preferences on a form provided for the purpose. The interests of the pupils, expressed in this way, serve as the basis for organizing the club activities of the school.

Stimulating Pupil Membership in Clubs. Should all pupils be expected to belong to a club? If so, how should they be encouraged to join? How many clubs should a pupil be permitted to join? These are some of the questions that are raised with respect to pupil membership in club activities.

Writers on the subject agree that all pupils should belong to a club, but they differ regarding the methods of encouraging them to join. Ideally, club activities should be so attractive and so varied that every child in school will find one that appeals to him. Some schools have been quite successful in developing such an attractive program. For instance, in one school, all except 15 pupils from an enrollment of more than 600 joined clubs voluntarily, and later these 15 formed a club of their own which became one of the most successful in the school.

Another common policy with respect to pupil membership is to require pupils to join at least one club. Although such a requirement may be advisable in some schools, it can only be interpreted as a sign of weakness in the club program if pupils fail to participate unless compelled. A club program so attractive that all pupils will participate voluntarily should be the ambition of every junior high school staff.

Effective publicity is one of the best ways of stimulating pupil interest in the club program. The most appropriate time for such publicity is when the pupils are making their choice of clubs. Mimeographed materials describing the various clubs, statements in various pupil publications, and presentations in assemblies and homerooms are valuable channels for arousing pupil interest in the various clubs. The most effective publicity, however, is the work carried on by the clubs themselves. If a club is doing interesting things, pupils will want to join. Every club should become aware of the value of publicity concerning its program for maintaining an adequate, interested membership from year to year. The various clubs should be encouraged to use the school paper, the bulletin boards, and assembly programs to inform the school of their activities; they should invite other pupils as guests to meetings, especially pupils who are not in a club; and they should assist homeroom teachers and officers in explaining the club program at the time that pupils make their club choices. Activities such as these will help considerably to stimulate pupil interest in the club program.

Limiting Membership in Clubs. There is some question regarding the number of clubs a pupil should be permitted to belong to at one time. Although, for purposes of exploration, it is to the pupil's advantage to have membership in several clubs, he may profit little from them by thus dividing his interests and efforts. Most junior high schools limit the number of clubs a pupil may join, although this policy is applied in several different ways. The most common practice is to have a maximum number of clubs to which a pupil may belong at one time. In junior high schools that follow this plan, membership is usually limited to one club, and rarely exceeds two. In schools with an activities period for club meetings, pupils are automatically restricted in the number of clubs they may join because of conflicts in meetings. It is difficult to see how a pupil could receive much benefit from club activities if he belongs to more than two clubs at a time. From an educational standpoint, it seems best for a pupil to put all his energies into one club activity. He can explore other clubs by changing his membership from year to year.

Prerequisites for Club Membership. In some schools pupils must meet scholarship prerequisites or demonstrate special talents before gaining admission to certain clubs, such as art, music, tumbling, dramatics, leadership, and journalism clubs. For certain types of clubs, such prerequisites are desirable, providing they are applied intelligently. It would be unwise, for instance, to admit pupils to certain music clubs without sufficient talent to work effectively with the other members. But, frequently, such prerequisites exclude from membership the very pupils who can profit most from the club. A more desirable policy is to so organize a club that there will be a place for pupils of all talents.

In a few schools, popularity demonstrated by a vote of approval from present members is a prerequisite for admission to certain clubs. It is difficult, indeed, to defend this practice. Frequently, the unpopular pupil is most in need of the socializing opportunities offered by club membership. Furthermore, this practice is totally inconsistent with our democratic philosophy concerning education in the public schools. Interest in a club is the only prerequisite for membership which is in harmony with our present philosophy of education.

Suggestions for Club Sponsors. The success of a club depends largely upon the enthusiasm, skill, and judgment of the faculty sponsor, and his relations with the pupil members. If the sponsor dominates the club—dictating its policies, organizing and planning its activities, performing administrative details, and restricting the initiative of the members—then the members of that club may profit little from it. But if the sponsor is one who can remain in the background, and yet stimulate and guide the interests and activities of the group into desirable channels, the club may prove exceedingly worth while. The following suggestions may be helpful to the faculty sponsor:

1. The sponsor should bring prospective members of the club together for organizational purposes, but he should have a definite plan for placing the club under temporary officers, and, as soon as possible, in the hands of a permanent pupil organization.
2. The sponsor should inform the officers regarding their duties, instruct them in the techniques and responsibilities of leadership, and familiarize them with the essentials of parliamentary procedure.
3. The sponsor should assist the pupil officers in formulating a program of activities for the year—including objectives, group and individual projects, programs for club meetings, and entertainment.
4. The sponsor should assist the pupil officers in planning each club meeting to assure the efficient dispatch of club business and the effective conduct of the program and other activities.
5. The sponsor should attend all club meetings, but he should be definitely in the background, participating only when necessary.
6. The sponsor should encourage the pupil officers to manage the conduct of the members. He should take over conduct problems only if the situation threatens to get out of hand.
7. The sponsor should gain the confidence of pupil officers and members so that they will voluntarily seek his suggestions on important matters before they are presented to the entire group.
8. The sponsor should encourage all pupils to participate in projects, programs, business meetings, and other club activities.
9. The sponsor should frequently suggest activities for the club to the pupil officers and members, but should attempt to do it in such a way that the pupils are likely to develop these ideas as their own.

10. The sponsor should see that pupil officers and members are informed regarding the courtesies that should be extended to visitors and to other club members, including courtesies to guest speakers and entertainers, retiring pupil officers, and club members who have performed some special service.

New Developments in Club Activities. For some time, many educators have felt that we have gone too far in providing a wide variety of club activities in junior high schools. They believe that it is better to have only a few clubs, but to devote more time and energy to those we have.

Certainly, much support can be given this point of view. It is difficult to find teachers who are competent to serve as sponsors for all the different clubs in which pupils may have an interest. Furthermore, there is a serious question concerning the value of having a club meeting only once a week, or even less frequently.

Consequently, in quite a few schools the number of clubs has been reduced, but these have been given a place in the daily schedule much like any subject. The photography clubs provide an excellent example of this new approach. For years, in most schools this has been a hobby club which met only occasionally like other clubs. In some schools today, the photography club has become a photography class, meeting on a regular schedule like any other class. Under this new arrangement, a competent teacher is provided, and there is sufficient time to make a reasonably thorough study of photography. It becomes in effect a course in science, with the hobby aspects of the photography club being retained. Other clubs have been changed in much the same way. This practice is being used in a sufficient number of schools, especially in the Far West, to justify the conclusion that it is of more than passing interest.

Another development in club activities is to combine some of these activities with regular classwork in various subjects. For instance, knitting, crocheting, and similar hobbies are being brought into the homemaking classes; airplane-building is included in industrial arts classes; and music and art hobbies are being included in those subjects. This is made possible particularly in schools where teachers use the experience-centered approach to teaching. Where this approach is used, the learning situation is sufficiently flexible to permit pupil participation in planning and directing learning activities much as in school clubs.

By bringing these activities into the regular classes, more thorough attention can be given them than in infrequent club meetings. Care must be taken, however, to retain the same freedom for pupils to plan and direct these activities as they have in the effective club program.

3. The School Assembly

Objectives of School Assemblies. Like other extraclass activities, assemblies provide educational experiences which have a bearing on most or all of the ultimate goals of education. In the junior high school, certain immediate purposes that are served by school assemblies include the following:

1. To aid in unifying the student body and in developing wholesome school spirit and morale
2. To stimulate pupil interest and participation in all phases of the life and program of the school
3. To provide opportunities for pupils to gain experience in organizing and directing those group activities appropriate in school assemblies
4. To provide opportunities for pupils to gain poise, ease, and self-confidence before large groups
5. To assist pupils to develop a sense of courtesy and desirable conduct in large group meetings
6. To provide opportunities for pupils to explore and develop individual talent and interests
7. To provide guidance for pupils in meeting some of their educational, vocational, social, and personal problems
8. To provide opportunities for group guidance
9. To provide opportunities for pupils to learn more about the school and all phases of its work
10. To suggest worth-while leisure activities
11. To promote the feeling of "belonging" on the part of each pupil

Sources of Assembly Programs. If pupils "learn best by doing," then the chief source of assembly programs should be the pupils themselves. Clubs, homeroom groups, classes, and music organizations, as well as individual pupils, are specific sources within the school from which appropriate assembly programs may be obtained. Concerts by the school band, orchestra, or glee clubs, a fire-prevention program by a citizenship club, a Latin play by a Latin class, a demonstration by a tumbling club, and a "talent" program under the sponsorship of the student council—these are a few examples of programs that may be presented by pupil groups from the school itself. In cities with two or more junior high schools, assembly programs that are especially good may be exchanged between the schools, thus providing additional stimulation and experience for the participants.

The senior high school is a second source for assembly programs in the junior high school. In most senior high schools there are dramatics clubs, music organizations, debating teams and other speech groups, and individual pupils with special talents who can provide such programs. Aside from their entertainment value, such programs are helpful for guidance purposes because they bring junior high school pupils into contact with senior high school activities. There are also many values for the senior high school pupils in such a cooperative plan for arranging assembly programs.

Individuals and groups within the community and commercial lyceum agencies are other sources of assembly programs. Because of the expense and the difficulty of obtaining suitable programs, the lyceum agencies are not employed as much in the junior as in the senior high schools. But one or two such programs a year may add a great deal to the assembly activities of the school. The community itself is usually a better source of programs than lyceum agencies; for every community has speakers, musicians, and entertainers who are willing to contribute their talents to the schools. Such speakers and entertainers must be carefully selected, however, in terms of the appreciation levels of junior high school pupils.

Pupil Participation in Assemblies. If participation in assembly programs is an educational experience, then every child in school should take part actively in planning and presenting them. This means that the entire program of assembly activities must be so planned that pupils of every talent, interest, and ability can find a place in them. In small schools, this can be arranged without too much difficulty, but in medium-sized and large schools careful planning and much encouragement will be required to bring all pupils into the assembly activities.

It must be recognized that the interests and abilities of pupils with respect to participation in assemblies differ widely. Some have considerable leadership ability and therefore should take an active part in arranging and directing assembly programs; a few possess special talents appropriate for particular types of programs; others would do well as master of ceremonies, assembly chairman, or stage manager; and still others may prefer to participate only in group activities, such as a concert by the glee club, band, or orchestra. The faculty should be continually on the alert for such ways of encouraging different pupils to participate. The following suggestions may be helpful for extending participation to more pupils:

1. An inventory should be prepared every year of all pupil talent which can be used in assemblies. This inventory can be made through the homerooms by questionnaire or in other ways.
2. An inventory should be prepared every year of ways in which pupils would like to participate, including such responsibilities as

chairman of an assembly, stage manager, usher, and in the program itself.

3. Most responsibilities in assemblies should be distributed, instead of being assigned to the same person for an extended period. For instance, it is better to have new chairmen or masters of cermonies from time to time, instead of assigning this responsibility to the student council president or some other pupil officer.
4. Participation should be distributed systematically among pupils in the various grades, rather than confining it largely to upper-grade pupils.
5. Faculty sponsors of assembly programs should see that less talented pupils do the easier things, reserving pupils with special talents for more important responsibilities.
6. In medium-sized and large schools, grade assemblies make it possible to distribute participation to more pupils.

Pupil Participation in Planning and Conducting Assemblies. Pupil participation in school assemblies should not be confined to taking part in programs, but should extend also to the selection and planning of those programs. In most junior high schools today, such participation is the established policy. Pupils may assist in selecting and planning assemblies as follows: (1) by cooperating with a faculty committee or a director of assemblies in arranging the schedule of programs for the year, (2) by calling on pupil and faculty groups to request their aid or participation in certain programs, (3) by interviewing persons in the community to request their appearance at school assemblies, (4) by serving on pupil committees to plan and direct programs presented by pupil groups, (5) by taking charge of guest speakers and entertainers, and (6) by greeting and extending the usual courtesies to parents and friends who attend assemblies.

There should be pupil representation in the group which arranges the programs for the year. In some schools the student council has this responsibility; in others, there is a joint faculty-pupil committee; and in still others, a faculty committee or director arranges the schedule of assemblies after consultation with certain pupil leaders. Occasionally, a school has a plan of divided responsibility for assemblies, the faculty arranging certain programs, while some assembly dates are assigned to a pupil committee to arrange more or less as they wish. *It should be clear, however, that any plan for pupil participation in planning assembly programs should be subject to the supervision of a faculty adviser who has the confidence of the pupils concerned.*

Preparing Pupils for Participation in Assemblies. If pupil participation in assembly programs is to be a worth-while experience, careful thought must be given to preparing pupils for such participation. In too many schools, a pupil is asked to preside at an assembly only a day or two ahead, and then with little or no help in preparing for it. Almost any junior high school pupil can preside satisfactorily at a grade or all-school assembly if someone assists him in planning for that responsibility. Similarly, pupils should be adequately prepared for any part in the program itself, no matter how small it may be. Everyone has seen a school pep meeting when the football captain or some player stumbled through an impromptu talk. Such an experience is indeed unfortunate for any boy. The pupil speakers, the song leader, the accompanist, the yell leader, and the others who participate in such a program, should know precisely what they intend to do before the assembly begins. Other responsibilities related to school assemblies for which pupils should be adequately prepared include interviewing persons regarding their appearance on assembly programs, serving on assembly committees, serving as ushers, and greeting parents and other guests.

In some schools a faculty committee or director of activities is responsible for assisting pupils to prepare for their parts in school assemblies. Frequently, the training of pupils for the various responsibilities is assigned to different faculty members. For instance, one teacher may be responsible for working with the stage group, another with the ushers, and a third with the masters of ceremonies. Sometimes the faculty sponsor for each program is expected to take care of training all participants. Whatever means is used, the faculty members concerned should recognize their responsibility for helping pupils profit from participation in assembly programs by preparing them adequately.

Administrative Arrangements for Assemblies. The schedule of assemblies should be planned well in advance, preferably for the entire school year. In too many schools, assemblies are arranged week by week or month by month, with the frequent result that they are too hurriedly prepared to be of much educational value. Advance planning of the assembly schedule is desirable, not only for participating pupil groups within the school, but also for senior high school groups and members of the community who appear at school assemblies. Better programs are likely to result if the schedule is arranged far ahead.

The place that assemblies are given in the daily schedule has not always been well chosen. Until recently, assemblies in most schools interfered with classes and other school activities because no time in the schedule was reserved specifically for them. Assembly activities are sufficiently worth while to be assigned a regular place in the schedule so as to avoid interference with other phases of the school's program. In many junior high schools today, assemblies are held during a scheduled activities period. This is perhaps the most satisfactory arrangement for scheduling assembly programs.

In the past, the school assembly was a convenient place for making announcements, explaining administrative policies, and lecturing pupils on matters of conduct. In many schools, this practice still persists. Authorities on the subject generally agree that using the assembly for such administrative purposes may discourage pupil interest and enthusiasm for assembly activities. The homeroom period is far more appropriate for the reading of announcements and the discussion of administrative policies. The setting for pupil assemblies should not be disturbed by the introduction of such administrative matters.

4. Social Activities

Objectives for Social Activities. Social functions in the secondary school too often are arranged primarily for recreational purposes. Although their recreational values are perfectly acceptable, these activities also offer many opportunities for worth-while educational experiences. It is important that the junior high school faculty analyze the educational values of social activities and plan them accordingly. The first step in that direction is to formulate an acceptable statement of objectives for social activities. For the junior high school level, the following objectives are suggested:

1. To give pupils opportunities for developing poise, good taste, and self-confidence at various types of social functions
2. To give pupils opportunities for acquiring desirable social skills and graces
3. To extend the interests of pupils in wholesome recreational activities of a social nature
4. To provide opportunities for individual pupils to develop special talents for the social entertainment of their fellows in such areas as music, declamation, dramatics, and certain hobbies
5. To encourage the development of democratic social attitudes and relationships among pupils as opposed to snobbishness and class consciousness
6. To assist pupils to develop leadership abilities through participation in the planning and direction of social activities
7. To encourage the development of favorable pupil attitudes toward the school program as a whole through enjoyable social experiences

Types of Social Activities. Three types of social activities are common in the junior high school: (1) informal social activities carried on in clubs, homerooms, or classes, and ordinarily held during the school day; (2) more formal parties, usually grade or all-school affairs, which are held in late afternoon or evening; and (3) outdoor activities, such as picnics, field days, and similar outings. Schools should have more of the informal activities than of any other type, especially in homerooms, clubs, and other pupil groups. At informal social functions, there should be well-planned and interesting programs, but the more elaborate entertainment and refreshments that characterize formal parties should be avoided. Such informal activities afford splendid socializing experiences for all pupils and add a great deal to their enjoyment of school life. The more formal social functions in late afternoon or evening, as well as school outings, demand considerable preparation by both pupils, room mothers, and teachers, and consequently must be held less frequently. All three types of social functions, however, have a place in the program of extraclass activities.

The educational values of the various social activities depend largely on how they are planned and conducted. If they are planned largely by a faculty committee or sponsor, with little pupil assistance, their educational value may be small indeed. But if the pupils themselves, under competent faculty supervision, arrange the social activities, they can be an exceedingly worth-while phase of the pupil's educational experience. The responsibilities with respect to social activities most often assumed by the pupils include planning and serving refreshments, planning programs and games, directing and presenting the entertainment at the party, preparing invitations to guests, serving as official hosts and hostesses, and providing publicity for the party. At school picnics and outings, the responsibilities assumed by pupils may differ from those in the planning and direction of parties, but their nature and purpose are essentially the same.

Preparation of Pupils for Social Activities. Perhaps the most important single reason why school parties fail is the students' ignorance of ordinary party courtesy. Knowledge of what is correct and the ability to put this knowledge into practice make for confidence and poise. Fear of doing the incorrect thing prevents many students from entering party activities. Unfortunately, the child who needs socializing experiences the most is least likely to attend. *Pupils, therefore, not only should be urged to attend social functions, but they should also be given assistance in preparing to participate in them and enjoy them when they do attend.* In many schools, such preparation is given through a study of good manners in the homerooms which precedes the important social functions. This study covers such topics as how to dress, how to ask a girl for a dance, how the girl should respond, how to introduce one person to another, what to do after the party, and numerous other questions that ordinarily disturb junior high school youth. Appropriate channels for the study of such problems, other than the homeroom, include clubs, assemblies, and English, social studies, and home economics classes.

Some problems other than good manners also deserve attention in preparing pupils for participation in social functions. If there is to be social dancing or other entertainment that requires some skill, pupils should be given sufficient previous instruction to be able to participate. Then, too, certain pupils must be taught how to write invitations to guests, how to prepare and serve refreshments, how to direct games, and how to act as master of ceremonies. These are only a few of the things that must be done to prepare the pupils for effective participation in social activities.

The preparation of pupils in the various social skills and graces is especially important in the junior high school because, at this age level, children ordinarily participate for the first time in adult types of social activities. As they grow older, they tend to become self-conscious about their shortcomings in social relationships, thus making it more difficult to discuss these matters. It cannot be urged too strongly that, in the junior high school, the various social activities should serve as a laboratory for pupils to develop desirable social skills, habits, and attitudes.

5. Speech Activities

Neglect of Speech Activities. The organization of speech activities in the junior high school has lagged considerably behind other phases of the extraclass program. The failure to develop speech activities in more schools is attributable at least in part to the fact that the traditional pattern of formal speech activities in the high school—debate, oratory, and declamation—was not appropriate for the junior high school, especially in view of the phenomenon of changing boys' voices. A type of activities had to be developed which was better suited to the interests and abilities of junior high school youth.

Objectives of Speech Activities. There are several objectives for speech activities which are generally accepted in the junior high school. These include:

1. To provide opportunities for pupils to develop skill in those forms of speech commonly employed in the activities of everyday life

2. To provide opportunities for pupils to develop public-speaking skills desirable for certain educational and vocational activities

3. To help pupils develop poise and self-confidence in appearing before groups of their fellows

4. To provide opportunities for pupils to explore their interests and aptitudes in those vocations and avocations where certain speech abilities are desirable for success

Characteristics of Speech Activities. Any description of speech activities in the junior high school must be made with some reservation because so few schools have a well-organized speech program. There are certain policies and practices, however, that are quite common in the schools which have such a program.

1. *The speech program is largely—often entirely—intramural.* Interschool competition is usually limited to schools within the same community. Pupils also appear occasionally before groups in the local community, such as the service clubs, and before assemblies, clubs, and similar groups in other schools of the city.

2. *The speech program as a rule is not highly competitive.* Although school and grade winners in certain speech activities are occasionally chosen, pupil speakers and speech groups make many appearances at grade assemblies, club meetings, etc., which are not competitive at all. The emphasis is placed on participation for its own sake, rather than participation to win. When there are competitive activities, they are, of course, largely intramural.

3. *The speech program is usually the outgrowth of other pupil activities, like clubs, homerooms, and social studies or English classes.* Speech activities separate from other phases of the extraclass program, like the traditional high school debating teams, are uncommon in junior high schools. In many schools, there are clubs in such speech activities as debate, oratory, declamation, dramatics, after-dinner speaking, impromptu speaking, oral reading, play-reading, and story-telling. Then, too, in competitive speech activities, pupils frequently represent their homerooms, classes, or clubs.

4. *The speech activities are conducted largely during school hours.* Work on these activities is ordinarily carried on in club meetings or class periods, while performances usually are held in assemblies, at club meetings, before classes, and at other regularly scheduled pupil sessions. After-school practice sessions, however, are definitely the exception.

5. *The speech activities are usually so organized that all interested pupils may participate.* In other words, participation ordinarily is not limited to a few talented pupils who are selected through tryouts, nor are participants as a rule required to meet certain scholarship standards

or other prerequisites. Furthermore, the program is usually broad enough to provide activities for all interested pupils. For instance, instead of one all-school debate team or one team for each grade, as many teams may be organized as necessary to take care of all pupils who want to participate.

6. *The speech activities are often conducted on an all-pupil basis.* Not only are there pupil participants in the activity itself, but pupils act as chairmen, judges, timekeepers, and other officials. Such participation gives experience to a larger number of pupils, frequently those who have insufficient talent to engage in the speech activity itself.

7. *The speech program ordinarily is characterized by a high degree of informality.* The highly organized and carefully regulated speech program so prevalent in the senior high school is practically unknown in junior high schools. Rules and regulations restricting the freedom of the participants are kept to a minimum, and the activities ordinarily are adapted to the interests of the pupils who are participating.

Types of Speech Activities. Activities in the junior high school include debating, declamation, oratory, dramatics, and informal speaking. Although they resemble in name the speech activities usually found in the senior high school, they are, as the preceding discussion indicates, much more informal in most respects. The most popular of these activities is debating, with declamation next in popularity. The selections presented in declamatory and oratorical contests are seldom original with the participants.

In quite a few junior high schools, there are contests of informal speeches prepared by the pupils themselves. The topics of these speeches may be chosen by the pupils or assigned by a faculty sponsor, but they are confined to subjects which are at the appreciation level of junior high school pupils. Although the details of these informal speech contests vary from school to school, the tendency is to have them conform as much as possible to the type of public speaking which is demanded of citizens in life outside the school.

Dramatics, as an extraclass speech activity, is found in many junior high schools, especially in dramatics clubs. Unlike the class plays and other formal dramatic presentations in the senior high school, the dramatic performances in the junior high school are quite informal, consisting mostly of short plays at assemblies, social functions, P.T.A. meetings, and similar gatherings. The formal public performance before a paying audience is quite uncommon and should probably be discouraged at this grade level.

6. Other Extraclass Activities

Competitive Sports Activities. The chief characteristic of the competitive sports program in the junior high school is its intramural organization. In many large communities, there is intracity competition between junior high schools, although competition with schools in other communities is also common. But the basic characteristic of the sports program is the fact that it usually provides broad intramural participation for all interested and physically able pupils.

A study by Fennell of types of athletics found in the programs of 224 junior high schools gives some indication of the breadth of these activities.[1] The number of schools offering each of these types is:

Boys' basketball	221
Girls' softball	197
Boys' softball	196
Football	173
Girls' basketball	170
Track	166
Table tennis	138
Soccer	86
Tennis	78
"Pep" club	75
Wrestling	55
Swimming	51
Archery	44
Field hockey	41
Boxing	40
Bowling	35
Winter sports	29

There is evidence that, in most junior high schools, there is extensive pupil participation in both intramural and interscholastic athletics. In the survey of 370 schools by the authors, it was found that the following proportions of all pupils in school participated in at least one intramural or interscholastic sport, in the percentage of schools indicated:

Pupil Participation	Schools
76-100%	39%
51- 75%	30%
26- 50%	18%
1- 25%	10%
No estimate	3%

[1] Edward Glenn Fennell, "An Analysis of Programs of Outstanding Junior High Schools in the United States" (Unpublished doctoral thesis, Cornell University, Ithaca, N. Y., 1953), p. 158.

Pupils frequently participate in the sports program of the junior high school in ways other than as contestants. It is the usual policy in intramural contests to have pupils serve as officials, such as timekeeper, scorekeeper, umpire, and referee. Sometimes pupils are given definite training for these responsibilities, either through a sports officials' club or through brief courses conducted by the physical education staff. The policy of having pupils assume such responsibilities, if it is under intelligent faculty supervision, is indeed a desirable one.

Participation in School Management. There are two general practices with respect to pupil participation in the management of school affairs: (1) participation through a formal pupil organization, such as a student council, which has specified and continuous responsibilities and duties in the management of school affairs; and (2) participation through various pupil committees and groups that are created from time to time to meet specific needs in school management. Both of these practices are employed quite extensively in the junior high school.

The formal type of pupil organization takes various forms. The most prevalent one is the student council, as it is usually called, which ordinarily consists of a representative pupil group that is given certain duties and responsibilities in the management of the school. The members are usually chosen by the various homeroom groups and serve for a semester or a school year. The duties of the council vary considerably from school to school, but ordinarily are limited to those responsibilities which pupils of junior high school age are sufficiently mature to discharge effectively.

Pupil Responsibilities in School Management. The responsibilities which pupils assume in the management of school affairs vary widely. Usually, they include responsibility for planning and conducting such pupil activities as assemblies, clubs, social functions, pupil elections, and certain school publications.

Pupils in junior high schools, according to the authors' survey, assist in school management as homeroom officers in nearly all the schools, as corridor monitors in a great majority of schools, and as schoolground monitors or office assistants in about half the schools. A minority, but an increasing number, of schools are assigning pupils to traffic and safety patrols.

Educators do not agree with respect to the responsibility that pupils should have in the making of school policies and regulations and in the correction of pupil offenders. Some believe that, while it is proper to delegate matters of administrative detail and routine to the pupils, the formulation of the policies and regulations of the school should be made by the professional staff with little or no pupil participation. The trend at the present, however, is toward having pupils share in formulating those policies and regulations which have a direct bearing on pupil conduct.

At the junior high school level, the advisability of delegating disciplinary responsibilities to the pupil council or some other pupil group is indeed open to question. Although, in some schools, pupil organizations have satisfactorily discharged such responsibilities, in others pupil participation in disciplinary activities has been quite unsatisfactory. If pupils are given responsibility for disciplinary action, it is important that (1) these responsibilities be clearly defined, (2) that they be limited to matters which pupils can be expected to manage successfully, (3) that any action by the pupils be subject to review by the principal or some other representative of the faculty, and (4) that there be intelligent supervision by competent faculty sponsors.

The Student Council. A few junior high school administrators and faculties have taken the position that junior high school pupils are too young to have an effective student council. Nothing could be farther from the truth. In fact, most junior high schools in the United States have some kind of a student council, in many schools an exceedingly successful one. Furthermore, the number of junior high schools with student councils are increasing, and the councils are assuming an increasing amount of responsibility for pupil affairs in those schools where they already exist.

An interesting development in student councils in the junior high school is the tendency to make them a more significant avenue for learning experiences than has often been true in the past. This is done in the following ways: (1) more time is being assigned for student council meetings, (2) student councils are frequently combined or correlated with social studies or English, and (3) more competent faculty sponsors are being selected. As a result, student council activities are providing better experiences in citizenship; they are helping pupils improve in poise, personality, and leadership qualities; and they provide many functional experiences in both oral and written expression.

The effort to make student councils more effective has made most progress in the Far West. In many California junior high schools, the student council meets daily like classes in any subject. At the Lafayette Junior High School, Los Angeles, pupils elected to the student council are scheduled for it as an elective subject, meeting a full class period daily. At the Charles A. Lindbergh Junior High School, Long Beach, the student council is combined with English and social studies, three class periods daily being assigned these subjects. In situations such as these it is possible to make the student council a more significant part of the educational program.

Pupil Publications. The publications most common in the junior high school are the school paper, the pupil handbook, and the school magazine. Of these, the newspaper is the most popular. Both the paper and the magazine are usually edited either by a journalism club or by one of the English classes. The appointment or election of an editorial staff which serves for a semester or a year, as is common in high school and college, is not favored in the junior high school, primarily because it limits participation to a few pupils. This is in harmony with the present tendency to give all interested pupils some part in the preparation of school publications.

Music Activities. The music organizations of the junior high school are quite different from some of the other extraclass activities. Not only do they demand more time than many of the other activities, but they also do not lend themselves so readily to pupil participation in planning, organizing, and directing the work. The trend at present, especially in the Middle West and the Far West, is to give music organizations, such as the glee club, chorus, orchestra, and band, a regularly scheduled place in the daily program, much like any subject in the school curriculum. The music activities, therefore, are becoming class, rather than extraclass, activities. The success which this policy has had in schools where it has been employed is sufficient justification for recommending it as a desirable practice in the junior high school.

7. CONCLUSION

The program of extraclass activities continues to develop as a significant part of the educational program of the junior high school. It is being integrated more fully with the rest of the educational program. A greater variety of activities is being offered, there is wider pupil participation, and the activities are being given a regular place in the schedule. Finally, they are now being used to make the curricular program more interesting and functional. We need to continue to study the program of extraclass activities to make it more meaningful in the educational growth of the junior high school child.

Questions and Exercises

1. Write out in your own words the more important underlying principles for extraclass activities in the junior high school.

2. Be able to discuss clearly the contribution of extraclass activities to the various functions of the junior high school.

3. Write out ten or twelve important suggestions for a program of clubs in the junior high school.

4. Prepare a plan for the administrative organization of club activities in the junior high school, including membership, time and frequency of meetings, pupil choice of clubs, club dues, etc.

5. How can each of the following contribute to the effectiveness of the club program: (a) assemblies, (b) school paper, and (c) homeroom?

6. Would you charge dues and fees for the various extraclass activities? If so, would you place a limit on the amount to be charged?

7. Plan a program of assembly activities for a given school for an entire semester. Have at least one assembly program a week.

8. Give suggestions for carrying on assembly activities so that the greatest number of pupils in all three grades can participate.

9. How can senior high school activities contribute to the program of assemblies in the junior high school?

10. Plan a program of social activities for a given school for the entire year, indicating the number and types of activities you would have for each grade.

11. What should be the objectives for the social activities of the junior high school?

12. How may each of the following contribute to the effectiveness of the social activities: (a) homeroom, (b) clubs, (c) English class, (d) school paper, and (e) music programs?

13. Plan in detail a program of speech activities for the junior high school, including debate, declamation, and dramatics.

Part IV

ORGANIZATION
AND ADMINISTRATION

Chapter 14

EVALUATING, REPORTING, AND
RECORDING PUPIL PROGRESS

1. Basic Points of View

Purposes of Education Have Broadened. When the first junior high schools were established, the purpose of education was centered largely in the mastery of subject matter. In fact, the development of the junior high school was in part a protest against such a narrow purpose for education of young adolescents. We have indeed come a long way since that time in our thinking with respect to the purposes of education, particularly those that apply to young adolescents.

The broadened purposes of education have a direct bearing on the procedures that are appropriate for evaluating, marking, and reporting the progress of pupils. When the junior high school was concerned primarily with the mastery of subject matter, it was relatively easy to measure progress. Either the pupils could do the problems in arithmetic or they could not; they could spell the words correctly or they could not; either they knew the facts of history which they were to memorize or they did not; and so with other subject-matter skills and information.

We are still concerned, of course, with the acquisition of certain subject skills and basic information. But now the evaluation of pupil progress is much more difficult because of our concern for character and personality development, for developing wholesome citizenship attitudes, for helping pupils learn how to work together effectively, for developing desirable attitudes toward people of other races, religions, and points of view, and for helping the child to grow in emotional and social stability. It is not easy to formulate tests for measuring the growth of pupils toward these objectives, or to mark them on the growth which they make. We need to find ways of evaluating the growth of pupils in personality and character qualities, social and citizenship attitudes, and emotional development, as well as in subject-matter backgrounds.

Growing Concern for the Individual. The change from the regimented classroom with uniform assignments for all pupils, to the individualized approach to teaching, has likewise created serious problems in the evaluation, marking, and reporting of individual progress. Today we are less concerned about how the pupil's progress compares with that of his classmates than we are about the use he is making of his abilities. We realize that a child of high intelligence who earns a mark of B may still be achieving far below his capacity, while the slow-learning child with a mark of D may be doing his very best. Somehow, we must find a way of evaluating the growth which a child is making in terms of individual potentialities, and then we must be able to report that information to the child and his parents.

The individualized approach to teaching in other ways has complicated still further the evaluation, marking, and reporting of progress. The teacher who has three or four reading groups in the same class, each one working with different materials and at a different level, has difficulty indeed in evaluating and marking pupils by a common standard. Similarly, in arithmetic, spelling, and oral and written expression, pupils in an individualized classroom will be working with different materials. This is as it should be. But it also means that we must recognize these different approaches as we evaluate, mark, and report the progress of the pupils.

Concern for the Pupil's Mental Health. Every experienced teacher knows that more emotional upsets are caused by examinations, marks, report cards, and promotion practices than perhaps by anything else in school. We have come to attach so much importance to examinations, marks, and report cards that in some schools the whole purpose of education seems to be centered there. This problem is not confined to the slow-learning pupils alone. In fact, sometimes the better students, who are competing with each other for marks and are pointing toward school honors, college admission, and other goals based primarily on marks, become much more disturbed about examinations, marks, and report cards than the average or slow-learning pupils.

Unfortunately, parents often are of little help with this problem. In fact, frequently the pressure for pupil achievement from parents intensifies the tension at examination or report-card time. The tensions pupils develop from examinations, marks, and report cards may indeed have a serious effect on their mental and physical health. For young adolescents, this situation is sufficiently serious to justify a study of these practices to see how they can be modified in the best interests of the child's mental and physical health.

Parents Need More Information. Although some parents may not realize it, the traditional percentage or letter mark gives very little information about the progress which their child is making in school. If there is to be cooperation between the home and the school, parents need to be well informed concerning all aspects of their child's growth and development. They need to have the answers to questions such as these:

1. How well does my child cooperate with the teacher, the principal, and other pupils in school?
2. Does my child show as much leadership as he should in working with his classmates?
3. Is my child well adjusted in various social situations in the classroom, in the school as a whole, and in various school activities?
4. Is my child accepted by other pupils?
5. Is my child developing wholesome and effective personality qualities?
6. Does my child have wholesome moral character qualities?
7. Is my child prompt, neat, and careful about details of his work?
8. Is my child's achievement in the various subject areas commensurate with his abilities?
9. What are the specific strengths and weaknesses of my child in the language arts, arithmetic, social studies, and other subjects?

Unless parents have information such as this, it is difficult for them to cooperate with the school in helping their children make satisfactory progress. The traditional percentage or letter mark certainly does not give that information. In fact, traditional marks do not even give much information about growth in subject matter. For instance, if the child has a mark of B in language arts, the parents know little about his progress in spelling, penmanship, neatness, grammar, oral expression, written expression, reading, and literature appreciation. When we develop policies and procedures for evaluating, marking, and reporting pupil progress, we need to be aware of the importance of giving parents much information about the growth that their child is making in school.

Unique Position of the Junior High School. In evaluating, marking, and reporting pupil progress, the junior high school is indeed in a unique position. In the elementary school, the teacher ordinarily has only thirty pupils or so; he has quite frequent contacts with parents; and he need not be unduly concerned about college-entrance requirements. Consequently, in the elementary as compared with the secondary school, it has been much easier to develop new procedures for evaluating, marking, and reporting pupil progress. The situation is quite different in the junior high school. There a number of conditions obtain which indeed make it difficult to develop satisfactory marking and reporting procedures. Some of the conditions peculiar to the junior high school that bear on this problem are as follows:

1. *The junior high school is an articulating unit between the elementary and the senior high school.* This means that the procedures for evaluating, marking, and reporting pupil progress must provide for articulation between the elementary and the senior high school practices. The junior high school should not introduce an abrupt change in marking and reporting procedures as pupils enter the seventh grade. And before they leave the junior high school they should be ready for practices in the senior high school. This suggests that in some schools it may be desirable to have marking and reporting practices in the seventh grade which are different from those in the ninth grade.

2. *Teachers in the junior high school usually have many different pupils in their classes as compared with those in the single class of the typical elementary teacher.* In such subjects as English, social studies, mathematics, and science, the teacher may have 150 to 175 different pupils during the week. In such subjects as industrial arts, art, music, and physical education, the total pupil load may be even greater, especially if classes in these subjects do not meet daily. Individualized procedures for evaluating, marking, and reporting pupil progress become more difficult as the pupil load of teachers increases.

3. *In many junior high schools, pupils in the ninth grade choose the elective curriculum which they will take in the senior high school.* For instance, they have a choice between such curriculums as the college preparatory, general, business, and others. As a basis for making such a choice, marks based on a competitive grade standard are sometimes considered desirable. If competitive marks are not used, parents, pupils, and counselors may need other information which is useful in making decisions concerning college admission and vocational choices.

4. *In many school systems, the work of the ninth grade is a part of that which leads to a high school diploma and to college admission.* Where this is the case, the procedures for marking and reporting pupil progress in the ninth grade may need to be in harmony with those of the senior high school.

Principles Basic to Evaluation, Marking, and Reporting Procedures. There are a number of principles which are generally accepted as basic to any study of evaluation, marking, and reporting procedures. Those which are especially appropriate for the junior high school are:

1. *The procedures for evaluating, marking, reporting, and recording pupil progress should be developed as a whole.* That is, a faculty should not develop new pupil-progress report forms, without also

examining the procedures for evaluating and marking pupil progress. Furthermore, the system of pupil records may also need to
be modified when changes are made in evaluation, marking, and
reporting procedures. In other words, a faculty should not make
a piecemeal approach to the development of these procedures.

2. *Pupil progress should be evaluated, marked, and reported in terms
of the total objectives of the school and the objectives in each
subject area.* The child's progress toward educational objectives is
what we should evaluate and report to his parents. This means
that our evaluation practices, the marking system, and the procedures for reporting to parents, must all recognize the educational
objectives of the school. Certain objectives obtain throughout
the entire school program, such as personality, character, and
citizenship objectives. Others are achieved primarily in certain
subject areas. Pupil progress toward all-school objectives and
subject objectives should be evaluated and reported to the pupil
and his parents.

3. *The evaluation, marking, and reporting of pupil progress should
recognize differences in pupil abilities.* Unless that is done, any
attempts to individualize the program of the school will be a
mockery indeed. Furthermore, it is desirable that the parent be
informed concerning his child's potentialities, and the extent to
which he is using them.

4. *There should be some record of the pupil's achievement as compared with his fellows as a basis for guidance, graduation from
high school, admission to college, and recommendations for jobs.*
College admissions boards and prospective employers may be interested in knowing how the applicant stands in comparison with
his classmates. Such information should be accumulated and become a part of the permanent records of the school.

5. *The use of competitive marks for achievement, based on the same
standard for all pupils, should be delayed as long as possible.* It is
doubtful that competitive marks serve any significant purpose in
the seventh grade, and perhaps even in the eighth grade. Because
of the present practice of including the work of the ninth grade
in the requirements for graduation from high school and for admission to college, it may be desirable to begin competitive marks
in the ninth grade. Certainly competitive marks are not necessary
before the ninth grade and may even be delayed to the senior high
school.

6. *The pupil and his parents should have as much information as
possible about the child's progress in school.* A subject-matter
mark alone gives little information. The pupil and his parents
should have information about the child's progress toward all the
objectives that form a part of the school's educational program.

7. *The pupil and his parents should be fully informed at all times*

about the pupil's progress, instead of just at report-card time. The
shock of report-card day is educationally unsound and unjustifi-
able. The child should know day by day how well he is doing,
with any formal report at the end of a marking period merely
making it a matter of record. Furthermore, there should be some
provision for informing parents immediately if there is any serious
change in the child's progress between the formal periodic reports.

8. *Any procedures for evaluating, marking, reporting, and recording
pupil progress should be simple, understandable, and easily administered.* They certainly need to be readily understood by parents; otherwise, they have little value. They should also not place
an undue burden on the teacher. Furthermore, there should be
provision for simple and objective pupil records in the principal's
office.

2. Evaluating Pupil Progress

Evaluation by the Teacher. Much of the evaluation of the pupil's
progress in school always has been, and no doubt always will be, made
by the teacher. That certainly is true of tests and examinations, but it
is also true of many other evaluation devices.

Much of the evaluation of a child's work by the teacher is of an
informal nature. It may be a follow-up to some activity in which the
child has participated or some project he has prepared. Sometimes
the teacher's informal evaluation takes the form of a comment or two,
but at other times it may consist of a formal conference with a pupil.
Some teachers have periodic conferences with all their pupils. Such
conferences to evaluate pupil progress are particularly common in
core classes.

Much of the teacher's evaluation is quite subjective. Like tests and
examinations, subjective evaluation by the teacher of the pupil's participation and progress has distinct values for improving the pupil's
work.

Evaluation by the Group. Especially in core classes, there is much
emphasis today on evaluation by the group, both of activities in which
the entire group engages, and of participation by individuals. Such
evaluation is usually planned by the group. It may be a formal evaluation, through the use of such instruments as checklists, or it may be
carried on through an informal group discussion.

Evaluation by the group means in effect that the members of the
group from time to time answer these questions: How well are we
doing? Are we achieving the objectives that we set up? In what
ways are we doing especially well? In what respects might our work
be improved? If the class is divided into committees or groups, each
group is encouraged to evaluate its progress periodically. Further-

more, at the end of a unit of work there is usually some evaluation of the work of the class by the entire group. Self-evaluation by the group should preferably be planned by the teacher and pupils together. It can provide splendid motivation for the work of the group and may contribute much toward improving the effectiveness of its learning activities.

Self-Evaluation by the Pupil. Every pupil should be encouraged to evaluate his own progress toward the objectives of every learning activity, every subject, and the school program as a whole. Tremendous motivation and much help in improving his work may result if the pupil knows what progress he is making. Self-evaluation is particularly appropriate in core classes, English, social studies, science, industrial arts, home economics, art, and physical education. In such skills as arithmetic, spelling, and penmanship, self-evaluation may be objective and formal, but in creative activities it may be quite subjective and informal. Self-evaluation by the pupil should be employed whenever it may contribute to more effective learning.

Evaluation Through Tests and Examinations. When the mastery of subject matter was the chief purpose of education, tests and examinations were the chief devices for evaluating pupil progress. Although many different evaluation procedures are used today, tests and examinations continue to be more widely used than any other. This is, of course, not necessarily undesirable. Acquisition of certain subject-matter skills and information continues to be an important function of the junior high school program.

However, as with the objectives of education, we have expanded the purposes which examinations should serve and the manner in which they should be given. A few years ago the chief purpose of tests and examinations was to serve as a basis for marks, progress reports, and promotions. Today, there are many purposes for which tests and examinations are used, including the following:

1. To measure the effectiveness of the instructional procedures employed by the teacher
2. To provide information for diagnosing the difficulties of individual pupils and for planning remedial activities to improve deficiencies
3. To measure the progress of the class as a whole on a unit or block of work as a basis for planning further learning activities
4. To help pupils evaluate their individual progress on a unit of work and plan for the improvement of the work
5. To ascertain the effectiveness of the study habits and procedures of individual pupils
6. To assist the pupil in summarizing the significant things gained from a unit of work

Reduced Emphasis on Final Examinations. Those examinations which have been given at the end of a marking period or a school term—commonly called final examinations—were particularly over-emphasized in the past. In many schools the pupil's promotion or failure depended entirely on his performance on the final examinations. This alone magnified the significance of these examinations in the minds of teachers, pupils, and parents, all out of proportion to their actual educational value. The way in which the examinations were approached and the manner in which they were administered added to the dread that surrounded this phase of the child's educational experience. The setting aside of special examination days, the comprehensive reviews, the warnings of the teacher, and the formal examination atmosphere—all these were part of a pattern which led pupils to approach final examinations with varying degrees of concern.

There is a growing recognition among junior high school teachers of the undesirable emotional effects of final examinations. Furthermore, many teachers doubt that such examinations of the older type are of sufficient educational value to justify as much time of teacher and class as has been devoted to them in the past. Consequently, there has been a tendency to reduce the emphasis on final examinations in the junior high school. In fact, in many schools today final examinations are not given at all. Instead, pupil achievement is measured through more frequent unit tests covering shorter periods of time. Teachers should study methods of preparing such tests, and they should learn how to use the results for improving the achievement of pupils. A comprehensive testing program which includes various types of standard and teacher-prepared tests has been introduced in some schools. If such a program is carefully planned and properly carried out, it should have much greater educational value than the traditional final examinations.

3. Marking and Reporting Pupil Progress

Present Marking Practices. In most junior high schools a formal marking system is still employed. Letter marking systems are the most common, with the letters A, B, C, D, and F being most often used. In a few schools, a percentage system of marks is still in use. Frequently percentage and letter systems are combined, the letters designating the pupil's mark within a certain percentage range.

In recent years many junior high school faculties have been experimenting with new types of marking practices. Such experimentation is usually done as part of an over-all study of the evaluation, marking, and reporting of pupil progress. Sometimes a new marking system merely provides for the substitution of one letter system for another. For instance, one school replaced an A, B, C, D, F system with H-honors, S-satisfactory, and U-unsatisfactory. It is doubtful that changes in letters alone will do much to bring the marking system more in harmony with our present philosophy of education. In quite a few schools, however, a marking system as we commonly think of it has been discontinued, and a detailed analysis of each child's work has been substituted for it. Usually this takes the form of a checklist which includes the learning outcomes for a given subject, and is closely tied in with the pupil-progress report forms.

New Reporting Procedures. Many kinds of new reporting procedures have been introduced in junior high schools throughout the United States. Some are still in the experimental stage, but others have been used successfully for some years. Although the new reporting procedures have taken a variety of forms, they usually provide for the following:

1. An evaluation of pupil progress in terms of the objectives of the total educational program and the various subjects in that program.
2. An evaluation of pupil progress in terms of the ability of the individual child rather than on the basis of a uniform standard for the group.
3. An analysis of the child's progress toward specific objectives in a subject, rather than one over-all mark for the subject as a whole.
4. An evaluation of the pupil's progress on aspects of development such as attitudes, character, and personality qualities, citizenship traits, and study habits.
5. Separate report forms for the different subjects.
6. Less frequent reports to parents than with the traditional report cards, but a more detailed report when one is made.
7. Teacher-pupil conferences to discuss with the individual pupil the progress he is making.
8. Teacher-parent conferences to discuss the child's progress in school. In some schools, such conferences are held at regular intervals, but in others they are at the request of either the teacher or the parent.

Procedures for Developing New Types of Pupil-Progress Reports. In many junior high schools, where new types of progress-reporting procedures have been introduced, there has been serious opposition or misunderstanding by parents, teachers, and pupils. Frequently this can be ascribed to the way in which the new procedures were introduced. Certainly, if new reporting procedures are developed by the principal or a supervisor without the help of the faculty, they may not receive the support of the teachers.

BATTLE CREEK PUBLIC SCHOOLS

Battle Creek, Michigan

19___–19___

JUNIOR HIGH SCHOOL
PROGRESS REPORT TO PARENTS

ARTS AND CRAFTS

Name ....

Grade........... Home Room....................

School ....

....
Teacher's Signature

Dear Parents:

The purpose of this report to the home is to inform you as fully as possible about the progress of your child in the junior high school.

This report card was designed by a committee of parents and teachers. It reports an academic grade which is determined on a competitive basis and indicates whether social and personal development are satisfactory or unsatisfactory.

The best education for your child results from the cooperation of the home and school. If you desire further information about the progress of your child, please call the school your child is attending and arrange for a conference with the teacher.

First Period Comments

....
Parent Signature

Second Period Comments

....
Parent Signature

FIG. 1. Pupil Progress Report Form in Arts and Crafts (Outside), Junior High Schools, Battle Creek, Michigan

ENGLISH-SOCIAL STUDIES, GRADES 7 and 8

Final Grade..............

PROGRESS IN:	MARK			COMMENTS	COMMENTS	COMMENTS
	1st	2nd	3rd	1st	2nd	3rd
Academic grade						
Effort						
Getting along with others						
Work and study habits						
Taking part in class activities						
Understanding current events						
Reading with understanding						
Finding and using resource materials						
Effective writing						
Effective speaking						
Listening effectively						
Spelling in all written work						
Respect for property and rights of others						
Times Absent						
Times Tardy						

FIG. 2. Pupil Progress Report Form in English-Social Studies (Inside), Junior High Schools, Battle Creek, Michigan

HOMEMAKING

Final Grade................

PROGRESS IN:	MARK			COMMENTS	COMMENTS	COMMENTS
	1st	2nd	3rd	1st	2nd	3rd
Academic grade						
Effort						
Courtesy						
Following directions						
Work habits						
Care of equipment						
Cooperation with others						
Written work						
Food preparation						
Sewing skills						
Class participation						
Completing projects						
Times Absent						
Times Tardy						

Fig. 3. Pupil Progress Report Form in Homemaking (Inside), Junior High Schools, Battle Creek, Michigan

Similarly, parents are not likely to understand or approve new reporting procedures about which they have not been consulted. Perhaps the chief purpose of pupil-progress reports is to bring information to parents concerning the progress of their children in school. In no other school practice is the understanding and cooperation of the parents so urgently needed. Where parent participation has not taken place, it is difficult to see how a new progress-report plan could meet with success.

In developing new procedures for reporting pupil progress to parents, attention should be given to the way in which principals, teachers, and parents might best bring about such changes. The following are some suggestions:

1. All teachers in the school need to participate in developing the new marking and reporting procedures.
2. A representative group of parents should participate from the very beginning in studying the present procedures for marking and reporting pupil progress and in developing new procedures. These parents should be of different backgrounds and points of view. Furthermore, other parents should be consulted to ascertain the type of information they would like to have about their children's progress in school and the procedures for bringing that information to them.
3. Pupils should have some part in studying present marking and reporting procedures and in developing new ones. This does not necessarily mean that the pupils should give their approval to any plan that is ultimately adopted. Rather, it means that the thinking of the pupils concerning marking and reporting procedures may be of help to teachers and parents as they study present procedures and develop new ones.
4. Any new reporting procedure should be employed experimentally for a year or two, with a careful evaluation by teachers, parents, and pupils.
5. A new plan for marking and reporting pupil progress should be finally adopted only when a great majority of teachers and parents feel that it is more satisfactory than the plan which has been in use. Even then, there should be continuous evaluation of the reactions of teacher, parent, and pupil as a basis for further changes.

Examples of New Reporting Procedures. Many educators believe that the only satisfactory way for reporting pupil progress to parents is through teacher-parent conferences. Although this plan is used in a few junior high schools, it is usually employed along with other reporting devices. For instance, in the Jonathan Weeks Junior High

School, Newton, Massachusetts, homeroom teachers are encouraged to have conferences with parents several times during the year. Because most homeroom teachers have two groups, which include sixty to seventy pupils, it is difficult to have these conferences as often as may be desirable. For that reason, a progress report on a printed form is sent home periodically for each pupil so that parents receive a report on their child's progress whether or not they are able to come for a conference.

Teacher-parent conferences are used frequently in core classes as a means of reporting pupil progress to parents. In fact, the objectives are so broad and the nature of the work so varied in the effective core class that it is difficult to report pupil progress except through such conferences. Furthermore, the fact that the core teachers have fewer pupils for longer blocks of time makes it easier for the teacher to arrange conferences with parents.

In many schools new printed or mimeographed progress report forms have been developed to achieve the purposes suggested earlier in this chapter. These forms differ widely from one school to another, some of them being relatively simple, while others are detailed and complex. In a few schools, the teacher writes a brief note or letter describing a pupil's progress in a given subject. Although such a note permits the evaluation of the child's work to be highly individualized, it places a tremendous burden on the teacher in a departmentalized school. Consequently, the teacher's notes often fall into stereotyped patterns which give little information to parents.

In schools where teachers write notes to parents, these are usually combined with a checklist or some other printed form on which the teacher may indicate the pupil's progress. The teacher then may write a comment only for those pupils for whom it seems especially appropriate. The printed form with an optional teacher comment seems preferable in a departmentalized school where teachers have many different pupils in their classes.

The report forms presented here are typical examples of the new ones which are being developed. At Battle Creek, Michigan, there is a separate form for each subject, with an academic mark, marks on specific objectives, and space for comments by both teacher and parent. The forms for two subjects are presented here (Figures 1, 2, and 3).

In the junior high schools of Springfield, Massachusetts, pupils are given a letter mark based on a group standard, but they are also checked in each subject on certain qualities which may be lacking in the pupil's work (Figures 4 and 5).

ATTENDANCE	ABSENT	TARDY	DISMISSED
FIRST REPORT			
SECOND REPORT			
THIRD REPORT			
FOURTH REPORT			
FIFTH REPORT			
SIXTH REPORT			
TOTALS			

PARENT'S SIGNATURE

FIRST REPORT ______

SECOND REPORT ______

THIRD REPORT ______

FOURTH REPORT ______

FIFTH REPORT ______

PROMOTION RECORD

THIS IS TO CERTIFY THAT ______ IS

PROMOTED TO GRADE ______

HOME ROOM TEACHER'S SIGNATURE ______

______ 195__

SPRINGFIELD PUBLIC SCHOOLS

SPRINGFIELD, MASSACHUSETTS

JUNIOR HIGH SCHOOL REPORT CARD

NAME ______

GRADE ______ HOME ROOM ______ 195____195__

SCHOOL ______

HOME ROOM TEACHER ______

PRINCIPAL ______

TO PARENTS:

A report of your child's progress in Junior High School should indicate:

1. General achievement in each class

2. Comprehension and mastery of Fundamentals (skills and basic knowledge) in each class.

3. Attitude, or disposition to learn, in each class.

This report card is designed to give you this information. The Period Mark of A, B, C, D, or E measures general achievement in each class. Check marks show how your child's attitude, comprehension and mastery of fundamentals compare with the average for his class.

WILLIAM J. SANDERS,
SUPERINTENDENT

FIG. 4. Pupil Progress Report Form (Outside), Junior High Schools, Springfield, Massachusetts

A—EXCELLENT
B—ABOVE AVERAGE
C—AVERAGE
D—LOWEST PASSING MARK

E—NOT PASSING
I—INCOMPLETE WORK—DUE TO
CONDITIONS BEYOND THE CON-
TROL OF THE PUPIL

NAME

GRADE

ROOM — 1 2 3 4 5 6 FINAL

ENGLISH
— EFFORT
— FUNDAMENTALS
— COMPREHENSION
— PARTICIPATION
— CONDUCT

FRENCH—LATIN
— EFFORT
— FUNDAMENTALS
— COMPREHENSION
— PARTICIPATION
— CONDUCT

MATHEMATICS
— ARITHMETIC — ALGEBRA — GENERAL
— EFFORT
— FUNDAMENTALS
— COMPREHENSION
— PARTICIPATION
— CONDUCT

SCIENCE
— EFFORT
— FUNDAMENTALS
— COMPREHENSION
— PARTICIPATION
— CONDUCT

SOCIAL STUDIES
— EFFORT
— FUNDAMENTALS
— COMPREHENSION

1 — ABOVE AV. / AVERAGE / BELOW AV. / POOR
2 — ABOVE AV. / AVERAGE / BELOW AV. / POOR
3 — ABOVE AV. / AVERAGE / BELOW AV. / POOR
4 — ABOVE AV. / AVERAGE / BELOW AV. / POOR
5 — ABOVE AV. / AVERAGE / BELOW AV. / POOR
6 — ABOVE AV. / AVERAGE / BELOW AV. / POOR

FUNDAMENTALS—BASIC KNOWLEDGE AND SKILLS
COMPREHENSION—UNDERSTANDING
PARTICIPATION—TAKING PART IN CLASS ACTIVITIES
OMISSION OF CHECK (√) MARKS INDICATES SUBJECT MARK IS SATISFACTORY

PARTICIPATION
CONDUCT

INDUSTRIAL ARTS

METAL WORK — PRINTING — WOODWORK
EFFORT
APTITUDE
INTEREST
CONDUCT

MECH. DRAWING
EFFORT
APTITUDE
INTEREST
CONDUCT

HOME ECONOMICS

FOODS — CLOTHING
EFFORT
APTITUDE
INTEREST
CONDUCT

ART
EFFORT
APTITUDE
INTEREST
CONDUCT

MUSIC

VOCAL — INSTRUMENTAL
EFFORT
APTITUDE
INTEREST
CONDUCT

PHYSICAL ED.
EFFORT
APTITUDE
INTEREST
CONDUCT

HOME ROOM ATTITUDE

Fig. 5. Pupil Progress Report Form (Inside), Junior High Schools, Springfield, Massachusetts

At the Weeks Junior High School, Newton, Massachusetts, the objectives for each subject are given on the progress report form. Pupils are given letter marks on each objective. Because of the large number of pupils which teachers have in physical education and music, the symbols S-satisfactory and U-unsatisfactory are used in these subjects (Figures 6 and 7).

Suggestions for Pupil-Progress Report Forms. A printed report form of one kind or another continues to be the chief, if not the only, device for reporting pupil progress to parents in most schools where new reporting procedures have been developed. Because of the difficulties in arranging teacher-parent conferences and the time needed for writing individual letters, the printed form will perhaps continue to be the most important part of reporting procedures. It seems appropriate, therefore, to offer some suggestions for developing satisfactory pupil progress report forms. The following may be helpful:

1. The report form should be sufficiently simple that it is readily understood by the parents.
2. The report form should be sufficiently brief that parents may examine it carefully in a reasonable length of time.
3. The report forms should be such that the teacher can prepare them carefully for all his pupils in a reasonably short period of time.
4. The report form should be such that there will be reasonable uniformity in the way it is prepared and used by different teachers.
5. The report form, if it is a new one, should be introduced only after considerable preliminary study by parents and teachers.
6. The report form should not be changed too often, lest it confuse parents, pupils, and teachers.

The principal weakness of the new types of marks and reports lies in the fact that it is very difficult for teachers to rate pupils on many of the important qualities which the school seeks to develop. Adequate means of observing and evaluating growth in character and personality traits, attitudes, and ideals, are not available to many teachers. Perhaps marks and reports should be attempted only upon those items on which the teacher appears to be in good position to pass judgment. This will vary from school to school and will depend upon a number of factors, particularly upon whether departmental teaching is employed and upon class size. Teachers should be trained in making judgments about traits which the school seeks to develop among its pupils.

4. Recording Pupil Progress and Other Information

Purposes of Cumulative Records. Up to this point, we have discussed methods of evaluating pupil progress and reporting it to the pupil and his parents. Repeated reference has been made to the importance of procedures for recording that information for future use. It is almost general practice to maintain a record of each pupil's progress in the administrative offices of the junior high school. Most systems have cumulative records which follow the child through school from kindergarten to graduation from high school. The cumulative records include, of course, information about the pupil's work in junior high school.

Cumulative records serve many purposes other than providing information for promotions, graduation, and college admission. In the junior high school, the information in the cumulative records is particularly helpful for such purposes as the following:

1. To help entering pupils become adjusted to the junior high school
2. To help pupils choose elective courses and curriculums, both for the junior high school and before entering the senior high school
3. To help pupils succeed in school
4. To help pupils with personal, social, and emotional problems
5. To help teachers in planning individualized learning situations
6. To provide necessary information for a pupil's work in senior high school and college
7. To provide information for vocational guidance and placement

Information in the Cumulative Record. A few years ago, the National Committee on Cumulative Records, appointed by the United States Office of Education under the chairmanship of Dr. David Segel, made an extensive survey of cumulative records in cities of 2,500 and over, and in all counties of the United States. As part of the study they prepared a rather complete and detailed list of items that should be included on cumulative record forms. This list is as follows: [1]

Personal

    Name
    Date of birth
    Place of birth
    Sex
    Color or race
    Residence of pupil and/or parents

[1] *Handbook of Cumulative Records,* A Report of the National Committee on Cumulative Records, United States Office of Education Bulletin No. 5 (Washington, D.C.: Government Printing Office, 1944).

TOWARD SUCCESSFUL LIVING

Through

SKILLS
SUBJECT MATTER
ARTS

NAME

GRADE

DIVISION

COAT ROOM

To Parents:

The purpose of this report is to inform the pupil and his parents regarding his achievement in the subjects he is now studying. For the purpose of this report, his standing is evaluated in terms of comparison with other members of his group.

This form is only one way of reporting pupil progress. Comment slips, telephone calls, and personal conferences are used by the teacher when a pupil's work shows marked deterioration or improvement. A conference between the teacher and parent probably is the best way to report pupil progress. Such conferences are encouraged.

THE FACULTY OF THE WEEKS JUNIOR HIGH SCHOOL

RAYMOND W. BLAISDELL, *Principal*

HAROLD B. GORES, *Superintendent of Schools*

WEEKS JUNIOR HIGH SCHOOL

195...... – 195......

NEWTON CENTRE - - - MASSACHUSETTS

FIG. 6. Pupil Progress Report Form (Outside), Weeks Junior High School, Newton, Massachusetts

IN NEWTON JUNIOR HIGH SCHOOLS

The pupil who receives an "A" does outstanding work in his group; his work is neat, accurate and thorough; he promptly makes up work he has missed, without being reminded; he is self-reliant in his work, depending on his own efforts with a minimum of help; he faithfully completes regularly assigned work of superior quality and often carries through to completion projects beyond the assigned work; in class discussion he contributes much of value, expressing himself clearly and forcefully; in tests he ranks at or near the top of his group.

The pupil who receives a "B" does good work in his group; he has the qualities of the "A" pupil in slightly lesser degree. He may equal the "A" pupil in some ways, but falls short in others.

Note: Colleges which admit without examination require a mark of "B" or better in the ninth grade.

The pupil who receives a "C" does fair work in his group; he contributes to class discussions but not always to the point; his accuracy, his achievements on tests are only fair; regularly assigned work is reasonably well done; he needs considerable supervision and help; he makes up work he has missed, though sometimes he must be reminded to do so.

The pupil who receives a "D" has the lowest passing rating. In the ninth grade a "D" rating received in Algebra 1, Latin 1, or French 1 admits to Math. 15, Latin 15, or French 15 only in Curriculum I. It does not admit to Math. 2, Latin 2, or French 2 in Curriculum I. It does admit to Latin 2, French 2, Geom. X in Curriculum II.

The pupil who receives an "F" does failing work; he contributes practically nothing to the class discussion; he is below the average of his grade in the mastery of the mechanics of written work; he makes up the work he has missed only when he is compelled to do so; he achieves a low rating on his tests and completes the regular assignments unsatisfactorily.

The pupil is marked "Incomplete" only when he has missed work because of excused absence. He must complete such work within a specified time if credit is to be given.

"S" and "U" ratings are given in physical education and music. A rating of "S" indicates that the pupil is making satisfactory progress. A rating of "U" indicates he is not making satisfactory progress. Teachers may give an "A" to particularly outstanding pupils.

Signature of Parent or Guardian:

Your signature merely indicates that you have examined this report. Space is provided for you to comment if you wish.

November ....

....

....

January ....

....

....

April ....

....

....

....

Fig. 6. Pupil Progress Report Form (Outside), Weeks Junior High School, Newton, Massachusetts (*Continued*)

Name.. Division.............. Coat Room...........

The most recent rating represents the pupil's achievement to date

ENGLISH Times/week.........

Teacher.............................

	NOVEMBER	JANUARY	APRIL	FINAL
Oral expression of ideas				
Written expression of ideas.............				
Application of principles of good usage...............				
Efficiency in reading skills...........................				
Range and quality of reading materials..............				
Listening habits				

SOCIAL STUDIES Times/week.....

Teacher.............................

	NOVEMBER	JANUARY	APRIL	FINAL
Knowledge and understanding of current problems........				
Knowledge and understanding of the unit being studied....				
Acceptance of his responsibilities throughout the school.....				
Participation in class discussion and activities............				

SCIENCE Times/week.........

Teacher.............................

	NOVEMBER	JANUARY	APRIL	FINAL
Reading science materials..........................				
Understanding science principles				
Solving science problems..........................				

MATHEMATICS Times/week........

Teacher.............................

	NOVEMBER	JANUARY	APRIL	FINAL
Understanding of fundamental operations..............				
Use of skills applied to everyday exercises..........				
Reading and organization in problem solving........				
Development of independent work habits..............				

ART Times/week.........

Teacher.............................

	NOVEMBER	JANUARY	APRIL	FINAL
Knowledge and use of the many art materials............				
Creative development of ideas......................				
Quality of finished product........................				

FIG. 7. Pupil Progress Report Form (Inside), Weeks

MUSIC   Times/week.........

Teacher.............................

	NOVEMBER	JANUARY	APRIL	FINAL
Vocal work, including tone, rhythm, melody, and harmony...				
Listening				
Performance (only pupils who perform will be marked in this)..				
Written work				

LATIN OR FRENCH   Times/week.......

Teacher.............................

	NOVEMBER	JANUARY	APRIL	FINAL
Mastery of basic facts and skills....................				
Vocabulary building..........................				
Ability to use and apply these fundamentals intelligently...				
Effective oral expression........................				
Effective written expression......................				
Reading comprehension..........................				

GENERAL BUSINESS   Times/week.......

Teacher.............................

	NOVEMBER	JANUARY	APRIL	FINAL
Knowledge and understanding of the unit being studied....				
Acceptance of responsibility in the practice of various business methods, procedures, and skills...............				

HOME ECONOMICS   Times/week.......

Teachers.............................

.. . .

	NOVEMBER	JANUARY	APRIL	FINAL
Knowledge and practical application of subject matter.....				
Reading and following directions....................				
Quality of finished product......................				
Development of poise and competence in social graces of home living				

INDUSTRIAL ARTS   Times/week.......

Teachers.............................

....

	GRAPHIC ARTS	GENERAL WOODS	GENERAL METALS
Competence in planning work......................			
Knowledge of materials, equipment, and products........			
Production of an article with evidence of craftsmanship.....			

PHYSICAL EDUCATION Times/week.......

Teacher.............................

	JANUARY	FINAL
Performance of basic physical skills..................		
Knowledge and application of rules for each activity......		
Recognition of need for leadership and organization.......		
Attitudes of good sportsmanship......................		

Junior High School, Newton, Massachusetts

Home and community

Names of parents or guardians
Occupation of parents or guardians
Are parents alive or deceased
Ratings of home environment and/or economic status
With whom does pupil live
Birthplace of parents
Language spoken in home
Marital status
Number of siblings, older and younger

Scholarship

School marks by years and subject
Special reports on failures
Record of reading
Rank in graduating class (with number in class)

Test scores and ratings

General intelligence test scores
Achievement test scores
Other test scores
Personality ratings

School attendance

Days present or absent each year
Record of schools attended, with dates

Health

The following types of items are desirable if a school has a health program in which physicians and nurses are a part:
Complete health record, to be filled in by physician or nurse
Record of physical disabilities
Vaccination record
Disease census

Anecdotal records

If an anecdotal records system is to be used, a special form should be developed. Anecdotal reports may be kept easily if filed in a folding type of cumulative record or where records are kept in envelopes.

Miscellaneous

Employment record during school years
Vocational plans
Counselor's notes
Extracurricular activities
Follow-up record after leaving school
Space for notations by teachers and others

Since the precise nature of the cumulative record must vary from school to school, this list of items should merely be considered a suggested one. Furthermore, some of them are not particularly appropriate at the junior high school level. It is an excellent list, however, to serve as a guide for the preparation of a satisfactory cumulative record form.

Maintaining Cumulative Records. Although excellent cumulative record forms are available in many school systems, they frequently fail to serve their purpose satisfactorily because of the manner in which they are prepared and the way in which the information is used. The same care should be given to developing a plan for recording the desired information on the record forms as to the preparation of the form itself. In some school systems there is a carefully prepared mimeographed or printed statement to guide staff members in preparing and maintaining the cumulative records. For instance, in the junior high schools of the City of New York, a sheet of instructions to teachers which corresponds to the pupil personnel record form shows item for item how that form is to be filled in. In the Stamford, Connecticut, public schools a printed booklet of instructions has been prepared to assist teachers in filling in and using the cumulative records. Such a plan for recording the information on the record forms should give attention to the following:

1. Any key or code that is used should be placed on the forms, as well as in a statement of instructions.
2. All staff members who place information on the forms should be thoroughly informed concerning the purpose and nature of the information desired. These instructions should be reviewed each time that information is recorded.
3. There should be careful definition of each item in the record form so that the information from year to year may be uniform.
4. There should be a definite time during the school term for recording each of the various items so that some of them will not be overlooked.
5. Provision should be made for recording the various items in such a way as to assure the accuracy of the records.

Using Cumulative Records. Some thought should also be given to the availability of cumulative pupil records for teachers, counselors, and other staff members. All too frequently such records are placed in a central office where they may not be readily available to teachers. In the survey of 370 junior high schools by the authors, 60 per cent have cumulative records available only in the central office. However, in 20 per cent of the schools they are placed in the hands of all teachers who need them. Much of the value of cumulative records is lost if they are not readily available to the faculty. These records should be placed where they can be reached easily by all staff members.

One practice that might be suggested for making this information available is to prepare summaries of the most significant information, have these summaries typed or mimeographed, and then place them in the hands of all the teachers. One danger in this practice is that the summaries may get into the hands of the pupils. Care needs to be taken that this does not occur. Another possibility is to set aside a certain time during the first week or two of school when teachers should come to the office where the records are kept and take down pertinent information about their pupils. In school systems where teachers return several days before classes begin, this would be an especially appropriate procedure. In a few schools, duplicate cumulative records are kept by the homeroom teacher. This is of no help, however, to other teachers who should have information about their pupils.

5. CONCLUSION

In this chapter only a brief summary was presented of the methods of evaluating, reporting, and recording pupil progress. For a more detailed study of these problems, books in various special fields should be examined. It should be emphasized, however, that the philosophy of the junior high school demands that considerable attention should be given to the techniques of evaluation, the types of pupil-progress reports, and the plans for recording pupil progress that are employed. The traditional practices in these matters are still widely employed and no doubt have some value. But they fail in many instances to meet the needs of a forward-looking junior high school program. Thoughtful attention should be given to the practices most appropriate for evaluating, reporting, and recording pupil progress in the junior high school.

QUESTIONS AND EXERCISES

1. Prepare a statement of suggestions for making good test items of the following kinds: (a) true-false, (b) multiple choice, (c) yes-no, and (d) matching.

2. Should final examinations each semester or year be given in the junior high school? If so, how much emphasis should be placed on them?

3. For what purposes are essay questions especially appropriate?

4. What are the objections to the percentage marking system?

5. Should factors other than subject matter achievement be taken into consideration in the marking system? If so, what factors would you consider? How much weight would you give to each?

6. What are the more important characteristics of the new types of pupil-progress reports?

7. What are the advantages and the disadvantages of the traditional pupil-progress reports?

8. What are the advantages and the disadvantages of the new pupil-progress reports?

9. Prepare a pupil-progress report form which you consider is appropriate for the junior high school in terms of our modern philosophy of education.

10. What are present trends in cumulative record forms for the junior high school?

11. Prepare a cumulative record form that you consider acceptable.

12. How would you employ anecdotal records in the junior high school so that they would be helpful in the guidance program?

13. Prepare a health record form for junior high school pupils.

14. How would you place in the hands of homeroom and classroom teachers the information about pupils which is usually found in the cumulative records in the principal's office?

Chapter 15

PROBLEMS OF ORGANIZATION
AND ARTICULATION

1. Grade Organization

Development of the 6-3-3 Plan of Organization. Before 1905, the emphasis on the shortening of the period of elementary education and on the earlier beginning of secondary education had so dominated the discussions on reorganization that a 6-6 division seemed to be the most logical plan of grade arrangement. It was not until about 1906 that some proponents of reorganization began to suggest that the six-year secondary school be divided into two parts—a junior school and a senior school. Consequently, the first reorganized schools included several different plans of grade organization, of which the most common were the 6-6, 6-3-3, and 6-2-4.[1]

In the decade or so after 1910, however, the junior high school—both the two- and the three-year types—spread rapidly in certain sections of the United States. But, by 1920, it was quite clear that the three-year school was to be the more popular plan of grade organization. By that time it was also obvious that the two-year school was, in most instances, a transitional arrangement in communities where the housing facilities, the preparation of teachers, or other factors were at the time unsuited to the 6-3-3 plan.

In Chapter 3, reference has already been made to the opinions of leaders in secondary education concerning the various types of grade organization. Of 66 recognized authorities, almost all (90 per cent) preferred the 6-3-3, the 6-4-4, or the 6-6 plan of organization. Not one gave the 8-4 plan as his first choice.[2] *In other words, authorities on the subject are in almost complete agreement that some form of a junior high school organization is desirable and that it is certainly preferable to the 8-4 plan.* It is seldom that there is such complete agreement on any issue in American education.

[1] See Chapter 1 for a more complete account of the grade organization found in the early junior high schools.
[2] See Table 2 in Chapter 3.

The Four-Year Junior High School. In the earlier years of the junior high school movement, a considerable number of authorities in secondary education expressed themselves as favoring the 6-4-4 plan of organization, which included a four-year junior high school and a four-year senior high school–junior college. Not many of those people who expressed themselves as favoring the four-year junior high school have since indicated that they have changed their minds. Indeed, it is likely that a majority of them still believe the 6-4-4 plan is at least as good as the 6-3-3 or 6-3-3-2 plan. Even so, the number of communities which adopted the 6-4-4 plan was never large. It has been more popular in California than in any other state. In the last decade, the number of school systems on the 6-4-4 plan has slowly but steadily declined.

The principal reasons educational leaders gave for favoring the 6-4-4 plan include the following: (1) the three-year unit is somewhat too short, both for adequate use of the plant and equipment and for an adequate educational program; (2) there is a much better chance for a bright student to gain a year—that is, to do four years in three—in the four-year than in the three-year unit; (3) there is likely to be good articulation between the courses in the senior high school and those in the junior college, especially in such subjects as physics, history, and literature, in which investigations have revealed an undesirable amount of duplication between the eleventh and twelfth grades of the high school and the first two college years; and (4) in small communities it is easier to extend the program of education to include grades thirteen and fourteen with a four-year combined senior high school–junior college, than with a two-year junior college.

The conditions which have led to the abandonment of the 6-4-4 plan in a number of cities, and which no doubt prevented its adoption in other cities, are as follows: (1) the desire of junior college teachers and administrators to be regarded as college educators; (2) the difficulty in organizing competitive sports programs; (3) the conservatism of the people of the community who have been accustomed to thinking of the high school as ending with the twelfth grade, with long-standing traditions of high school commencement exercises; (4) the feeling on the part of some junior college teachers that it is difficult to develop college morale for youth in grades thirteen and fourteen when they are housed in the same building with grades eleven and twelve; and (5) the belief of some educators and parents that the age spread included among youth in the four-year schools, namely, from about sixteen to twenty years, is not a desirable one.

Since the four-year junior high school seems to be practical only in communities with a public junior college, there has really been little experience with this grade arrangement in the junior high school. Where communities have either introduced or rejected the 6-4-4 plan, the decision seems to have been based most often on the merits of the four-year high school–junior college, rather than on those of the four-year junior high school.

Advantages of the Six-Year School. The chief reason for the rapid growth of the six-year high school, as compared with the segregated junior high school, is the fact that the six-year school is particularly adapted to the needs of small communities, of which there are so many. The advantages of the six-year high school that apply especially to small communities include:

1. Building costs can be reduced by constructing one large building instead of two small ones.
2. Economies can be effected in the assignment of administrative, supervisory, and teaching staffs, and in the adjustment of class size and teaching load.
3. The facilities of certain departments—such as science, music, art, home economics, and industrial arts—can be used by both the junior and senior high schools.
4. Economies may result from the joint use by the junior and senior high schools of the gymnasium, auditorium, library, and administrative offices.
5. Broader curricular and extraclass offerings are made possible by a larger teaching staff.

There are other advantages of the six-year high school which pertain to large as well as small communities:

1. It is easier to develop a well-articulated junior-senior high school program.
2. It is easier to retain pupils in school if the break between the junior and the senior high schools is eliminated.

Disadvantages of the Six-Year School. There are also several disadvantages of the six-year high school which apply particularly to the junior high school grades, including the following:

1. There is a tendency for pupils in grades seven, eight, and nine to become prematurely sophisticated through close contact with senior high school pupils.
2. There is a tendency to give preference to the pupils in the upper grades in both curricular and extraclass activities.
3. There is a tendency for the upper-class pupils to dominate positions of leadership in school activities.
4. There is a tendency to pattern the curricular and extraclass activities of the lower grades after those of the upper grades, rather

than to develop a program suited especially to the needs of the younger pupils.

5. There is a tendency to select teachers who are well qualified to teach in the upper grades, but without sufficient preparation, experience, and interest for the junior high school grades.

Whether for grades seven, eight, and nine, the six-year high school is inferior to the segregated junior high school remains, therefore, a moot question. From the standpoint of administrative efficiency, the answer depends largely upon the size of the pupil population for grades seven to twelve, as well as other purely local considerations. So far as the educational program for grades seven, eight, and nine is concerned, either the six-year or the segregated plan may be satisfactory, providing that the advantages and limitations of each are carefully considered in developing the program for the school. *It is the opinion of many educators, however, that, where the pupil population is sufficiently large to justify separate schools, pupils in grades seven, eight, and nine fare better in a separate junior high school than in a six-year high school.*

Psychological Considerations in Grade Organization. The junior high school, according to some educators, is primarily a school for pubescents. According to this point of view, the grades which should be included in the junior high school are those in which the pupils are becoming physiologically mature. There is considerable variation, however, in the age at which youngsters mature. The grades in which the largest percentage of boys mature are six through nine, while for girls they are five through eight. For the two sexes combined, they are grades six, seven, and eight. Obviously, with such variation in the ages when boys and girls mature, this factor cannot be considered a particularly satisfactory basis for determining the grades to be included in the junior high school.

The social maturity of the pupils is another consideration in deciding what grades are most satisfactory for the junior high school. Many educators and parents believe that children of twelve, thirteen, and fourteen are not sufficiently mature to participate in the social activities that are interesting and appropriate for sixteen- and seventeen-year-olds. Although objective evidence on this point is lacking, experience with junior and senior high school youth shows that, for girls, the end of the eighth grade might be a good dividing point between the junior and the senior high school, while for boys the end of the ninth grade probably is better. Obviously, it would create administrative and educational difficulties to have different grade arrangements for boys and girls.

Desirable Enrollment for a Junior High School. It is difficult to suggest what enrollment is most desirable for a segregated junior high school. Some objections to an exceedingly small school are as follows: (1) it is difficult to provide an adequate educational program, (2) the cost of the building and of equipment may be excessive, (3) it may be difficult to attract the best teachers, and (4) administrative and supervisory services may be inadequate. But an exceedingly large school also may be undesirable, because of such reasons as the following: (1) there may be excessive walking distances for many pupils, (2) there may be insufficient opportunity for all pupils to participate in extraclass activities, and (3) there may be too impersonal a relationship between pupils and faculty.

With these factors in mind, a reasonable estimate perhaps can be made regarding the most satisfactory enrollment for a junior high school. For instance, it is doubtful whether an effective junior high school program can be provided in a three-year school which does not have at least three class groups in each grade, or a minimum total enrollment of 250 to 300 pupils. On the other hand, little is to be gained in educational opportunities by having a three-year junior high school of more than 600 or 700 pupils, and a school of more than 1,000 pupils seems definitely too large. The most desirable enrollment for a junior high school therefore probably is about 600 to 700 pupils, with 1,000 pupils a desirable maximum.

Housing of the Junior High School. Of the 370 junior high schools included in the survey by the authors, the housing arrangements are as follows, for the percentage of schools indicated:

Building of its own	75%
Same building with elementary school	12%
Same building with senior high school	11%
No reply	2%

While there are advantages to being housed in the same building with either the elementary school or the senior high school, the disadvantages of this type of housing, except for very small junior high schools, seem to outweigh the advantages. Nevertheless, separate housing calls for special attention to problems of articulation.

2. THE JUNIOR HIGH SCHOOL DAY

Trend Toward Long Class Periods. In the seventh and eighth grades of the traditional elementary school, the number of subjects increased until, by 1900, there were classes in grammar, composition, reading or literature, spelling, arithmetic, music, art, penmanship, science, home economics, industrial arts, one or two of the social studies, physical education, health and hygiene, and sometimes other subjects. Many of these subjects were taught daily, while others came only two or three times each week. Such was the schedule of courses in the upper-elementary grades when the junior high school movement began about 1910.

The organization of subjects in the junior high school has been influenced considerably by the high school policy of having fewer subjects and longer class periods. The trend toward the fusion of specific courses in such subject areas as English, social studies, and science has also contributed greatly to a decrease in the number and an increase in the length of class periods. Other factors which led to a longer class period in the junior high school are the use of the project method, the long-unit assignment, introduction of laboratory methods in certain subjects, and supervised study in the classroom.

Class periods of 50 to 60 minutes are certainly preferable to shorter ones. Present practices in the junior high school support this suggestion. In the survey of 370 junior high schools by the authors, the percentage of schools having various lengths of class periods was as follows:

Minutes	Schools
Less than 41	5%
41-45	21%
46-50	30%
51-55	28%
56-60	15%
More than 60	1%

The most common practice is to have a 50-minute period, with 23 per cent of the schools reporting it; the 55-minute period is next, in 22 per cent of the schools; the 45-minute period is third, in 16 per cent; and the 60-minute period is fourth, in nine per cent. In other words, it is clear that a class period of 50 to 55 minutes is by far the most popular in the junior high schools today.

The trend toward core classes is another expression of the desire to have more time with a group of pupils. In the core classes, pupils have the opportunity to remain with the same teacher for two or more class periods. *More time with a group of pupils for a teacher is essential if we are to achieve satisfactorily the recognized functions of the junior high school.* The trend toward longer class periods and block scheduling of core classes should contribute toward achieving that result.

Number of Periods in the School Day. The typical daily school schedule in the junior high school provides for six periods daily, each

50 to 60 minutes long. Sometimes there are short homeroom and activity periods in addition to the regular class periods. In some schools, however, the activity period is a part of the schedule of regular class periods.

In the survey of 370 schools by the authors it was revealed that, although the most common practice is to have six class periods daily, quite a few schools have a seven-period day. The percentage of schools having various numbers of periods each day is as follows:

Periods Daily	Schools
4	1%
5	6%
6	53%
7	30%
8	9%
9	1%

Length of School Day. Before 1940 there was a tendency in all types of secondary schools to lengthen the school day. The reasons for this trend include the following:

1. The increasing preference for supervised study in school as compared with study at home
2. The introduction into the school program of more physical activity and also more self-directed activity, tending to make a longer school session less tedious
3. The increasing number of boys and girls continuing beyond the sixth grade who come from homes of low economic and cultural levels where home study conditions are not favorable
4. The increasing tendency to live in apartments and other types of crowded quarters not conducive to effective study at home
5. The greatly increased competition for the pupil's out-of-school time in the form of radios, the automobile, social life, the movies, dance halls, and television
6. The decreasing amount of time needed to go to and from school because of (a) better roads, (b) more automobiles, and (c) transportation provided by the school
7. The lessened opportunity for young people to get jobs after school
8. The increasing number of extraclass activities in the regular program of the school day

Beginning in the 1940's, the trend to lengthen the school day began to disappear, and indeed in many schools the day was actually shortened. In view of the growing belief that home study may have limited value, as well as the interference of television and other out-of-school interests, there is reason to believe that the trend toward lengthening the school day should be revived.

The typical junior high school day is slightly longer than that of the senior high school, if one takes into consideration only the time spent in classes. To compensate for this in part, extraclass activities in the senior high school occupy a greater amount of time after regular school hours. In the junior high school, the school day is usually from 5¾ to 6¼ hours in length as compared with 5 to 6 hours in the senior high school. The longer school day in the junior high school is due, in part, to the greater prevalence of supervised study in school, with less home work expected of the pupils. Other factors that contribute to a longer day in the junior high school are the proximity of the school to the homes of the pupils, less likelihood of after-school employment for pupils, and the larger number of subjects ordinarily included in the pupil's daily program.

In Fennell's doctoral dissertation, referred to several times previously in this volume, it was found that the over-all school day in the 224 junior high schools he studied was usually between six hours and thirty minutes and six hours and forty minutes, with a fifty-minute lunch period. This means a net school day of five and one-half to six hours.[3]

In any case, it should be clear that a short school day cannot be justified in the junior high school today. The day should be sufficiently long to provide adequate time for supervised study in the curricular program, for guidance, and for those extraclass activities which should be included in the regular day. *For such a program, the school day in the junior high school should be not less than five and a half hours; a six-hour day would be even better; and a six and a half hour day in many communities would not be excessive.* This time is exclusive of the lunch hour.

Typical School Hours. Among factors influencing the opening and closing hours of school are transportation facilities available for pupils, cafeteria, or lunch arrangements, and the program of athletics and other extraclass activities. In some communities, junior high school hours are influenced by those of the senior high school and the elementary school. Especially is this so if all pupils come on the same buses, if teachers or pupils shift from one school to the other, or if there are other administrative relationships among the various school units which may have a bearing on school hours.

[3] Edward Glenn Fennell, "An Analysis of Outstanding Junior High Schools in the United States" (Unpublished doctoral thesis, Cornell University, Ithaca, N. Y., 1953).

In recent years there has been a tendency for schools to begin a little earlier and to dismiss earlier. In most communities today the opening hour of the junior high school is 8:30 to 8:45 in the morning, and the closing hour about 3:30 in the afternoon. Also with more schools having cafeterias and a larger percentage of children having lunch at school, the time between the opening and the closing hours of school has been shortened to compensate for the shortened lunch recess. No recommendation can be made concerning the most desirable opening and closing hours because this depends so much on local considerations.

Provision for Noon Intermission. The length of the noon hour depends upon such factors as the distance most pupils live from school, prevailing weather conditions, and facilities for lunch in school. If adequate lunch facilities are available, the noon intermission may be rather brief, on the assumption that all pupils except those living within the immediate neighborhood of the school should remain for lunch. Ordinarily, junior high school pupils can be expected to walk a mile and return in a total of 45 minutes or a little less. Since they need at least 15 minutes for lunch, the noon hour in schools where most pupils go home should be at least 60 minutes long.

Numerous administrative problems are created in schools that provide lunchroom facilities for the pupils. One of these results from a lack of adequate lunchroom space, a situation found in many schools. Frequently in such schools there are several staggered lunch periods. The student body is divided into two or three groups which go to lunch in shifts, usually beginning at 11:30 or 12 o'clock. There may be still another group of pupils who live near the school that are assigned a longer period so that they may go home for lunch. The chief difficulty with schedule arrangements for staggered lunch periods lies in the fact that these periods are usually shorter than the regular class periods. Consequently, in schools with staggered lunch periods, schedule arrangements such as the following frequently must be made:

1. *The activities period, according to one plan, is scheduled for the noon hour, one group of pupils having lunch while the other has the activities period.* This plan is fairly practical if there are only two shifts. It is not very satisfactory, however, from the standpoint of the activities period. Assemblies, clubs, and other activities for which it is desirable to have the entire student body available, cannot conveniently be arranged for such an activities period. Other objections include the difficulty in arranging for programs from outside the school during the noon hour and lack of pupil interest in extraclass activities at that time of day.

2. *In schools with three shifts, a common plan is to split a class period for the middle lunch group.* That is, for the classes concerned, one-half of the class period precedes and the other half follows the lunch period. In schools where this plan is employed, the middle group is usually scheduled for a study period during the noon hour so as to avoid interrupting regular classes. But, even so, it is usually necessary in these schools to have some classes meet during the middle lunch period. Obviously, this arrangement can be defended only on the basis that no other solution to the noon schedule is possible.

3. *A third plan is to have the lunch periods the same length as the regular class periods.* In schools where provision is made for social activities during the noon hour, this plan provides a splendid solution for staggered lunch periods. Usually, this plan is not favored by school authorities where there are long class periods—that is, 50 minutes or more in length. Furthermore, it is not desirable for more than two lunch shifts because it spreads out the total time that is needed for lunch.

Pupil Activities During Noon Hour. In most schools, the pupils who remain for lunch provide a serious supervisory problem for the faculty. If the noon hour is too brief, the pupils may be so hurried that they will acquire undesirable eating habits and be deprived of the relaxation that is desirable after a meal; and if it is too long, it may be difficult to keep the pupils properly occupied after they finish their lunch.

In many junior high schools, the lunch period is considered an opportunity to provide appropriate social and health training. For instance, in connection with the lunch program, pupils are encouraged to acquire desirable eating habits, they are taught good table manners, and they are helped to break undesirable food prejudices. In schools that capitalize on the noon hour for social training, there are also well-planned activities for pupils as soon as they finish lunch. These activities include social dancing, library reading, chess, checkers, bridge, hobby work, music, movies, and library service. Various rooms are assigned for activities such as these, under the supervision of interested and trained faculty sponsors. For junior high school pupils, certain physical activities are especially appropriate for the noon hour, such as ping-pong, darts, and shuffleboard. In good weather, the playgrounds may also be used. On the playground, there should be organized activities and adequate faculty supervision. The key to the success of a noon-hour program with such varied activities is proper organization and adequate faculty supervision. A program such as this offers splendid possibilities for social and health education.

3. Registration and Schedule-Making

Importance of the Schedule. In schools with a departmentalized program, like that in most junior high schools, the problem of schedule making is quite complicated. Furthermore, once the schedule is made, it must be followed much more closely than in a nondepartmentalized school. It is exceedingly important, therefore, that serious consideration be given to the factors involved in preparing an efficient schedule.

The nature of the schedule in a junior high school should be determined primarily by the type of educational program which the faculty intends to provide. Unfortunately, educational considerations have not always been the dominating factor in schedule-making. Too often the nature of the schedule has been influenced more by administrative than educational considerations.

Pre-registration of Pupils. In recent years, the more progressive secondary schools have adopted the practice of pre-registration before the close of school in the spring. There are, of course, several important administrative advantages for pre-registration, chiefly the fact that it furnishes information concerning the registration for various courses which is essential for the preparation of the class schedule. But an even greater advantage of pre-registration lies in the opportunity it affords for advising pupils concerning their educational careers and related problems. The educational-guidance values of pre-registration should be kept in mind in planning activities of this kind in the junior high school.

A period of several weeks may well be employed for the pre-registration of pupils. Typical of the better schools is the practice of setting aside a period of six to eight weeks during March and April for educational-guidance activities leading to the choice of electives and the planning of the pupil's program for the next year. The activities in such a program for educational guidance might well include the following:

1. An introductory lecture in grade assemblies on the importance of educational planning
2. A talk by the principal or counselor on the values and importance of the required subjects
3. A series of talks by teachers of the various elective courses, explaining the values of these courses, the aptitudes desirable for satisfactory achievement, and the educational and vocational goals to which they lead
4. A series of homeroom discussions on the elective courses so as to answer any questions pupils may wish to raise

5. A talk by the principal or counselor on the extraclass activities of the school
6. Distribution among pupils and parents of information on registration, requirements for graduation, and course offerings. This may be done through such channels as the school paper, mimeographed and printed booklets, group conferences with parents, and the local newspaper
7. An individual conference between the homeroom teacher and every pupil, at which time the pupil's individual program is actually planned
8. Conferences for parents with homeroom teachers, principals, or counselor
9. Signing of registration cards by pupils, parents, and homeroom teachers
10. Weekly assemblies during this period, presented largely by various junior or senior high school groups—such as the band, orchestra, dramatic groups, glee clubs, declamation winners, and debate teams—to create interest in extraclass participation

Since the program in grades seven and eight is usually the same for all pupils, guidance concerning elective courses and pre-registration are not so important in these grades. However, in schools with several elective music organizations and a broad program of extraclass activities scheduled during the school day, guidance in planning the pupil's program and pre-registration become as important in grades seven and eight as in grade nine.

Schedule Construction: Mosaic Plan. There are two methods of schedule construction suitable for use in the junior high schedule: (1) the mosaic method and (2) the block method. For junior high schools with less than 400 to 500 pupils, the mosaic plan is most suitable and the most widely employed.

For the mosaic method, the materials needed include an ordinary drawing board, thumbtacks, a large sheet of white drawing paper, a T-square, and as many different colors of drawing or construction paper as there are grades in school. A grid outline for the schedule is first drawn on the white drawing paper, which has been attached to the drawing board. This outline should have enough columns to equal the number of periods in the school day, with one or two extras. There should be sufficient rows so that there is one for every teacher.

The name of each teacher is then placed in the left-hand column, and the number of each class period is filled in across the top. Next, slips are cut from the colored drawing paper the approximate size of each small rectangle on the schedule board, making a few twice that size for double-period classes, should there be any. A different color is used for each grade. The name of the class sections and the days of the week when the class meets are placed on these slips. After the slips are arranged in some convenient form, they are thumbtacked on the schedule board.

Courses which have no duplicate sections and those which require double periods should be scheduled first. It might be well to begin with the classes for the ninth grade, then proceed to the eighth grade, and finally to the seventh. The class slips are placed in the row with the name of the appropriate teacher and in the column for the period considered most desirable for that section. The colored slips assist in avoiding conflicts during any one period. The courses with two or more sections are blocked in last, since they usually cause the least difficulty.

Rarely can all conflicts in pupil schedules be prevented in the first attempt. The person preparing the schedule can quickly sort out and check for conflicts those pre-registration cards which appear irregular. As a rule, the entire schedule should not be disrupted to take care of the conflicts of a few pupils. With proper counseling at pre-registration, many conflicts can be avoided. If it is necessary to change the tentative schedule, care should be taken to keep a record of the original positions of all section slips that are shifted. Frequently, a better schedule can be arrived at in the process of changing sections. If the schedule cannot be conveniently changed, pupils with conflicts may have to make shifts in their elective courses.

Schedule Construction: Block Method. Under the block method of schedule construction, a group of pupils who are together in one subject, let us say English 7A, Section II, continue together in most or all of their classes. In some schools, the homeroom groups serve as the basis for the block method. The block method has these advantages: (1) it provides an easy method of equalizing the size of sections, (2) it tends to prevent conflicts, and (3) it makes possible the automatic assignment of pupils in groups rather than necessitating the making of an individual program for each pupil. The block method is better for junior high schools of more than 500 or 600 pupils. Procedures for employing the block method are given in most standard books on high school administration.

4. Problems of Articulation

Break Between Elementary and Secondary Schools. One of the chief reasons for dissatisfaction with the 8-4 plan was the lack of articulation between the elementary and secondary schools. Under the 8-4 system, there usually are abrupt changes in administrative practices and in the curriculum between the eighth and the ninth grades. For instance, when pupils enter the ninth grade, they find many practices which are quite different from those of the elementary school, among them: (1) they now have several teachers during the day instead of one, (2) they take fewer subjects, (3) many subjects are entirely new, such as algebra and foreign languages, (4) they have greater responsibility for the independent completion of their school work, (5) they study under teachers who tend to place more emphasis on scholastic achievement, (6) there is a large and more impersonal administrative organization, and (7) less personal attention and guidance are given pupils by the faculty. These are a few of the differences between the elementary school and the secondary school which, under the 8-4 plan, create a break between the eighth and ninth grades.

One reason for the introduction of the junior high school early in this century was this lack of articulation between the elementary and the secondary schools. But the introduction of the junior high school does not automatically lead to better articulation. In fact, it may result in two breaks in the school program instead of one. It is, therefore, exceedingly important to explore every possibility for employing the junior high school to smooth the transition from the elementary to the secondary school.

Articulation in Instructional and Administrative Practices. There are certain administrative and supervisory practices that have a direct bearing on the problem of articulation. From the standpoint of articulation, it is important that the change in these practices between the elementary and the secondary school should not be too abrupt. The following recommendations are made to improve the articulation in such practices:

1. *Satisfactory articulation demands a definitely formulated statement of ultimate educational goals and a basic educational philosophy for the entire program of elementary and secondary education.* Obviously, there cannot be satisfactory articulation between the elementary and secondary schools until a common purpose dominates the entire program of these schools. It is true, however, that the administrative authorities in many school systems feel that, even though such statements are not definitely formulated, the ultimate goals of education and a basic educational philosophy are generally agreed upon by their elementary and secondary school teachers. But it seems important, as a basis for effective articulation, that there should be a well-formulated statement of educational philosophy and objectives for every school system.

2. *Satisfactory articulation demands that the teachers in each school unit be kept informed regarding the objectives, learning activities, and instructional methods of other school units.* For instance, the junior high school should be sure that its staff, especially new teachers, is thoroughly familiar with the work of the elementary and the senior high schools. There are definite activities in many schools to bring about this understanding. Visitation by teachers among the various school units is one. Such visitation, to be effective, should be very carefully planned by the various teachers concerned.

The exchange of material explaining courses of study between the junior high school and other school units is another practice for improving articulation in the instructional activities. In many junior high schools today material of this type is exchanged between the junior high school and the elementary schools and between the junior high schools and the senior high schools.

Shifting teachers from one school unit to another is a third method for bringing about closer articulation in the instructional program. Teachers from the elementary school may be shifted to the junior high school, while some in the junior high school may be assigned to the senior high school. Once the teacher has been shifted he is usually left there indefinitely. Although this policy has some commendable aspects, its chief weakness lies in the fact that teachers are generally willing to be "promoted" to a higher unit, but they resent being "demoted" to a lower unit in the system. Even so, shifting teachers "upward" has some values from the standpoint of articulation.

3. *Satisfactory articulation demands that teachers from all three school units—elementary, junior high, and senior high—be kept informed when any considerable modification or reorganization is made in the instructional program of any one of these units.* This means, for instance, that major curriculum or course-of-study revision in any of the school units should be made only with the knowledge and participation of representatives from the others. This policy is fairly common in junior high schools, since in more than one-third of them curriculum and course-of-study committees include representatives from the elementary and senior high schools. In a few school systems, junior high school teachers are also invited to serve on the curriculum committees in the elementary and senior high schools. Cooperative efforts of this kind should be the usual practice, not only in curriculum and course-of-study development, but in any other modifications of the school program.

4. *Satisfactory articulation demands a gradual transition from the nondepartmentalized organization of the elementary school to the departmentalized plan of the secondary school.* It is certainly unwise

to have pupils taught by only one teacher in the elementary school, and then to place them abruptly in the seventh grade under the supervision of six, eight, or even more teachers. That is the situation, however, which pertains in most junior high schools today. Although most junior high schools are departmentalized in all grades, very few of them introduce pupils gradually to the departmentalized system. For better articulation in this respect it is urged that, in the seventh grade, pupils spend the greater part of the school day with the same teacher. For instance, they may have one teacher for homeroom and the basic subjects, while music, physical education, industrial arts, and home economics may be taught by different teachers, as under the departmentalized plan. Certainly each seventh-grade pupil should have at least two subjects, if not three or four, taught by the same teacher. In the eighth grade, departmentalization may be extended further, but not to all subjects, while in the ninth, the program may be as fully departmentalized as in the senior high school. This plan would avoid the abrupt change which pupils now experience when they enter the junior high school.

The core curriculum organization, with blocks of time of two periods or more, provides an excellent transition from little or no departmentalization in the elementary school to complete departmentalization in the senior high school. There are other features in the core curriculum that assist pupils in making the transition from one school unit to another. These were mentioned in the chapter on the core curriculum which appeared earlier in the book.

5. *Satisfactory articulation demands a gradual transition from the supervised study of the elementary school to the more independent study expected of pupils in the secondary school.* In the elementary grades, the pupil's study is usually done under the supervision of his regular teacher. But in the secondary school, it is customary to have library or study periods where pupils work without the help of the teachers. Since they are not accustomed to independent study in the elementary grades, the pupils should be introduced gradually to such independent study hall and library periods. Furthermore, there should be organized activities to teach the pupils how to do independent study efficiently.

6. *Satisfactory articulation demands a gradual transition from the common education required of all pupils in the elementary school to the elective courses and curriculums of the secondary school.* This recommendation contradicts the point of view on this subject held by many in the first decade of the junior high school movement. In fact, many early advocates of the junior high school considered the introduction of elective courses in grades seven and eight an essential

feature of a good junior high school organization. Current professional thought, however, holds that we should not go too far in the offering of elective courses in the secondary school. In the junior high school, a desirable policy is to have few, if any, electives in the seventh and eighth grades, but offer a limited number of electives in the ninth.

7. *Satisfactory articulation demands a gradual transition from the administrative policies and practices of the elementary school to those of the secondary school in such matters as attendance, home work, marks, report cards, and discipline.* In almost every high school, some teacher informs entering pupils that they need not expect the "spoon-feeding" methods of the elementary school in his classes. This point of view suggests that pupils will be expected to change greatly and suddenly in their conduct in school. Furthermore, it suggests that the high school will be much different in its method of discipline, as well as in other matters, from the elementary school. The junior high school faculty should study carefully the practices of both the elementary and the senior high school in such matters as discipline, attendance, home work, marks, and report cards. It should attempt to develop practices in the junior high school which will provide an easy transition in these matters from the elementary school to the senior high school.

Survey of Articulation Practices by Byers. A comprehensive survey of articulation practices in 130 junior high schools located in various parts of the United States was made recently by Richard S. Byers at the University of Connecticut.[4] In addition to making a survey of articulation practices, Byers also asked the opinions of leaders in elementary and secondary education on the articulation practices which they considered to be most desirable. His study led to certain conclusions which are appropriate here:

1. In the junior high schools studied, more attention is given to articulation practices between grades six and seven than between grades nine and ten. Furthermore, the leaders in elementary and secondary education were more interested in articulation between the elementary and the junior high school than between the junior and the senior high school.

2. There is wider use, in the 130 junior high schools, of articulation practices that bring people together from various school units to work on common problems than there is of practices to exchange information and materials. For instance, there is a wide use of workshops, teacher study groups, joint committee activities, and

[4] Richard S. Byers, "Articulation in the Junior High School" (Unpublished doctoral thesis, University of Connecticut, Storrs, Conn., 1955).

intervisitation by teachers. The leaders in elementary and secondary education also indicated a decided preference for activities which bring teachers together from the elementary, the junior, and the senior high school. It was believed that such activities lead to a better understanding of the philosophy, curriculum, and methods of each of the three school units by the teachers concerned.

3. In the junior high schools studied, the adjustment of pupils to a new situation is accompanied by a greater number of different articulation practices than any other articulation problem. The most common practices to help pupils make such an adjustment include (1) orientation of sixth-grade pupils before and after entering the seventh grade, (2) obtaining information about entering pupils, and (3) guidance practices to ease the transition from the elementary to the junior high school.

5. Conclusion

It is quite clear from this brief survey of the administrative problems of the junior high school that this institution has developed some rather distinct administrative characteristics. Both as a segregated school and as part of a six-year high school, the junior school generally has come to include grades seven, eight, and nine. The school day is long compared with four-year and senior high schools, but the registration and scheduling practices are very much like those of the senior high school.

In the articulation practices of the junior high school, there is an urgent need for improvement. In many schools, there have been determined efforts to bridge the gap between the elementary and the secondary school. But, considering that the lack of articulation was one of the chief reasons for the introduction of the junior high school, the progress that has been made in meeting this problem is far from satisfactory. Both in administrative practices and in the instructional program, most schools need to give more attention to providing a smooth transition from the elementary to the secondary school.

Questions and Exercises

1. What type of secondary school is likely to develop in the greatest numbers in the next decade or two—the six-year high school or the separate junior and senior high school? Justify your answer.

2. Be able to state the advantages and the disadvantages of the six-year high school as compared with separate junior and senior high schools.

3. What should be the minimum and the maximum size of a junior high school? Give reasons for your answer.

4. Prepare a bell schedule which you consider appropriate for a junior high school, in which you show such things as the following: (a) opening and closing of school day, (b) length and number of class periods, (c) length and number of homeroom periods, and (d) noon period.

5. What are the advantages of a class period of 60 minutes as compared with a 40-minute period?

6. What are the principal arguments for and against a four-year junior high school?

7. How would you arrange the daily schedule to provide for a long or double period for an integrated course in English–social studies in each grade?

8. What plan of scheduling would you employ to provide sufficient time for industrial arts, home economics, physical education, and similar subjects?

9. Suppose that you have a lunchroom or cafeteria which accommodates only one-third of the pupils at a time. How would you arrange your lunch schedule and schedule of classes to provide for all the pupils?

10. What extraclass activities would you include in the regular daily schedule? How would you provide adequate time for them in the schedule? What activities would you have outside the regular school hours?

11. Prepare a plan of pre-registration for a junior high school of a given size of your choice.

Chapter 16

STAFF PROBLEMS

1. Size and Pattern of Staff

Desirable Pupil-Teacher Ratio. There is no precise mathematical approach to the problem of how large a staff should be for a school with a given enrollment. Certainly one teacher for every 15 pupils, were it educationally desirable, would involve an expense much greater than the taxpayers in most school districts would feel that they could afford. On the other hand, administrators and teachers would readily agree that only one teacher to every 40 pupils or more would mean that a school is badly understaffed. It seems desirable to consider 25 pupils per teacher as a reasonable maximum load in staffing a school. Administrative, supervisory, and guidance staff should not be included in computing this ratio.

It is quite generally agreed, however, that 25 pupils is a desirable average class size for most subjects in the junior high school, with 30 as the maximum. In such laboratory subjects as industrial arts and home economics, it is best to have classes somewhat smaller, with 25 pupils as the maximum.

Unfortunately, there is a tendency to exceed these class sizes in many junior high schools. In fact, some educators believe that one can justify larger classes in the junior than in the senior high school. One school system, for instance, specifies that in the junior high school the average class size should be 30, with 35 as the maximum; for the senior high school, however, it provides for an average size of 25, with 30 as a maximum.

Pattern of Personnel. The staff of a secondary school in the late nineteenth century consisted almost entirely of classroom teachers. Only in large systems were there a superintendent, principals, and an occasional supervisor who did little or no classroom teaching. But, since 1900, marked changes have taken place in our philosophy of education and in the educational program offered in the secondary schools. To meet the needs created by these changes, many high school faculties began to include such staff members as an assistant principal, director of guidance, dean of girls, counselor, school nurse, director of extraclass activities, curriculum director, research worker, visiting teacher, and supervisors of special subjects.

Several factors have a direct bearing on the number and pattern of the professional staff that are desirable for a specific school, including particularly the funds available and the nature of the school's program. Since these factors vary considerably from school to school, it is difficult to formulate precise standards for the composition of the professional staff. A staff which may be recommended for a school with a forward-looking educational program is presented in Table 4. It should be understood that the recommended staff does not represent either prevailing practice or the ideal situation. It is a suggested pattern that should be attainable in a modern, well-supported junior high school.

TABLE 4

RECOMMENDED JUNIOR HIGH SCHOOL STAFF, ACCORDING TO SIZE OF SCHOOL

Position	Schools of 101-300	Schools of 301-600	Schools of 601-1,000	Schools of 1,001-2,000
Principal	⅓ to ⅔	⅔ to 1	1	1
Assistant principal		¼ to ½	½ to 1	1 to 2
Counselors	⅓ to ⅔	⅔ to 1	1 to 2	2 to 4
Librarian	⅓ to ⅔	1	1 to 2	2 to 3
School nurse	¼ to ½	½ to 1	1 to 1½	1½ to 2
School physician		¼	¼	½
Psychologist		¼	½	1
Attendance officer, office clerks, secretaries	½ to 1	1 to 2	1½ to 3	3 to 5
Supervisors and curriculum director	½	1	2	3 to 6
Classroom teachers	5 to 12	12 to 24	24 to 40	40 to 80
Total	7 to 16	17 to 32	33 to 53	55 to 105

Entries refer to number of full-time individuals or the equivalent total of fractions of the time of different individuals who work in the positions indicated. Totals for the school are given in nearest whole number.

The part-time specialists suggested in Table 4 may devote some of their time to teaching duties or may divide their time among several schools. The school nurse, physician, or psychologist may well divide time between two or more small schools. Special staff members who ordinarily may be expected to do part-time teaching in small schools include the assistant principal, counselor, librarian, and activities director. Still another possibility for the small school is to combine certain of these positions, such as those of assistant principal and counselor.

Some idea of the prevalence among junior high schools of various types of specialized personnel is given by Fennell from his study of practices in 224 schools, with the number of schools as follows: [1]

Boys' physical education teacher	208
Music teacher	207
Girls' physical education teacher	203
Home economics teacher	193
Art teacher	193
Industrial arts teacher	190
School nurse	174
Attendance officer	107
Guidance counselor	105
Vice-principal	85
Guidance director	73
Reading specialist	73
Speech therapist	65
Visiting teacher	58
Athletic director	58
Supervisor	50
Psychologist	44
Agriculture teacher	28
Curriculum director	24

2. PROFESSIONAL AND PERSONAL QUALIFICATIONS OF TEACHERS

Need for Adequate Training. The success of any school depends more upon the type of teacher employed than upon any other single factor. This is particularly true in a new type of school organization, like the junior high school, where a new educational program is being developed. In the early junior high schools there were few teachers specially trained for junior high school work. Most of them had training and experience in the philosophy and the program of the traditional elementary and secondary schools. Frequently, they were the "culls" from the high school faculty or from the applicants for high school positions. In many instances, the teachers in the early schools were skeptical about the junior high school idea, while some were actually opposed to it. In the selection of the teaching staff for the junior high school, it is exceedingly desirable to secure persons who not only have superior intellectual and personal qualities, but also have training and experience in the type of work to be done.

Fennell reported in his study of 224 junior high schools that approximately 95 per cent of the junior high school teachers had at least

[1] Edward Glenn Fennell, "An Analysis of Programs of Outstanding Junior High Schools in the United States" (Unpublished doctoral thesis, Cornell University, Ithaca, N. Y., 1953), p. 197.

a bachelor's degree, and of these more than a third had a master's degree. In general, the larger the school, the more people with master's degrees would be found on the faculty.[2] Although advanced degrees do not necessarily lead to better teaching, it is generally true that the teacher with the most preparation has professional skills, understandings, and backgrounds which enable him to be more effective in his work.

Nature of College Education. It was indicated in an earlier chapter that four years of college education is quite generally accepted today as the minimum standard for the preparation of junior high school teachers, while many of them have five years or more of college. But adequacy of preparation cannot be measured alone by years of college training. In recent years, it has become exceedingly easy to get a degree at many institutions of higher education. Therefore, in selecting junior high school teachers, it is important to consider the type of institution and the nature of the college program, as well as the period of training.

In the early years of the junior high school, there was much discussion as to whether the junior high school teacher should be trained in a normal school or teachers college rather than a liberal arts college or university. Some educators felt that in the teachers college too much attention was given to methods and other professional studies at the expense of subject matter, while others believed that in the college or university the reverse was true.

Today, educators feel that the more important consideration is not so much which *type* of institution but which *institution* offers the best training opportunities. Many teachers colleges have strengthened their program of subject-matter training, while many colleges and universities include more professional subjects in their teacher-education programs and permit the student a wider variety of subject-matter courses. At the University of Colorado, for example, students may take a "distributed major" for the A.B. degree, consisting of work in several departments, like English, history, economics, and sociology. This improvement in the teacher-education programs, both in the teachers colleges and in the liberal arts colleges and universities, has largely dissipated the discussion regarding the effectiveness of one type of institution as compared with another for the preparation of junior high school teachers.

Academic Preparation of Teachers. The junior high school teacher of today should be a person of broad interests and back-

[2] Fennell, *op. cit.*

grounds. He not only should be well prepared in the subjects he is to teach, but he also should be interested and well informed in economic, political, and social problems, international affairs, literature, music, art, and the theater. The development of such broad cultural interests should be the first consideration in the preparation of the junior high school teacher.

Preparation in specific teaching fields, likewise, should not be narrow and overspecialized. The teacher of science should have at least some preparation in botany, zoology, chemistry, and physics, and preferably in geology, geography, bacteriology, and astronomy as well. The preparation of the social studies teacher should include history, sociology, political science, economics, and geography. Teachers of English, the foreign languages, and other subjects also should be prepared in broad subject areas.

In examining the applicant's subject-matter preparation, little reliance can be placed by employing authorities on the "majors" and "minors" which serve as a basis for course selection in many colleges and universities. Both the requirements and the scope for a college "major" or "minor" vary so much from school to school that they have little meaning as a basis for teacher selection or assignment. In some institutions a "major" consists of as much as 40 to 50 semester hours of work in one department, while in others it may be as little as 20 to 25 semester hours. Then, too, the departmental organization is by no means uniform among all institutions. Some of them have a highly specialized departmental organization with courses grouped in such narrow areas as history, economics, and government, while in others the courses are grouped for majors and minors into broad fields, like the social sciences, the physical sciences, and the biological sciences. It is important, therefore, to examine with some care the subject-matter training of applicants for teaching positions in the junior high school.

Since degrees, credits, and marks do not give much assurance of the prospective teacher's professional preparation and interest, professional examinations are being used increasingly to supplement college records as a basis for employing teachers. Many of the larger school systems require applicants to take either examinations prepared locally or the National Teacher Examinations.[3] These examinations give some measure of the teacher's interest and preparation in broad cultural areas, in specific subject fields, and in professional subjects. Properly used, they can be helpful in selecting teachers.

[3] Prepared and administered by the Educational Testing Service, Princeton, New Jersey.

Professional Preparation of Teachers. The professional preparation of the junior high school teacher today is considered to be fully as important as training in subject areas. The teacher's professional study should include, as a minimum, some attention to each of the following: (1) philosophy of education; (2) educational sociology; (3) principles and problems of curriculum development; (4) psychology of growth and learning, including a study of motivation and interest, individual differences, and problems of pupil growth and development; (5) mental hygiene; (6) the history, objectives, organization, and curriculum of the secondary school in America; (7) the history, functions, organization, and curriculum of the junior high school; (8) the philosophy, organization, and procedures for guidance and extraclass activities; and (9) methods of teaching and of evaluating pupil growth in the junior high school. Entire courses in each of these areas are impossible, and, for that matter, not desirable. But a reasonable minimum of professional preparation for the junior high school teacher demands some familiarity with all these areas.

The junior high school teacher who intends to be a master in his profession, of course, should go beyond the minimum in professional preparation. In addition to the basic preparation outlined above, it would be desirable for him to do some study in the following professional areas: (1) the use and interpretation of intelligence tests, (2) organization and techniques of guidance, (3) psychology and measurement of personality, (4) advanced educational psychology, (5) history of education, (6) workshop experience in curriculum development and guidance, and (7) school and community relations.

The program of professional education for the junior high school teacher, as just outlined, should culminate in carefully planned and well-supervised experience in a typical junior high school teaching situation. That experience, usually called observation and student teaching, should include: (1) extended and varied classroom teaching opportunities; (2) observation and participation in the supervision of extraclass activities; (3) the direction of homeroom and other guidance activities; (4) practice in the administrative duties of the teacher; (5) participation in such professional and community activities as faculty meetings, faculty committees, and the Parent-Teacher Association; and (6) conferences with parents and contacts with the pupils' homes.

Preparation in Extraclass Activities. The educational responsibilities of the junior high school teacher, like those of teachers in other secondary schools, have long since ceased to be confined to the classroom. Most teachers in the junior high school supervise one or more pupil activities—a club, speech activities, assemblies, competitive sports, music, dramatics, social functions, the student council, or a school publication. The employing authority in selecting his staff should consider their capacity for leadership in such activities. He should exercise care in building his staff so that, taken as a whole, it is prepared to assist in a well-balanced program of activities.

The best evidence of the beginning teacher's preparation to supervise extraclass activities is previous participation in high school and college activities. For the experienced teacher, previous success in supervising activities is, of course, the most satisfactory basis for judging ability to assist with the extraclass program. The qualifications of prospective teachers in this respect should be carefully examined by the employing official.

Previous Experience of Teachers. Two decades or more ago, when it was difficult to find teachers trained or experienced in junior high school work, there was much discussion as to whether these teachers should be recruited from the elementary school or from the high school. Authorities on the junior high school objected to the employment of too many inexperienced teachers and also to the transfer of mediocre ones from the high school. Today, the objection to inexperienced teachers is not so valid because they have more adequate professional training as part of their college work.

There is still the question as to whether elementary or high school experience is best as preparation for work in the junior high school. But the place in the school system where the junior high school teacher received his previous experience is really of secondary importance. Of far greater importance is the nature and quality of that experience. *Those teachers should be recruited for junior high school work whose personality, interests, philosophy of education, and teaching skills are favorable for contact with boys and girls in early adolescence.* Both the elementary and the senior high school faculties should be studied to locate such teachers.

The policy of "demoting" mediocre teachers from the senior high school, and "promoting" the more successful ones from the junior high school, cannot be justified. Educational authorities generally agree that the trying years of early adolescence demand fully as great, or even greater, teaching skill than the later years in the senior high school. Furthermore, the attitude on the part of administrators that the junior high school is the proving ground for teachers who want senior high school positions has a very undesirable effect on the morale of the junior high school staff. Capable teachers should be encouraged to make the junior high school their career.

Proportion of Men and Women Teachers. One of the arguments for the junior high school advanced early in the movement was that men teachers could be attracted in desirable numbers. A larger representation of men teachers, it was believed, would: (1) bring pupils into desirable contact with masculine personalities, (2) induce older boys to remain in school, (3) bring about a better disciplinary situation, (4) bring into the learning situation the points of view and experiences of men, and (5) provide men for those guidance and extraclass activities which they can supervise more effectively than women.

Although there is no scientific evidence to substantiate this position, some authorities believe that at least a third of the teachers of boys and girls over ten years of age should be men. Fennell reported that, in 1953, in the 224 junior high schools he studied, nearly 40 per cent of the teachers were men.[4]

Because of the increasing interest of men in teaching in the junior high school, some schools are exceeding considerably the proportion of men which has just been suggested. In fact, an occasional junior high school has more men than women. It seems appropriate to suggest, therefore, that it is also good practice to have at least one-third of the faculty consist of women. The talents of women and their influence on early adolescents are fully as important as those of men.

Desirable Personal Qualities of Teachers. Although school administrators are constantly looking for teachers with good personalities, few of them could explain what a good teaching personality is. Unfortunately, there are no scientific data to show what personal qualities are particularly desirable for junior high school teachers. Experience would indicate that the personal qualities of these teachers should include: (1) attractive facial expression, voice, and general appearance; (2) a sense of humor; (3) interest in individual children; (4) patience with the irritating peculiarities and manifestations of the adolescent personality, such as lack of interest in school, desire to clown or show off, emotional "tail spins," display of temper or sulking, and deliberate antisocial behavior; (5) tolerance of the points of view and skepticism of youth; (6) understanding of the interests and problems of young people; (7) freedom from vindictiveness; (8) enthusiasm for teaching; (9) desire and capacity to meet parents and become acquainted in the community; and (10) effective leadership qualities. Although few people possess all of these qualities, an intelligent and sympathetic supervisor can help most teachers improve themselves in these respects.

[4] Fennell, *op. cit.*

Basic Philosophy and Understandings. High on the list of factors contributing to the success of junior high school teachers is their possession of a sound philosophy of education and an understanding of the responsibility of the school for participation in guiding and stimulating all-round growth of young adolescents—social, emotional, physical, and intellectual. Truly successful teachers should also understand the responsibility of the school for the preparation of young people to take their appropriate place in American society. They should recognize not only that the public school system exists to benefit the young people who attend it, but also that it is a social institution and its program must be developed to meet the needs of the society in which our youth will live.

In-Service Growth. It is clear that in the junior high school, as in the elementary and the senior high school, teachers cannot be fully prepared for their responsibilities before they accept their first position. A fully competent junior high school teacher should make every effort to grow from year to year after he begins teaching. While opportunities for in-service growth include extension, summer school, and correspondence courses, they are not confined to those areas. Indeed, in recent years, another type of in-service activity has come to be regarded as exceedingly valuable for the professional improvement of the teacher. This is the work by faculties on projects for the improvement of the curriculum and other aspects of the program of the school. Such work may be done through committees, workshops, and faculty study groups, especially organized and conducted to study specific problems in the program of a given school.

The Junior High School Principal. In the past, a common practice was to select a senior high school teacher with administrative qualities for the junior high school principalship. Sometimes an elementary school principal was "promoted" to the principalship of the junior high school. Little can be said in favor of either of these practices. In general, such principals have little background in the philosophy, problems, and educational program of the junior high school. Often the junior high school principalship became the proving ground for the principalship of a senior high school. Furthermore, the effect on the morale of the junior high school faculty of these practices is anything but good.

In recent years, however, the quality of junior high school principals has improved tremendously. More and more, superintendents are insisting that the principal have some experience and background in junior high school work. The more forward-looking superintendents are "grooming" young men and women for administrative and supervisory positions by giving them opportunities to gain experience under the supervision of a competent junior high school administrator. Professional study in junior high school education and the problems of young adolescents is also being required. Furthermore, more principals have master's degrees, and a significant number have a sixth year of professional study or the doctorate.

It used to be fairly common in the junior high school to have a principal who is also assigned to the elementary or senior high school. The policies employed in the assignment of principals, for the percentage of schools indicated in 1940 and 1954 are as shown below:

	1940	1954
Principal assigned only to junior high school	63%	85%
Principal assigned also to elementary school	29%	9%
Principal assigned also to senior high school	5%	4%
Principal assigned also to both elementary and senior high school	1%	0%

Many of the arguments regarding the assignment of teachers to more than one school unit apply also to the principal. Better articulation in the entire educational program is certainly a good argument for a common administrative authority for either the elementary and junior high schools or for the junior and senior high schools. But in some systems which have one principal for the junior and senior high schools together, there has been the complaint that he devotes the greater part of his attention to the upper grades. Some schools avoid this difficulty by placing an assistant principal in charge of the junior high school division.

Staff for the Six-Year School. The principal of a six-year secondary school should be selected partly on the basis of his understanding of the philosophy and program of the junior high school, and he should have a deep interest in early adolescents and the work of the junior high school grades. Teachers in the six-year schools should have qualifications, interests, and backgrounds appropriate for responsibilities with the young as well as the older adolescents. It is good practice to select some teachers for six-year schools with experience in the junior high school or the elementary school, and to assign them primarily to the junior high school grades.

3. Teacher Salaries and Loads

Prevailing Salaries. For the country as a whole, salaries for junior high school teachers were, for many years, about midway between those of the elementary school and the senior high school. In recent years, the salary situation for junior high school teachers has changed sufficiently so that their median salaries now are much closer to those of the high school than the elementary. The percentage improvement in salaries of junior high school teachers from 1930 to 1955 was much larger than for high school teachers, though not so large as for elementary teachers. The relative salaries for teachers at the elementary, junior high, and high school levels, with the percentage of increase from 1930-31 to 1954-55, are as follows: [5]

School	Median Salaries		Percentage of Increase
	1930-31	1954-55	
Elementary school	$1,162	$3,465	198.3%
Junior high school	1,360	3,579	163.2%
High school	1,547	3,848	148.7%

Furthermore, it is shown in the same study that median salaries for junior high school teachers increased considerably more from 1930 to 1950 than was true for senior high school teachers. But during this period median salaries for elementary school teachers in all types of cities increased more than those for teachers in both the junior and senior high schools.

Importance of Equal Salaries. Many educators believe it unfortunate that teachers in the junior high school are paid less than those with similar training and experience in the senior high school. Aside from salary, the traditional attitude in the public schools of America has attached more prestige to teaching positions at the upper-grade levels. The higher pay, as well as the added prestige, has encouraged junior high school teachers to seek "promotions" to the senior high school. In any case, the salary policy in a school system should be such as to encourage good teachers to remain in the junior high school and to improve themselves for the professional responsibilities at that grade level.

An increasing number of school systems have adopted such a salary policy in the form of a single salary schedule for all grade levels. Under this plan, salaries are fixed in terms of such factors as the teacher's training, experience, and skill, rather than the grade level. This trend toward equalized salaries for teachers at all grade levels should contribute much toward obtaining a competent faculty for the junior high school.

In some ways, the situation is even more serious with the salaries for principals than for teachers. There is no doubt that the character

[5] National Education Association, "Salaries and Salary Schedules of Urban School Employees, 1954-55," *Research Bulletin*, XXXIII (April, 1955), 70.

of a junior high school program is determined more by the administrative and supervisory leadership than by any other factor. Although the salaries of junior high school principals are higher, on the average, than those of elementary principals, they are lower than those of principals in the senior high school. Until this situation is changed, principals will continue to move from the junior to the senior high school.

In some communities there is a single salary schedule for both junior and senior high school principals, which is based on education and experience. That is as it should be. Sometimes, however, the schedule is also based on school enrollments or the number of teachers under the principal's supervision. Since the senior high school is usually larger than the junior high school, this practice tends to create a differential in the salary of the principals in the two types of schools. Furthermore, it is doubtful that one can defend the practice of paying higher salaries in the same community for administrative and supervisory leadership in the larger schools. It would seem that, in a given community, all schools should have a right to the same quality of leadership. Therefore, the practice of considering size of school as a basis for determining the principal's salary does not seem to be a desirable one.

Factors in the Teaching Load. The effectiveness of the instructional program is determined not only by the skill and diligence of the teacher, but also by the weight of his teaching assignments and responsibilities, which we commonly call his teaching load. Hence, it is exceedingly important that careful consideration be given to the proper adjustment of the teaching load.

The factors which form a part of the total teaching load are numerous and varied indeed. The more important factors affecting the teaching load may be summarized as follows:

1. Number and type of classes and pupils
2. Use and care of instructional facilities and equipment
3. Requirements of instructional planning and class preparations
4. The nature of classroom methods and procedures
5. Administrative, supervisory, and clerical responsibilities
6. Responsibilities for extraclass activities
7. Guidance and pupil-adjustment responsibilities
8. Required or expected community relationships
9. Professional-improvement requirements [6]

It is of value to know what teachers believe can be done to improve the teaching load. In a survey in the Research Division of the Na-

[6] National Education Association, "The Teacher Looks at Teacher Load," *Research Bulletin*, XVII (November, 1939), 267-68.

tional Education Association, secondary school teachers made the following recommendations when asked what they thought might be done to improve teaching load: [7]

Recommendations	Percentage of Teachers
Try to improve the scheduling of the program	47
Try to secure additional personnel	41
Try to improve the administrative management of the school	35
Try to improve the school plant	16
Other suggestions	9

Desirable Class Size. The teacher's load is affected directly by class size. Furthermore, class size also influences considerably the nature of the learning situation. As noted above, it is quite generally agreed that a desirable average class size in most subjects is 25 pupils, with 30 pupils as a maximum. In such laboratory subjects as industrial arts and home economics classes smaller than 25 are desirable, with 25 pupils as the maximum number.

Unfortunately there is a tendency to exceed these class sizes in many junior high schools. In the study by the authors of 370 schools the following typical class sizes were reported from the percentage of schools indicated:

Typical Class Size	Schools
Less than 25	3%
25-29	15%
30	33%
31-35	40%
More than 35	9%

It was reported from a number of schools that 40 pupils constituted the typical class size. Certainly, either from the standpoint of the teacher's load or the effectiveness of the instructional program, the typical class size should not exceed 30.

In some junior high schools, class sizes are especially large in physical education and music. Physical education classes of 40 to 60 pupils are not at all uncommon, and in some schools they are even larger. *If pupils are to receive the individual attention which they need in these subjects, classes in physical education and music should not exceed 30 pupils.*

Number of Classes. Perhaps the most important single factor in the teacher's load is the number of classes he teaches daily. Because

---

[7] National Education Association, "Teaching Load in 1950," *Research Bulletin,* XXIX (February, 1951), 30.

class periods vary so much in length from school to school, it is difficult to make a recommendation applicable to all schools. In schools with six class periods 50 to 60 minutes long, the teacher's load should not exceed on the average five class periods daily. This number should be reduced for teachers who have major responsibilities for counseling, administration, or extraclass activities.

In the survey of 370 junior high schools by the authors, five class periods were reported most often as the daily class load. Although the following summary does not take into consideration the length of class periods, it is some indication of current practice. The percentage of schools which have various average numbers of class sections per teacher is as follows:

Classes Taught	Schools
4	9%
5	71%
6	18%
Other	2%

Departmentalized Assignments. A strong argument for the establishment of the junior high school was that it would lead to improved instruction through departmentalized teaching. The basis for this argument was that teachers in a departmentalized organization could concentrate on one or two subject fields, while in a nondepartmentalized school they would spread their energies over a wide range of subjects. Furthermore, it was believed that the departmentalized school could command the services of teachers with specialized training in subjects to which they were to be assigned. But, even before the time of the junior high school, there was much disagreement regarding the desirability of departmentalized teaching in the secondary school.

There are some valid arguments that can be advanced both in favor of and against departmentalization. The more important of those for departmentalization may be summarized as follows:

1. It facilitates the use of special teachers for music, art, home economics, industrial arts, and other subjects.
2. It facilitates the fixing of responsibility for growth in a particular subject field over a period of years.
3. It simplifies the work of supervision.
4. It prepares the pupil better for departmentalization in the senior high school.
5. It is likely to attract more specialized and better prepared teachers, at least in so far as subject preparation is concerned.
6. It lessens the load of the teacher as compared to the load involved in teaching several subjects.

7. The influence of an unusually poor teacher is spread out over several groups of pupils as compared with a school where one teacher teaches all the subjects.
8. There is relief from monotony and physical relief for the pupils by changing rooms and teachers.
9. Because of the variety of teachers each pupil has, he is more likely to find at least one teacher who understands him and to whom he may talk freely.

Arguments against departmentalization are as follows:

1. It brings about rigidity in the schedule. On the other hand, if teachers teach two or more subjects in consecutive periods, they may spend both periods on one subject, or divide the time among the subjects as they see fit.
2. It makes it difficult for the teacher to bring about correlation and integration between two or more subjects.
3. It creates difficulties in arranging after-school conferences with pupils because two or more teachers may schedule a conference with the same pupil the same afternoon.
4. It results frequently in an overload of pupils with homework and other preparation on some days, and an underload on others since, under the departmentalized plan, no teacher knows what homework and other preparations are being assigned by other teachers.
5. It tends to encourage subject-matter specialization and an undue emphasis on subject matter as such.
6. It tends to lessen the interest of the teachers in pupils as individuals, since they have so many that it is difficult to know them well.
7. Some pupils find it difficult to adjust to the methods of teaching and standards of conduct of several teachers, who may differ widely in these matters.
8. Many junior high school pupils, especially those in the seventh grade, are not ready for independent work in specialized fields under departmentalized teachers.
9. No one may assume responsibility for such things as penmanship, English usage, courtesy, personal appearance, and other matters which do not clearly belong to a specific subject area.

With the trend in recent years toward "integrated courses" which cut across traditional subject-matter lines, there has been a reaction against departmentalized teaching, particularly in the junior high school. This trend has been especially pronounced in the seventh and eighth grades. For instance, in many schools today seventh- and eighth-grade pupils have the same teacher for two or three different subjects, such as English and social studies or mathematics and science. In a few junior high schools this practice has been carried even further, all subjects being taught by one teacher, except for the "special" subjects—physical education, art, music, home economics, and industrial arts. A great deal can be said in favor of this trend away from extreme departmentalization, especially in the seventh and eighth grades.

Other Factors in Teacher Assignments. There are several other factors which should not be neglected in making faculty assignments for courses and extraclass activities. These factors include: (1) the teacher's subject preparation, (2) interest and previous participation in certain extraclass activities, (3) professional preparation for guidance and other special services, (4) previous experience and success in teaching the various subjects and in supervising various extraclass activities, and (5) the teacher's preference for the various subjects and for other professional responsibilities. Before making faculty assignments the administrator should obtain complete information on these items and give them careful consideration.

Faculty Assignments to Other Schools. Although the great majority of the junior high schools have a faculty separate and distinct from those of the elementary and senior high schools, in a few communities teachers are assigned to more than one school unit. Usually, according to the survey by the authors, in systems with separate junior high schools, staff members teach only in the junior high school. Occasionally they teach also in the elementary school. These are usually teachers of art, music, or physical education. On the other hand, about one teacher in ten in the separate junior high school teaches one or more subjects in the senior high school. This is usually in buildings which house both the junior and the senior high schools or in cities where the junior and the senior high schools are located close to each other.

It is difficult to say whether it is advisable to have the junior high school staff teach also in the elementary and senior high schools. In a six-year high school much can be said in favor of assigning teachers to courses in both the junior and senior high school divisions. Where that policy is employed, one might expect to find (1) better articulation in the philosophy, curriculum, and methods between the various grades; (2) less duplication in the curriculum; (3) better understanding of pupils through contact with them over a period of years; and (4) more complete departmentalization, especially in smaller schools.

In practice, there are objections to the assignment of teachers to both the junior and senior high schools. Some authorities contend: (1) that teachers so assigned tend to take more interest in the upper grades to the disadvantage of the junior high school classes; and (2) that there is a tendency to employ teachers trained in senior high school work with little understanding and sympathy for the junior high school pupil. These objections are perhaps less valid today than formerly, since the amount of professional training of junior high school teachers now compares favorably with that of the senior high school staff.

As a matter of general policy, it seems best to have at least a few teachers assigned to both junior and senior divisions in six-year schools and in schools where the two divisions are housed in the same or adjacent buildings. This policy is particularly appropriate for subjects requiring unusual teacher talents or peculiar building facilities and equipment, such as music, art, industrial arts, and home economics. The teaching assignments under this plan would be made in terms of the teacher's preparation and preference, as well as the best interests of the pupils concerned. This policy would necessitate a uniform salary schedule and other administrative practices that grant equal prestige to teachers at all grade levels.

Assignment in the Six-Year School. There are a great variety of interests and considerable differences in maturity and general behavior of pupils in a school that has six grades. There may be some teachers who are able to adjust to youngsters at all six grade levels, but the majority of teachers will find it quite difficult to do so. Some teachers, therefore, should be selected primarily for grades seven, eight, and nine, and others for grades ten, eleven, and twelve. The smaller the school, the more difficult it is to assign teachers within one subject field to one or two grade levels. In the assignment of teachers, it should be clear that those assigned to the lower grades in the six-year school are in no way inferior. Indeed, it should be emphasized that greater teaching ability and understanding of children are necessary for success in the junior high school than in the senior high school grades.

Basic Principles. Great care should be exercised in the assignment of teachers to subjects for which they are prepared by education, experience, and personal interest. An excellent statement of principles underlying better practice in the assignment of teachers is that of the Commission on Research and Service of the North Central Association of Colleges and Secondary Schools. The eight principles below are quoted from that statement:

1. There should exist in every secondary school a definitely formulated policy relative to the combinations of duties assigned to teachers, together with long-term plans for its progressive realization.

2. Individual teaching assignments should be considered as reasonably flexible, and subject to change in accordance with the best interests of the school.

3. Every secondary school position should be held by a teacher who is qualified for the total combination of duties assigned to it.

4. Every secondary school teacher should be assigned to subject-matter fields in which he possesses broad, as well as concentrated, preparation.

5. Every teaching assignment in the secondary school should be limited to not more than two broad fields of subject matter.

6. As nearly as possible, each teacher should be assigned in conformity with the most frequently occurring teaching combinations.

7. The extraclass responsibilities in a school should be regarded as a part of the teachers' assignments and should be considered in determining their total loads.

8. Whenever possible, new and inexperienced teachers should be assigned relatively light loads in comparison with their colleagues.[8]

QUESTIONS AND EXERCISES

1. Examine carefully the recommended junior high school staff for different sizes of schools given in this chapter and criticize it. Give reasons for your criticisms. If you disagree seriously with the recommended plans, prepare one of your own.

2. What do you consider an appropriate minimum size for classes in the junior high school? An appropriate maximum size? Defend your answers.

3. Write out in summary form your ideas of an ideal and well-trained junior high school teacher.

4. How well are junior high school teachers paid as compared with elementary school and other high school teachers? Is this as it ought to be?

5. What do you consider the most important arguments for and against departmentalized teaching in the junior high school? Are you in favor of or against departmentalization?

6. For the three junior high schools in a certain community there is only one junior high school principal. In each school there is an assistant principal. Evaluate this plan. Tell what should be the responsibility of the principal and each assistant principal.

7. Prepare a rather complete statement of the ideal qualifications of a junior high school principal.

[8] *Assigning Teachers in the Secondary School: A Guide to Better Practice*, Report of the Subcommittee on High Schools of the Committee on Preparation of High School Teachers, North Central Association of Colleges and Secondary Schools (Minneapolis: College of Education, University of Minnesota, 1945).

Part V

LOOKING AHEAD

Chapter 17

PROBLEMS FACING THE
JUNIOR HIGH SCHOOL

A number of problems face junior high school educators today, as they go about developing a program that is suited to the needs of young adolescents. Some of these problems are new, while others are of long standing. Some of them have come to our attention because of changing points of view concerning junior high school education, while others have developed as we have come to know better the needs of young adolescents. These problems, and others like them, need to be given careful study as we develop programs for the new schools that are being built and as we improve the programs in the schools that are already established.

Most of these problems have already been discussed in previous chapters in this book. In this chapter they are presented more or less as a summary of things that need to be done in junior high school education.

1. Problems in Administration

1. *How can we prepare administrators and supervisors to provide leadership for junior high schools and for six-year high schools?* This problem is already critical, but it will increase in seriousness as new junior high schools are built. The problem is intensified by the fact that men and women with backgrounds in junior high school education are needed for administrative and supervisory positions in the many new junior-senior or six-year high schools that are being established. The problem cannot be solved alone by the teacher education institutions. Because we need men and women with experience in junior high school education, school administrators should encourage able young people to obtain experience in junior high schools and to prepare themselves for administrative and supervisory positions at that level. Furthermore, these positions need to be sufficiently attractive, both in salary and prestige, to prevent the present migration of able junior high school administrators and supervisors to the senior high school level.

2. How can we prepare enough competent and interested teachers who are willing to make the junior high school their careers? There are two aspects to this problem. First, we need to develop more effective programs at our teacher education institutions for the preparation of junior high school teachers. Teachers for this level need to understand the philosophy of the junior high school, the needs, interests, and abilities of young adolescents, and the type of learning activities and program which are most effective for junior high school youth. Second, we need to make the junior high school sufficiently attractive to young teachers so that more of them will find an interest there instead of continually pointing toward the senior high school grades. This is more than a matter of salary and professional prestige. It is largely a matter of helping young people develop an interest in the needs and characteristics of young adolescents.

3. What kind of a building and other facilities should we have to provide for an adequate program of education for young adolescents? All too often our junior high school buildings are patterned after those of the senior high school, without sufficient thought to the characteristics of a program of junior high school education. In some of the new junior high school buildings, splendid things are being done. These need to be studied by administrators who are responsible for shaping the plans for new buildings both for junior high schools and for junior-senior high schools. Those aspects of the junior high school building which need particular study are the library, the auditorium, facilities for corrective physical education, industrial arts shops, homemaking laboratories, arts and crafts rooms, general science rooms, rooms for core classes, guidance facilities, and facilities for pupil activities.

4. How can we provide for better articulation between the elementary and the senior high schools through the junior high school program? This problem is indeed older than the junior high school itself, but it continues to deserve prominent attention. It is common knowledge that the junior high school often produces two breaks in the school system where previously there was one. This need not be so. Through workshops, study groups, and other activities, teachers from the elementary, the junior high, and the senior high school levels are being brought together in many communities to study common problems. More activities such as these need to be carried on if we are going to do an adequate job of developing a school system from kindergarten through the twelfth grade which has no unnecessary breaks along the way.

5. How can we provide an adequate educational program for junior high school youth within the framework of a six-year high school? At the present rate of increase, there is reason to believe that, in a few years, the number of six-year high schools in the United States will exceed all other types of secondary schools combined. It is common knowledge that, in the six-year high schools, many aspects of the program for the junior high school are seriously overshadowed by the program for the senior high school grades. That is not only true with respect to the assignment of facilities for certain extraclass activities, such as athletics, but in many schools it is even true with respect to the assignment of teachers to the various grades. There is every reason to believe that a program for the junior high school grades can be provided as well, if not better, within the framework of a six-year secondary school as in a separate junior high school. But if this is to be accomplished, it needs the interest, understanding, and attention of administrators and teachers in our six-year high schools.

6. *How can we provide greater flexibility in the daily class schedule?* The type of educational program that we want to develop in the junior high school today demands a variety of activities. The rigid class schedule with relatively short periods, which is so common in the junior high school, makes it difficult to carry on some desirable activities. Laboratory activities, field trips, the use of certain audio-visual materials, and cooperative group activities make it desirable at times to have longer periods than are now provided in most schools. It is not only the length of class periods, but also flexibility in class periods which is important. There needs to be experimentation with the junior high school schedule to see how such flexibility may better be provided.

7. *How many periods weekly should classes meet in the various subjects?* This question is raised particularly by administrators who are concerned with introducing a variety of subjects into the weekly schedule, and by teachers of such subjects as music, art, physical education, general science, industrial arts, and homemaking. In some schools, such subjects are taught once, twice, or three times a week, with the result that the teachers have several hundred different pupils. The task of knowing these pupils and individualizing instruction to meet their various needs and interests is indeed an impossible one. We need to decide whether it is better to have some of these subjects taught more frequently, perhaps even daily, but for only one semester, rather than to have them meet less frequently, but for the entire year. This problem has been particularly accentuated by the current interest in teacher-pupil planning, individualizing instruction, creative activities in the various subjects, modifications in our practice for evaluating, marking and reporting pupil progress, and other similar developments.

8. *How should we group pupils for instructional purposes?* This raises immediately the perennial problem of homogeneous versus heterogeneous grouping. We need to study the entire educational program of the junior high school in the light of modern thinking with respect to the education of young adolescents, and then develop an approach to grouping that is in harmony with that thinking.

9. *What is the best grade arrangement for elementary and secondary education—6-3-3, 6-4-4, 6-6, or some other plan?* In most communities, this question is decided on the basis of administrative rather than educational considerations. However, in some communities, particularly the large ones, any one of these plans would be appropriate. It is important, therefore, to have some understanding of the relative effectiveness of the various plans of grade organization. This has not yet been satisfactorily done.

10. *What is a desirable load for teachers, including responsibilities for guidance and extraclass activities as well as classroom instruction?* In many schools, five class periods daily is considered to be a desirable teaching load. But this does not take into consideration responsibilities for a homeroom, clubs, social functions, student council, and a host of other activities that have been added to enrich the program of the junior high school. Some of the new activities demand more time, energy, and resourcefulness than classroom teaching. We need to study the appropriate class load for teachers and the consideration which should be given other responsibilities in arriving at desirable total teacher load.

2. Problems in the Curriculum

11. *What should be the program for the ninth grade in the junior high school?* In more and more schools, the ninth grade is clearly becoming a part of a unified junior high school program rather than continuing the program and administrative characteristics which it had at one time as part of a four-year high school. This has a bearing on such matters in the ninth grade as college admission, the offering of elective courses, the number of courses a pupil is to take, study halls, and participation in some pupil activities. There is little doubt in the minds of educators concerning the desirability of making the ninth grade clearly a part of the junior high school program. At the same time, it is difficult to accomplish this goal so long as the work of the ninth grade counts toward high school graduation and college admission. We need to study ways of separating the ninth grade in the junior high school from such requirements.

12. *What is a reasonable approach to departmentalization in the junior high school?* The present trend toward core classes, block scheduling, and other forms of double or triple period classes is in part the answer to this question, at least in some schools. The problem of departmentalization needs to be studied in terms of its appropriateness at the various grade levels—seventh, eighth, and ninth. That is, should pupils in the junior high school be introduced gradually to departmentalization? Furthermore, how does its appropriateness differ from one subject to another? Should departmentalization, for instance, be carried further in music, art, industrial arts, and homemaking, than in language arts, social studies, and mathematics? Questions such as these are basic to the problem presented by departmentalization.

13. *How much should pupils specialize in their junior high school program?* For the seventh and eighth grades, the thinking and practice nationwide has pretty much resolved this problem; namely, it is generally believed that pupils should not begin to specialize, but should all take a common program of general education, until they enter the ninth grade. But with respect to the ninth grade, the point of view concerning specialization is not clear. Many educators believe that pupils should not begin specialized curriculums leading to college admission or preparation for a specific vocation before the senior high school. And yet, in many junior high schools, some specialized curriculums, particularly the college-preparatory curriculum, are begun in the ninth grade. The problem of specialized curriculums and courses, especially in the ninth grade, needs to be given further study.

14. *What is the place of exploratory or try-out courses in the junior high school?* There is little question about the importance of exploratory activities, but there is no agreement on the way in which they should be provided. In the early junior high schools exploration was provided primarily through exploratory or "try-out" courses. In these courses, pupils usually had contact with various subjects or activities during the year, devoting a few weeks to each. Even though some educators question the value of such "short courses," they are still the practice in many schools. We need to find out what values, if any, there are in courses which give pupils a series of short term try-out experiences.

15. *What should be the place of elective curriculums and courses in the junior high school?* This problem seems to be quite clearly resolved as far as grades seven and eight are concerned. In most schools, elective courses in grades seven and eight are confined to such subjects as music, where pupils may choose between orchestra, band, glee club, chorus, and similar activities. The situation is different, how-

ever, in the ninth grade. There, elective courses are quite commonly given according to the senior high school pattern. We need to study the situation particularly in the ninth grade with respect to elective courses and curriculums, and decide to what extent they are appropriate there.

16. *How may we effectively teach the fundamentals in the junior high school?* Although this problem at present is of interest at every grade level from the first through the twelfth, it is particularly pertinent in the junior high school. There is a question in the minds of some people whether it is advisable to teach such courses as arts and crafts, industrial arts, and homemaking, apparently at the expense of the fundamental skills. Although junior high school educators agree that subjects other than the traditional fundamentals are essential, they are also concerned with teaching the fundamental skills effectively. Although some of the fundamental skills are being taught more effectively today than ever before, many educators believe that we have the professional knowledge to do even better.

3. Problems in Teaching Methods

17. *How may parents and other citizens contribute to the development of the junior high school curriculum?* This problem is not peculiar to the junior high school. At all grade levels, laymen are being asked to work cooperatively with the professional staff in studying the curriculum. In many schools, however, the procedures for such cooperative lay-professional activities are not clear. For instance, what is the responsibility of each group? How many laymen should participate? How should they be chosen? What should be done if teachers and laymen disagree on basic issues? Questions such as these concern administrators and teachers as they work cooperatively with laymen on curriculum problems.

18. *What is the place of study periods and study halls in the junior high school?* In practice, there has been quite a decline in the use of study halls in grades seven and eight. In some schools, they have also been discontinued in grade nine, although they still are quite common in that grade. Many educators feel that a study period in a study hall supervised by a teacher other than the one who gave the assignment is not appropriate in the junior high school. They believe that, instead of separate study periods, there should be longer class periods where learning activities may be planned, carried on, and completed with the help of the teacher responsible for the subject.

19. *How may the library be used most effectively in the junior high school?* In the past, it was quite common to have combined

library-study periods for pupils in all three grades. Today, some educators feel that a separate library period is not the most effective way
to use library facilities. We need to study ways of using the library
as a laboratory for entire class groups, for small groups of pupils, for
committee activities, for listening to audio materials, for viewing
visual materials, for the investigation of individual problems, and for
pleasure reading. We also need to study ways of bringing the library
into the classroom by having library centers in the various rooms
where library materials may be placed which are appropriate for the
learning activities that are underway.

20. *How should we mark and report pupil progress so that these
procedures will be in harmony with our individualized approach to
teaching and our points of view concerning the education of young
adolescents?* This is one of the most discussed and controversial
questions facing educators today. It is quite generally agreed that the
older forms of marking and reporting pupil progress are not consistent
with our present-day points of view about education. At the same
time, we have not yet developed a new approach to marking and reporting which is generally acceptable to parents and educators. In
some schools much progress has been made with this problem. In any
case, we know that this problem must be resolved at the local level,
since procedures that seem to be effective in one school may not be
acceptable in another. The problem is such an urgent one that we
need to continue to give it our attention.

21. *How can we effectively evaluate the progress of pupils?*
Tests and examinations still are the prevailing devices for evaluating
the progress of pupils. For evaluating growth in subject matter they
serve a real purpose. We need to study other means of evaluation,
however, so that we may know what progress pupils are making in
aspects of the school program other than subject-matter skills and information. We also need to develop skill in self-evaluation by pupils,
both evaluation by the group as a whole and by individual pupils.

22. *What should be the attitude toward home work for junior
high school pupils?* As is true of some other problems, this one has
been discussed again and again through the years. Frequently the
answer is based on senior high school practice and thinking rather than
on what seems best for young adolescents. We need to decide how
much home work is appropriate, what type of work pupils may do
effectively away from school, and what help pupils need to prepare
them for learning activities that are to be done at home.

23. *What should be the policies for promoting pupils from grade
to grade in the junior high school?* At present, in many junior high
schools, two policies seem to be in effect. In grades seven and eight,

it is quite generally the practice, though not universally so, to promote pupils on the basis of what seems best for the individual child. In other words, the welfare of the individual child rather than a grade standard is used as a basis for promotions. In the ninth grade, however, promotions are generally based on a grade standard that is the same for all pupils. We need to study the policies and practices employed in promoting pupils, and then modify these policies so that they are in harmony with the best interests of young adolescents.

24. *How can we best meet the interests, needs, and abilities of different pupils in our classes through the teaching methods that are employed?* In the elementary school, teachers have developed more skill in individualized methods than in either the junior or the senior high school. In the junior high school, we have tended to emphasize administrative practices, rather than teaching methods, in individualizing instruction. We need to develop skill in classroom methods which are effective in meeting the different needs, interests, and abilities of young adolescents.

4. Problems in Guidance

25. *How can we improve the effectiveness of the homeroom?* The nature of the homeroom has not changed a great deal since its introduction in the junior high school many years ago. Educators still feel that it is an exceedingly important part of the junior high school program, but some believe that its effectiveness should be improved. For instance, the homeroom needs to be more than an administrative device, where announcements are made and attendance is taken. If the homeroom is to be an effective avenue for guidance in the school, there needs to be sufficient time for group guidance activities and for individual teacher-pupil conferences. Furthermore, the homeroom at present tends to be set off from the rest of the school program. We need to find ways of making the homeroom a well integrated part of the total educational program of the school.

26. *How can we find adequate time for guidance during the school day?* This problem is similar in some respects to the one that has been just mentioned. Homeroom teachers, classroom teachers, and counselors have difficulty in working with pupils on guidance problems during the school day. In most schools, the only way that counselors can see pupils is to take them out of classes. Homeroom teachers usually find it difficult to meet with pupils on guidance problems except during the noon hour, before school, or after school. Classroom teachers also find it difficult to have conferences with individual pupils. One of the significant contributions of the core classes is that they

provide more time for guidance conferences with pupils. The guidance program will be lacking in effectiveness until adequate time for guidance conferences is available during the school day.

27. *What should be the teacher's part in guidance?* Although this does not seem to be a problem to some educators, in many schools there is not a clear definition as to what part the homeroom and classroom teachers should take in guidance activities. Some believe that guidance is a specialized job which should be carried on only by those with special experience, training, and backgrounds. Others contend, however, that anyone who comes in contact with pupils should be ready and able to consult with them on some of their problems. We need to study the part that individual teachers should take in the guidance program, and then we should help them prepare for that responsibility.

28. *How can we provide teachers with adequate information about individual pupils?* Both as a basis for guidance and for effective teaching, this problem is an important one. Usually information about pupils is available in junior high schools, but that information is located in the office of the principal, the nurse, or the counselor. If it is to be used by homeroom and classroom teachers, that information needs to be in the hands of all the teachers for all their pupils. This presents a difficult administrative task, but we need to find ways of resolving it.

5. Problems in Extraclass Activities

29. *How extensive a program of extraclass activities should there be in the junior high school?* There was a time when educators believed that this program should be as extensive as possible. In some schools, however, we seem to have gone too far. For instance, a pupil may belong to the student council, play in a music organization, serve on the staff of the school paper, belong to a club or two, and participate in assemblies and social functions. With his class activities and out-of-school responsibilities, a pupil may gain little from such wide participation. Teachers likewise may be asked to sponsor so many different extraclass activities that they can give little time and energy to each one. We need to decide whether it is better to have many different activities and have both pupils and teachers devote only a little time to each, or to concentrate on a more limited number.

30. *How can we bring about better integration between extraclass activities and other aspects of the program of the school?* From the very beginning, the extraclass activities in the junior high school have been set apart from the rest of the program of the school. In recent

years, more and more activities have been brought within the school program. That has been especially true of music activities, but also of clubs, assemblies, student council, and some other activities. Nevertheless, much of the program of extraclass activities continues to be set apart from the rest of the school program. We need to find ways of integrating these activities more fully with other aspects of the educational program.

31. *How can we find adequate time for extraclass activities?* For many years it has been agreed that most of the extraclass activities should be carried on during the regular school day. Few schools have found satisfactory ways of doing so. In some schools there is an activities period which meets this situation in part, while in other schools the number of activities has been reduced so that they may be scheduled during the day like regular classes. We need to see if we can find school time for more extraclass activities.

32. *What is the place of interscholastic athletics in the junior high school?* This is one of the most controversial problems in the junior high school today. Many junior high school leaders are opposed to interscholastic athletics of any kind, favoring instead a broad intramural program that provides a place for every interested boy and girl. But many junior high schools do have interscholastic athletics. We need to study the schools that engage in interscholastic competition, to see if such competition is appropriate for young adolescents.

33. *How much and in what ways should junior high school pupils participate in national, state, and local contests which are sponsored by nonschool organizations and agencies?* For many years, contests under the auspices of nonschool organizations have presented quite a problem to the senior high school. In recent years, these contests are being extended more and more to include the junior high school. Many of these organizations have the best of intentions, wanting to provide some educational service. Others sponsor contests purely for advertising or propaganda purposes. Since the function of the school is to provide the best educational experiences for our children, these contests raise some difficult questions. Which contests serve significant educational purposes? How many contests are appropriate in a given year? Should the teachers merely bring the contest to the attention of their pupils, or should some pressure to participate be exerted? Should participation at times be compulsory, or always voluntary? Should school credit be given for participation in these contests? These are some of the questions which confront the school administrator and faculty as they study the problem presented by contests sponsored by nonschool organizations.

34. *How can we build an effective school community?* From the earliest history of the junior high school, it was believed that, in every school, there should be a community of teachers and pupils who work happily and effectively together. In such a school, all pupils and teachers have much loyalty to the school community, they participate in many of its activities, and they contribute toward improving its effectiveness. It is not easy to achieve such a community spirit in a school. In many schools, pupils go from class to class and room to room without any awareness that they belong to a school community. Administrators, teachers, and pupils need to study ways of bringing about a community atmosphere and feelings of loyalty and belonging-ness to a community within the school.

SELECTED READINGS

CHAPTER 1

BUNKER, FRANK FOREST. *The Junior High School Movement: Its Beginnings.* Washington, D.C.: F. W. Roberts Co., 1935.

An excellent history of the early development of the junior high school in the United States. An especially good statement of the introduction of the junior high school in Berkeley.

CUBBERLEY, ELLWOOD P. *Public Education in the United States.* Boston: Houghton Mifflin Co., 1919, chaps. viii, ix.

A summary of the development of the elementary school in America, with particular reference to the eight-year school.

FRAZIER, G. W. "The Junior High School as an Educational Problem," *California Journal of Secondary Education,* XXVII (February, 1952), 112-15.

Traces the history of junior high schools and discusses the extent to which they have either achieved their reasons for being or have changed them.

GAUMNITZ, WALTER, and HULL, J. DAN. "Junior High Schools Versus the Traditional (8-4) High School Organization," *Bulletin of the National Association of Secondary-School Principals,* XXXVIII (March, 1954), 112-21.

Contains statistical data on the growth of the junior high school and suggestions on the relative advantages of the 8-4 and the 6-3-3 plans for early adolescents.

GAUMNITZ, WALTER H., and OTHERS. *Junior High School Facts—A Graphic Analysis.* United States Office of Education, Misc. No. 21, November, 1954. Washington, D.C.: Government Printing Office, 1955.

Presents a statistical summary of the origin and growth of the junior high school; present status of and trends in the junior high school; attendance, retention, and employment facts related to junior high school youth; and other pertinent information concerning the junior high school and its program.

GRIZZELL, E. D. *Origin and Development of the High School in New England Before 1865.* New York: The Macmillan Co., 1923.

A comprehensive history of the early development of the high school in New England.

HARTWELL, CHARLES S. "Economy in Education," *Educational Review,* XXX (September, 1905), 159-77.

One of the first articles to recommend a separate junior high school, with particular reference to New York City.

HERTZLER, SILAS. *The Rise of the Public High School in Connecticut.* Baltimore: Warwick & York, Inc., 1930, chap. iv.

Presents a summary of the grade organization of the early high schools in Connecticut.

JONES, ARTHUR J. "The Junior High School: Past, Present, and Future," *Bulletin of the National Association of Secondary-School Principals,* XXVIII (March, 1944), 3-14.

A review of early developments, an appraisal of the present program, and predictions of future developments of the junior high school.

JUDD, CHARLES H. "Shall We Continue to Imitate Prussia?" *School and Society,* VII (June 29, 1918), 751-54.

Suggests that the eight-grade elementary school was transplanted to the United States from Prussia.

MONROE, PAUL. "Shall We Continue to Advocate Reforms by False Arguments?" *School and Society,* VIII (September 8, 1918), 290-94.

Contends that the eight-grade elementary school was American in origin.

MULHERN, JAMES. "The Beginnings of the Junior High School," *Educational Outlook,* VII (March, 1934), 159-71.

Presents some information on the early history of the junior high school.

SUNDERLAND, ALBERT, and DRAKE, LELAND N. "The Junior High School, Yesterday and Today," *Bulletin of the National Association of Secondary-School Principals,* XXXIX (February, 1955), 63-80.

A summary of developments in basic point of view for the junior high school.

CHAPTER 2

BRIGGS, THOMAS H. *The Junior High School.* Boston: Houghton Mifflin Co., 1920, chap. v.

One of the best statements of functions of the junior high school developed some years ago by an early leader in the movement.

DOUGLASS, HARL R. "The Function of the Modern Junior High School," *Bulletin of the National Association of Secondary-School Principals,* XXXIV (April, 1950), 119-27.

A discussion of the functions of a modern junior high school program.

EDUCATIONAL POLICIES COMMISSION. *Education for All American Youth.* Washington, D.C.: National Education Association, 1944.

Presents a point of view, with suggestions for implementation, of a program that meets the needs of adolescent youth of all abilities, interests, and backgrounds.

GRUHN, WILLIAM T. "The Purposes of the Junior High School After 40 Years," *California Journal of Secondary Education,* XXVII (March, 1952), 127-32.

Traces the changes that have taken place in our thinking with respect to the basic functions of the junior high school.

KOOS, LEONARD V. *Junior High School Trends.* New York: Harper & Bros., 1955, chap. ii.

A discussion of the purposes of reorganization, summarizing some of the statements of needs, objectives, and purposes of several authors.

————. *The Junior High School.* Boston: Ginn & Co., 1927, chaps. ii, iii.

Summarizes the opinions of educators concerning the peculiar functions to be served by the junior high school. Although this study was made many years ago, it is helpful in understanding the present philosophy of the junior high school.

NATIONAL EDUCATION ASSOCIATION, COMMISSION ON THE REORGANIZATION OF SECONDARY EDUCATION. *Cardinal Principles of Secondary Education.* United States Bureau of Education Bulletin No. 35. Washington, D.C.: Government Printing Office, 1918.

Presents a comprehensive statement of the objectives of secondary education, prepared as part of an extensive study of the reorganization of secondary education.

NATIONAL EDUCATION ASSOCIATION, DEPARTMENT OF SUPERINTENDENCE. *The Junior High School.* Fifth Yearbook. Washington, D.C.: The Association, 1927, chap. i.

A good summary of opinions concerning the purposes of the junior high school.

NATIONAL SOCIETY FOR THE STUDY OF EDUCATION. *Adolescence.* Forty-third Yearbook, Part I. Chicago: University of Chicago Press, 1944.

Brings together much information on youth in adolescence. Although it covers the entire period of adolescence, it is helpful in understanding the early adolescent period.

NOAR, GERTRUDE. *The Junior High School—Today and Tomorrow.* New York: Prentice-Hall, Inc., 1953, chaps. i, ii.

A discussion of the functions of the junior high school and of the needs of junior high school youth.

RICE, THEODORE D., and FAUNCE, ROLAND C. "Education for All Junior High School Youth," *Bulletin of the National Association of Secondary-School Principals*, XXIX (April, 1945), 40-45.

Adapts the point of view expressed in *Education for All American Youth*, by the Educational Policies Commission, to junior high school youth.

SMITH, WILLIAM A. *The Junior High School*. New York: The Macmillan Co., 1925, chap. v.

An excellent early statement of the purposes to be served by the junior high school.

CHAPTER 3

BEATLEY, BANCROFT. *Achievement in the Junior High School*. Harvard Studies in Education, Vol. 18. Cambridge, Mass.: Harvard University Press, 1932.

A study of the effect on pupil achievement of the reduction in time devoted to the fundamentals in the junior high school.

CLEM, O. M., and ROBERTS, H. M. "The Tenth Year Progress of Junior High School and Elementary School Pupils," *Journal of Educational Research*, XXI (April, 1930), 288-99.

Reports the results of a study in which the tenth-grade marks of two groups of pupils were compared, one group including 432 junior high school graduates, and the other 426 graduates of eight-grade elementary schools.

GAUMNITZ, WALTER H., and HULL, J. DAN. "Junior High School versus the Traditional (8-4) High School Organization," *Bulletin of the National Association of Secondary-School Principals*, XXXVIII (March, 1954), 112-21.

Besides giving statistics on the status of various types of grade organization, it gives some of the advantages of each.

LAUCHNER, A. H. "What Are the Characteristics of a Modern Junior High School?" *Bulletin of the National Association of Secondary-School Principals*, XXXIV (March, 1950), 10-16.

Points out reasons why the junior high school has accomplished its purposes, with suggestions as to how those purposes may be achieved.

MACKIE, R. H. "Why the Junior High School?" *Education*, LXXIII (February, 1953), 374-77.

Reviews the psychological arguments advanced for the junior high school by early advocates.

SMITH, HARRY P. "The Relative Efficiency of the Junior High School vs. the Conventional 8-Grade Type of School," *Journal of Educational Research*, XXVI (December, 1935), 276-80.

A study to find out how well pupils in the junior high school achieve in the basic subjects, as compared with pupils in other types of schools.

SMITH, WILLIAM A. *The Junior High School*. New York: The Macmillan Co., 1925, chap. v.

An excellent early statement of the purposes to be served by the junior high school.

TUTTLE, HAROLD S. "Has the Junior High School Kept Its Promise?" *Clearing House*, XIV (January, 1940), 263-66.

A review of the aims, accomplishments, and problems of the junior high school.

"Types of High School Organization," *The School Executive*, LXVIII (October, 1948), 63-76.

This is a symposium participated in by ten school administrators who present the points of view concerning the various types of high school organization.

WITHAM, ERNEST C. "Holding Powers of Junior and Non-Junior High School Cities," *The School Executive*, XLVIII (January, 1929), 451-53.

Reports a study in which the holding power is compared for cities with junior high schools with those which have the traditional grade organization.

CHAPTER 4

ALBERTY, HAROLD B. *Reorganizing the High School Curriculum.* New York: The Macmillan Co., 1953.
A comprehensive treatment of curriculum development in the secondary school, with particular attention to the core curriculum.

ANDERSON, VERNON E., GRIM, PAUL R., and GRUHN, WILLIAM T. *Principles and Practices of Secondary Education.* New York: The Ronald Press Co., 1951, chaps. iv-vi.
A presentation of new curriculum concepts, the teacher's place in curriculum development, and the framework for a modern curriculum.

ASSOCIATION FOR SUPERVISION AND CURRICULUM DEVELOPMENT. *Developing Programs for Young Adolescents.* Washington, D.C.: National Education Association, 1954.
Presents a statement of principles for a program for young adolescents, and examples of programs from schools in the South and the Middle West.

BRIGGS, THOMAS H. "The Secondary School Curriculum, Yesterday, Today, and To-morrow," *Teacher's College Record,* LII (April, 1951), 399-448.
A critical analysis of the philosophies underlying the secondary school curriculum and problems in developing the secondary school curriculum.

DOUGLASS, HARL R. *Secondary Education.* New York: The Ronald Press Co., 1952, chaps. vii, viii.
An overview of the approach to curriculum development in the secondary school.

EDUCATIONAL POLICIES COMMISSION. *Education for All American Youth—A Further Look.* Washington, D.C.: National Education Association, 1952.
This volume is a further development of the point of view concerning the program for the secondary school which was presented in the earlier one, *Education for All American Youth,* which appeared in 1944.

FEATHERSTONE, WILLIAM B. *A Functional Curriculum for Youth.* New York: American Book Co., 1950.
An excellent discussion of the curriculum from the functional approach.

LEONARD, J. PAUL. *Developing the Secondary School Curriculum.* New York: Rinehart & Co., Inc., 1953, chaps. xi-xiii.
A discussion of recent developments in the curriculum of the secondary school.

LEWIS, GERTRUDE M. *Educating Children in Grades Seven and Eight.* United States Office of Education Bulletin No. 10. Washington, D.C.: Government Printing Office, 1954, pp. 1-36.
A report of practices in the program for grades seven and eight, based on observations in 31 elementary and 45 junior high schools.

ROMINE, STEPHEN A. *Building the High School Curriculum.* New York: The Ronald Press Co., 1954, chaps. vii-xi.
A comprehensive discussion of procedure for developing the curriculum in the high school.

SMITH, B. OTHANIEL, STANLEY, WILLIAM O., and SHORES, HARLAN J. *Fundamentals of Curriculum Development.* Yonkers-on-Hudson, New York: World Book Co., 1950, chaps. xi-xv.
A good discussion of principles and procedures in curriculum development.

SPEARS, HAROLD. *The High School for Today.* New York: American Book Co., 1950.
The entire volume presents a forward-looking approach to developing a curriculum for the secondary school.

STRATEMEYER, FLORENCE, and OTHERS. *Developing a Curriculum for Modern Living.* New York: Bureau of Publications, Teachers College, Columbia University, 1947.
This volume presents a forward-looking approach to the development of the curriculum. Although it deals with curriculum development at all levels, the point of view expressed is especially appropriate for the junior high school.

CHAPTER 5

ANDERSON, VERNON E., GRIM, PAUL R., and GRUHN, WILLIAM T. *Principles and Practices of Secondary Education.* New York: The Ronald Press Co., 1951, chaps. vi, vii.
A discussion of the common learnings, with suggestions for the core curriculum type of organization.

BESVINICK, SIDNEY L. "Planning and Operating a Good Core Program," *Clearing House,* XXVIII (December, 1953), 219-22.
Describes a core program as to how it developed, and its advantages and disadvantages.

CAPEHART, BERTIS E., HODGES, ALLEN, and BERDAN, NORMAN. "An Objective Evaluation of a Core Program," *School Review,* LX (February, 1952), 84-89.
Report of an experimental study of the effectiveness of the core program in the high school at Oak Ridge, Tennessee.

CRAMER, ROSCOE V. "Common-Learnings Program in the Junior High School," *Bulletin of the National Association of Secondary-School Principals,* XXXV (April, 1951), 158-66.
A description of the introduction of a common learnings or core program in the West Junior High School, Kansas City, Missouri.

DEANS, HELEN E. "Student Self-Evaluation in a Core Program," *Social Studies,* XLV (March, 1954), 83-91.
Suggests the usefulness of self-ratings in a core class concerned with the personal problems of students.

DEATON, J. C., SR. "A Core-Organized School in Action," *California Journal of Secondary Education,* XXVII (March, 1952), 133-38.
A description and appraisal by the principal of the core program in the Yosemite Junior High School, Fresno, California.

EDUCATIONAL POLICIES COMMISSION. *Education for All American Youth.* Washington, D.C.: National Education Association, 1944, chap. iv.
Presents a basic plan for common learnings, or the core program, from grades seven to fourteen. Gives a division of time at the various grade levels between common learnings and other aspects of the school program. Presents particularly well the core plan for the junior high school grades.

FAUNCE, ROLAND C., and BOSSING, NELSON L. *Developing the Core Curriculum.* New York: Prentice-Hall, Inc., 1951.
This is a comprehensive treatment of the core curriculum, including its philosophy, planning of the core, learning activities, developing a core program, and evaluation procedures.

HARVILL, HARRIS. "Eight Advantages of the Core Organization," *Social Education,* XVIII (January, 1954), 4-6.
As its title suggests, this article presents some of the advantages of a core type of curriculum organization.

KECK, MALCOLM. "We Get to Know Joe," *NEA Journal,* XLI (December, 1952), 562-63.
Describes the double period classes in English and social studies in the Folwell Junior High School, Minneapolis, Minnesota.

LEONARD, J. PAUL. *Developing the Secondary School Curriculum.* New York: Rinehart & Co., Inc., 1953, chap. xiv.
A discussion of the core curriculum including characteristics, advantages, present status, and a number of examples.

NOAR, GERTRUDE. *The Junior High School—Today and Tomorrow.* New York: Prentice-Hall, Inc., 1953, chaps. ix-xi.
These chapters present suggestions for a core program in action.

ROMINE, STEPHEN A. *Building the High School Curriculum.* New York: The Ronald Press Co., 1954, chap. xii.

Discussion of the status and nature of the core curriculum, with examples of core programs in operation.

SMITH, B. OTHANIEL, STANLEY, WILLIAM O., and SHORES, J. HARLAN. *Fundamentals of Curriculum Development.* Yonkers-on-Hudson, New York: World Book Co., 1950, chaps. xx, xxi.

An especially good discussion of the theoretical bases and the characteristics of the core curriculum.

VARS, G. F. "Problems of a Beginning Core Teacher," *Educational Leadership,* IX (October, 1951), 12-16.

Presents problems faced by a teacher of core in the Junior-Senior High School, Bel Air, Maryland.

WRIGHT, GRACE S. *Core Curriculum Development: Problems and Practices.* United States Office of Education Bulletin No. 5. Washington, D.C.: Government Printing Office, 1952.

Report of a study of status and practices of core programs in secondary schools. Provides an excellent classification of the different types of core programs and gives numerous examples of the various types.

CHAPTER 6

1. Industrial Arts

AMERICAN VOCATIONAL ASSOCIATION. *A Guide to Improving Instruction in Industrial Arts.* Bulletin, June, 1953. Washington, D.C.: The Association.

This booklet, prepared for the Association by a committee of leaders in industrial arts education, gives the philosophy, objectives, and subject content of the various areas in the industrial arts.

ERICSON, E. E. *Teaching the Industrial Arts.* Peoria, Ill.: Charles A. Bennett Co., 1946.

Explains the practical phases of teaching industrial arts including curriculum, equipment, and method.

NEWKIRK, LOUIS V. *Organizing and Teaching the General Shop.* Peoria, Ill.: Charles A. Bennett Co., 1947.

This is a teacher's professional book which explains the objectives, content, methods, and equipment necessary to teach the general shop.

NEWKIRK, LOUIS V., and JOHNSON, H. W. *The Industrial Arts Program.* New York: The Macmillan Co., 1948.

Describes in detail a program of industrial arts from the kindergarten through high school including the objectives, content, shop plans, and methods of teaching.

WILBER, GORDON O. *Industrial Arts in General Education.* Scranton, Pa.: International Textbook Co., 1954.

Gives the objectives of industrial arts and discusses the problems of equipping and teaching industrial arts subjects.

2. Physical Education

AMERICAN ASSOCIATION FOR HEALTH, PHYSICAL EDUCATION, AND RECREATION. *Developing Democratic Human Relations.* First Yearbook. Washington, D.C.: National Education Association, 1951.

An exceptionally fine source for ideas relative to the cultivation of social behavior through the physical education experience.

BRACE, DAVID K. *Health and Physical Education for Junior and Senior High Schools.* New York: A. S. Barnes & Co., 1948.

An excellent statement of suggestions for the curriculum in grades seven through twelve.

DANIELS, ARTHUR S. *Adapted Physical Education.* New York: Harper & Bros., 1954.
Contains many practical suggestions for dealing with physically handicapped children in the physical education program.

ERWIN, LESLIE W. *The Curriculum in Health Education and Physical Education.* St. Louis: C. V. Mosby Co., 1951.
Descriptions and suggestions for class organization and the physical education curriculum in secondary schools.

FORSYTHE, CHARLES L. *The Administration of High School Athletics.* New York: Prentice-Hall, Inc., 1954.
Excellent suggestions and standards for junior high school programs which include interscholastic athletics.

FORSYTHE, CHARLES L., and DUNCAN, RAYMOND O. *The Administration of Physical Education.* New York: Prentice-Hall, Inc., 1951.
Practical suggestions from two authors with wide experience in the field. Contains good suggestions for secondary schools.

HUGHES, WILLIAM L., and FRENCH, ESTHER. *The Administration of Physical Education.* Philadelphia: W. B. Saunders Co., 1954.
Good suggestions for standard practice in administration of programs for all levels.

KOZMAN, HILDA, CASSIDY, ROSALIND, and JACKSON, C. O. *Methods in Physical Education.* Philadelphia: W. B. Saunders Co., 1952.
Gives suggestions on class organization and the approach to teaching skills.

MEANS, LOUIS E. *The Organization and Administration of Intramural Sports* (2d ed.). St. Louis: C. V. Mosby Co., 1952.
Practical suggestions for the teacher in the organization of competitive and individual sports within the school program.

OBERTEUFFER, DELBERT. *Physical Education.* New York: Harper & Bros., 1951.
A book of principles which underlie the development of a program of physical education at any level, with specific suggestions for program-building.

VOLTMER, EDWARD F., and ESSLINGER, ARTHUR A. *The Organization and Administration of Physical Education.* New York: Appleton-Century-Crofts, Inc., 1949.
A standard work in administration of the physical education program. Contains excellent suggestions for program organization.

3. Mathematics

BUTLER, CHARLES H., and WREN, F. LYNWOOD. *The Teaching of Secondary School Mathematics.* New York: McGraw-Hill Book Co., Inc., 1951.
A comprehensive discussion of the mathematics curriculum in the secondary school, with special reference in some chapters to the junior high school.

GROSSNICKLE, FOSTER E. "Teaching Arithmetic in the Junior High School," *The Mathematics Teacher,* XLVII (December, 1954), 520-27.
Suggests the factors which influence the teaching of arithmetic in the junior high school, including (1) acceptance of a theory of learning which emphasizes meaning and understanding, (2) continuous promotions, and (3) gradual deferment of certain topics to higher grades.

HOUSTON, LUCILLE. "Articulating Junior High Mathematics with Elementary Arithmetic," *School Science and Mathematics,* LI (February, 1951), 117-21.
Suggests that articulation with the elementary school might be improved by (1) a gradual shift from the work of the elementary school, (2) an understanding of the content of the elementary school program, and (3) an emphasis on meanings and understandings.

KINNEY, LUCIEN B., and PURDY, RICHARD C. *Teaching Mathematics in the Secondary School.* New York: Rinehart & Co., Inc., 1952.
Although the discussion pertains to the mathematics curriculum in the secondary school, there is reference in some chapters specifically to the junior high school.

KINSELLA, J. J. "Some Reflections on the General Mathematics Situation," *School Science and Mathematics*, LIV (June, 1954), 431-38.

The author suggests that two or three types of general mathematics programs may be necessary, the type being adapted to the abilities and goals of individual pupils.

REEVE, WILLIAM D. *Mathematics for the Secondary School*. New York: Henry Holt & Co., Inc., 1954.

A comprehensive discussion of the mathematics curriculum in the secondary school, with particular references in some chapters to the junior high school.

4. Art

BALLINGER, THOMAS O. "Some Problems and Issues in Art Education with Special Consideration of the Junior High School Level," *Education*, LXXV (February, 1955), 379-82.

Discusses the weaknesses of the junior high school art program with particular reference to the attitudes of administrators, training of teachers, and the philosophy of art teachers.

FITZGERALD, LOLA. "Sketching Our Surroundings," *School Arts*, LIII (January, 1954), 19-22.

Points out that making sketches of things in the community often causes junior high school pupils to discover things previously overlooked.

GIBBS, JAMES. "Not Why But How," *California Journal of Secondary Education*, XXVIII (April, 1953), 186-88.

Emphasizes the importance of maintaining a free, spontaneous and creative approach in the art education program of the junior high school. Suggests that pupils should not be made to stress the end results, but rather should concentrate on the sheer thrill of the experience of doing.

MACHEK, KATHRYN, and COCKFIELD, DOROTHY. "Functional Creativity in the Junior High School," *School Arts*, LI (March, 1952), 226-27.

Emphasizes the part art can play in all areas of the junior high school curriculum. Describes some of the integrative activities carried on in the Rockford Junior High School, Rockford, Illinois.

CHAPTER 7

5. Home Economics

ADAMS, LELA. "Family Living in the Junior High School," *California Journal of Secondary Education*, XXVI (April, 1951), 220-21.

Presents a program used in grades seven and eight, in Moline, Illinois, consisting of courses in homemaking, experiences in personal and group relationships, and the sharing of home and family duties.

AMERICAN HOME ECONOMICS ASSOCIATION. *Strengthening the Family Relationships Aspects of Home Economics Teaching at the Secondary Level*. Washington, D.C.: The Association, 1953.

Material developed in a workshop to serve as a guide to secondary school teachers in developing sound programs in family relationships for different age groups.

DAY, E. G. "We Use the Whole School for Our Classroom," *Practical Home Economics*, XXXI (May, 1953), 10-11.

A description of interschool projects in home economics.

DOUGLASS, HARL R. *Secondary Education*. New York: The Ronald Press Co., 1952, pp. 360-67.

A summary of trends in home economics education in grades seven through twelve.

EIFLER, ANNE G. "Working Together," *Forecast for Home Economists*, LXIX (October, 1953), 28-29.
　　Shows how preparation for successful family life can begin in the junior high school.

LURRY, LUCILE L., and ALFORD, B. "Home Economics in a Core Program," *Practical Home Economics*, XXIX (May, 1951), 222-23.
　　A description of home economics in a core program at the University of Florida.

RICCI, V. G. "What Are We Eating Today?" *Practical Home Economics*, XXXIX (September, 1952), 39-40.
　　A description of a boys' foods class in a junior high school in California.

UNITED STATES OFFICE OF EDUCATION. *Home Economics for Boys and Girls in 7th, 8th, and 9th Grades*. United States Office of Education, Division of Vocational Education, Home Economics Education Branch, Misc. 3422, October, 1952. Washington, D.C.: Government Printing Office.
　　Descriptions of promising practices in home economics in grades seven, eight, and nine.

6. The Language Arts

ADAMS, FAY, GRAY, LILLIAN, and REESE, DORA. *Teaching Children to Read*. New York: The Ronald Press Co., 1949, chap. x.
　　A summary of ways of improving the reading skills of pupils in the secondary school.

ANDERSON, IRVING H., and DEARBORN, WALTER F. *The Psychology of Teaching Reading*. New York: The Ronald Press Co., 1952.
　　A comprehensive treatment of the psychological aspects of the teaching of reading.

CARLSEN, GEORGE ROBERT. "Behind Reading Interests," *The English Journal*, XLIII (January, 1954), 7-12.
　　A short discussion of the reasons for the reading choices that prevail among junior and senior high school students.

DEBOER, JOHN, KAULFERS, WALTER, and MILLER, HELEN R. *Teaching Secondary School English*. New York: McGraw-Hill Book Co., Inc., 1951.
　　One of the most complete general methods books in the field of language arts.

MARVEL, GEORGE W. *The Reading Interests of Young People*. New York: D. C. Heath & Co., 1950.
　　The results of an intensive investigation of what 50,000 adolescents choose as reading preferences.

NATIONAL COUNCIL OF TEACHERS OF ENGLISH, COMMISSION ON THE ENGLISH CURRICULUM. *The English Language Arts*. New York: Appleton-Century-Crofts, Inc., 1952.
　　A most significant statement about the teaching of the language arts today. Includes discussion of point of view and methodology from kindergarten through the graduate school.

POOLEY, ROBERT C. *Teaching English Usage*. National Council of Teachers of English, Monograph No. 16. New York: Appleton-Century-Crofts, Inc., 1946.
　　While somewhat older, this short book is the best statement of the implications of recent linguistic research for methodology and content that has yet been written.

STRANG, RUTH, McCULLOUGH, CONSTANCE, and TRAXLER, ARTHUR. *Problems in the Improvement of Reading* (2d ed.). New York: McGraw-Hill Book Co., Inc., 1955.
　　A revision of an older book dealing primarily with the problem of giving instruction in reading at the junior and senior high school levels.

7. Foreign Languages

ANDERSON, THEODORE. *The Teaching of Foreign Languages in the Elementary School.* Boston: D. C. Heath & Co., 1953.

A concise discussion of aims, content, and methods of teaching foreign languages in the lower as well as upper elementary grades, and in junior high schools.

DOUGLASS, HARL R. *Secondary Education.* New York: The Ronald Press Co., 1952, 347-55.

A summary of trends in the foreign language programs in grades seven through twelve.

KAULFERS, WALTER V. *Modern Languages for Modern Schools.* New York: McGraw-Hill Book Co., Inc., 1942.

A comprehensive textbook on aims, content, and methods, carefully illustrated with examples from five languages. Chapters ix and x present cultural orientation courses and general language offerings in junior high schools.

————. *Modern Spanish Teaching.* New York: Henry Holt & Co., Inc., 1947.

A practical manual of methods for junior high school Spanish, with bibliographies of suitable audio-visual aids, language games, and books for outside background reading.

8. The Social Studies

ALDRICH, JULIAN C. (ed.). *Social Studies for Young Adolescents: Programs for Grades Seven, Eight, and Nine.* Washington, D.C.: National Education Association, 1951.

A bulletin prepared for the National Council for the Social Studies, which identifies major curriculum trends in the social studies for the junior high school grades. Special attention is given to the social studies in a common learnings program.

CARPENTER, HELEN McCRACKEN. *Skills in Social Studies.* Twenty-fourth Yearbook of the National Council for the Social Studies. Washington, D.C.: National Education Association, 1953.

Gives suggestions based on current practice for teaching skills in reading, writing, using maps, and other social studies skills.

MICHAELIS, JOHN U. *Social Studies for Children in a Democracy.* New York: Prentice-Hall, Inc., 1950.

A comprehensive book on the social studies in the elementary school, with much that is useful for the junior high school grades.

QUILLEN, I. JAMES, and HANNA, LAVONNE A. *Education for Social Competence.* Chicago: Scott, Foresman & Co., 1949.

Although this book deals with the subject of teaching for social competence at all grade levels, it is particularly useful for the junior high school grades.

SARAFIAN, ARMEN (coordinator). "Symposium: The Social Studies in California's Secondary Schools," *California Journal of Secondary Education,* XXX (May, 1955), 280-311.

Various aspects of the social studies in California secondary schools are discussed by leading California educators.

STORE, H. F. "Junior High School Social Studies," *NEA Journal,* XXXVIII (March, 1949), 186-87.

Suggestions for teaching in a core program with emphasis on social learnings.

CHAPTER 8

9. Music

ADUBATO, LENORE. "Providing for Individual Differences in the Music Department," *School Activities,* XXV (December, 1953), 125-26.

Describes what music teachers may do to determine and help correct lack of interest and ability in music. Discusses both individual and group methods.

BEER, ALICE STEWART. "Teacher-Pupil Planning," *Music Educators Journal,* XXXVIII (June-July, 1951), 18-19.
   Describes the process one junior high school music class went through in planning, preparing, and presenting a musical program.
BELL, EVALENE. "Some Things to Try in Junior High," *Music Educators Journal,* XXXVIII (February-March, 1952), 38-40.
   Points out some of the difficulties of teaching music in the junior high school. Suggests music activities which are particularly suitable for the junior high school.
CHRISTENSEN, LORN E. "The Problems of Junior High School Music Teachers," *California Journal of Educational Research,* V (May, 1954), 111-15.
   Reports the results of a survey of problems encountered by junior high school teachers of music in Southern California.

10. Business Education

NICHOLS, FREDERICK G. *Commercial Education in the High School.* New York: Appleton-Century-Crofts, Inc., 1933, chaps. xv, xvii.
   The most challenging critique of junior business available.
TONNE, HERBERT A. *Principles of Business Education.* New York: McGraw-Hill Book Co., Inc., 1954, chap. xxiv.
   Opportunities and limitations of junior business as related to the entire school program.
TONNE, HERBERT A., POPHAM, ESTELLE L., and FREEMAN, M. HERBERT. *Methods of Teaching Business Subjects.* New York: McGraw-Hill Book Co., Inc., 1949, chaps. xiii, xiv.
   A discussion of practical teaching procedures in the business subjects.
WALTERS, R. G., and NOLAN, C. A. *Principles and Problems of Business Education.* Cincinnati: South-Western Publishing Co., 1950, chap. iv.
   A discussion of how junior business subjects fit into the entire business education program.

11. Science

ANDERSON, H. S. "A Key to the Science Interests of Junior High School Students," *The Science Teacher,* XXI (October, 1954), 227-30.
   Describes a science interest questionnaire which can be useful in ascertaining the science interests of junior high school pupils.
BLANC, S. S. "Science Interests of Junior High School Pupils," *School Science and Mathematics,* LI (December, 1951), 745-52.
   Reports the results of a questionnaire study of the science interests of 486 pupils in the Denver junior high schools.
BLOUGH, GLENN O., and HUGGETT, A. J. *Methods and Activities in Elementary School Science.* New York: The Dryden Press, 1951.
   Contains many suggestions for methods of teaching science in the junior high school grades.
BURNETT, R. W. *Teaching Science in the Elementary School.* New York: Rinehart & Co., Inc., 1953.
   A comprehensive discussion of the science program in the elementary school, with many suggestions that are appropriate for the junior high school grades.
EVANS, HUBERT M. "Some Significant Trends in Science Education," *Teachers College Record,* LIV (May, 1953), 424-29.
   Trends in enrollment, course offerings, subject matter, and teaching methods are discussed.
HEISS, ELWOOD D., OBOURN, ELLSWORTH S., and HOFFMAN, C. WESLEY. *Modern Science Teaching.* New York: The Macmillan Co., 1950.
   Discusses present practices and trends in science teaching and the facilities, equipment, and instructional materials needed in the program.

MALLINSON, GEORGE GREISEN, and BUCK, JACQUELINE V. "Some Implications and Practical Applications of Recent Research in the Teaching of Science at the Secondary-School Level," *Science Education*, XXXVIII (February, 1954), 58-81.

A review of outstanding research studies in junior and senior high school science during the years 1949 to 1952, with a statement of conclusions useful in developing teaching practices.

NATIONAL SOCIETY FOR THE STUDY OF EDUCATION. *The Content and Method of Science in the Junior High School.* The Forty-sixth Yearbook. Chicago: University of Chicago Press, 1947, pp. 152-82.

A summary of research studies on the development, content, and methodology of science education in the junior high school.

POWERS, L. S. "The Correlation of Science and Mathematics in the Junior High School," *School Science and Mathematics,* LIV (October, 1954), 571-73.

Explains how mathematics may be correlated with certain units of science, such as weather, birds, insects, and measurement of time.

CHAPTER 9

BROWN, EDWIN J. *Managing the Classroom.* New York: The Ronald Press Co., 1952, chaps. xvi-xx.

Especially good as a source of ideas on the teacher's place in the learning situation.

BURTON, WILLIAM H. *The Guidance of Learning Activities.* New York: Appleton-Century-Crofts, Inc., 1952, chaps. xi-xvi.

Presents various aspects of teaching methods that affect the setting for learning.

BUSH, ROBERT N. *The Teacher-Pupil Relationship.* New York: Prentice-Hall, Inc., 1954.

This is a well-written report of an investigation of teacher-pupil relationships in the classroom in grades seven through fourteen, in a variety of subjects.

GILES, H. H. *Teacher-Pupil Planning.* New York: Harper & Bros., 1941.

Although one of the older books on methods, it is still an excellent practical statement of suggestions on teacher-pupil planning. Especially appropriate at the junior high school level.

GRUHN, WILLIAM T. *Student Teaching in the Secondary School.* New York: The Ronald Press Co., 1954, chaps. iv-viii.

A discussion of various aspects of methods from the standpoint of the beginning teacher.

INGRAM, CHRISTINE P. *Education of the Slow-Learning Child.* New York: The Ronald Press Co., 1953, chaps. x-xiii.

Presents a discussion of methods for the slow-learning child, with examples of units especially planned for this type of child.

LANE, HOWARD, and BEAUCHAMP, MARY. *Human Relations in Teaching.* New York: Prentice-Hall, Inc., 1955.

An excellent, comprehensive discussion of human relations as related to teaching, with suggestions for developing effective relations in the classroom.

LEONARD, J. PAUL. *Developing the Secondary School Curriculum.* New York: Rinehart & Co., Inc., 1953, chaps. xv-xvii.

Presents suggestions for organizing resource units and developing classroom units.

OLSEN, EDWARD G. (ed.). *School and Community.* New York: Prentice-Hall, Inc., 1954, chaps. v-xiv.

Presents a discussion of various ways of using the community in the instructional program of the school, such as field trips, people as resources, school camping, work experiences, and community service projects.

STRANG, RUTH. "What About Homework?" *The School Executive*, XIV (July, 1955), 39-42.

Presents a good discussion of the pros and cons of home work, with suggestions for giving some home work in such a way that it will be most effective.

WHEAT, HARRY GROVE. *Foundations of School Learning*. New York: Alfred A. Knopf, Inc., 1955.

This is a different approach to the study of teaching methods, emphasizing the positive program of developing pupils that the learning situations of the school can provide.

WILES, KIMBALL. *Teaching for Better Schools*. New York: Prentice-Hall, Inc., 1952.

A practical presentation of some of the new approaches to teaching. Especially helpful on small group activities and on helping the class function effectively as a group.

CHAPTER 10

ASSOCIATION FOR SUPERVISION AND CURRICULUM DEVELOPMENT. *Fostering Mental Health in Our Schools*. 1950 Yearbook. Washington, D.C.: National Education Association, Part III.

This part, "Knowing and Helping the Child," has specific suggestions for obtaining information about individual children and using it to foster mental health.

BURTON, WILLIAM H., and BRUECKNER, LEO J. *Supervision: A Social Process*. New York: Appleton-Century-Crofts, Inc., 1955, chap. x.

A comprehensive discussion of ways of diagnosing the learning difficulties of individual pupils.

EDUCATIONAL POLICIES COMMISSION. *Education of the Gifted Child*. Washington, D.C.: National Education Association, 1950.

Presents a discussion of the importance of educating the gifted child, identification of the gifted, and suggested provisions for the education of the gifted.

FEATHERSTONE, WILLIAM B. *Teaching the Slow Learner*. New York: Bureau of Publications, Teachers College, Columbia University, 1951.

A practical discussion of teaching the slow learner, adapted especially to the needs of the classroom teacher.

HILDRETH, GERTRUDE H. *Educating Gifted Children*. New York: Harper & Bros., 1952.

An excellent discussion based on experiences with gifted children in the Hunter College Elementary School. Although it is written primarily from the point of view of the elementary school, there is much that is equally appropriate in the junior high school.

INGRAM, CHRISTINE P. *Education of the Slow-Learning Child*. New York: The Ronald Press Co., 1953.

A comprehensive work covering all aspects of a program for the slow-learning child, including the child's needs, the curriculum, and methods of teaching.

JEWETT, ARNO, and HULL, J. DAN (coordinators). *Teaching Rapid and Slow Learners*. United States Office of Education Bulletin No. 5. Washington, D.C.: Government Printing Office, 1954.

Report of a questionnaire study of practices in regular, junior, and senior high schools with an enrollment over 300. Covers administrative practices, techniques for discovering rapid and slow learners, and instructional procedures.

JUSTMAN, JOSEPH. "Academic Achievement of Intellectually Gifted Accelerants and Non-accelerants in Junior High School," *School Review*, LXII (March, 1950), 142-50.

Evaluates the part of the special progress class in improving academic achievement in the basic subjects.

KIRK, SAMUEL A., and JOHNSON, G. ORVILLE. *Educating the Retarded Child.* Boston: Houghton Mifflin Co., 1951.

A comprehensive discussion of the classification, programs, and methods for the mentally retarded. Special attention is given to the mentally retarded in the secondary school and special teaching procedures in the various subject areas.

LAUCHNER, A. H. "How Can the Junior High School Curriculum Be Improved?" *The Bulletin of the National Association of Secondary-School Principals,* XXXV (March, 1951), 296-304.

Suggests how the curriculum could be adapted to meet the needs of both rapid and slow learners by introducing more flexibility.

NOAR, GERTRUDE. *The Junior High School—Today and Tomorrow.* New York: Prentice-Hall, Inc., 1953, chap. xiv.

A practical discussion of the needs of the gifted and the slow pupils, with numerous examples of how these needs may be met in the classroom.

ROGERS, JAMES FREDERICK. *What Every Teacher Should Know About the Physical Condition of Her Pupils* (rev. ed.). United States Office of Education, Pamphlet No. 68. Washington, D.C.: Government Printing Office, 1945.

An excellent guide for the homeroom and classroom teacher in studying the physical condition of her pupils.

ROTHNEY, JOHN W. M. *The High School Student: A Book of Cases.* New York: The Dryden Press, 1953.

The entire volume is devoted to case studies of individual high school students. It is helpful both in understanding students and in developing ways for studying them.

SCHEIFELE, MARIAN. *The Gifted Child in the Regular Classroom.* New York: Bureau of Publications, Teachers College, Columbia University, 1953.

A practical discussion of things that can be done to meet the needs of the gifted child in the regular classroom situation.

"The Education of Handicapped and Gifted Pupils in the Secondary School," *Bulletin of the National Association of Secondary-School Principals,* XXXIX (January, 1955), 3-232.

This issue, which is devoted to the handicapped and gifted pupils, was prepared by a committee appointed for this purpose. Various aspects of the problem are presented by principals and others who have had experience with it in the secondary school.

VREDEVROE, L. E. (coordinator). "Symposium on Current Theory and Practice in the Grouping of Pupils in Secondary Schools," *California Journal of Secondary Education,* XXX (January, 1955), 22-59.

Various points of view concerning homogeneous grouping and other types of grouping are discussed by leaders in secondary education.

WITTY, PAUL (ed). *The Gifted Child.* Boston: D. C. Heath & Co., 1951.

The report of a committee for the American Association for Gifted Children. An excellent presentation of many aspects of the problem of meeting the needs of the gifted child.

CHAPTER 11

ANDERSON, VERNON E., GRIM, PAUL R., and GRUHN, WILLIAM T. *Principles and Practices of Secondary Education.* New York: The Ronald Press Co., 1951, chaps. xiii, xiv.

A discussion of the guidance program with particular attention to the place of the teacher in guidance.

BEALS, LESTER M. "The Guidance Program in Colin Kelly Junior High School," *Bulletin of the National Association of Secondary-School Principals,* XXXIV (January, 1950), 248-57.

An overview of a forward-looking guidance program in a junior high school.

DRISCOLL, GERTRUDE. *How to Study the Behavior of Children.* New York: Bureau of Publications, Teachers College, Columbia University, 1941.
Practical suggestions for teachers in studying the behavior of children.

ERICKSON, CLIFFORD E. *A Practical Handbook for School Counselors.* New York: The Ronald Press Co., 1949.
As the title implies, this is a practical handbook which provides much valuable information on interviewing, counseling, informational services, the guidance staff, and organization for guidance.

FROELICH, CLIFFORD P., and DARLEY, JOHN G. *Studying Students.* Chicago: Science Research Associates, Inc., 1952.
The emphasis in the entire volume is on ways of studying individual pupils as a basis for teaching and guidance.

HYMES, JAMES L., JR. *Effective Home-School Relations.* New York: Prentice-Hall, Inc., 1953.
An excellent discussion of home-school relations, with many suggestions for developing such relations.

KNAPP, ROBERT H. *Practical Guidance Methods for Counselors, Teachers and Administrators.* New York: McGraw-Hill Book Co., Inc., 1953.
As the title indicates, this book presents practical suggestions on guidance, helping the slow learner, helping the superior pupil, etc.

LANGDON, GRACE, and STOUT, IRVING W. *The Discipline of Well-Adjusted Children.* New York: The John Day Co., Inc., 1952.
A discussion of discipline based on what the parents of 414 well-adjusted children said they did in bringing them up.

LEWIS, GERTRUDE M. *Educating Children in Grades Seven and Eight.* United States Office of Education Bulletin No. 10. Washington, D.C.: Government Printing Office, 1954, pp. 37-44.
A report of guidance practices in grades seven and eight, based on observations in 31 elementary and 45 junior high schools.

"Orientation of Pupils for the Secondary School," *The National Elementary Principal,* XXXI (February, 1952), 3-43.
The entire issue is devoted to problems of preparing children of the elementary grades to enter the junior and senior high school grades.

THOMASSON, A. L. "How May Guidance Be Effective in the Junior High School?" *Bulletin of the National Association of Secondary-School Principals,* XXXVI (March, 1952), 234-42.
The steps taken to develop an effective guidance program in the junior high school at Champaign, Illinois, are described.

TRAXLER, ARTHUR E. *Techniques of Guidance.* New York: Harper & Bros., 1945.
The entire volume deals with a discussion of tests, records, and counseling as a part of the guidance program.

CHAPTER 12

ANDERSON, VERNON E., GRIM, PAUL R., and GRUHN, WILLIAM T. *Principles and Practices of Secondary Education.* New York: The Ronald Press Co., 1951, chap. xiv.
A statement of principles and practices in guidance by the homeroom and classroom teacher.

DAVIS, FRANK G. *Guidance Handbook for Teachers.* New York: McGraw-Hill Book Co., Inc., 1949, chaps. iv, v.
A discussion of the organization of the homeroom and cumulative records for the homeroom teacher.

DOUGLASS, HARL R. *Modern Administration of Secondary Schools.* Boston: Ginn & Co., 1954, pp. 204-12.
An overview of the purposes, organization, and program of the homeroom.

DUNSMOOR, C. C., and MILLER, LEONARD M. *Principles and Methods of Guidance for Teachers.* Scranton, Pa.: International Textbook Co., 1949.
   This volume is written especially for homeroom and classroom teachers, and contains many practical suggestions concerning their guidance responsibilities.
FEDDER, RUTH. *Guiding Home Room and Club Activities.* New York: McGraw-Hill Book Co., Inc., 1949.
   An excellent treatment of the role of the teacher-sponsor in homerooms and clubs.
LITTLE, WILSON, and CHAPMAN, A. L. *Developmental Guidance in Secondary School.* New York: McGraw-Hill Book Co., Inc., 1953, chap. xi.
   Discussion of the place of the homeroom as a guidance center.
VAN POOL, GERALD M. "The Home Room," *Bulletin of the National Association of Secondary-School Principals,* XXXVI (February, 1952), 150-56.
   A discussion of the objectives, administration, and internal organization of the homeroom.

CHAPTER 13

ANDERSON, VERNON E., GRIM, PAUL R., and GRUHN, WILLIAM T. *Principles and Practices of Secondary Education.* New York: The Ronald Press Co., 1951, chap. x.
   An overview of the program of extraclass activities in the secondary school.
EDUCATIONAL POLICIES COMMISSION. *School Athletics: Problems and Policies.* Washington, D.C.: National Education Association, 1954.
   A statement of policy and desirable practices for athletics in elementary and secondary schools. One chapter is devoted to the junior high school.
FULLER, KENNETH A. "Finance—An Area for Junior High School Participation," *Bulletin of the National Association of Secondary-School Principals,* XXXVII (December, 1953), 57-73.
   Presents the purposes and basic principles of pupil participation in financing extraclass activities. Describes a plan that is being used in one junior high school.
JOHNSTON, EDGAR G., and FAUNCE, ROLAND C. *Student Activities in Secondary Schools.* New York: The Ronald Press Co., 1952.
   A comprehensive discussion of student activities in the secondary school, including clubs, assemblies, publications, student councils, athletics, speech, music, and camping.
LEWIS, GERTRUDE M. *Educating Children in Grades Seven and Eight.* United States Office of Education Bulletin No. 10. Washington, D.C.: Government Printing Office, 1954, pp. 44-81.
   A report of practices in grades seven and eight, based on observations in 31 elementary and 45 junior high schools.
LUDDEN, WALLACE. "How Extensive an Activities Program in the Junior High School?" *Bulletin of the National Association of Secondary-School Principals,* XXXVI (March, 1952), 257-62.
   Describes the pupil activities program in the junior high school, Rome, New York.
McCOMANGHEY, SUSANNE. "Where the Kids Live and Learn," *Coronet,* XXI (January, 1947), 51-55.
   Describes pupil activities in the Skokie Junior High School, Winnetka, Illinois, where pupils have organized insurance services, a credit union, a labor union, a bank, a cooperative store, and other similar activities.
McKOWN, HARRY C. *Extracurricular Activities* (rev. ed.). New York: The Macmillan Co., 1952.
   A comprehensive treatment of extracurricular activities, including philosophy, organization, and types of activities. Although it is not directed primarily at the junior high school, it is fully appropriate for that level.

McKown, Harry C., and Bailard, Virginia. *So You Were Elected!* New York: McGraw-Hill Book Co., Inc., 1946.

An excellent practical presentation of the responsibilities and duties of pupil officers in school organizations, written primarily for the pupils.

National Association of Student Councils. *Student Council Handbook.* Washington, D.C.: National Association of Secondary-School Principals, 1949.

Contains numerous descriptions of student council projects and sample constitutions. Discusses basic principles for student council organization.

Smith, Joe. *Student Councils for Our Times: Principles and Practices.* New York: Bureau of Publications, Teachers College, Columbia University, 1951.

A comprehensive discussion of the purposes and procedures of student councils.

Watkins, J. H. "Intramurals in the Junior High School," *Journal of the American Association of Health, Physical Education, and Recreation,* XXI (May, 1950), 28-82.

Describes how an intramural athletics program can be scheduled in the regular school day.

Chapter 14

Anderson, Vernon E., Grim, Paul R., and Gruhn, William T. *Principles and Practices of Secondary Education.* New York: The Ronald Press Co., 1951, chap. xii.

A statement of principles on evaluating and reporting pupil progress, with examples of some new type forms.

Brown, Edwin J. *Managing the Classroom.* New York: The Ronald Press Co., 1952, chap. x.

Presents suggestions for grading, recording, reporting, and promoting.

Burton, William H. *The Guidance of Learning Activities.* New York: Appleton-Century-Crofts, Inc., 1952, chaps. xix, xxi.

A discussion of the evaluation of learning outcomes in chap. xix, and of marking and reporting pupil progress in chap. xxi.

Burton, William H., and Brueckner, Leo J. *Supervision: A Social Process.* New York: Appleton-Century-Crofts, Inc., chap. ix.

A thorough discussion of various techniques and procedures for appraising the educational product.

Froelich, Clifford P., and Darley, John G. *Studying Students.* Chicago: Science Research Associates, Inc., 1952, chaps. x, xi.

A discussion of techniques for measuring scholastic ability and scholastic achievement.

Langdon, Grace, and Stout, Irving W. *Teacher-Parent Interviews.* New York: Prentice-Hall, Inc., 1954.

A comprehensive, practical discussion of the purposes and procedures for teacher-parent interviews.

Odell, C. W. *How to Improve Classroom Tests.* Dubuque, Iowa: Wm. C. Brown Co., 1953.

Provides practical suggestions for constructing and using informal tests of achievement.

Thut, I. N., and Gerberich, J. Raymond. *Foundations of Method for Secondary Schools.* New York: McGraw-Hill Book Co., Inc., 1949, chaps. v, viii, xi, xiv.

Discusses the appraisal of pupil growth in the daily-assignment method, the subject-matter unit, and the experience unit.

Traxler, Arthur E. *Techniques of Guidance.* New York: Harper & Bros., 1945. chaps. xii, xiii.

A discussion of cumulative records and progress reports to parents.

TRAXLER, ARTHUR E. "The Use of Tests in Differentiated Instruction," *Education,* LXXIV (January, 1954), 272-78.

Discusses the use of tests in planning differentiated instruction and checking on the growth of pupils as a result of differentiated procedures.

WRINKLE, WILLIAM L. *Improving Marking and Reporting Practices in Elementary and Secondary Schools.* New York: Rinehart & Co., Inc., 1947.

A report of experience with various practices in marking and reporting over a period of years in the secondary school of the Colorado State College of Education at Greeley.

CHAPTER 15

ANDERSON, VERNON E., GRIM, PAUL R., and GRUHN, WILLIAM T. *Principles and Practices of Secondary Education.* New York: The Ronald Press Co., 1951.

A discussion of the relationship between the organization of the school and the instructional program, with a statement of basic principles bearing on the subject.

ESSEX, MARTIN W., and SPAYDE, PAUL E. "Junior High School Is Here to Stay: A Study of the First Forty Years Based on Practices in Forty Cities," *The Nation's Schools,* LIV (August, 1954), 31-34.

A study of practices in 40 cities on organization of the school day, study halls, guidance, curriculum, class size, and core programs.

HERRIOTT, M. E. (chairman). "Organizing the Junior High School," *Bulletin of the National Association of Secondary-School Principals,* XXXV (December, 1951), 6-112.

A comprehensive statement of the organization of a junior high school prepared by the Committee on Junior High School Problems of the California Association of Secondary-School Administrators.

KOOS, LEONARD V. "Superiority of the Four-Year Junior High School," *School Review,* LI (September, 1943), 397-407.

A comparison of the four-year and three-year junior high schools, based on a questionnaire study and interviews of a number of each of the two types of schools.

MCCOMB, STUART F. "Why Pasadena Dropped 6-4-4 Plan," *The Nation's Schools,* LIV (November, 1954), 60-61.

Presents arguments for and against the 6-4-4 plan and reasons for shifting to the 6-3-3-2 plan in Pasadena.

STEWART, LYLE. "Seattle Sets Pattern for Future Junior High Schools," *The Nation's Schools,* LI (March, 1953), 59-64.

Describes the features of the Nathan Eckstein Junior High School, one of Seattle's new junior high schools.

"Types of High School Organization—Their Advantages and Disadvantages," *The School Executive,* LXVIII (October, 1948), 63-76.

Seven leading school authorities discuss the merits of the more common forms of grade reorganization, such as the 6-3-3, 6-6, and 6-4-4.

YOUNG, IRVIN F. "What Are the Most Significant Functions of the Six-Year School?" *Bulletin of the National Association of Secondary-School Principals,* XXXVI (March, 1952), 304-11.

Presents the advantages in cost, administration, and educational opportunities of the six-year school as compared with separate junior and senior high schools in small school systems.

CHAPTER 16

ANDERSON, VERNON E., GRIM, PAUL R., and GRUHN, WILLIAM T. *Principles and Practices of Secondary Education.* New York: The Ronald Press Co., 1951, chaps. xviii, xix, xx.

The pre-service and in-service education of the teacher are discussed, and the responsibilities of the teacher in the secondary school are summarized.

BURTON, WILLIAM H., and BRUECKNER, LEO J. *Supervision: A Social Process.* New York: Appleton-Century-Crofts, Inc., 1955, chap. xviii.
    Presents procedures for evaluating the effectiveness of teachers and teaching.
DOUGLASS, HARL R. *Modern Administration of Secondary Schools.* Boston: Ginn & Co., 1954, chaps. iv-vi.
    A discussion of various problems of the staff in the secondary school, including load, selection, assignment, and supervision.
GRUHN, WILLIAM T. *Student Teaching in the Secondary School.* New York: The Ronald Press Co., 1954, chaps. xi, xii.
    The responsibilities of the beginning teacher in the secondary school and suggestions for participating in the life of the community.
HAMMOCK, ROBERT C., and OWINGS, RALPH S. *Supervising Instruction in the Secondary Schools.* New York: McGraw-Hill Book Co., Inc., 1955, chaps. vi, vii.
    Suggests ways for the faculty to work together on school problems and on developing an effective school program.
JACOBSON, PAUL B., REAVIS, WILLIAM C., and LOGSDON, JAMES D. *The Effective School Principal.* New York: Prentice-Hall, Inc., 1954, chap. xvi.
    A comprehensive discussion of staff problems in elementary and secondary schools, including supply, selection, retention, salaries, and in-service education.
MELBY, ERNEST O. *Administering Community Education.* New York: Prentice-Hall, Inc., 1955, chaps. xv, xvi.
    Presents suggestions for administrators, teachers, and lay people to work together on problems in education.
MENGE, J. WILMER, and FAUNCE, ROLAND C. *Working Together for Better Schools* New York: American Book Co., 1953.
    The entire volume is devoted to a discussion of ways for teachers, administrators, and laymen to work together for better schools.
"Salaries and Salary Schedules of Urban School Employees, 1954-55," *Research Bulletin of the National Education Association,* XXX (April, 1955), 60-88.
    A study of salaries of school employees in urban communities, arranged by type of position, type of school, and city population.
"Teaching Load in 1950," *Research Bulletin of the National Education Association,* XXVI (February, 1951), 1-51.
    Report of a questionnaire study of facts and opinions on teacher load, as reported by 2,200 elementary and secondary school teachers. Data are reported for junior high school teachers.
WEBER, CLARENCE A. *Personnel Problems of School Administrators.* New York: McGraw-Hill Book Co., Inc., 1954.
    This volume presents a comprehensive discussion of various problems of the teaching staff. Of particular interest at the junior high school level are the discussions on selection, in-service education, and load.
———. "Reactions of Teachers to In-Service Education in Their Schools," *School Review,* LI (April, 1943), 234-40.
    A report of a survey on this subject.

CHAPTER 17

ANDERSON, VERNON E., GRIM, PAUL R., and GRUHN, WILLIAM T. *Principles and Practices of Secondary Education.* New York: The Ronald Press Co., 1951, chap. xxi.
    Suggests some of the needed changes in secondary education in the years ahead.
ANDREEN, EARL P. (coordinator). "Symposium: The Challenge Facing the Junior High School," *California Journal of Secondary Education,* XXIX (May, 1954), 263-301.
    A description of policies and practices in California junior high schools, with emphasis on practices that are new and forward-looking.

DOUGLASS, A. A. "Persistent Problems of the Junior High School," *California Journal of Secondary Education*, XX (February, 1945), 110-20.

Presents the original purposes of the junior high school, changes that have occurred, and the problems that persist.

LAUCHNER, A. H. "A Study of Trends in Junior High School Practices in Twenty-Four States," *Bulletin of the National Association of Secondary-School Principals*, XXXV (December, 1951), 120-25.

A report of trends in junior high school practices after visits to 71 schools in various parts of the United States.

LONG, FORREST E. "Trends in Junior High School Education," *Bulletin of the National Association of Secondary-School Principals*, XXXV (April, 1951), 143-51.

A summary of trends in guidance, curriculum, marking and reporting, athletics, and other aspects of the junior high school program.

NAME INDEX

Adams, Fay, 399
Adams, Lela, 398
Adubato, Lenore, 400
Alberty, Harold B., 394
Aldrich, Julian C., 400
Alford, B., 399
Anderson, H. S., 401
Anderson, Irving H., 399
Anderson, Theodore, 400
Anderson, Vernon E., 394, 395, 404, 405, 406, 407, 408, 409
Andreen, Earl P., 409

Bailard, Virginia, 407
Baker, James H., 14
Ballinger, Thomas O., 398
Beals, Lester M., 404
Beatley, Bancroft, 49, 393
Beauchamp, Mary, 402
Beer, Alice Stewart, 401
Bell, Evalene, 401
Berdan, Norman, 395
Besvinick, Sidney L., 395
Billett, Roy O., 212
Blanc, S. S., 401
Blayne, Thornton C., 146
Blough, Glenn O., 401
Bossing, Nelson L., 395
Brace, David K., 396
Briggs, Thomas H., 392, 394
Brown, Edwin J., 402, 407
Brown, Kenneth E., 119 f.
Brown, Stanley B., 169
Brueckner, Leo J., 403, 407, 408
Buck, Jacqueline V., 402
Bunker, Frank F., 7, 15, 391
Burnett, R. W., 401
Burton, William H., 402, 403, 407, 408
Bush, Robert N., 402
Butler, Charles H., 397
Byers, Richard S., 38, 82, 198, 239

Capehart, Bertis E., 395
Carlsen, G. Robert, 136 ff., 399
Carpenter, Helen McCracken, 400
Carpenter, L. H., 49
Carr, Edwin R., 147
Cassidy, Rosalind, 397
Chapman, A. L., 406

Childs, Hubert G., 49
Christensen, Lorn E., 401
Clem, O. M., 50, 393
Cockfield, Dorothy, 398
Cramer, Roscoe V., 395
Cubberley, Ellwood P., 391

Daniels, Arthur S., 397
Darley, John G., 405, 407
Davis, Frank G., 405
Day, E. G., 398
Deans, Helen E., 395
Dearborn, Walter F., 399
Deaton, J. C., Sr., 395
DeBoer, John, 399
Douglass, A. A., 410
Douglass, Harl R., 392, 394, 398, 400, 405, 408
Drake, Leland N., 392
Driscoll, Gertrude, 405
Duncan, Raymond O., 397
Dunsmoor, C. C., 406

Eifler, Anne G., 399
Eliot, Charles W., 7
Erickson, Clifford E., 405
Ericson, E. E., 396
Erwin, Leslie W., 397
Essex, Martin W., 408
Esslinger, Arthur A., 397
Evans, Hubert M., 401

Faunce, Roland C., 393, 395, 406, 409
Featherstone, William B., 394, 403
Fedder, Ruth, 406
Fennell, Edward G., 69, 249, 305, 347, 361 f., 366
Fitzgerald, Lola, 398
Forsythe, Charles L., 397
Frazier, G. W., 391
Freeman, M. Herbert, 401
French, Esther, 397
Froelich, Clifford P., 405, 407
Fuller, Kenneth A., 406

Gaumnitz, Walter H., 19, 391, 393
Gerberich, J. Raymond, 407
Gibbs, James, 398
Giles, H. H., 402

411

Glass, Lillian, 50
Gray, Lillian, 399
Greenwood, James M., 15
Grim, Paul R., 394, 395, 404, 405, 406, 407, 408, 409
Grizzell, E. D., 391
Grossnickle, Foster E., 397
Gruhn, William T., 392, 394, 395, 402, 404, 405, 406, 407, 408, 409

Hammock, Robert C., 409
Hanna, Lavonne A., 400
Hartwell, Charles S., 391
Harvill, Harris, 395
Heck, Arch. O., 227
Heiss, Elwood D., 401
Herriott, M. E., 25, 408
Hertzler, Silas, 391
Hildreth, Gertrude H., 403
Hodges, Allen, 395
Hoffman, C. Wesley, 401
Hollingworth, Leta S., 218
Hopka, Erich, 169
Houston, Lucille, 397
Huggett, A. J., 401
Hughes, William L., 397
Hull, J. Dan, 19, 391, 393, 403
Hymes, James L., Jr., 405

Ingram, Christine P., 226 f., 402, 403

Jackson, C. O., 397
Jacobson, Paul B., 409
Jewett, Arno, 403
Johnson, G. Orville, 404
Johnson, H. W., 396
Johnston, Edgar G., 406
Jones, Arthur J., 391
Judd, Charles H., 391
Justman, Joseph, 403

Kaulfers, Walter V., 143 ff., 399, 400
Keck, Malcolm, 395
Kinney, Lucien B., 115 ff., 397
Kinsella, J. J., 398
Kirk, Samuel A., 404
Knapp, Harriet E., 123
Knapp, Robert H., 405
Koos, Leonard V., 31, 392, 408
Kozman, Hilda, 397

Landsittel, F. C., 50
Lane, Florence R., 221
Lane, Howard, 402
Langdon, Grace, 405, 407
Lauchner, A. H., 393, 404, 410
Leonard, J. Paul, 394, 395, 402

Lewis, Gertrude M., 394, 405, 406
Little, Wilson, 406
Logsdon, James D., 409
Long, Forrest E., 410
Ludden, Wallace, 406
Lurry, Lucile L., 399

McComanghey, Susanne, 406
McComb, Stuart F., 408
McCullough, Constance, 399
Machek, Kathryn, 398
Mackie, R. H., 393
McKown, Harry C., 406, 407
Mallinson, George Greisen, 402
Marvel, George W., 399
Means, Louis E., 397
Melby, Ernest O., 409
Menge, J. Wilmer, 409
Michaelis, John U., 400
Miller, Helen R., 399
Miller, Leonard M., 406
Mills, H. C., 49
Monroe, Paul, 392
Morrison, Gilbert B., 12
Mulhern, James, 392
Murchison, Carl, 219
Mursell, James L., 161 ff.

Nelson, Howard H., 100 ff.
Nelson, V. Ronald, 169
Newkirk, Louis V., 396
Nichols, Frederick G., 165, 401
Noar, Gertrude, 392, 395, 404
Nolan, C. A., 401

Oberteuffer, Delbert, 108 ff., 113, 397
Obourn, Ellsworth S., 401
Odell, C. W., 407
Olsen, Edward G., 402
Owings, Ralph S., 409

Pooley, Robert C., 399
Popham, Estelle I., 401
Porter, W. A., 49 f.
Powers, L. S., 402
Purdy, Richard C., 397

Quillen, I. James, 400

Ransom, William L., 24
Reavis, William C., 409
Reese, Dora, 399
Reeve, William D., 398
Ricci, V. G., 399
Rice, Mabel C., 145
Rice, Theodore D., 393
Richards, Ellen H., 129

Roberts, H. M., 50, 393
Rogers, James Frederick, 404
Romine, Stephen A., 394, 396
Rose, Ella J., 128 ff.
Rothney, John W. M., 404
Ruffini, Elise, 122 ff.

Sarafian, Armen, 400
Scheifele, Marian, 404
Schweickhard, Dean M., 105
Shores, Harlan J., 394, 396
Smith, B. Othaniel, 394, 396
Smith, Harry P., 50, 393
Smith, Joe, 407
Smith, William A., 393
Spayde, Paul E., 408
Spears, Harold, 394
Stanley, William O., 394, 396
Stewart, Lyle, 408
Store, H. F., 400
Stout, Irving W., 405, 407
Strang, Ruth, 399, 403
Stratemeyer, Florence, 394
Sumption, Merle R., 219, 222
Sunderland, Albert, 392

Terman, Lewis, 219
Thomasson, A. L., 405

Thut, I. N., 407
Tonne, Herbert A., 164 ff., 401
Traxler, Arthur E., 399, 405, 407, 408
Tuttle, Harold S., 393

Van Pool, Gerald M., 406
Vars, G. F., 396
Voltmer, Edward F., 397
Vredevroe, L. E., 404

Wachner, Clarence, 143
Walters, R. G., 401
Watkins, J. H., 407
Weber, Clarence A., 409
Wesley, Edgar B., 152
Wheat, Harry Grove, 403
Wilber, Gordon O., 396
Wiles, Kimball, 403
Willis, Charles F., 219
Witham, Ernest C., 393
Witty, Paul, 404
Wood, W. C., 51 f.
Wren, F. Lynwood, 397
Wright, Grace S., 396
Wrinkle, William L., 408

Young, Irvin F., 408

SUBJECT INDEX

Aberdeen, South Dakota
  core course, 131
Ability grouping; see Homogeneous
  grouping
Acceleration of gifted pupils, 220 f.
Achievement, pupil
  considerations relative to, 49 ff.
  factors influencing studies of, 50 f.
  in junior high, 49 f.
  in senior high, 50
Activities, class
  in experience-centered approach,
    184 ff.
  in industrial arts, 103 f.
  in language arts, 141 f.
Activities, extraclass
  assemblies, 296 ff.
  audience activities, 288 f.
  basic point of view, 284
  clubs, 290 ff.
  cost of, 286 f.
  development of, 47
  during noon hours, 349
  for every child, 285 f.
  for gifted pupils, 224
  guidance through, 259
  how extensive, 387
  in six-year high schools, 289 f.
  in the homeroom, 264, 278
  preparation of teachers for, 364
  prerequisites for, 287
  social, 300
  speech, 302 ff.
  sports, 305 f.
  time for, 286, 388
Activities, extracurricular; see Activities,
  extraclass
Activity-centered teaching, 179 f.
Administration
  for assemblies, 299 f.
  pupil participation in, 306 f.
Administrators; see Principal
Adolescents, school for, 26
Advantages, of junior high
  discussion of, 45 ff.
  six-year high schools, 342
  summary of, 57 f.
Advisers, homeroom
  pupil data for, 276 f.

retention of, 270
selection of, 273
teaching load for, 276 f.
Aims; see Objectives
Allentown, Pennsylvania, program of
  studies, 80 f.
Art; see Arts and crafts
Articulation
  break after elementary school, 352 f.
  current practices, 356 f.
  improvement in, 54
  in administrative practices, 353 ff.
  in industrial practices, 353 ff.
  more emphasis on, 37
  problems of, 353 ff., 380
  statement of function, 32
Arts and crafts
  basic principles, 122 f.
  curriculum areas, 124 ff.
  offerings in, 123
Assemblies
  objectives of, 296
  pupil participation in, 297 f.
  sources of programs, 296 f.
Athletics
  competitive, 305
  participation in, 305 f.
  problem of interscholastic, 388
Audio-visual materials
  production of, 193 f.
  use of, 192 f.

Battle Creek, Michigan, pupil progress
  reports, 322 ff.
Berkeley, junior high school in, 17 f.
Buildings
  better in junior high, 56
  need for study, 380
  separate for junior high, 344
Business education
  early trends, 164 f.
  junior business, 165 f.
  offerings, 167
  typewriting, 169

Child growth, emphasis on all aspects of,
  27
Citizenship, preparation for, 72 f.

Class size
  present practice, 371
  recommended size, 371
Club activities
  faculty sponsors, 294 f.
  growth of, 290 f.
  meeting pupil interests, 291 f.
  membership in, 292 ff.
  new developments, 295
  objectives of, 291
  prerequisites for, 293 f.
College preparation, postponement of, 73 ff.
Columbus, Ohio, junior high school in, 17 f.
Committee on College Entrance Requirements, recommendations of, 10 f.
Committee on Economy of Time in Education, recommendations of, 13 f.
Committee of Fifteen, recommendations of, 9 f.
Committee of Ten
  appointment of, 7 f.
  recommendations of, 8 f.
Committee on Six-Year Courses, recommendations of, 11 ff.
Community, school as a, 30 f., 389
Community resources, 191 f.
Consumership preparation for, 71, 149
Core curriculum
  basic point of view, 82 ff.
  definition of, 82
  development of, 82 f.
  discipline in, 99
  evaluation of, 97
  facilities needed, 95 f.
  guidance in, 85 f., 257 f.
  individualization through, 85
  introduction of, 93
  summary of purposes of, 86 f.
  trend toward, 67 f.
  types of, 87 ff.
Correlation
  trend toward, 66
  with real-life activities, 70 f.
Costs of junior high, 56 f.
Course offerings
  art, 123
  business, 167
  foreign languages, 144
  home economics, 133
  industrial arts, 102
  language arts, 137
  mathematics, 174 f.
  music, 164
  physical education, 110
  science, 172

  social studies, 147 f.
Cumulative records
  information on, 331 f.
  maintenance of, 337
  purposes of, 331
  use of, 337 f.
Curriculum
  broader in junior high, 46
  change in concept of, 61
  changes in, 46
  characteristics of good, 77 f.
  guidance through, 257
  lay participation in, 68 f., 384
  philosophy of, 61
  principles of, 76 f.
  pupil participation in, 68
  relation to objectives, 63
  summary of trends, 78
  terminology, 63 ff.
  trends in, 65 f.
  trends in mathematics, 118
  types of organization, 75 f.

Danielson, Connecticut, cooperative teacher planning, 92
Darien, Connecticut, core program, 88
Deep River, Connecticut
  core program, 88
  use of library, 196
Democracy
  methods for teaching, 188 f.
  teaching for, 149
Denver, Colorado, social studies program, 154 f.
Department of Secondary Education, recommendations of 6-6 plan by, 11 f.
Departmentalization
  advantages of, 372
  disadvantages of, 373
  overemphasis on, 83 f.
  reasonable approach to, 383
Differentiation; see also Individualized teaching
  more attention to, 35
  statement of function of, 32
  within curriculums, 75
Disadvantages
  of junior high school, 45 ff.
  of six-year high schools, 342 f.
Discipline, better in junior high, 55

Economy of time in education
  emphasis on, 13 f.
  not achieved, 55

Educational guidance; *see* Guidance; Orientation activities
Educational Policies Commission, objectives of education, 23 f.
Efficiency, of junior high school, 51 f.
Eight-four plan
  attacks on, 6
  departure from, 16
  dissatisfaction with, 6 f.
  origin of, 5 f.
Elective courses
  desirability of, 383
  meeting individual differences through, 23 f.
English; *see* Language arts
Enrichment
  for gifted pupils, 221 f.
  in regular classes, 223 f.
  in special classes, 222 f.
  through extraclass activities, 224
Enrollment, desirable for junior high, 344
Eugene, Oregon, social studies program, 155 f.
Evaluation
  basic point of view, 313
  group evaluation, 318 f.
  principles for, 316 f.
  problem of, 385
  pupil self-evaluation, 319
  teacher evaluation, 318
  through tests, 319
Examinations; *see* Tests
Experience-centered teaching
  activities in, 181
  appropriateness of, 187 f.
  characteristics of, 180 f.
  definition of, 180
  group activities in, 184 f.
  individualized teaching, 183 f.
  planning for, 181 f.
Exploration
  better opportunities for, 53 f.
  emphasis on, 33
  exploratory courses, 383
  statement of function, 31
Extraclass activities; *see* Activities, extraclass
Extracurricular activities; *see* Activities, extraclass

Foreign languages
  enrollments in, 143
  objectives, 144 f.
  offerings in, 143 f.
  status of, 145 f.
  trends in, 146 f.
Four-year high schools, 19

Four-year junior high school, 341 f.
Functions
  changes in, 32 ff.
  meaning of, 30 f.
  statement of, 31 f.
Fundamentals
  emphasis on, 29 f.
  in core curriculum, 97
  in experience-centered approach, 186 f.
  method of teaching, 384
Fusion, of related subjects, 66 f.

General education, emphasis on, 28 f.
Gifted pupils
  acceleration of, 220 f.
  characteristics of, 219 f.
  enrichment for, 221 ff.
  in small schools, 224 ff.
  meeting needs of, 220
  methods for, 224
  neglect of, 218 f.
  provision for, 218 ff.
  special classes for, 222 f.
Grade organization
  best plan, 382
  development of, 340
  preferences for, 52
  psychological considerations in, 343
  types of, 19
Granite School District, Salt Lake City, Utah, combination subjects, 91
Group activities
  class as a group, 189 f.
  in experienced-centered approach, 184 ff.
Grouping, within classes, 207 f.; *see also* Homogeneous grouping
Guidance
  avenues of, 257 ff.
  better facilities for, 52
  educational guidance, 239 ff.
  health guidance, 248 ff.
  in core curriculum, 85 f.
  in the homeroom, 265 f.
  individual, 260
  information about pupils, 255 f.
  personal guidance, 34, 254 f.
  philosophy of, 237 ff.
  preparation of teachers for, 245 f.
  recreational guidance, 252 ff.
  social guidance, 252
  statement of function, 32
  teacher's part in, 386
  through social studies, 148
  time for, 386
  vocational guidance, 246 ff.

Health education
    principles of, 113 f.
    program in, 112 f.
Health guidance
    need for, 248
    practices in, 248, 250
    preparation of teachers for, 251
    sex problems, 250
History, content of courses in, 151 ff.; see also Social studies
Home economics
    curriculum content of, 131
    examples of programs, 134 f.
    influences on, 128 f.
    teaching methods, 131
    trends in, 129 ff.
Home visitation, 274
Home work
    attitude toward, 385
    hours per day, 198
    suggestions for, 198 f.
Homerooms
    activities in, 278
    advisers for, 270, 273 ff.
    committees in, 271 f.
    composition of, 269 f.
    contributions of, 264 ff.
    frequency of periods, 267 f.
    functions of, 263 f.
    guidance through, 257 f.
    improvement of, 386
    length of periods, 267 f.
    officers for, 271
    permanence of, 270
    planning for, 277 ff.
    procedures for, 281 f.
    pupil participation in, 282
    time for, 269
Homogeneous grouping
    avoidance of undesirable pupil attitudes, 215 f.
    desirability of, 212 f.
    development of, 209
    effective grouping practices, 214 f.
    extent of, 211 f.
    purposes of, 210
    recommended approach to, 216 f.
    special classes for gifted pupils, 222 f.
    studies of, 213 f.
    types of, 210 f.

Individual differences; see Differentiation; Individualized teaching
Individualized teaching; see also Differentiation
    better provision for, 53
    emphasis on, 27 f.

for gifted pupils, 218 ff.
for mentally retarded pupils, 226 ff.
improvement of, 386
in core curriculum, 85
in experience-centered teaching, 183 f.
in language arts, 142 f.
knowledge of pupils, 85, 202 ff., 255 ff.
methods of, 205 ff.
remedial instruction, 208 f.
within classes, 35
Industrial arts
    activities in, 103 f.
    experience areas in, 104 f.
    grade placement, 107
    objectives of, 100 ff.
    offerings in, 102
    suggested programs, 105 ff.
Instructional practices
    advantages and limitations of, 46 ff.
    criticism of, 48
Integration
    importance of, 84 f.
    improvement of, 387
    statement of function, 31
    through extraclass activities, 290
    trend toward, 32, 67 f.
Intramural competition, 288

Junior business
    content of, 167 f.
    early trends in, 165 f.
    modern courses in, 166 f.
Junior high school
    definition of, 3 f.
    desirable enrollment for, 344
    growth of, 3, 16 ff.
    growth since 1910, 18 f.
    housing for, 344
    influence of committees on, 14 f.
    introduction of, 17 f.
    number of, 19
Junior-senior high school; see Six-year high schools

Kansas City, Missouri, 7-4 plan in, 15

Language arts
    basis for program, 137 ff.
    individualized teaching, 142 f.
    language skills, 141
    offerings in, 137
    organization of, 140 f.
Lawrence, Kansas, junior high school in, 17
Laymen, participation in curriculum planning, 68 f.
Library, use of, 195 f., 384 f.

Limitations of junior high school
  discussion of, 45 ff.
  summary of, 57 f.
Long Beach, California, social studies
  program, 158
Los Angeles, California, student council
  in, 307 f.
Lunch period
  activities during, 349 f.
  arrangements for, 348 f.

Marks
  adaptation to individual differences,
    231 f.
  present practices, 320 f.
Mathematics
  curriculum trends in, 120 f.
  functions of, 115 f.
  offerings in, 117 f.
  problems in, 120 f.
  trends in ninth grade, 119 f.
Mental health, pupil progress reports, 314
Mentally retarded pupils
  characteristics of, 227 f.
  in small schools, 230
  intelligence of, 226
  methods for, 228 f.
  needs of, 228
  problem of, 226
  special classes for, 229 f.
Methods of teaching
  democratic relationships, 188 ff.
  flexible methods, 205
  for gifted pupils, 224
  for mentally retarded pupils, 228 f.
  importance of, 178
  in core curriculum, 86
  in social studies, 150
  in the homeroom, 277 ff.
  individualized methods, 205 f.
Minnesota, State of
  home economics program, 134 f.
  industrial arts program, 105 f.
Music education
  activities, 308
  basis for program, 161 ff.
  features of, 163 f.
  offerings, 164

Needs of youth, 24 ff.
New Britain, Connecticut, program of
  studies, 79 f.
New Mexico, State of, home economics
  program, 134 f.
New York, City of
  homeroom programs, 280 f.
  junior high school in, 17

New York, State of, home economics
  program, 134 f.
Newton, Massachusetts
  cooperative teacher planning, 91
  development of philosophy, 40 f.
  philosophy of, 41 f.
  pupil progress reports, 332 ff.
Ninth grade
  mathematics trends in, 119 f.
  problems in, 120 ff.
  program for, 382

Objections to junior high, discussions of,
  45 ff.
Objectives
  cardinal principles of secondary educa-
    tion, 22
  Educational Policies Commission, 22 ff.
  foreign language, 144 f.
  industrial arts, 100 ff.
  of assemblies, 296
  of club activities, 291
  of homerooms, 263 f.
  of social activities, 300
  of speech activities, 302 f.
Officers, homeroom, 271 f.
Orientation activities
  for parents, 242
  for pupils, 242
  to new school, 240
  types of, 239 f.
  units on, 241 f.

Parent-teacher relationships, 267
Parents, pupil information for, 314 f.
Periods, class
  length of, 345
  number of, 345 f.
Personnel; see Staff
Philosophy
  developing a school, 37 ff.
  elements of, 38
  examples of, 41 ff.
  implementation of, 39 f.
  importance of, 37 f.
  junior high school, 26 ff.
  of curriculum, 61
  of guidance, 237
  of science education, 170 f.
  percentage of schools having, 38
  procedures for formulation, 38 f.
Physical education
  offerings in, 110
  principles of, 108 ff.
  problems in, 110 f.
  typical program, 111 f.

Planning
    educational programs, 243 f.
    for assemblies, 298 f.
    in the homeroom, 277 f.
    pupil participation in, 181 f., 207
Principal
    assignment of, to schools, 368
    preparation of, 367 f., 379
Program of studies, examples of, 79 ff.
Progress reports, pupil
    adaptation to individual differences,
        231 f.
    basic point of view, 213
    concern for the individual, 313 f.
    developing new types of, 321 f.
    examples of, 322 ff.
    mental health, 314
    new practices, 321
    parents need for information, 314 f.
    principles for, 316 f.
    problem of, 385
    suggestions for, 330
Promotion
    by subject, 232
    problem of, 385
Publications, pupil
    guidance through, 258 f.
    types of, 308
Pupil-teacher ratio, desirable for junior
    high, 359
Pupils
    concern for, 313 f.
    data about, 275 f.
    elimination studies, 15 f.
    information about, 203 ff.
    mentally retarded, 226 ff.
    participation in assemblies, 298 f.
    participation in curriculum planning,
        68
    participation in social activities, 301 f.
    retardation of, 55 f.
    retention of, 54

Recreational guidance
    need for, 252
    practices in, 253 f.
Registration, pre-registration of pupils,
    350 f.
Remedial teaching, 208 f.
Reorganization movement
    beginning of, 7
    Committee of Ten and, 6 f.
    influence of Eliot, 7
    influence of pupil elimination studies,
        15
Retardation, in junior high, 54
Retention of pupils, in junior high, 54

Richmond, Indiana, junior high school in,
    17 f.

Salaries
    importance of improvement, 369 f.
    increase in, 369
Schedule; see also School day
    construction by block method, 352
    construction by mosaic plan, 351 f.
    importance of, 350
    need for flexibility, 381
    weekly periods needed, 381
School day
    length of, 346
    noon intermission, 348 f.
    number of periods, 345 f.
    typical hours, 347 f.
Science education
    early developments, 169
    later developments, 169 f.
    philosophy of, 170 f.
    problems in, 176
    trends in, 172 ff.
Secondary schools
    number of, 19
    preference for various types, 52
    types of, 19
Senior high schools, number of, 19
Seven-four plan, experience with, 15
Shaker Heights, Ohio, philosophy of, 42 f.
Six-three-three plan, development of, 340
Six-year high schools
    adequate program, 380 f.
    advantages of, 342
    disadvantages of, 342 f.
    early development, 4 f.
    extraclass activities in, 289 f.
    number of, 19
    recommendations for, 10 f.
Social activities
    objectives of, 300
    preparation of pupils for, 301 f.
    types of, 301
Social studies; see also History
    examples of programs, 154 f.
    methods in, 150 f.
    offerings, 147 f.
    trends in, 148 f.
Socialization
    statement of function, 32
    teaching for, 36
Speech activities
    characteristics of, 303 f.
    neglect of, 302
    objectives of, 302 f.
    types of, 304
Sports; see Athletics

Springfield, Massachusetts, pupil progress
    reports, 327 ff.
Staff, professional; *see also* Teachers
    desirable size of, 360
    for six-year high school, 368
    types of personnel, 361
Student council, 307 f.
Study halls
    future of, 384
    trends in, 196 f.
Study skills, teaching of, 199 f.
Subject-centered teaching, 178 f.
Supervised study, new approach, 194 f.

Teachers
    academic preparation of, 362
    as classroom leader, 189
    assignments to schools, 374 f.
    better qualified, 47
    cooperative planning by, 91
    desirable qualities of, 366
    experience of, 365
    in-service growth of, 367
    in six-year high schools, 375
    nature of college education, 362
    need for training, 361
    preparation of, 364 f., 380
    principles for assignment of, 375 f.
    proportion of men and women, 366
    salaries, 368 ff.
Teaching load
    desirable load, 382
    factors in, 370 f.
    for homeroom advisers, 276 f.

improvement of, 371
    number of classes, 371 f.
Teaching materials
    audio-visual, 192 f.
    community resources, 191 f.
    textbooks, 190 ff.
Tests
    purposes of, 319
    reduced emphasis on, 320
Textbooks, 190 ff.
Typewriting, 169

Unified studies, trend toward, 67 f.; *see*
    Core curriculum
Unit organization, trend toward, 69 f.
Unit planning
    activity-centered, 179 f.
    experience-centered, 180
    for individualized teaching, 206 f.
    subject-centered, 178 f.

Vocational guidance
    counseling in, 247 f.
    reduced emphasis, 246 f.
    vocational information, 247

Washington, D. C., social studies pro-
    gram, 156 f.
Washington, State of, home economics
    program, 134 f.
Wauwatosa, Wisconsin, program of
    studies, 79
Wellesley, Massachusetts, philosophy of,
    42